THE MIGHTY CONTINENT

The Mighty Continent

A Candid History of Modern Europe

Walter A. McDougall

CREED &
CULTURE

NASHVILLE, TN

Copyright © 2026 Walter A. McDougall

All rights reserved. Except for brief quotations in review, neither this book nor any parts thereof may be reproduced in any form without the publisher's permission. Contact the publisher at creedandculture.com.

All images courtesy of Wikimedia Commons, except those on pages 4 and 51, which are courtesy of Google Art Project.

First published 2026 by Creed & Culture Books

Hardback ISBN: 9781967613007
E-book ISBN: 9781967613052

Library of Congress Control Number: 2025944212

The study of the past with one eye upon the present is the source of all sins and sophistries in history.

—Herbert Butterfield

What has been is what will be, and what has been done is what will be done, and there is nothing new under the sun.

—Ecclesiastes 1:9

Contents

	Preface	ix
1	The Classical Origins of European Civilization	1
2	The Biblical Origins of European Civilization	15
3	Faith Based on Reason: The Medieval Millennium	31
4	Renaissance! Humanism and the Classical Revival	45
5	"A Mighty Fortress Is Our God": The Protestant Reformation	61
6	"Set All Aflame!" The Catholic Reformation	77
7	Spices, Specie, and Souls: Europe Goes Global	91
8	Two Cardinals and a Sun King: Absolutism in France	107
9	Parliaments Triumphant: Absolutism Thwarted in England	123
10	To Probe the Mind of God: The Scientific Revolution	137
11	Soldiers, Serfs, Icons, and Axes: The Rise of Prussia and Russia	155
12	Reason Based on Faith: The Competing Enlightenments	171
13	Competition for Empire: Britannia Rules the Waves	185
14	Liberty, Equality, Fraternity Betrayed: The French Revolution	201

15	A World Restored: The Birth of Conservatism and Liberalism	217
16	Machines in the Garden: Four Industrial Revolutions	233
17	1848 and After: Romantic Revolutions and Realistic Reforms	247
18	"Nothing to Lose but Your Chains": The Rise of Socialism	263
19	Fluttered Folk and Wild: Europe's New Imperialism	277
20	The Snake That Ate Its Tail: The Culture of Modernity	291
21	"Human, All Too Human": The Descent into World War I	305
22	Storm of Steel: The Traumas of War and Peace	319
23	Class War: Marxism-Leninism Captures Russia	333
24	Race War: Fascism and Nazism Capture Italy and Germany	347
25	Years the Locust Hath Eaten: The Great Depression	363
26	Descent into Hell: World War II and Its Holocausts	377
27	Echternach Dance: The Cold War and the Revival of Europe	393
28	Be Not Proud, Be Not Ashamed: In Defense of the West	409
	Index	423

Preface

Europeans invented the modern world. These days that undeniable truth makes numerous people uncomfortable, to the point that, as objectively undeniable as it may be, it is in fact strenuously denied by most academic historians, even (or especially) in those portions of the globe where those of European ancestry reside. That is because the anti-intellectual trends which have captured the historical profession over the past sixty years—trends such as postmodernism, deconstructionism, critical race theory, radical feminism, and "wokeness" in general—condemn Western civilization for having produced most of the ills besetting the world in the twenty-first century.

This is a comparatively new perspective. As recently as sixty years ago, when I studied history in school, survey courses on Western civilization in general, and the ascent of Europe in particular, celebrated those persons and nations who had invented, defended, and spread such ideas and institutions as limited government, the rule of law, religious liberty, popular sovereignty, capitalist economics, industrialization, and the unprecedented prosperity to which they gave rise, not to mention universities, the scientific method, serial technological revolutions, maritime explorations, and globalization. Teachers and textbooks of that era did not overlook or minimize the nearly constant warfare, imperialism, racism, and social oppression that tarnished European history, yet they still depicted Europeans and their overseas descendants as leaders in humanity's grand march of progress.

My own exposure to the subject of this book first occurred at New Trier Township High School in Winnetka, Illinois, a suburb of Chicago. I enrolled in a freshman survey on world history, then a sophomore survey on modern Europe. My teacher in the latter course assigned a textbook authored by a prominent twentieth-century historian named Carl Becker. That text, the subjects it dealt with, and my inspiring teacher hooked me on European history. Indeed, I became so fascinated by the excitement, pathos, glory, and tragedy of modern Europe that I later majored in history at Amherst College, even though I had no expectation that it would lead to a successful career. My minor fields, German and classical music, supplemented my studies of French, British, German, Austrian, Italian, and Russian history. During 1967 and 1968, my senior year, the Vietnam War was at its peak and American boys of my age group faced conscription. Upon graduation I enlisted in the army, more out of duty than patriotism, but not before applying to graduate programs in history. I figured that by the time my tour of duty was over I would have reached a decision about what I *really* wanted to do with my life—not realizing that soldiers at war do not think about anything other than coming home in one piece. So when I did return safely (thank you, Lord!) I matriculated at the University of Chicago.

Only a couple weeks passed before I knew that this was exactly where I belonged. The University of Chicago's faculty was uniformly outstanding, and I took full advantage of lecture classes and seminars offered by esteemed scholars such as William H. McNeill, Donald Lach, Michael Confino, S. William Halperin, Peter Novick, and F. Gregory Campbell. I added a reading knowledge of French to the Latin I had learned in high school and the German I had learned in college. After passing my oral exams I undertook dissertation research at the Quai d'Orsay, the French foreign-ministry archives in Paris, and in libraries and archives elsewhere in London, Brussels, and Bonn, then the capital of West Germany. So tirelessly did I labor that I was awarded the doctoral degree in 1974, after just four and a half years of graduate school.

The academic job market was already poor for aspiring historians. The baby-boom generation had grown up, and college and university faculties were stagnant, if not shrinking. Nevertheless, I was fortunate to be recruited by two

Preface

institutions: Clemson University in South Carolina and the University of California at Berkeley. Needless to say, I accepted an assistant professorship in the world-class history department at UC Berkeley, and I distinctly recall driving my rental car from the San Francisco airport across the Bay Bridge, singing "California, here I come!"

Nevertheless, I was apprehensive in September 1975 when the fall semester began. Since the University of Chicago's undergraduate college was small, its faculty did not employ graduate students as teaching assistants. As a result, when I arrived to deliver my initial lecture at Berkeley, it was the first time I had ever faced students. Would I enjoy teaching history? Would I be any good at it? After ten minutes I learned the answers were yes and yes. Once again, I knew that I was precisely where I belonged. My primary responsibility was to teach a two-semester sequence on European diplomatic history from the French Revolution to the Cold War (then in full flush). Within two years my reputation had spread across campus such that my course enrollments surpassed three hundred students per semester.

Perhaps that popularity aroused the envy of some of my colleagues, or perhaps they judged a Vietnam veteran who taught about power politics to be reprehensible (don't forget this was Berkeley in the 1970s!), so I had to struggle for no less than nine years before the provost promoted me to associate professor with tenure. It was during those years that another popular professor named William Slottman decided to retire. He had taught History 5, a survey of modern Europe from the Renaissance to the present. Since I liked and admired him, I decided to attend his last lecture and pay my respects. I took a seat near the back of the large lecture hall, expecting my presence would go unnoticed. Imagine my surprise when Slottman ended his lecture with these words: "As you all know I shall be retiring at the end of this year, but I am pleased to report that I shall be placing History 5 in the capable hands of Professor McDougall." I have been teaching versions of that course for forty years, not only at Berkeley but throughout the decades following 1988, when I accepted a chair at the University of Pennsylvania. That course inspired me to write the book you are now reading.

The contents of my lectures have been periodically updated as new scholarship has appeared and new themes have become relevant, among them the end of the Cold War in 1989–91 and the onset of wars against Islamic terrorists after September 11, 2001. My lectures have also integrated several generations of new technology, especially PowerPoint. I know many audiences consider slide presentations a MEGO ("my eyes glaze over"), but my PowerPoint presentations are not at all boring. I carefully select colorful images of people, events, battles, maps, and other images illustrating the times and places described in the lectures. The slides contain informative captions as well. To purchase the rights for the enormous variety of images that accompany this course would take years and cost a small fortune. But I have nevertheless included one image in each chapter of this book, and I encourage readers to Google anyone or anything that strikes their fancy or about which they desire to have visual aids. In live lectures I also screen ten-minute YouTube clips of classical music in the hope of interesting college students in the rich repertory of European orchestral music. Readers of this book may enjoy Googling masterworks by Monteverdi, Bach, Mozart, Beethoven, and Brahms as accompaniments for those chapters which discuss the Renaissance, Baroque, Neoclassical, and Romantic eras of European culture.

Nowadays grand surveys of modern European history are seldom if ever published, while academic monographs on aspects of European history are often arcane, tendentious, and theoretical rather than descriptive. Too often academic treatises these days are insufferably "woke" or even unreadable, thanks to their postmodern jargon. This book, by contrast, consists of old-fashioned, meat-and-potatoes history. Rudyard Kipling (1865-1936), the poet laureate of the British Empire, once said that if history were taught in the form of stories, it would never be forgotten. Long before I knew of that precept, I was practicing it. Narrative history, loaded with drama, tension, passion, and irony, is what most readers crave. To be sure, textbooks that describe the sweep of European history in chronological fashion are still being published. But textbook authors and editors tend to strangle drama, tension, passion, and irony by chopping up their subjects into short sections and by interrupting the flow with numerous boxes, charts, tables, and snippets from primary sources. Moreover, textbooks these days are compiled by teams of scholars and therefore lack a clear narrative voice.

I could have coauthored a textbook, which would have been far more lucrative. But I have no interest in collaborative projects that entail tedious debates with one's colleagues over what to include and what to omit. Hence this volume is one historian's earnest effort to tell the tale of the ascent of Europe from the

Preface

fifteenth to the twenty-first century. The tale is highly stochastic, which is to say too complex to be understood through simple patterns of cause-and-effect, much less reductionist "laws." I have tackled the chore of telling the tale in the faith that history, when all is said and done, amounts to far more than Macbeth's "tale told by an idiot, full of sound and fury, signifying nothing." That faith is the reason why I dedicate this volume to the real and abiding Author of history.

I wish to express my sincere gratitude to the mentors, colleagues, students, and staff members who have taught me and assisted me so very much over my fifty years as a working historian. Special thanks are due to Jeremy Beer, president of Creed & Culture; Robert Banning, who served as this book's expert copy editor; and the entire production staff at Creed & Culture.

Walter A. McDougall
Bryn Mawr, Pennsylvania
June 2025

Chapter 1

The Classical Origins of European Civilization

What does it mean to be civilized—to be civil, to practice civility, to belong to a civilization? How did human beings first become civilized, and why have civilizations taken such multifarious forms?

In the 1930s a famous historian named Arnold J. Toynbee theorized that the principal factors which shaped the world's nineteen (by his count) civilizations were topography and climate. He theorized that complex cultures arose through a process of challenge and response whereby creative minorities interacted with their people's habitats to provide food, shelter, and defense. He believed the first civilizations arose in the valleys of the Nile and Tigris/Euphrates rivers because their fertile soil and abundant water made possible productive agricultural societies, so long as the inhabitants constructed elaborate systems of irrigation, which in turn required complex social, economic, and political systems, plus military organization to defend the land and resources.

A surplus of food production was an obvious prerequisite for the articulation of civilizations, because if all the people had to spend all their time on agricultural labor, then by definition they all must be hunters, gatherers, herdsmen, or farmers. But if a portion—say, 80 percent—of the population could raise enough food for everyone, then 20 percent might serve the community as craftsmen, artists, priests, soldiers, lawyers, or bureaucrats. Their activities, in turn, gave rise to government, law, commerce, religion, and all the other features we associate with higher civilizations.

Another esteemed world historian named William H. McNeill (my mentor at the University of Chicago) added to the prerequisites for civilization a predictability of behavior, by which he meant human beings' adherence to common laws and shared customs, habits that allowed them to anticipate the behavior of others. We take this adherence for granted, of course, as we do the very air we breathe. But consider how long our cities and towns would remain civil if people suddenly quit going to work, quit obeying traffic laws, quit maintaining utilities, or quit respecting each other's property and lives. Hence, for McNeill, the abstract mechanisms of social control are just as essential to the rise and maintenance of civilizations as are material resources.

Still, all these criteria—surpluses of food, shelter, and clothing; division of labor; law and order; political, social, military, and technical power achieved through human organization—leave out something important. They have nothing to say about the quality of civilizations as defined by their principles of authority, the ethical foundations, cultures, and religions that regulate the behavior of everyone from kings and priests to soldiers, workers, and slaves—the principles of authority that endow behavior with meaning.

All civilizations, from ancient Egypt to late modern Europe, have possessed spiritual as well as material components. What is the link between them? Toynbee wasn't sure. He wrote the first five volumes of his epic history of world civilizations on the assumption that the creative minorities of emerging civilizations create religions in order to justify hierarchical social orders and to exercise discipline over other people. Then, toward the end of his fifth volume, Toynbee abruptly changed his mind and wrote five more books in which he argued that in fact religions create civilizations, not the other way around. Whatever the case, the spiritual need for meaning and purpose seems to be as intrinsic to human nature as is the need for food and shelter.

Harvard sociologist Daniel Bell, in a seminal book called *The Winding Passage*, elaborated on these timeless issues by asking what distinguished twentieth-century people from the inhabitants of ancient Greece. Modern technology would certainly be regarded by the ancients as magical, he answered. But otherwise we moderns live on the same earth, scan the same skies, wonder where it

The Classical Origins of European Civilization

all came from, wonder what meaning, if any, our lives possess, and wonder what happens, if anything, after we die. The ancient Greeks, explained Bell, summed up the attributes of civilization in the words *techne* and *themis*. *Techne* referred to those arts of survival and manipulation of nature which endow societies with power—power to manipulate the natural world and each other as symbolized in Greek mythology by Hephaestus, the blacksmith god (whom the Romans called Vulcan). *Techne*, needless to say, is the root of our words technique, technician, technical, and technology. The second word, *themis*, was the name of the mythological titaness Justitia. She personified order, law, and custom and sat on the right hand of Zeus, king of the gods. *Themis* was therefore the realm of justice, philosophy, religion, and art—in other words, cult and culture. The things of *themis* address the mysteries and problems common to all men and women in all times and places—such as how to love and be loved, how to cultivate virtues, how to cope with suffering and injustice, and how to escape the boredom of poverty and the boredom of riches. In sum, how to live a good life. Those are questions which all human beings have asked, even we moderns. Different civilizations and different generations within each civilization have addressed the timeless mysteries in strikingly different ways. Indeed, those different ways are what make history, the study of change over time, so fascinating.

Where should we look for the roots of the particular civilization that emerged in the western fringes of the Eurasian landmass and came to be called European? A professor of linguistics at Amherst College once taught his students (me included) that as offshoots of Europe's civilization, we could never consider ourselves educated unless we knew the Greeks and the Bible. Of course, really knowing the Greeks and the Bible would require a lifetime of study, but it is clear what he meant. Just as a biographer begins by studying the youthful influences that shaped his subject's personality, so the chronicler of a civilization must begin by studying the early influences that shaped its language, mentality, and attitudes toward the things of *techne* and *themis*.

In the case of Europe, those influences mostly originated from three ancient peoples living around the Mediterranean Sea. The first called themselves Hellenes. We know them as the Greeks who lived in city-states such as Athens, Sparta, and Corinth, in addition to the border provinces of Macedonia. The second called themselves Israelites. We know them also as Hebrews or Jews. The third called themselves Latins. We know them as the Romans who

The Architect's Dream, an 1840 oil painting by the American Romantic Thomas Cole, celebrates the great civilizations that gave birth to modern Europe.

conquered Greece (only to be conquered themselves by Greek culture), then conquered Judea (only to be conquered themselves by the obscure Jewish sect they called Christian). In the fullness of time, the Roman Empire fell. But the Christian church survived and thrived as a rich synthesis of Jewish theology, Greek philosophy, and Roman polity. Accordingly, this book shall begin with three introductory chapters briefly describing the Graeco-Roman, biblical, and medieval roots from which modern European civilization sprang forth.

One final word about the value of "old-fashioned" methodology. In an era shaped by the Internet, Wikipedia, social media, and artificial intelligence it may seem passé to commit to memory facts that can be accessed by a few clicks on your smartphone or computer. Why not just cut to the chase and study history through the application of theories, categories, and models that serve as frameworks for making sense of the infinite number of facts about humanity's past? The answer is that if theories are promoted at the expense of facts, then the study of history suffers in two debilitating ways. The first is that we become so focused on abstract processes that we lose sight of the fact that real men and women lived real lives in which their own intelligence or folly, energy or passivity, perseverance or despair, created those processes. For instance, the

The Classical Origins of European Civilization

industrial revolution did not just happen. It was wrought by human agency, by inventors and entrepreneurs and mechanics and factory workers. The second danger is that theorizing about impersonal forces to the exclusion of human facts tempts us to think we know something about history when in fact we have only learned some buzzwords. For instance, to say that royal state-building or the scientific revolution profoundly changed early modern Europe is all very well, but if you cannot name a single king who built a centralized state, or a single scientific idea that altered the way Europeans looked at their world, then you are faking it.

Honest historians employ both deductive reasoning—beginning with a theory, then testing it against the facts—and inductive reasoning—beginning with the facts, then asking what theories they suggest. Both facts and concepts are important. How do they fit together? In pragmatic terms, historians of all specialties meld data and theories together by seeking to discern patterns of human behavior over time. Depending on their areas of specialization, historians seek such patterns in one or more of five basic relationships.

First, the relationship between man and nature that gives rise to technology, from the first stone axe or plow to the space satellite or silicon chip. Is this solely a matter of *techne*, or does it involve *themis* as well?

Second, the relationship between men and women, which gives rise to the family and other kinship patterns that regulate procreation and the inheritance of property. Is this relationship solely within the realm of *themis*, or does it involve *techne* as well?

Third, the relationship between families and other families, which gives rise to clans and tribes, linguistic and religious groups, and finally whole nations. Are societies and their politics an expression of *techne*, *themis*, or both?

Fourth, the relationships among multiple polities, which give rise both to commerce and conflict and serve to diffuse ideas, institutions, and technologies around the world. Clearly *techne* and *themis* are all mixed up here.

Fifth, the relationship of all the above to noumenal realities such as the meaning of life and death, love, justice, beauty, freedom, eternity, God. This is the thematic relationship which impels humankind to transcend material civilization and create culture.

All these interactions are the stuff of economic, social, political, diplomatic, military, intellectual, and cultural history. What most historians do is to invoke facts drawn from one field in hopes of discerning patterns in some other branch. Thus, any synthetic work of history is likely to argue how social change at some given time and place helped to bring about political change, or how military conflict bred economic change, or how economic development sparked intellectual change, and so on. To be sure, many historians since the nineteenth century belong to some ideological school holding that one of these human activities—for instance, economics—determines developments in all the others, which means they are determinists. But determinists such as the Marxists, even though they are thoroughly secular, make a leap of faith as great as do religious believers who explain history as the unfolding of Providence. That, too, will be one of the abiding themes of this book, for the tensions in human philosophy are not between those who put their faith in religion and those who put their faith in science, but rather those whose faith is in the City of Man and those whose faith is in the City of God.

The earliest civilizations sprang up in the irrigated valleys of the Nile River in Egypt and the valleys of the Tigris and Euphrates rivers in Mesopotamia. But by the Bronze Age (about 2000 to 1000 BC) several smaller civilizations thrived on the island of Crete (such as the Minoan culture with its great palaces, artful depictions of marine life, and mysterious languages Linear A and B), Greece's Peloponnesian peninsula (Mycenae), and the coast of Asia Minor (Troy). Alas, Cretan culture was destroyed in a mighty earthquake around 1500 BC (quite possibly the origin of the Atlantis legend). Troy was destroyed by the Myceneans during the Trojan War. And the Peloponnesian cultures were destroyed, apparently by barbarian invaders from the north, around 1200 BC. The myths and epic poems of those cultures—especially the *Iliad* and *Odyssey*, both of course attributed to the legendary blind poet Homer—were filled with references to their departed glories.

Over the following centuries the first Hellenic peoples entered Greece from the north, their main language and culture groups being the Doric, Ionic, and Corinthian. Most people today are familiar with those terms as types of classical architecture. During the eighth century BC the Hellenes began to establish a uniquely creative civilization based on rain-watered agriculture rather than irrigation and far-flung commercial networks. Those were the principal sources of the wealth which enabled urban Greek scholars to devote their lives to study and contemplation, and over time to realize a golden age of science, architecture, sculpture, philosophy, politics, and military organization. To this day, historians of science cannot begin to explain the spontaneous *ex nihilo* creativity of the city-states in their golden age. They simply refer to the "Greek Miracle."

One major influence on the politics and economics of Greece was likely its geography. The country is divided by mountains and jagged coastlines into self-contained valleys that inhibited the development of centralized government along the lines of Egypt, Mesopotamia, or Persia. Instead, the Hellenic tribes founded self-governing city-states such as Athens, Corinth, Sparta, and Thebes. The name for such a state was *polis*, the root of our word *politics*.

A military invention called the phalanx was another important influence on Hellenic civilization. Phalanxes were formations of foot soldiers called hoplites who were equipped with armor and spears and who rigorously drilled to maneuver as one body. The hoplites' bristling spears provided a rugged defense against enemies, whether those enemies were on foot or on horseback. Moreover, since the Greeks were among the pioneers of the Iron Age, the iron-tipped spears, swords, and armor forged by their blacksmiths were superior to those of soldiers whose weapons were made of bronze.

The social effects of the phalanx must have been enormous. It required voluntary cooperation among the hoplites, and thus encouraged a concept of reciprocal rights and duties unprecedented in the ancient Mediterranean. After all, the survival in battle of each citizen-soldier depended in large part on the shields and swords of his comrades on either side. Hence, a phalanx bred mutual trust and solidarity. Since the defense of each polis was largely a function of the size and training of the phalanx, the pressure for social equality must have been irresistible. Sparta, the most militant city-state, even suppressed all marks of difference based on rank or wealth and declared all male citizens equal. Males were also subject to rigorous military training from the age of seven. The Spartan phalanx soon became the greatest in Greece and allowed Sparta to conquer the Messenes in the next valley. That was an important event, for the Spartans made the Messenes slaves on their farms and transformed themselves into a rigidly democratic, if militaristic, ruling class. The Spartans even forbade themselves the art and philosophy cultivated in other city-states, deeming such pursuits to be effete and corrupting. In this case *techne* clearly triumphed over *themis*.

In Athens, by contrast, reliance on the phalanx inspired social reforms and a highly creative culture devoted to art, philosophy, and political experimentation, as when the Athenians gave the wise philosopher Solon authority to reform their laws in the name of justice. Among other things, Solon proceeded to forgive the debts of small farmers and to elevate to full citizenship all adult males. But over the course of the fifth century BC the Athenians succumbed to an excess of democracy, as manifested in episodes of mob rule, a turn of events that enabled demagogues and dictators, including the infamous Alcibiades, to seize power.

Greek democracy was never universal. All the city-states possessed slaves whom they captured abroad, while women had no political status, being sheltered by their male kinfolk. Still, Athens was the original source of our modern notions of democracy and political science. Thus did Protagoras, Plato, and Aristotle perceptively analyze the cycles whereby polities tended to pass from monarchy to aristocracy to oligarchy to democracy to anarchy or tyranny, then either to extinction or back to monarchy.

During the Greek Golden Age the Athenians reached their peak of power and prosperity. Their naval and commercial expansion dominated the Aegean Sea. But Athenian imperialism was also a source of danger, since the city gradually absorbed a large underclass of foreigners and slaves captured in foreign wars. As in Sparta, the Athenians put the slaves to work on their farms and over time ceased to perform the labor they had previously considered character-building. Instead, Athenians increasingly engaged in political rivalries, indulged in abstract speculation, and subscribed to various philosophical cults such as the Stoics, Epicureans, and Pythagoreans.

The ancient Greeks were the original source for many diplomatic terms and techniques that persist to this day. They developed diplomatic immunity and embassies, commercial law, and a precocious balance-of-power system among their fiercely competitive city-states. During the latter stages of the Greek Golden Age an existential threat arose when a "clash of civilizations" occurred. In 482 BC the armies of the mighty Persian emperor Darius, commanded by his general Xerxes, crossed the Hellespont (the "Greek bridge" now called the Turkish Straits), and invaded the Greek peninsula. The city-states were alarmed but quarreled among themselves. Defeatists advised capitulation and throwing themselves on the mercy of the Persians. Cynics hoped the Persians would crush their Greek rivals while leaving their own polis alone. But the Athenians determined to resist, forged alliances with several other city-states, and in 490—thanks to some shrewd strategy—routed the Persian army at the Battle of Marathon. Legend had it that a messenger ran nonstop the twenty-six miles to Athens only to drop dead after delivering the good news.

Alas, it proved only a respite. Ten years later Xerxes returned and defeated the Greeks in the Battle of Thermopylae. Then, a reversal. The Athenian navy—thanks again to some clever deception—destroyed the Persian fleet in the Battle of Salamis, which forced the Persian army, whose supply lines were now threatened, to retreat. Thus the Greeks managed to preserve what they self-consciously called *eleutheria* (liberty). Indeed, the Greeks had a word for liberty during an era when few other Near Eastern peoples had an equivalent.

Sadly, the political morality play did not end there. For soon after the Persian wars ended, Athens and Sparta fell into a savage twenty-seven-year conflict known as the Peloponnesian Wars, during which both city-states succumbed to political tyranny and both cities were laid waste.

Those dramatic stories are known to us in great detail because Greek culture also gave rise to the study of history, which is to say genuine chronological narrative, as opposed to myth or hagiography. Herodotus, known as the father of history, chronicled the Persian wars and introduced a theme that has resonated throughout European history and into our own day through books and movies such as *The Lord of the Rings* and *Star Wars*. That was the theme that free peoples always prevail over evil empires because they fight, not as slaves, but for each other and for freedom itself. A second great historian named Thucydides chronicled the Peloponnesian Wars. Not surprisingly his principal theme was how the abuse of freedom can sometimes lead to folly, ambition, and self-destruction.

What lofty ideals other than patriotism inspired the Greeks? Toynbee divided the history of all religions into four stages. He said the first awakening of mankind to spirituality during the Neolithic Age was through nature worship, in which the sun or rain or rivers or animals were considered divine. During the second stage, nature worship became personified in anthropomorphic gods such as Apollo the sun god and Demeter goddess of the harvest, or in the worship of spiritual qualities such as Athena the goddess of wisdom and Aphrodite the goddess of beauty. But the development of civilization, involving as it does the local conquest of nature by technology and organization, and the emergence of human political authority in the forms of kingdom, empire, or city-state, inevitably led to a third stage characterized by civil religions that venerated human rulers and states. The fourth stage arrived with the advent of monotheism and the so-called higher religions.

Since Toynbee drew many of his notions from ancient Greece, it is not surprising that Greek mythology reflected the higher phases of religious sensibility. Greek mythopoeia reflected this pattern. It drew on many sources, including the gods of the earlier Myceneans, the Greeks' own gods of war and fertility, and at length the pantheon of Olympian deities. But in daily religious life people showed less piety to Zeus, Hera, Poseidon, and the other Olympian gods than they did to local divinities. Each family had "household gods" that were placed above the hearth and served as guardian angels. Over time city-states adopted one or another deity as their patron. Athena was obviously the patron of Athens, Artemis was the patron of Sparta, and Poseidon, the god of the ocean, was the patron of the port city of Corinth. Festivals were dedicated to particular gods—for example, to Artemis the goddess of hunting, or to Dionysius (the Roman Bacchus) the god of wine.

How was it that brilliant Greek philosophers could have believed such silly myths? First, they mostly did not believe, and second, the gods were not silly. Paganism can be a beautiful, profound form of worship. When the natural world itself is deemed to be divine, or under divine blessing, human beings cannot fail to revere nature and treat it with awe and respect. The pious pagan can imagine a one-to-one connection between human events and the benign or capricious actions of gods—and imagine also that mortals might solicit divine assistance through piety and sacrifice. Even the skeptical philosopher must have whispered a prayer to Poseidon when threatened with shipwreck by a storm. Pagan belief also encouraged divination according to omens such as the flight of an eagle, a particular pattern of animal entrails, the Delphic Oracle of Apollo, or the mystical haunt of the Cumaean Sibyl in a quest for what the future may hold.

The Greek myths also expressed a deep and ironic understanding of the reality of the human condition. Consider the tale of Pandora's Box, which illustrates the wicked fruits of the lust for power; the myth of Prometheus, which depicts the dangers of attempting to play god; or the myth of Daedalus and Icarus, which depicts the perils of prideful technology. Indeed, the richness of metaphor in Greek mythology would make it one of the two principal sources of literary and artistic inspiration throughout European history. The other, of course, is the Bible.

Myths were common to all ancient cultures. What made the Greeks unique was their miraculous invention of science and secular philosophy. No one can explain what inspired Miletus to ask, "What are things made of, how do things change, and for that matter, how can we really be sure that we know anything?" That last question posed the problem of epistemology, the science of knowing. The Greeks assumed the universe to be a cosmos, or an orderly system, as opposed to chaos. If the world is a cosmos, then it must have patterns that can be observed or deduced. Surely one path toward knowing is the evidence of our five senses and logic. (The Hebrews had a second answer to the question of how we know what we know, which we will consider in the next chapter.)

The first Milesian thinkers, later known as philosophers (a word that means "lovers of wisdom"), pondered the nature of earth and water, and even fire and air, which they proved to be material by the experimental inflation of wineskins. Zeno even rejected the idea of the infinite divisibility of matter, deducing instead that all matter must be composed by irreducible units he called atoms. Space consists either of atoms or the void, and all motion occurs for a reason. Thus did Zeno anticipate Sir Isaac Newton's Second Law of Motion by two millennia.

Pythagoras, who lived around 500 BC, carried such reasoning further through his discoveries in mathematics. (His disciples celebrated his famous Pythagorean theorem by sacrificing a bull.) He raised the atomic idea to a higher level of abstraction by asserting that all things ultimately can be reduced to numbers. And he endowed numbers with such a mystical aura that his school of philosophy became a religious cult. Pythagoras was also one of the first persons to idealize the philosophical life. For instance, he identified three types of people among the crowds at the Olympic Games. The lowest were the vendors, who came to the games merely to sell their wares. Next were the athletes, who deserved honor for their physical prowess. The loftiest class of people were the spectators, the *theoroi* (from the same root as *theoria*, from which we derive *theory*), for they exercised mental prowess in theorizing about the athletes' techniques and strategies.

From early Milesian philosophy emerged the two great branches of Greek thought that Europeans would later separate into the realms of science and philosophy. The first focused on *physis*, the physical world, and the second on *onomata* or *logos*, the world of names or words. During their Golden Age the Greeks produced a phenomenal array of physical scientists, including Euclid the founder of geometry, Strabo the geographer, Galen the anatomist, and Aristarchus, who used trigonometry to calculate the distance of the earth from the sun. Others calculated the size of the earth and proposed a heliocentric theory of the solar system. But the greatest organizer of knowledge was not an experimental, inductive thinker, but rather a contemplative, deductive one. That was Aristotle, who died in 322 BC, having codified Greek theories of physics, mathematics, astronomy, politics, rhetoric, and ethics. Although his a priori notions about nature were in many cases wildly wrong, his prestige was enormous, and he became the main authority on science throughout the ancient and medieval eras.

The tremendous achievements of Greek art also derived in part from science. The classical proportions of Greek sculptures and buildings were based on the mathematical golden mean of Euclidean geometry, plus a meticulous study of human anatomy. To be sure, the ancient Greeks did not discover perspective; their frescoes are as two-dimensional as Egyptian art. But their temples, such as the Parthenon, and their exquisite sculptures of the human form set standards for beauty that have been revived time and again throughout the course of European civilization.

The other branch of Greek thought, the one centered on concepts, logic, and moral philosophy, reached a culmination with Protagoras, who famously pronounced that man is the measure of all things and who denied the possibility of knowing whether or not the gods exist. A school called the Sophists embraced that skeptical philosophy and designed a mundane, practical curriculum designed to train Greek youths in law and rhetoric in preparation for careers in politics. The great opponent of the Sophists was Socrates, the hen-pecked genius who sat all day in the agora, or town square, refuting the logical certitudes of the Sophists. His method of inquiry—the method we know as Socratic—was simply to ask questions of his opponents, questions that seemed always to catch them in contradictions.

Socrates, who had no interest in power, contemplated the mysteries scorned by cynical Sophists, mysteries such as how to define beauty, love, justice, or virtue. Socrates became so influential that he was deemed subversive and sentenced to death for "corrupting the youth of Athens." Like a later body of judges in Jerusalem, the authorities considered it expedient that "one man should die for the people." And just as the four evangelists recorded the words of Jesus in the Gospels, so did Plato record for posterity the words of Socrates.

Plato's own prolific philosophical tracts helped prepare the pagan world for the advent of Judeo-Christian theology. Plato, like Socrates, rejected the Sophists' position that the physical world was all that existed. Rather, the *onomata* or *logos*—the names or words that expressed abstractions such as beauty, justice, and truth—proved that human beings possessed an intuitive knowledge of a higher, spiritual plane. In a famous metaphor Plato likened life as it is experienced to a cave that is but a shadow of reality, which in turn is the perfect mind of God. People, trapped as they are in one time and space as well as in their own imperfections, trudge through the cave as if in single file, chained together and capable only of seeing the shadows of images and hearing the echoes of voices. If human beings were to escape this cave and enter the light, the glaring truth they would encounter would surely blind them. And if they were then permitted to reenter the cave, they would be utterly incapable of describing to others the glory of that heavenly light.

The Christian evangelist Paul later wrote: "Now we see through a glass darkly, but then we shall see face to face." Thus did Paul, a Greek-educated Jewish Pharisee, address the ultimate question posed by Greek philosophy, which was how imperfect, mortal human beings can apprehend the perfect, immortal things they are capable of imagining.

Why should we regard ancient Greek politics and culture as so important? First, because in the fourth century BC the armies of King Philip of Macedonia swept down from the north and conquered the city-states, whereupon Macedonia embraced Greek culture wholesale. Philip even employed Aristotle to tutor his son Alexander, who became the Great. A military genius, Alexander then launched an unprecedented career of conquest that spread Greek culture throughout Asia Minor, Israel and Judea, Egypt, Mesopotamia, and Persia, ultimately penetrating as far east as the Indus River. Thus did the whole Middle East acquire a veneer of Greek culture, while Greek science reached its acme of influence, not least through the majestic library established in Alexandria, Egypt.

A second reason the Greeks demand our attention is that Greece itself was conquered in 146 BC by the Roman Republic, soon to become the Roman Empire. The Latins' genius was for the things of *techne*, especially government, engineering, and war. In cultural matters—the things of *themis*—the Romans, too, became Hellenized through the wholesale adoption of Greek mythology, literature, art, and philosophy. Although their common speech remained Latin, nearly all educated Romans spoke Greek and hired Greek tutors for their children.

Finally, Roman political history echoed that of the Greek city-states. Early on, the Latin polity abolished its primordial monarchy and founded a vibrant republic whose leaders extolled public virtue and whose motto was SPQR, *Senatus Populusque Romanus*, meaning "the Senate and Roman People." But by the first century BC—that is, just a century after the Romans had conquered Greece—their own institutions had decayed and their republic become corrupted by tyrants who not only governed by force but eventually styled themselves gods. Still, a remarkable era of peace—the so-called Pax Romana—prevailed for another two centuries, during which a second cultural revolution spread around the Mediterranean world. That second taproot of European civilization came from a highly unlikely source: the rustic, provincial, and fiercely monotheistic herdsmen of two little kingdoms called Judah and Israel. And it is to them that we must now turn our attention.

Chapter 2

The Biblical Origins of European Civilization

European civilization was a product of the merger between Greco-Roman culture and Hebraic or Judeo-Christian culture. Indeed, religion will be a major subject over the next several chapters of this book as it races through the medieval era, whose culture and politics were mostly shaped by the Roman Catholic church, and the early modern era, whose culture and politics were mostly shaped by the Protestant Reformation.

A deep dive into biblical religion may discomfit devout readers who take offense when theology is discussed in a secular setting, as well as skeptical readers who take offense when theology is discussed at all. But readers must bear in mind that most human beings, in virtually every culture and era, have subscribed to religious beliefs of one form or another; hence, historians cannot understand past cultures without delving into what they considered holy. Whether the Holy Bible contains literal, allegorical, and/or metaphorical truth is a profound question that will not be considered here. But as students of European history, we must appreciate that devout Jews and Christians over the centuries have taken the Bible to be the revealed word of God and have therefore tried to live by its commandments and promises, sometimes at the cost of their lives.

Indeed, Judaism and Christianity are unique among world religions insofar as their adherents emphasize their faith's genuine historical origins. That is, the Bible does not depict Judaism and Christianity as religious systems dreamed up by holy men. Rather, it depicts them as ex post facto interpretations of miraculous events that really happened to the Hebrew patriarchs and the disciples of Jesus: divine interventions in history that Jews and Christians gradually came to understand as providential. To put it another way, Jews did not invent Judaism; rather, Judaism invented the Jews. In fact, Jews did not even exist until the Lord made covenants with Abraham, his son Isaac, and his grandson Jacob (whom the angel renamed Israel, meaning "he who wrestles with God") and then made another covenant with the prophet Moses, whom the Lord called to liberate his people from bondage in Egypt and to lead their exodus to the promised land. Likewise, Christians did not invent Christianity: The Gospels make it abundantly clear that the twelve apostles had no clue what Jesus's earthly ministry was about until after his death and resurrection. History just *happened* to the characters described in the Bible. They were confronted by amazing events that only gradually made sense to them, as if they were clay in the hands of a divine sculptor. A profound sense of history was just as central to ancient Jewish and Christian consciousness as it was to the pagan Greeks, but for different reasons. The Greeks looked deep into history to discern human nature—and attributed most of life's perverseness to the capriciousness of the gods. The Jews looked deep into history to discern divine nature—and attributed most of life's perverseness to the sinfulness of man.

The Bible is a complex document that must be handled with extreme care. Counting the New Testament, its sixty-six books written over seven hundred years contain a rich mixture of history, prophecy, psalmody, poetry, theology, and eschatology. The authors and precise dates of numerous passages are unknown. The Torah, the first five books ranging from Genesis to Deuteronomy, records ancient oral traditions apparently not written down until the Babylonian captivity of the Jews during the sixth century BC. But however much scholars may argue about the authorship, dating, and correct interpretation of the Bible's various parts, the devout have believed, and continue to believe, that the Bible's human authors were divinely inspired. That suggests a second contrast with the pagans. Ancient Greek philosophers considered science and logic the only sure ways to "know" anything. Jewish prophets and scribes offered a second epistemological vehicle: revelation. After all, if God does exist, how else can he communicate with us mortals except by stooping down from heaven to talk to us—or through us—in our own languages? Not that, according to the Bible, revelation contradicts reason and logic. On the contrary: the Word of God is the very essence of reason and logic. That is why ancient Jews and Christians claimed that the quest for truth must start with God's word, to the content of which human beings could then apply their own God-given reason.

Much later in history, many Europeans did come to believe that faith and reason—or revelation and science—were contradictory. But in the ancient world, the Jewish belief in a God revealed through prophecy and Providence offered powerful answers to those ultimate questions which the Sophists and Platonists despaired of answering.

The Torah—or Pentateuch, as the Five Books of Moses were called in Greek—recounts Jewish traditions about the creation, the fall of Adam and Eve (the first man and woman) into sin, their expulsion from the garden of Eden, the multiplication of humanity until Noah's flood (a catastrophe echoed in Sumerian and Egyptian folklore), and the origins of God's chosen people in the divinely guided lives of Abraham, Isaac, and Jacob, whose twelve sons became the patriarchs of the twelve tribes of Israel. During a famine, the patriarchs migrated to Egypt, where they found divine favor because the Lord had arranged for Joseph—whom his brothers had exiled out of envy—to serve as prime minister under the Pharaoh himself.

Alas, according to the Bible, in the ensuing centuries subsequent pharaohs reduced the Israelites to slavery. This was the situation until around 1200 BC, when the Lord appeared in a burning bush and commanded Moses to demand that the all-powerful pharaoh "let my people go." Moses, like every other prophet in the Bible, was reluctant to assume this awesome responsibility and urged God to choose someone else. That dialogue is extraordinary, not least because Moses asks the Lord, "Who shall I tell my people you are?" That is: What's your name? To which the Lord replies "Jahweh"—later Latinized as Jehovah—which means simply (or perhaps not so simply) "I am that I am." That's an astounding, even heart-rending statement, as if the Lord had said: I made you, I love you, and you don't even know me. So whenever you think of me, remember, *I am*.

Moses persuades Pharaoh to let his people go only after the Lord visits a series of plagues on the Egyptians, the last of which is the death of every firstborn child and beast in the land. The Israelites were spared this horrifying tragedy because the Lord ordered Moses to instruct every family to take into its home a lamb, love the cuddly thing, then kill it, cook it with bitter herbs, and eat it with unleavened bread. Moses also ordered the Israelites to smear their lambs' blood over their doors, so that the destroyer would "pass over" Jewish homes during this final plague. That was the origin of the Jewish Passover.

Finally allowed to leave by the pharaoh, Moses then led the children of Israel through the Red Sea and across the Sinai Peninsula to the borders of the promised land. But along the way the Israelites lost heart and refused to trust that the Lord would enable them to conquer the land's Canaanite inhabitants. For forty years, until all the people still yearning for the "fleshpots of Egypt" had died, God made them wander in the desert. In the meantime, the Lord had given to Moses the Ten Commandments on Mount Sinai. Those commandments expressed a moral code unique in the ancient world. First, they taught monotheism. The Lord may be the tribal God of Israel, but he is also the only true God; all other gods are false. The Lord is sovereign of the universe, not made for our pleasure, but we for his. Recall how the Greek philosopher Protagoras boasted, "Man is the measure of all things." The Jews, by contrast, insisted that God is the measure of all things, as in Psalm 8:3–4: "When I consider the heavens, even the work of Thy fingers, I ask what is Man that thou are mindful of him?"

Second, the commandments taught that the one, true God is a lawgiver and judge who teaches right from wrong and blesses those who obey his precepts because they are meant to make people happy. Third, they conveyed an image of God, not as a mere personification of natural forces, but as master of nature itself, the very Creator of heaven and earth and of humanity in his own image. The Hebrew Bible's account of the exodus likewise depicts the Lord as the Author of History, as the literal Good Shepherd who frees his people from bondage, leads them through the wilderness with a pillar of smoke by day and a pillar of fire by night, feeds them with manna from heaven, and makes his presence known in the ark of the covenant, a sacred box containing the stones on which the Ten Commandments are etched.

Fourth, the commandments taught that the Lord is a jealous and just God who must chastise those whom he loves when they misbehave. Thus, Moses's farewell address in Deuteronomy, one of the most astounding passages in all literature, assures the Israelites that if they keep their covenant with the Lord, worshiping him alone and obeying his laws, they will prosper in the land of milk and honey he will bestow upon them. But Moses also warns the Israelites that if they transgress God's law and worship foreign idols, they will be cast out of the promised land. The implication that history has purpose and meaning could not have contrasted more sharply with pagan notions of history as endlessly and blindly cyclical, or as the product of the gods' capriciousness.

The exodus appears to end well when Joshua, Moses's successor, conquers the land of Canaan and divides it among the twelve tribes of Israel, who proceed to govern themselves under God's holy law for four hundred years. But at length the tribal leaders whine to the prophet Samuel that they desire a king "so to be like all the other nations," the Gentiles that surround them. Samuel is displeased, but the Lord assures him the people are not rebelling against him, but against the Lord himself. Nevertheless, he instructs Samuel to anoint for the Israelites a king. Sure enough, Saul, the first king, proves to be both foolish and wicked.

Over time, the Israelites as a whole fall into apostasy, intermarry with Gentiles, and worship pagan idols. Even the good kings, such as David, who captures the city of Jerusalem, and Solomon, who builds the great temple, repeatedly fall into sin. The Lord nevertheless displays nearly infinite patience with his chosen people. Nobody knew that better than David, the shepherd, warrior, king, and poet who praised God's mercy in words unlike any others throughout the ancient world. Consider his famous Twenty-Third Psalm:

> The lord is my shepherd, I shall not be wanting. He causes me to lie down in green pastures; he leads me beside still waters. He restores my soul. He leads me in the paths of righteousness for his name's sake. Yea, though I walk through the valley of the shadow of death, I shall fear no evil, for you, Lord, are with me, your rod and thy staff they comfort me. You prepare a table before me in the midst of my enemies; you anoint my head with oil and my cup runs over. Surely goodness and mercy shall follow me all the days of my life, and I shall dwell in the house of the Lord, forever.

So: a God of mercy, but also of justice, because the human race, steeped in sin, cannot survive unless their Maker is both. A God who cared only for justice and for whom "the wages of sin are death" must rightly condemn the human race. A God who cared only for mercy would permit people to magnify their selfishness and violence to the point where the human race destroyed itself. From a biblical perspective, history emerges as a sort of curriculum designed to educate a stiff-necked humanity until it learns—as the prophet Micah wrote— "to do justice, love mercy, and walk humbly with your God."

Under David and Solomon a unified kingdom arose around 1000 BC that elevated the Israelites to the heights of power and wealth. Solomon made Jerusalem a splendid capital and built a great temple to serve as the shrine for the ark of the covenant and the locus for the ritual sacrifice of animals whose blood atoned for the people's sins.

That was another stunning Hebrew novelty. Pagans sacrificed animals all the time, but for the purposes of currying favor with a particular god or goddess, to advertise their piety, and to give themselves occasions for a feast, perhaps even an orgy. Jews, by contrast, accompanied their sacrifices with prayer, fasting, and confessions of their own impiety.

The biblical account of Adam and Eve postulated that humanity was made in the image of God, which is usually understood to consist in self-consciousness and free will. That was why Adam and Eve had the choice of disobeying the Lord and committing the original sin, which is pride. Now, the Hebrew word for sin literally means "missing the mark," as when an archer repeatedly fails to hit the bull's-eye. Through its historical narratives, the Bible suggests that all human beings are prone to being more or less willful, selfish, and disobedient, not least in their refusal to admit their own sins. But since a just and holy God requires that disobedience be paid for, he mercifully provided through the Mosaic law a means for substitutionary atonement. The temple sacrifices of animals such as sheep and cattle were administered by the priestly tribe of Levites, who were supported by donations of a tithe, or tenth, of the produce of the other eleven tribes. As early as David's time, however, pious Jews had already begun to spiritualize sacrifice, as we read in Psalm 51: "Were I to give a burnt offering you would not be pleased. The sacrifice acceptable to God is a broken spirit: a broken and contrite heart you will not despise." The notion that spiritual repentance was more pleasing to God than material sacrifice was yet another novelty destined to shake the Judeo-Christian world over and over again, most obviously in the Protestant Reformation of the sixteenth century.

The Biblical Origins of European Civilization

The lips of the prophet Isaiah anointed by an angel, as painted by American artist Benjamin West in 1782 (*Isaiah's Lips Anointed with Fire*).

In the fullness of time the law, the prophets, and the temple cult could not immunize the Hebrews from the sort of political and moral decay that befell the Greek city-states. The historical books of the Bible record that in the centuries following Solomon's death the now-divided and rival kingdoms of Judah and Israel suffered a virtually unbroken succession of kings who took foreign wives, worshiped idols, forgot the Mosaic law, and placed their trust in foreign alliances instead of the Lord's protection. In 721 BC the cruel Assyrian Empire conquered the northern kingdom of Israel, and in 586 BC the Babylonian Empire conquered the southern kingdom of Judah, razed the walls and temple of Jerusalem, and carried large numbers of Jews into exile. That was the famous Babylonian captivity referred to in Psalm 137: "By the rivers of Babylon we lay down and wept, when we remembered Zion. . . . How shall we sing the Lord's song in a strange land?"

Here we come to another astounding novelty: the Jews, unlike the pagan tribes, did not blame or reject their God when he failed to defend his people. Instead, they interpreted their defeat as the Lord's judgment upon themselves! The Jews imagined history quite literally to be a morality play, an idea that would become another powerful theme in subsequent European history. The Babylonian exile was also the context in which the messianic tradition matured. The

Hebrew word from which we get *messiah* means "anointed one," as when a king or prophet is anointed with holy oil. Hence messiah had both royal and priestly connotations, and during the Babylonian captivity there spread a belief that the Messiah would someday redeem Israel and establish the kingdom of God. The Greek translation of messiah is *christos*, from which we get the title Christ.

The psalms of David hinted at a future messiah. Later, the prophet Jeremiah leavened his fierce "jeremiads" with the hopeful prophecy of a new David who would restore to Israel a righteous and everlasting kingdom. In that glorious day, he explained, the Lord would write his law on human hearts, not just tablets of stone, and reconcile man and God forever. But the messianic age was most explicitly described by Isaiah, whom the early Christians interpreted as prophesying around the year 700 BC that a young woman (or virgin) would someday bear a son called Immanuel, or "God is with us." Some 2,400 years later the great composer George Frideric Handel put verses from the ninth chapter of Isaiah to music in his magnificent oratorio *Messiah*: "For unto us a child is born, unto us a son is given: and the government shall be upon his shoulder: and his name shall be called Wonderful, Counsellor, The mighty God, The everlasting Father, The Prince of Peace."

Elsewhere in the Hebrew Bible appear prophecies to the effect that the messiah would be a descendant of David, that he would be born in Bethlehem, and that through him the deaf would hear, the blind would see, and the gospel (or "good news") would be preached to the poor. Suffice it to say that rabbinical scholars ever since have disputed which passages of prophecy truly refer to the Messiah. They stress especially the many verses that specify that the Messiah would be a conquering king who established a holy realm in Jerusalem. Christian scholars, by contrast, have emphasized those passages which describe the Messiah as a "suffering servant" who would be despised and rejected by men, bear their iniquities, and die for their redemption.

In approximately 550 BC the Babylonians themselves were conquered by that same Persian Empire which had invaded Greece. Emperor Cyrus showed mercy on the Jews, permitting them to return to Jerusalem and rebuild the city of Jerusalem under the direction of the prophets Ezra and Nehemiah. Two centuries later, in 332 BC, Israel was swallowed up in the empire of Alexander the Great. At that point the stories of Greece and Israel begin to converge. The appeal of Greek culture was so strong that many educated Jews became Hellenized.

The Biblical Origins of European Civilization

Thousands more Jews emigrated abroad during this era. Their diaspora led to the erection of synagogues in the cities of Egypt, Syria, Asia Minor, and Greece. Meanwhile, during this so-called Maccabean era, bitter strife erupted in the Holy Land between those who remained faithful to Mosaic law—chiefly, the Pharisees—and those who embraced Greek philosophy—chiefly, the Sadducees, who followed the Sophists in rejecting belief in divine justice in this life or the hereafter (in which the Sadducees also did not believe).

Confusing matters further, the young Roman Empire conquered the Holy Land in 63 BC. The Romans did not know what to do with the obstreperous monotheists who resided there, so they endeavored at least to keep them quiet by governing them indirectly through a Hellenized Jewish elite called the Herodians. Most Judeans tolerated this collaborationist regime, but patriotic zealots, the rural poor, and the pious Pharisees despised the Romans and rekindled the hope that the Messiah would soon come to restore the kingdom of David. As we know from the Dead Sea Scrolls discovered at Qumran in the mid-twentieth century, still other Jewish sects, such as the Essenes, promoted mysticism and martyrdom and had apocalyptic expectations similar in some respects to those of the Christian movement about to be born. One desert-dwelling holy man called Jews to repentance and claimed that the kingdom of God was at hand. He was known as John the Baptist, and he ritually washed away the sins of penitents in the River Jordan while promising that soon, soon, the Messiah was coming.

To believing Christians it is a truism that Joshua bar Joseph—*Iesous*, in the Greek, from which we get the name Jesus—was charismatic, since the Greek word *charisma* means "gift" and, in the New Testament, acquired the connotation of "gift from God." But this is not a mere pious belief. From the Gospel accounts it is clear that disciples and opponents alike were amazed by this man Jesus. He inspired extremes of fear and love; his sermons were piercing yet humble; he appeared to fulfill the Mosaic law yet also to transcend it; he preferred to associate with the dregs of society; he behaved in ways both mysterious and magnetic. "No man speaks like this man does," said his disciples. "He speaks with authority."

Indeed, Jesus not only inspired the growth of a great world religion in the manner of Moses, Buddha, or Muhammad; he also threw believers and unbelievers alike into an agonizing debate over where ultimate authority lies. He denounced the Jewish priests and Pharisees, the holiest men of his day, as fools and hypocrites. Yet he claimed to have come not to overthrow the law of Moses, but to fulfill it. He spiritualized atonement by summing up the Law and Prophets in two quotations from Moses: "You shall love the Lord your God with all your heart and with all your soul and with all your mind," and, "You shall love your neighbor as yourself." He called the temple in Jerusalem "my Father's house" and wrathfully cleansed it of money changers. He challenged the authority of all earthly governments by invoking a kingdom of heaven, yet he told his disciples to render unto Caesar that which is Caesar's, and he rejected armed rebellion. He claimed to be the messiah in no uncertain terms. Yet he told the Roman prefect Pontius Pilate that his kingdom was not of this world, and he submitted meekly when he was unjustly condemned to torture and death.

Why was Jesus of Nazareth killed? His preaching against the priests and Pharisees understandably earned him hatred and fear among the local elites. His mass following and talk of a messianic kingdom understandably panicked the Herodians and their Roman patrons. But the refusal of Jesus to take up arms also caused many of his own followers to decide he must be a false messiah. Finally, when Jesus refused to deny the claim that he was truly the Son of God, the Jewish religious court understandably accused him of blasphemy and insisted that Pilate pronounce a death sentence. In hindsight, all those events make perfect sense in the political context of first-century Judea, not to mention the theological context of later Christian belief, which held that the Son of God had come to earth for the very purpose of sacrificing himself to atone for the sins of the world. But the events seemed like an inexplicable tragedy to his disciples . . . until, as the New Testament records, Jesus rose from the tomb on the third day in a bodily resurrection. Suddenly the ceremony he had performed at the Last Supper took on transcendent meaning.

Jewish priests in the temple and rabbis in diaspora synagogues habitually displayed bread and wine symbolizing the presence of God. But at the Passover meal prior to his crucifixion, the Gospels record, Jesus gave bread and wine to his disciples while uttering the words, "This is my body, which is given for you," and "This is my blood of the New Covenant shed for you and for many for the forgiveness of sins." That was the origin of the Christian rite known variously as Communion, the Eucharist (meaning "gift"), the Lord's Supper, or the Mass. It is, of course, a resounding echo of the Passover. According to Christian theology, Jesus himself is the spotless Lamb of God, whose sacrifice performs once and for all the same function as the slaughter of the lambs back in Egypt. His shed blood washes away the sins of the world so the destroyer will "pass over" the faithful and bring them to everlasting life in the ultimate promised land—heaven.

The Gospels also claim that at the moment Jesus died, the veil of the temple was rent in twain. That was the curtain which shrouded the holy of holies, where only the high priest could set foot once a year, and its rending symbolized for Christians the collapse of all barriers between God and man. Through Christ sinful man now had access to the one, true, all-holy God. The Jewish dispensation had been spiritualized and universalized for the entire human race.

Throughout the ensuing two millennia pious Jews have categorized Christianity as a Jewish heresy based on a false messiah, while pious Christians have categorized Judaism as a Jewish heresy based on rejection of the true messiah. Jewish scholars argued that Jesus failed to fulfill the messianic prophecies promising a conquering king. Christian apologists retorted that Jesus fulfilled the messianic prophecies concerning a suffering servant during his time on earth and that he will fulfill the rest upon the *parousia* (his second coming).

Judaism and Christianity are thus separated by a chasm impossibly deep, despite being as similar to each other as any two religions could possibly be.

Here is what Abba Eban, the former Israeli ambassador to the United States, wrote in his book *My People: The Story of the Jews*, in 1968:

> Both Christian theologians and Orthodox Jews have underestimated the original Judeo-Christian affinity. . . . Besides Jesus himself, Judaism gave Christianity the One, the living God. Judaism contributed a Sacred Book—the so-called Old Testament—and thereby paved the way for the New Testament. It passed on a tradition that made life purposeful and full of meaning. . . . Historians must in all objectivity include Christianity among the decisive achievements of the Jewish mind. Hebrew concepts and ethics permeated the faith and civilization which, with mysterious power, have dominated two millennia of human history. . . . [Indeed] the most significant feature of the Jewish heritage was its view of history. Other ancient peoples have believed in a golden age, but they have always located it in the present or past. Israel alone looked forward to a golden age in the future and interpreted history as a progressive movement toward Messianic consummation.

Still, the chasm exists, and nothing illustrates it so much as the Christian doctrine of the Trinity. After the resurrection, the Bible says, Jesus told his disciples to preach the gospel to all nations and baptize them in the name of the Father, the Son, and the Holy Spirit. That mystical doctrine of the Trinity was an abomination to Jews, for whom monotheism was the first principle. Christians insisted that they did not believe in three gods, but rather in three manifestations, or persons, of one God. But how could God be subdivided, much less die like a man? Over its first several centuries the church pondered such questions intensely until ecumenical councils of bishops reached a consensus on catholic (which means "universal") and orthodox doctrine. But to the rest of the ancient world the Trinity was a scandal. As the apostle Paul attested, "The Jews demand signs and the Greeks wisdom, but we preach Christ crucified, a stumbling block to the Jews, and a folly to the Greeks. But to those who are called, both Jews and Greeks, Christ is the power of God and the wisdom of God."

Jesus was Jewish, the early Christians were Jewish, and Jews composed nearly the entire New Testament. But they wrote those scriptures in Greek, not in Hebrew, and thereby intertwined the root beds of what would become European civilization. For it was in the Hellenized Jewish world, both in Israel and in synagogues around the Roman Empire, that Christianity made its first converts. There was great debate over who it was Jesus had meant to save. A party known as Judaizers insisted Gentiles must first become Jews before they could become Christians, implying (among other things) that grown men would have to get circumcised and obey Judaism's strict dietary laws. But at the first church council, in Jerusalem, the prestigious apostles Peter and Paul both testified that they had seen the Holy Spirit descend on Gentiles, while Peter received a revelation that God did not require converts to conform to Jewish dietary restrictions.

Peter and Paul carried the day, potentially turning Christianity into a world religion. For just as the coupling of Christian faith with Jewish concepts of *exodus*, *atonement*, and *messiah* spiritualized and universalized the new church, so the decoupling of Christian faith from the Jewish law, temple, and holy land spiritualized and universalized the new church. The most effective proponent of this doctrine was the apostle Paul. He had been a devout Pharisee and had even persecuted followers of Jesus prior to his miraculous conversion on the road to Damascus. He had been born Saul of Tarsus, a Hellenized city in Asia Minor. He had received an excellent Greek education and enjoyed the privilege of being a citizen of the Roman Empire. In other words, Paul was the ideal missionary to the Gentiles, and he did more than anyone to translate Jewish theology into philosophical language the Greeks could understand. He was aided in that task by a translation of the Hebrew Bible into Greek made by scholars at Alexandria in the third and second centuries BC, which meant Gentiles no longer had to learn Hebrew to access the Law and the Prophets. Nowhere was the Christian merger of the Greek and Jewish worlds better dramatized than in Paul's missionary journey to Greece and his arrival in the great *agora* (forum, or marketplace) of Athens, where Plato's academy was located and philosophical schools such as the Stoics and Epicureans debated in Socratic fashion. The account in the Acts of the Apostles reads as follows:

> Now while Paul waited for them at Athens, his spirit was stirred when he saw the city wholly given over to idolatry. So he argued . . . with the devout pagans daily. Some said, What does this babbler say? And others, He seems to be preaching strange gods. So they brought him to the Areopagus—the town square or judgment hall—saying, What is this new doctrine of which you speak (for Athenians were always eager to hear or to tell of some new thing). So Paul, standing in the midst of Mars Hill, proclaimed, "Men of Athens, I perceive that in all things you are very religious, for as I passed through the city I saw shrines to so many gods, even an altar inscribed: TO THE UNKNOWN GOD. That whom you therefore ignorantly worship, I now declare unto you. For the God who made the world, the Lord of heaven and earth, dwells not in temples made with hands and needs nothing from humans since He is the one who gives life and breath to all things. . . . For as some of your own poets have written, 'in him we live, and move, and have our being.'"

Another classic example of the Christian bridge between Athens and Jerusalem is the prologue to the Gospel of John, which expresses the Jewish messianic faith in terms of Greek *logos* philosophy, with a bow at the end to Plato's light at the end of the cave: "In the beginning was the Word, and the Word was with God, and the Word was God. The same was in the beginning with God. And all things were made by him, and without him was not anything made that was made. In him was life, and his life was the light of men."

Over the following three centuries Christian churches spread to the limits of the Roman Empire. Converts came from all classes, including the educated and wealthy, rather than simply the urban poor, as scholars once believed. Converts also included women, slaves, and pious Gentiles who had already been attracted by Jewish moral teaching. Likewise, over three centuries, the churches organized themselves into a catholic (universal) organization governed by a hierarchy of bishops, priests, and deacons and inspired by the books of the New Testament, which were canonized by ecumenical councils.

Periodically the Roman emperors, who claimed to be divine themselves, persecuted Christians. But the persecutions were sporadic and regional. Instead of stamping out the new faith, the martyrdom of Christians served to magnify the zeal of the church and increase the appeal of its religion. Above all else the early church preached love as the greatest commandment and practiced charity toward believers and unbelievers alike (something Emperor Julian could not understand). Christians founded the first hospitals and nursed the sick, even during epidemics, at the risk of their own lives. The churches welcomed everyone, be they male or female, slave or citizen, rich or poor, Jew or Greek, Roman or barbarian, and to all they promised access to eternal life. So even though the churches sometimes had to go underground, their membership increased exponentially.

These strengths of the early church also suggested temporal, historical tensions bound to emerge once Christianity became the established religion of the Roman Empire in the fourth century AD, and especially in the medieval kingdoms that arose in the wake of the empire's destruction. The first tension arose because Jesus and his disciples had gone out of their way not to endorse any specific social or political order. That left open questions of church and state and of how a Christian community should order itself. A second tension concerned how the church should evangelize once it had the secular powers behind it. In other words, how should church and state relate to nonbelievers, or those they deemed heretics, since Christians (like Jews before them and Muslims after them) claimed to have knowledge of and to worship the one true God?

A third implicit tension involved materialism. The Gospels inveighed against the worship of riches, or idolatry, and Jesus exhorted his disciples to "store up treasures in heaven ... for where your treasure is there will your heart be also." Yet the Gospels taught that the love of money (not money itself) was

The Biblical Origins of European Civilization

the root of all evil, and Matthew the evangelist quotes Jesus saying, "Seek first the kingdom of God and his righteousness, and all these things [other blessings] will be added unto you." Might that be construed to mean that wealth was not necessarily a temptation and might even be a sign of God's grace?

A fourth tension arose from disputes over the respective jurisdictions of the church and the state. Jesus famously declared, "Render unto Caesar the things that are Caesar's and unto God the things that are God's," implying a separation of church and state. But that begged the practical question: What exactly belongs to Caesar—the state—and to God—the church? Just how much authority should the state exercise?

Ambiguities also arose around the question of equality. Christians claimed that all human beings were equal in the sight of God and that all believers were children of God. Such radical democratization of human dignity was unimaginable elsewhere in the ancient world. But of course the church itself comprised sinful people tempted like everyone else by vice and hypocrisy. What sort of social order was least conducive to vice and most conducive to virtue? Christians have quarreled over the answer to that question for two thousand years.

War was the source of another conundrum. Jesus said, "Turn the other cheek," and, "He who lives by the sword dies by the sword." But what were Christians to do once they became secular rulers? Surely they had a duty to defend their people, land, and property. Moreover, the Hebrew scriptures included sophisticated rules about when wars are just, even or especially holy wars. Jesus commanded his disciples to love one another. But how does one institutionalize love? Christian pacifists and Christian crusaders would offer very different answers to these kinds of questions.

Tensions over how to reconcile spiritual values and secular institutions would contribute mightily to the restless vitality and experimentation that would characterize European history. They would become blindingly evident beginning in the year 312, when Emperor Constantine converted to Christianity, and again in the year 380, when Emperor Theodosius made Christianity the state religion. Suddenly the young church was flooded with thousands of prominent Romans, many of whom probably pretended to embrace the new faith out of conformity or ambition. As the English writer Charles Williams put it in his book *The Descent of the Dove*, after Constantine "all insincerity became Christian." That is what caused thousands of pious Christians to flee the cities and become prayerful hermits in the desert, or else monks secluded in rural monasteries unstained by the world.

Meanwhile, in the fifth and sixth centuries—the era when the Eastern Roman, or Byzantine, Empire reached its peak of power and splendor—the Western Roman, or Latin, Empire collapsed. Barbarian invaders plundered Western Europe for some time until, in AD 476, the last Roman emperor in Italy abdicated his throne. That calamity of civilizational proportions destroyed nearly all the achievements of Greece and Rome in both *techne* and *themis* throughout the western Mediterranean. St. Augustine of Hippo, the greatest theologian of late antiquity in the Western Roman world, had seen the catastrophe coming and was inspired to write his great treatise *The City of God* to reassure his fellow Christians that the church would survive even if the Roman state did not.

The church *did* survive, in the West, thanks in great part to St. Benedict of Nursia, a sixth-century Italian monk who began to organize ascetic Christians into disciplined monasteries devoted not only to prayer but to scholarship, worship, and charity. Beginning at Monte Cassino in southern Italy and spreading as far afield as Ireland, the Benedictine monasteries attracted orders of celibate monks who almost single-handedly preserved what remained of Greek and Roman culture. Some monks spent their entire lives meticulously copying ancient texts. Others risked martyrdom by serving as missionaries to pagan barbarians. In so doing, both laid the foundation for what historians call medieval Europe.

Chapter 3

Faith Based on Reason: The Medieval Millennium

Is it possible to summarize the history of a whole continent over a thousand years in a single chapter? Alas, such a hasty adumbration is too often the fate of the medieval era.

The first thing to know about the medieval millennium is that Europeans were not aware they were living in some "Middle Age." That notion was a conceit invented by savants of the fifteenth-century Renaissance who imagined their own age a rebirth of ancient glories, and it was later popularized by savants of the eighteenth-century Enlightenment who imagined their own age a new birth of reason. From their point of view, the era between the fall of the Western Roman Empire and their own seemed to have been an ignorant and superstitious one dominated by the church.

Such a notion was itself ignorant. To be sure, the territories of western and central Europe were overrun by barbarians during late antiquity, and as a result much ancient science, literature, and art disappeared along with the Roman Empire's roads and aqueducts. But thanks to the clergy—almost the only literate people left in Europe—some ancient learning survived. And thanks to the monasteries, new technologies would be pioneered during the medieval era. Historians even speak of a so-called "little Renaissance of the twelfth century," which preceded by three hundred years the Renaissance of which we typically speak. What is more, classical learning survived without interruption through the entire medieval millennium in the eastern Roman, or Byzantine, Empire based at Constantinople.

Beginning in the third century of the Christian era, the Western Roman Empire was invaded by waves of nomadic tribespeople who migrated west from the grassy steppes of central Asia into the continent later called Europe. Sometimes the migrations were caused by overpopulation and the quest for new pastureland, but often these Germanic tribes were forced westward by the territorial expansion of even fiercer tribes, such as the Huns, Avars, and Vandals. For two centuries the Roman Empire's legions held the barbarians at bay—or else permitted them to settle inside the empire in return for military service. But as Roman society grew increasingly decadent, the upper classes ceased to perform public service, or even reproduce, while the lower classes grew surly and rebellious. Population declined, partly thanks to Asian diseases spread along caravan routes. The economy shrank, too, even as the imperial budget grew out of control due to military expense, wasteful luxuries for the elites, and "bread and circuses" for the masses. By the later fourth century the imperial legions, whose soldiers were now mostly German, fought among themselves, overthrew emperors, and sapped what little Roman patriotism remained. In the year 410, Visigoths sacked the capital itself, and in 476 the last emperor, now based at Ravenna in northeastern Italy, abdicated his throne, whereupon the western empire splintered into rival kingdoms.

The fate of the eastern empire, anchored by its impregnable capital on the Hellespont where Asia Minor (the Anatolian peninsula or modern-day Turkey) and Europe meet, was decidedly different. The original name of that capital city was Byzantium, which is why the realm became known as the Byzantine Empire, but the city was renamed Constantinople by Emperor Constantine. After the fall of Rome, the Byzantine economy, army, and navy remained strong enough to reconquer parts of Italy during the reign of Justinian I from 527 to 565. It was he who built the magnificent Cathedral of St. Sophia (Holy Wisdom) in Constantinople, patronized art, and codified Roman law. Not surprisingly, the Greeks in the Byzantine Empire quickly came to look upon the now barbaric Latin West with contempt and soon drifted apart.

Gradually, two Christian cultures emerged—the Roman Catholic and

Justinian and Theodora briefly reconquered Italy in the sixth century, but the Byzantine Empire soon began to shrink under the assault of Arabs zealous for their new faith, Islam.

the Greek Orthodox—each with its own liturgical and theological variation. Another big difference lay in their ecclesiology, or theory of church government. The Byzantine emperors doubled as patriarchs of the eastern church, or else appointed the patriarchs who served as the eastern equivalent of the pope, a practice called caesaropapism. Over the centuries the eastern and western churches quarreled over missionary jurisdictions until 1054, when the pope in Rome and patriarch in Constantinople excommunicated each other on grounds of heresy and fell into schism. Incidentally, the boundary carved out by that rivalry persists to this day on the Balkan peninsula, where Greek Orthodox Serbs hate the Roman Catholic Croatians even though the two peoples are ethnic and linguistic cousins. The Serbs were converted by Greek missionaries from Constantinople and taught the Cyrillic alphabet, while the Croats were converted by Catholic missionaries and taught the Roman alphabet.

The Byzantine Empire began to experience its own great blow from external, non-Christian forces when the prophet Muhammad began to convert Arabs in the year 610 to the worship of Allah and the faith of Islam (which means "submission") and urged his converts to spread the new religion—by force, if necessary—through the Middle Eastern and Mediterranean regions.

In the centuries to follow, Muslims, as adherents to Islam were called, overran the Christian provinces of Egypt, Syria, and North Africa, and threatened the core of the Byzantine Empire. Far to the west, the Muslim tide even swept over Spain and crossed the Pyrenees into France before the Frankish king Charles Martel turned it back at the Battle of Tours in 732. The Muslims called Moors nevertheless held on to the Iberian Peninsula; it would take Christian rulers no fewer than seven hundred years to evict the Moors from what became Spain and Portugal.

Despite its collapse, memory of the Roman Empire persisted during the early medieval era because not only the church but also secular rulers dreamed of reconstituting a unified Christian empire. Among them was a grandson of Charles Martel, a man whose conquering armies subdued all of what is now France, the Low Countries, western Germany, and northern Italy. This man's military prowess, political skill, and personal piety were so great that in his own lifetime he came to be called Karl der Grosse—Charles the Great, or Charlemagne. One of his court poets even dubbed him "King and Father of Europe." Most famously, on Christmas Day in the year 800 the pope crowned Charlemagne Emperor of the West.

Charlemagne, though barely literate himself, was an avid patron of the arts. He brought learned monks to his imperial court at Aix-la-Chapelle (Aachen in German) in order to preserve what classical knowledge had survived. He codified laws and—by rewarding his chiefs with titles of nobility and land grants called fiefs of land—spread the feudal system across western Europe. But his empire did not last long. Charlemagne's grandsons quarreled over their inheritances until four treaties, the first of which was made at Verdun in 843, divided the empire's lands roughly along the lines of what centuries later would become France, Germany, the Netherlands, and Italy. It so happened that Louis the Pious was the grandson who inherited Charlemagne's imperial dignity, which is why his mostly German realm came to be known as the Holy Roman Empire. That accident was to have immense consequences for European history.

By historical convention Charlemagne's reign marks the transition from the early Middle Ages (pejoratively called the "Dark Ages") to the prosperous high Middle Ages, which lasted until the fourteenth century. During that era, western and central Europe consolidated into more or less stable political units ruled by the Holy Roman emperor, the kings of France, England, Castile and Aragon in Spain, Bohemia, and Hungary, plus various dukes, counts, and margraves who swore fealty to their superiors and in turn had vassals beneath them. Since almost all the princely states were dynastic, accidents of birth, death, and marriage sparked constant conflicts over the inheritance of lands and titles. Politically, therefore, Europe remained fractured. But culturally it became more united, thanks to the one holy, Catholic, and apostolic church governed by its own hierarchy, from the bishop of Rome, or pope, through archbishops, bishops, and monastic abbots down to parish priests. The clergy spoke and wrote in a common tongue—Latin—and had a common loyalty that, in theory at least, transcended politics and ethnicity. Over time, the clergy became responsible not only for religious functions but for all manner of social functions, including the administration of law and justice, charity, and education. In the course of the high medieval era the Catholic Church also acquired a substantial share of Europe's land and wealth, in large part because wealthy lords and merchants often made large bequests to the church out of concern for their immortal souls.

Finally, a new era dawned around the year 1000 because at about that time the barbarians in Europe were finally subdued. The last pagan holdouts in the forests of Saxony, Bohemia, Hungary, Poland, and Scandinavia (the homeland of the fierce Vikings and Norsemen) surrendered their worship of pagan gods under the influence of missionaries and crusading knights, which allowed a more mature and secure Christian civilization to emerge in western and central Europe, a civilization in which life itself was properly understood as a divine calling.

We conventionally imagine medieval society as comprising a rigid system consisting of three legal estates: the clergy, the nobility, and the commoners (mostly peasants). I say "legal estates" because these were not social classes of the modern sort. Social mobility barely existed outside the church, and one's status was defined by a feudal relationship, a sort of unwritten contract that stipulated everyone's rights and duties vis-à-vis everyone else. This feudal system developed during Charlemagne's reign and gradually spread throughout Europe. But it was not universal, and local variations abounded.

The word *feudal* is derived from *fief*, meaning a grant of land and legal rights from a ruler to a vassal, who in turn granted rights to cultivate land to *his* vassals, and so on down to the humblest peasant. The function of the feudal system was to provide military security—quite understandable, given that the five hundred years following the fall of the Roman Empire were ones of nearly constant danger. Barbarian invasions, including those of the Vikings in northwestern Europe, the Normans in western Europe and the Mediterranean, and the Magyars (Hungarians) and Bulgars in east-central Europe, vexed settled communities. Christian lords also warred against each other, most notoriously when the now-converted Normans from northwestern France conquered England in 1066. Incidentally, that French overlay on Anglo-Saxon England explains why the English language developed its extremely rich vocabulary, based as it is on Celtic, Germanic, and French words and grammar, seasoned with many other words derived from Latin and Greek.

Kings and emperors dealt with this violence by bestowing noble titles and local authority on trusted warriors in exchange for their military service in times of need. The nobility, in turn, bestowed rights and privileges on their own vassals in exchange for service. Even peasants were granted plots on which to support themselves in exchange for their service as workers and fighters.

But how did the fief as an economic system make sense? The answer is that its elaborate social and legal arrangements were needed to maintain the ultimate weapon of the day, a weapon its Byzantine inventors called the cataphract and that came to be known as the mounted knight. An armored warrior on horseback was impervious to the swords or spears of an enemy and was irresistible on the attack. Mounted knights were made possible by the invention of the stirrup, which passed into Europe from Asia via the Byzantine Empire. But they were expensive, especially in that primitive agricultural era. Knights needed armor, lances, swords, battle-axes, a retinue of esquires, and not least a stable full of powerful steeds. Their castles, too, were expensive, labor-intensive propositions. Yet they were necessary to protect a lord's household and property, as well as the lives of peasants and villagers during an enemy assault.

A supporting social structure therefore grew up around medieval Europe's warrior caste, the proud aristocracy or *noblesse d'épée* (nobility of the sword), and the nobility in turn contrived an array of social conventions to define gentlemanly behavior, especially in terms of honor, courage, honesty, piety, *courtoisie* (a French word derived from the "courting" of ladies), and chivalry (from the French *chevalier*, meaning "horseman"). Such "noble" behavior was celebrated in romantic myths such as those depicting King Arthur's Camelot with its round table of pious knights. The reality, of course, was different. Most knights were ignorant, loutish, and skilled mostly in the bashing of heads, and whenever no genuine enemies were at hand, these warriors grew restless. So they staged tournaments as a sort of moral equivalent of war, or "feuded" with each other, or rebelled against their own liege lords.

At the same time, the legal order based on personal oaths and contracts combined with the decentralized feudal system to bestow on the nobility certain rights that limited the authority of kings and emperor: rights the nobles defended through representative assemblies. The French called theirs the *États généraux*. The German principalities called theirs the *Landtag*, and the entire Holy Roman Empire had its *Reichstag*. Scandinavians simply called their assembly the Thing, while the English, of course, established Parliament, whose name derived from the French verb *parler*, "to talk." In the year 1215 the Anglo-Norman nobility and church even forced England's King John to accept Magna Carta—the great charter that limited royal power and granted Parliament the authority to make laws and impose taxation.

Indeed, the rule of law, human rights, checks and balances, separation of church and state, and representative government all emerged in their initial forms during the high medieval era.

Beneath the lords lay the great mass of peasants, often referred to as serfs, who existed only to serve. This is another misleading caricature, for in most parts of Europe peasants were not serfs in the Russian sense of being virtually owned by their masters or tied to the land by force. Although they were subservient, they were not slaves. They existed within a legal web of reciprocal rights and duties, just as their lords did.

There is no question that life in the medieval countryside was nasty, brutish, comparatively short, and subject to the whims of weather, disease, malnutrition, violence, ignorance, and a dreary sameness. But who is to say the lives of medieval peasants were worse than those of today's rural poor in Africa, Asia, or South America? In any event, medieval peasants knew no life other than the ones their parents and grandparents had also lived in the same village, tilling the same fields in the shadows of the same castles, chateaux, or monasteries. Moreover, even rural folk enjoyed market days and feast days, when the ale flowed freely and wandering jesters, dancers, and troubadours might perform. Rural families also knew times, such as high summer or the dead of winter, when there was far less work to do. Peasants were born into their stations, and their duty to their landlord, family, and indeed to God, was to be content and do the best with what they had.

Finally, what of the clergy? Their group alone recruited members from nobles and commoners alike, and among their number were wealthy bishops, poor parish priests, fat monks in monasteries, mendicant friars, comfortable clerks serving a lord or bishop, and missionaries risking their lives on pagan frontiers. The church was so diverse and mobile because it was the only estate a person was not born into but rather was *called* into. The church met people's spiritual needs by administering the sacraments. Its clergy also ministered to widows and orphans, the sick and the aged, and people of all legal stations seeking refuge from enemies or avengers.

That said, the church was just as susceptible to incompetence and corruption as was the nobility. Many medieval priests could barely stumble through the Latin mass, much less preach sermons or teach erudite theology. It may be apocryphal, but legend has it that the term *hocus-pocus* for magical nonsense is derived from the medieval mispronunciation of "Hoc est Corpus Meum"—a Latin phrase that means "This is my body," uttered by priests during the liturgy of the Eucharist. Bibles were rarely accessible, since books were extremely rare before the invention of printing and appeared only in Latin translation. Hence, religious observance during the medieval era was usually limited to the sacraments of baptism, marriage, communion, and absolution, plus whatever biblical stories might be depicted on church walls. Nevertheless, since the church possessed a monopoly on sacramental grace, all men and women—even, on a few occasions, the Holy Roman emperor himself—were obliged to bow to clerical authority lest they imperil their immortal souls. Over the centuries, various forms of corruption polluted the church. Some men joined the clergy out of ambition rather than piety, accepted bribes, neglected fasting and prayer, or pocketed the donations of pilgrims seeking miraculous cures or atonement in churches and monasteries that displayed allegedly holy relics, such as a bone fragment chipped from the skeleton of some martyred saint.

The saving grace of the medieval church was its power to generate reform from within, usually through new orders of "religious"—that is, monks and nuns. Among the greatest of high medieval reformers were the Franciscans and

Dominicans, orders whose names are familiar to this day because of the many Catholic schools and universities affiliated with those orders. St. Francis of Assisi (died 1226), the son of a prosperous merchant, wasted his youth on wine, women, and song until growing bored. He prayed for a spiritual calling, only to discover that many Italian clergy were as fond of the carnal pleasures as he had been. So Francis took vows of poverty and chastity, gave all his wealth to the poor, and founded an order of itinerant mendicant preachers. St. Dominic of Guzman (died 1221) was a Spaniard disgusted by the church's low standards. He, too, founded a mendicant order of scholarly preachers and teachers to tutor clergy and establish schools.

Another hugely important reform was launched at the French monastery at Cluny. Its leaders were appalled by the tendency of monks to pay more attention to their wine cellars than their chapels. The response of the Cluniacs and their imitators was to found monasteries rededicated to prayer and charity. The greatest bequest of their movement, however, was in the unlikely realm of *techne* rather than *themis*. Cluny's rule required monks to gather for prayer four times during the day and four times during the night. How could they know what times to come in from their fields, cells, or beds to gather for Vespers or Matins? The monks solved that problem by inventing the mechanical clock. Clockmaking, as refined over the twelfth through the fifteenth centuries, stimulated the spread of fine craftsmanship and helped to spark a host of technical inventions. Cluniacs pioneered or improved such technologies as water wheels, grist mills, carpentry, metallurgy, and glassblowing. Indeed, during the high medieval era the monks of Cluny and its offshoot abbeys imagined technology to be evidence of a divine spark, which meant that humanity was a sort of demiurge stimulating progress and even pursuit of an earthly paradise.

The reforming spirit of the high Middle Ages also inspired the creation of the College of Cardinals in the forlorn hope of insulating papal elections from outside pressures. The popes in turn tried to discipline secular rulers. They especially targeted the scandal of Christians fighting among themselves for power, wealth, and glory. One papal initiative was the Truce of God, which banned fighting on the Sabbath and saints' days and during penitential seasons such as Lent. A second, far more portentous initiative was to give restless knights a productive outlet for their belligerence. Beginning with Urban II in 1095, the popes promoted the Crusades.

These days, political correctness compels Europeans, especially Catholics, to condemn the Crusades. But they were conceived at the time as a highly moral enterprise meant to rekindle a spirit of piety and sacrifice among knights and kings, to end intramural strife among Christians, and to launch long overdue counterattacks against those Muslims who had conquered the Holy Land via their own crusades of the seventh century. Indeed, the First Crusade proved to be a remarkable success. But over several centuries the launching of crusades became habitual for the newly confident high medieval Europeans, partly because of the Crusades' commercial advantages. Kings and their knights became far more interested in plunder than in piety. Massacres of combatant and noncombatant Muslims and even Jews marred several Crusades. In the most scandalous case, a crusading army turned aside from its intended itinerary in order to sack the Greek Orthodox capital of Constantinople. The sole achievement of the campaigns, the Crusader kingdom established at Jerusalem, lasted from 1099 until 1187, when it was reconquered by the Kurdish Sultan Saladin.

However dysfunctional they eventually proved to be, the Crusades were of historic importance because they renewed European contacts with the Levant (the eastern Mediterranean littoral). Classical Greek literature and art, as well as Arabic science and mathematics, were now introduced into western Europe—including our "Arabic" numerical system, which originated in India. Caravan routes across Asia became known to Europeans and—in the case of Marco Polo in the 1200s—even made accessible the far distant and mysterious China. Trade in Asian spices and silks enriched Venice and other Italian city-states, whose wealth and cosmopolitan learning would lay the basis for the Renaissance.

Another source of strength for high medieval Europe was the sustained increase in crop yields achieved thanks to a favorable climate, a brilliant invention, and an equally brilliant breakthrough in agronomy. The meteorological boon was the fact that the northern hemisphere, from the eleventh to the fifteenth centuries, was unusually warm. Those higher temperatures were what allowed Vikings to sail in their open boats to Iceland, Greenland, and even Vinland in North America. Most importantly, hemispheric warming led to longer growing seasons and richer harvests. The brilliant invention, made by a blacksmith lost to history, was the moldboard plow. Its curved iron blade sliced easily through the crusty topsoil of northern Europe and left behind a deep furrow that captured rainwater for the thirsty seeds and shoots of grain planted within. Plows further increased yields and allowed farmers to cultivate marginal land. Finally, the advance in agronomy was the trial-and-error discovery that planting the same crop year after year wore out the soil. Medieval villagers responded by gradually adopting a three-field system in which crops were rotated and a third of their fields allowed to lie fallow each year. The result was a rapid growth in population, the clearing of forests from the Atlantic to Poland, and food surpluses that supported new, burgeoning towns.

Towns! People increasingly gathered by the hundreds and even thousands in urban markets to exchange goods, services, ideas, and money. In towns, people were not merely lords, peasants, or priests; they were craftsmen, merchants, scholars. The commercial activities of towns helped meet the growing demand for clothing, hardware, and luxury goods. For the first time since the fall of Rome a money economy emerged, and market towns won precious charters from the kings and emperor to govern their own affairs in exchange for a tax. Peasants might move to towns and apprentice themselves to cobblers, tailors, shoemakers, carpenters, or stonemasons. Artisans formed guilds to regulate the quality and prices of their goods. Collectively, townspeople came to be known in France as "bourgeois" and in Germany as "burghers," after the bourgs, or walled towns, they inhabited.

Because literacy and numeracy were indispensable to merchants and many artisans, this urban flowering revived learning outside the church. Last but not least, the precocious new towns competed for prestige, in hopes of attracting business to their annual fairs. Burghers chipped in to build elaborate town halls displaying magnificent clocks. Residents of larger towns aimed higher, pooling their wealth with the church to construct the most exquisite symbols of high medieval civilization: the Romanesque and Gothic cathedrals adorned with sculptured stone, carved wood, and stained glass. To build such magnificent monuments was the work of centuries, spanning as many as six generations, a testament to the medieval consciousness of the brevity of one's own lifespan, and therefore the need to focus on the eternal.

Yet another urban invention of the high medieval era was the university. These first associations of scholars and students were like guilds, except their product was intellectual rather than material. The University of Bologna was founded in 1158, the University of Paris in 1200, followed by Oxford, Cambridge, Heidelberg, Prague, Cracow, Salamanca, and dozens more in the following centuries.

Universities harbored colleges of theology, law, medicine, and philosophy. They also taught the seven liberal arts comprising the *trivium*—grammar, rhetoric, and logic—and the *quadrivium*—arithmetic, geometry, astronomy, and music. The universities fostered *techne* in the service of *themis*, not least because they were all affiliated with the Catholic Church. Far from being a principal opponent of science, the medieval church was the principal patron of science, even if the popes' embrace of many Aristotelian scientific doctrines turned out later to be wrong.

Eighteenth-century philosophers would bequeath to us moderns the myth that medieval schoolmen debated such silly questions as how many angels could dance on the head of a pin. But that was a canard, a malevolent falsehood. What thirteenth-century universities did produce was that era's greatest theologian in St. Thomas Aquinas, its greatest poet in Dante Alighieri, and perhaps its greatest philosopher in William of Ockham, whose epistemological principle known as Ockham's razor would lay an important foundation for the Scientific Revolution to come. Ockham postulated that whenever several theories might serve to explain a phenomenon, the simplest can be assumed to be right.

Indeed, so dynamic were the high Middle Ages that the even greater burst of creativity we call the Renaissance might have happened a century earlier than it did, had not the four horsemen of the apocalypse—War, Pestilence, Famine, and Death—struck Europe and hurled it into the crisis-torn late medieval era beginning in the middle of the fourteenth century.

First, interminable wars were provoked by kings and emperors determined to forge strong territorial states and expand at the expense of their neighbors. These wars were born of new national identities, and they were fueled by terrible new weapons such as gunpowder and cannons. Thus, for example, the *Reconquista* in Spain reached a crescendo of violence as the Christian Crusaders from Seville and Aragon fought to expel the Moors from their last stronghold in Granada, a goal finally achieved in 1492, ending a seven-hundred-year struggle on the Iberian Peninsula. And thus, for example, the kings of England, seeking to establish their claims to vast portions of France, triggered the savage Hundred Years' War from 1337 to 1453. People often associate that war with Joan of Arc, who saved the French cause but was abandoned to torture and death by the French king because he feared her popularity. But the war's important effects were to kindle national feelings in both countries at the expense of feudal and Christian loyalties and to introduce new weapons—artillery and the longbow—that could pierce a knight's armor and kill from a distance. The era of the mounted knight would soon come to its ignominious end.

A second cause of decline in the late medieval era was a crisis in the Catholic Church. Those Cluniac reforms, universities, Crusades, and the influx of new wealth had propelled the church to an apex of wealth and power, but the same factors had also planted the seeds of decay. The richer the church became, the more did young men with connections covet clerical posts. The mightier the church became, the more did secular rulers seek ways to control its clergy. The more independence university scholars achieved, the more did they conjure ideas the church deemed heretical. Historian Owen Chadwick shrewdly summed up these developments by observing that in the fullness of time the medieval church suffered from a multifaceted inflation of its power, wealth, and duties that was bound to corrode its spiritual purity.

The church's vulnerabilities were exposed in the 1290s when the French King Philip the Fair claimed the right to tax church property. Pope Boniface VIII replied with a thundering decree reaffirming the church's tax-exempt status. Philip's response was to march his army to Rome, and—when Boniface died—force the College of Cardinals to elect a pope of his choosing. Then he physically moved the papal court from Rome to the French town of Avignon, where it remained for over a century.

This "Babylonian captivity" of the papacy scandalized Europe, especially when the Holy Roman emperor sponsored the election of a second pope in 1378, whereupon a council of bishops deposed both sitting popes and elected a third! Finally, in 1414, another council persuaded all three popes to resign. But the damage done to the church's integrity and authority was immense.

Meanwhile, a third and most gruesome blow descended on medieval Europe. In 1348 the Black Death, a killer disease we know as the bubonic plague, arrived from Asia via the commercial routes. The bacillus was carried by fleas that lived in the hair of rats. It caused an infected person to develop bulbous black boils and a searing fever, and often to die within twenty-four hours. Europeans had no genetic defenses against this Asian plague and no understanding of how to prevent or cure it. So people perished. Whole villages perished. Whole urban neighborhoods perished. Whole provinces were ravaged until, as revealed in parish records, more than a third of all Europeans had died.

Imagine the psychological, social, and economic effects of such mortality. The plague brought down the curtain on the prosperity and self-confidence that had prevailed during the high medieval era and—together with terrible wars and the crisis of the papacy—primed the medieval mind and polity for radical change.

That was especially the case once a fourth crushing blow fell on the continent during the fourteenth and fifteenth centuries. That blow was delivered by the mightiest military threat Christendom had ever encountered: the Ottoman Turks. A warlike Muslim people armed with gunpowder and cannons, Turkish tribes ruled by Osman swept out of Asia to conquer the Byzantine provinces in Asia Minor and southeastern Europe, and finally Constantinople itself in the year 1453. The shock was incalculable. Yet, ironically, the flood of Byzantine refugees—carrying with them the treasures of Greek culture they had preserved for a thousand years—bestowed upon the urban centers of northern Italy the incentives and knowledge needed to embark on the artistic, literary, scientific, technological, and geographical voyages of discovery known to us today as the Quattrocento, the Italian Renaissance of the 1400s.

Chapter 4

Renaissance!
Humanism and the Classical Revival

This is an apt moment to cite one historian's description of the difficulty in employing historical labels.

> The prevalent notion that a Renaissance followed the medieval era was first expressed by Italians during the 1400s. According to them, a thousand years of unrelieved darkness had intervened between the ancient Roman era and their own times. During those so-called "dark ages" the Muses of art and literature had fled Europe before an onslaught of barbarism and ignorance. Almost miraculously the Muses returned and Italians happily collaborated with them to bring forth a glorious Renaissance, or rebirth. And ever since then historians have taken for granted the existence of a sort of rebirth that marked the transition from medieval to modern. Most famously, nineteenth century German historian Jacob Burkhardt popularized the idea that a unique Renaissance Spirit not only transformed culture, but political, social, and economic life as well. . . . In fact, however, the high Middle Ages witnessed no such "death" of classical learning. St. Thomas Aquinas, for instance, considered Aristotle the model Philosopher, and Dante thought Virgil the model Poet. Likewise, it would be false to imagine a revival of

paganism as opposed to medieval Europe's deep Christian faith, because however much Renaissance men and women loved the classics, no one revived the worship of pagan gods. Finally, all definitions of the Renaissance must be qualified by the fact that there was no single "Renaissance position" on any given subject.

So wrote John Merriman at the start of the chapter about the Renaissance in his textbook on modern history. The passage is highly instructive because it emphasizes the fact that fifteenth-century Italians and a nineteenth-century German invented the idea of a Renaissance in order to denigrate the medieval era. It thereby illustrates the problems historians confront whenever they try to label and periodize the past.

Merriman began his discussion of the Renaissance by qualifying the notion of a radical break. However, he proceeded to list some of the distinguishing traits that make the notion of a rebirth somewhat meaningful. First, there was indeed a quantitative explosion in classical knowledge during the fifteenth century. To be sure, medieval scholars had known a sizable number of ancient authors, but during the 1400s and 1500s many more works by Cicero, Ovid, Livy, Tacitus, Lucretius, and Greek philosophers and playwrights were rediscovered. Second, Renaissance thinkers not only had access to more classical texts than before, but they used them in new ways. Whereas medieval scholars tended to invoke ancient sources to complement and confirm their Christian and/or Aristotelian assumptions, Renaissance scholars drew on the classics to reconsider inherited ideas. Such determination to learn from classical antiquity was even more pronounced in architecture and art, contributing to a distinct "Renaissance style." Third, although European culture did not become pagan by any means, it certainly did become more secular than that of the Middle Ages. Indeed, the prosperity and cosmopolitanism of the Italian city-states in the fifteenth and sixteenth centuries created a supportive environment for attitudes that stressed the attainment of success in *this* life, in the commercial, political, and artistic arenas of *this* world.

Fourth, if one word comes closest to summing up the Renaissance ideal, it is humanism. In the technical sense, humanism was a curriculum designed to replace the medieval Scholastic emphasis on logic and metaphysics with studies of language, literature, history, and ethics. Humanist teachers stressed, well, the humanities—that is, those arts and sciences they believed would make students virtuous and prepare them to contribute to the public functions of their states.

Moreover, the broader sense of humanism stressed the dignity of humanity, the status of man as the most excellent of all God's creatures below the angels. Some Renaissance thinkers argued that human beings were excellent because, among all earthly creatures, they alone could apprehend the existence and nature of God, master their own fates, manipulate the natural world through technology, and thereby improve themselves and their surroundings. Humanists had a firm belief in the nobility and possibilities of the human race.

Nobility and possibility: think for a moment about the contrast between such humanist anthropology and the anthropology stressed by medieval civilization. The medieval church had boldly affirmed a concept of human dignity based on the biblical faith that men and woman were created in the very image of God. But the church also stressed the fallen condition of an imperfect human race. That is, human beings were possessed of a divine spark, but they were separated from God by willful sin and were incapable of improvement except by God's grace. The church also took the biblical prophets at their word when they predicted that history would end in a dreadful apocalypse prior to the triumphal return of the Messiah. Insofar as material progress was possible, it was doomed to be overcome by spiritual regress. Renaissance humanists, by contrast, tended to shrug off the medieval emphasis on sin and decay, choosing instead to praise humanity's virtues and powers.

The clash between those two images of humanity—the first humble regarding this life but hopeful regarding eternity, the second boastful regarding this life and complacent regarding eternity—characterizes the entire modern era of European history. That clash also expressed the growing tension between *techne* and *themis*. Should people be on guard against worshiping their technology, as taught by the cautionary myth of Icarus (who learned how to fly like a bird only to perish by coming too close to the sun), and thus take care always to keep *techne* subordinate to *themis*? Or should people have confidence that progress would render them not only more powerful but more virtuous and godlike, in which case *themis* should always be subordinate to *techne*?

Questions about progress will haunt this entire book, and readers must arrive at their own judgments. What, after all, does it mean to say that the world is getting better? Is the contemporary United States better than, say, medieval

Poland because Americans today have full grocery stores, jets, smartphones, and the right to vote? Or is the United States worse than medieval Poland because American society is tainted by crime, pollution, hedonism, runaway debt, and nuclear weapons? Are people today "better" because they are free to believe whatever they wish, or are they "worse" for believing in wicked things or, what is more likely, nothing at all? Is modern society superior because the average middle-class family today enjoys a standard of living far beyond that of a medieval king? Or is contemporary society more anxious and miserable than a medieval village because its people are addicted to their amusements and comforts and frightened of losing them?

The Renaissance was the era in which educated Europeans began to take progress for granted. The proud citizens of northern Italian towns, reveling in their commerce, art, technology, ancient knowledge, and new knowledge gained from exploration and science, imagined they were picking up the mantle of human progress after the long medieval hiatus. The sources of their pride were real. But their self-congratulation was also a species of vanity, because a fifth characteristic of Renaissance glory was how fleeting it proved to be, even or especially in the northern Italian cities that spawned such geniuses as Leonardo da Vinci and Michelangelo di Lodovico Simoni. For Italy's combination of commercial wealth and military weakness tempted outside powers—especially France's kings and Germany's Holy Roman emperors—to invade Italy beginning in 1494 and spark a century of war that sent Florence, Milan, Padua, and Verona into gradual but irreversible decline.

Yet a sixth characteristic of Renaissance humanism was the fact that north of the Alps cultural changes occurred on a more modest scale and displayed far different tendencies. Indeed, German, English, and Dutch humanists such as Desiderius Erasmus, far from embracing ancient pagan sensibilities, hoped to strengthen and purify Christian sensibilities. Seventh and finally, proponents of the idea of a sudden and wholesale rebirth of culture ignore the fact that historical change never happens overnight and that the changes we associate with Italy's Quattrocento really began in the late medieval era and then spread so unevenly that in remote parts of Europe a Renaissance can be scarcely detected at all.

The bottom line, therefore, is that whereas the genius and achievements associated with the Renaissance were certainly real, "the Renaissance" as a coherent era did not really exist. Historians continue to argue about its chronological starting and ending points, its territorial extent, and its causes, effects, and characteristics. Hence, those of us who are fascinated by history must come to appreciate that historical terminology is a slippery thing: conventional, artificial, oversimplified. Of course, we need to employ terms in order to communicate with each other at all, but we must never forget that they are merely shorthand for realities that are far more complex.

What we can do with assurance is to list some of the sources and preconditions for the phenomena collectively known as the Renaissance.

A first precondition was the flow of Byzantine and Arab science and art into northern Italy, a flow that stemmed initially from the Crusades but vastly increased when there arrived refugees fleeing from the Ottoman Turks, especially in the wake of the catastrophic fall of Constantinople in 1453. A second precondition was the influx into northern Italy of wealth from overseas commerce. The south Asian spice trade was especially important. It had also begun during the Crusades, and it helped create a prosperous urban culture of men and—significantly—women who devoted their leisure time to secular education and art. A third was a zesty lust for life that perhaps was a delayed psychological reaction to the remission of the Black Death. Indeed, the human urge to reproduce was so powerful among Europeans that the continent regained its preplague population of about seventy-five million by the year 1500. A fourth was the advent of mighty technologies such as gunpowder, cannons, mathematical and geometric advances, and new engineering techniques, especially in architecture and shipbuilding. Those tools of navigation in turn enabled the geographical explosion detonated by the kingdoms of Spain and Portugal when their ships (often commanded by mariners from northern Italian ports) first ventured onto the open oceans and discovered sea routes to Asia and the Americas. A fifth was the unique political organization, or rather disorganization, of northern Italy, divided as it was into rival city-states like ancient Greece. The city-states fiercely competed with each other in commerce and war, and thus sought to attract to themselves the most accomplished merchants, scientists, engineers, and soldiers, thereby stimulating material progress and the brilliant artworks that glorified their rulers.

All these preconditions made northern Italy fertile ground for discovery, and what did its scholars discover as they pored over ancient texts, many of which found their way to Italy following the fall of Constantinople? They discovered that Aristotle, Plato, and the other Greeks had disagreed with each other about all manner of things, which encouraged humanists to question all authority, be it intellectual, scientific, political, or religious.

The new interest in here-and-now questions affecting daily life, and the authority to pronounce on them, were the wellsprings of Renaissance humanism. Professor Merriman rightly cautioned against assuming that humanism was anti-Christian, but humanists did question the authority of a Roman Catholic Church whose clergy—especially those of the papal court—had become decadent, hypocritical, and corrupt. Without rejecting Christian faith, scholars nonetheless felt free to revisit many of the same questions that had vexed pagan philosophers, such as how to live a good life, which they defined as a creative life that celebrates the fullness of human nature. Surely, they said, Almighty God did not endow us with our five senses, reason, curiosity, appetites, and ambition only to have people stifle those gifts just because they could sometimes be sources of sinful temptations. Surely, God meant for people to experience his creation to the utmost, to embrace it, to study it, to harness it with technology, and to become subcreators in imitation of him.

The new humanism was the natural response of a new sort of European that included wealthy, educated merchants, artisans, and officials who stood outside both the church and the nobility and who possessed the means and motives to seek fame, fortune, and fulfillment in ways that broke with the medieval norm. Wealthy humanists acquired private libraries (a novelty in European history), including not only Greek and Latin texts but books in their own vernacular languages (yet another novelty in European history). The classics inspired them to emulate great men of antiquity such as Pythagoras, Cicero, and Marcus Aurelius: men of heroism, eloquence, aesthetics, and style. Humanists were further inspired to pursue fame through their achievements in politics, business, war, and patronage of the arts.

To be sure, wealthy humanists also displayed pomposity, greed, ambition, licentiousness, and cutthroat competitiveness—qualities the English playwright William Shakespeare would damn in tragedies and lampoon in comedies. Perhaps Jacob Burkhardt oversimplified things by suggesting that all Europe suddenly exhibited a bold individualism that stood in stark contrast to the communal ethos of the medieval era. But if we confine our view to the secular elites of northern

Renaissance!

Raphael's *The Alba Madonna* (1510) was one of many Quattrocento works of art that transcended the ancients.

Italy, we would be justified in saying that humanism focused on worldly ambition rather than the heaven to come, and on the self rather than God.

A Florentine named Matteo Palmieri summarized the new spirit of progress and self-gratification when he wrote in the 1430s: "It is but in our own days that men dare boast that they see the dawn of better things. . . . Now indeed may every thoughtful spirit thank God that it has been permitted him to be born in this new age, so full of hope and promise, which already rejoices in a greater array of nobly-gifted souls than the world has seen in the thousand years that preceded it!"

By now readers might have gotten the impression that the Italian Renaissance was, among other things, an enormous ego trip based on identification with—and blind imitation of—idealized images of ancient Greeks and Romans. But the greatest art of the Quattrocento, such as the paintings, sculptures, and architecture of Leonardo, Michelangelo, Raphael, Bernini, and Brunelleschi (whose exquisite dome capped the breathtaking cathedral in Florence)—went far beyond imitation and exceeded anything created by the ancients.

For instance, extraordinary achievements were evident in music. Renaissance composers such as Claudio Monteverdi in Italy and Josquin des Pres in the Netherlands invented entirely new genres of polyphonic musical forms both sacred and secular, instrumental and oral. Most radically of all, their instrumental music was often accompanied by voices. Ancient and medieval music had been exclusively monophonic, be it the Gregorian chants sung by monks or ballads crooned by wandering minstrels. By contrast, Renaissance madrigals, motets, and operas expressed complex harmonies and new worlds of sound, while establishing the eight-toned octave as the grammar and alphabet of European music.

The Renaissance love for the application of art to technology and technology to art was also on brilliant display in the invention or vast improvement of a whole array of musical instruments, including the violin and other strings, as well as the spinet or harpsichord and other keyboard ancestors of the *pianoforte*: a word that simply combines the Italian adjectives for soft and loud and that was later shortened to *piano*. Likewise in the plastic arts, which are surely the most familiar representations of the glory of the Renaissance. Thanks to Google, people in the twenty-first century may now access not only virtually the entire repertoire of European music but also the magnificent paintings of Leonardo, Michelangelo, Titian, and Tintoretto, not to mention the works of those other artistic schools that blossomed in Spain, the Netherlands, and Germany. The hallmark of all these artistic movements was something entirely new under the sun: *naturalism*. That is, the accurate representation of the human body and the natural world. Armed with geometry and mathematics inherited from the Greeks, Arabs, and Byzantines, Italian artists mastered perspective. By varying the sizes and angular relationships of objects in the foreground, middle ground, and background, Renaissance artists depicted them on their canvases the way they really appear to the eye. They also mastered the natural depiction of light by experimenting with *chiaroscuro*—a word that simply combines the Italian adjectives for light and dark. Similarly, their application of technology to art inspired the manufacture of more and better choices of pigments, brushes, marble, and tools to cut and shape stone.

Leonardo in particular engaged in an intensive study of human anatomy that not only revived the ancient learning of Galen, the Greek physician, but far exceeded him. He and his contemporaries learned not only how to depict naturalistic human figures in paint or stone but also how to express their subject's moods through body language and facial expressions. Doubtless the most celebrated example of that technique is Leonardo's haunting *Mona Lisa*.

Does all that mean that Renaissance artists were *better* than their forebears, given that their exquisite paintings of human forms were so much more alive than the stiff, symbolic figures of medieval art? Better in technique, certainly, but not necessarily better in an aesthetic sense, because the purpose of their art, the thematic value of it, was on an entirely different scale. The contrast between High Gothic art and Renaissance art is at bottom a function of what artists and their cultures deemed important enough to depict. To the medieval artist and his patrons (usually the church and/or the townspeople adorning a cathedral), what mattered most was the spiritual truth conveyed by the art, compared to which getting a landscape exactly right was secondary. Indeed, a certain democracy pervaded medieval art, inasmuch as people looked pretty much all the same. Only Jesus, the apostles, and martyrs might stand out from the crowd, and only then in a spiritual sense, as symbolized by their halos. Church icons were allegorical visual aids meant to encourage viewers to meditate on heavenly things. The same is true with respect to the vaulting naves and towering steeples of the cathedrals. In all respects the gaze of the medieval eye was *vertical*.

Renaissance artists, by contrast, shifted their gaze to the natural world and human society around them, depicting them from their own perspective rather than God's perspective. One might say that Renaissance art diverted the eye away from human souls and their heavenly Creator in order to gaze upon human bodies and earthly creation. Indicative of that naturalistic, *horizontal* gaze was the bold sensuality present in Renaissance art. The nude made a comeback after a thousand years. Hints of erotic love intruded upon the spiritual *agape* love of Christianity and the romantic love of medieval chivalry. Renaissance artists found in the ancient mythology of Greece and Rome scores of occasions to paint and sculpt nudes both male and female. The most striking evidence of the Renaissance's horizontal perspective and adoration of the human self is that its art not only depicted classical themes in addition to Christian ones but also depicted real, ordinary women and men as if they were gods or heroes themselves.

In the self-absorbed social whirl of the Italian city-states, a wealthy merchant or banker could claim no higher status than to commission a portrait or statue of himself or his wife by a celebrated artist. The artists in turn knew how to flatter their patrons. Indeed, another significant trait of the Renaissance was that elite women and beautiful models participated in the new spirit of individualism and self-promotion. Alessandro Botticelli's *Birth of Venus* is one of the most famous examples of the Renaissance fascination with the beauty, intelligence, and mystery of women. Finally, artists played games with chronology, often depicting some ancient or biblical scene in a contemporary Italian landscape or background, or depicting their contemporary subjects as entering a Greek temple or the Roman Senate dressed in togas. It made for terrific art, but also terrific vanity—a vanity that Europeans of a century earlier would have damned as idolatrous.

We must be careful to distinguish between the Renaissance styles of fifteenth-century Italy and those of other portions of Europe. The schools of Renaissance painting in Germany, as in the works of Albrecht Dürer and Hans Holbein, or in Spain, as in the works of Doménikos Theotokópoulos (El Greco), displayed the same astounding techniques the Italian painters had achieved, but without the Italians' hot-bloodedness. In art as in scholarship and philosophy, the Renaissance north of the Alps was tempered by a Christian humanism that was in good part a reaction against the excesses of Italy's classical humanism.

When one hears the phrase "Renaissance man," one thinks of an awesome polymath who soars above his (or her) contemporaries in the arts and sciences, technology, medicine, military science, or seemingly any branch of knowledge he (or she) chooses to pursue. For instance, Leonardo's sketchbooks contained elaborate designs of such inventions as flying machines, tanks, machine guns, water works, sewage systems, and clockwork contrivances that boggle the mind when we realize they were conceived in the 1400s. But should an era of history be judged by its geniuses? Most Europeans of the time were little (or not at all) affected by the fashions and feuds of the merchants and savants of Venice and Florence, while even the *cognoscenti* (a delightful Italian word connoting trendy, "in-group" sorts of people) were very often *poseurs* whose vanity, impatience, and occasional poor taste vexed the geniuses obliged to cater to their whims. Indeed, Renaissance Italians turned prestige into a veritable commodity, and the chief sources of prestige included money, power, high office, and above all a reputation for *virtú*.

Virtù is a curious term that must not be confused with the cardinal Christian virtues of prudence, justice, fortitude, temperance, faith, hope, and charity. Renaissance *virtù* derived from the notions of virtue celebrated in ancient Greece and Rome, whose citizens were admonished to cultivate loyalty, patriotism, boldness, leadership, eloquence, stature, and style. The Italian word *virtù* is derived from the Latin word *vir*, which simply meant man; hence, *virtù* implied a manliness very different from the godliness a saint, chivalrous knight, or pious ruler of the medieval era would characteristically aim to attain. On the contrary, true to their veneration of ancient culture, Renaissance Italians celebrated the sort of heroism honored in the ancient Greek *polis* or Roman *res publica*. They elevated heroes like the patriotic orators Pericles and Cicero, or heroes like the citizen-soldier Cincinnatus, who left his plow to lead the Roman army to victory in war, then humbly returned to his farm.

The contrast between Renaissance *virtù* and medieval virtue was on display, in the bold tones of *chiaroscuro*, in the politics of the city-states, politics that were ruthless, even vicious. Ambitious families such as the Borgias and Medicis, as well as individual demagogues and warlords, competed for prestige and power through deception, duplicity, and murderous violence. Daggers and poison chose the leaders of city-states as often as did elections and councils. But the mere fact of one's elevation to leadership proved one's *virtù*, whatever methods one employed to get there. Shakespeare's play *Macbeth*, although set in Scotland, was a northern humanist critique of the Machiavellian politics prevalent in southern Europe. Thus, the Quattrocento: so famous for its culture, it was also the era when clans ruled city-states through deception, betrayal, and bribery, when mercenary armies were hired to conquer neighboring cities, when foreign kings were bankrolled, and when conspiracies maneuvered kin into high office, including the papacy itself. To those who were daring, skillful, or lucky, life itself was a work of art that men, and to some degree women, were free to craft for themselves.

One Renaissance man who dared grandly, and was both skillful and lucky, hailed from the Italian port of Genoa, and he hit the jackpot in 1492 courtesy of the king and queen of Spain. That man was Cristoforo Colombo (Christopher Columbus), who will be discussed at some length in a subsequent chapter.

One of the ancient writers most revered by Italians was Plutarch. His biographies of great Romans, collected in an anthology called *Plutarch's Lives*, were rediscovered during the 1400s. They provided humanists with a ready-made standard for heroism, eloquence, and stature—in short, for *virtú*. The Renaissance French philosopher Michel de Montaigne even said Plutarch had raised Europeans out of the dirt. Italians, who especially identified with their Roman ancestors, revered Plutarch and cherished his explosive aphorism "'Tis better to will the good than to know the truth." Think about that. It sounds like a wise saying, even a natural conclusion for Renaissance scholars to reach, given their appreciation of how often ancient philosophers had disagreed with each other. It seemed self-evident that no one had a monopoly of truth, not even the Catholic Church, the corruption of whose hierarchy was never more on display than during the Renaissance. So perhaps it really was wiser to will the good—to display one's *virtú*—rather than fight over versions of truth.

Perhaps—if human beings are more adept at discovering and practicing "the good" than they are at discovering and accepting "the truth." But if human beings charge off in pursuit of the good while casting the truth underfoot, then Plutarch's maxim can easily become a formula for arrogance, self-delusion, and power unfettered by anything but will. It was Pontius Pilate, after all, who mockingly asked Jesus, "Quid est veritas?" (What is truth?). In modern times, bloodthirsty ideologues such as Cromwell, Robespierre, Lenin, and Hitler all claimed that their revolutions embodied the good, even as they trampled the truth.

That is why another wise adage teaches that "virtue is more dangerous than vice, because it isn't constrained by conscience." And why a second wise adage teaches that "hypocrisy is the tribute vice pays to virtue," for the hypocrite at least confesses the existence of truth.

In any event, the oligarchs whose *virtú* derived from their wealth, lineage, or, in the case of the mercenary *condottieri*, military prowess rose and fell in their city-states according to how well they mastered, not the good or the truth, but politics. Fortunately for their citizens, most oligarchs understood that their power derived in good part from how well their rule advanced the security and prosperity of their city-state. But over time their incessant intrigues and wars weakened Italy to the point that it became vulnerable to foreign invasion, even as its wealth made it a tempting victim. Those invasions began right on cue during the last decade of the magnificent Quattrocentro.

In retrospect, therefore, a great deal of irony surrounds *Oration on the Dignity of Man*, an essay written in 1486 by a young Florentine named Giovanni

Pico della Mirandola. He imagined that when God created man he placed him at the center of the universe, saying, "We have made you neither heavenly nor earthly, neither mortal nor immortal, so that as the free and honorable molder and maker of yourself, you may fashion yourself in whatever form you prefer. . . . To man it is granted to have whatever he chooses, to become whatever he wills." Free will to become whatever you will! As we know, the ancient Greeks and Hebrews had pondered free will at length. But the pagan stoics imagined human will to be circumscribed by irresistible fate and the caprice of the gods, whereas Jews and Christians identified human will with the propensity to sin. The novelty of Mirandola was his joyous, uncomplicated *celebration* of free will. Casting fate and sin to the winds, he imagined free will to be a divine promise of limitless power and self-gratification. Whether we think that healthy ambition or prideful self-worship, such an expression of faith in freedom and progress was a tocsin sounding the birth of the age we call modern.

Materialism, secular culture, sensuality, corruption, murderous politics, and idolatrous self-worship: What on earth happened to the church such that a reversal of medieval sensibilities occurred in cities just a few hundred miles from Rome? The short answer is not only that the late medieval and Renaissance papacy had become decadent, and had even suffered that schism in the early 1400s when two, and on one occasion three, popes contested for authority, but also that by the end of the fifteenth century popes were habitually elected through bribery and backroom deals manipulated by foreign monarchs and Italy's wealthy bankers and merchants. A few pontiffs even lived openly with their mistresses and had children by them. Many Renaissance popes hosted opulent feasts in the Vatican and even sponsored luxurious art and architecture paid for with the donations of the faithful. Simony—the selling of religious offices—was widespread. Moreover, since popes were also the temporal rulers of a province in central Italy known as the Papal States, they also engaged in war and diplomacy.

Hence it was understandable that toward the end of the hedonistic Quattrocento, in the very heart of Renaissance Italy, a frenetic religious revival occurred. It was sparked in Florence in 1494 by a fire-and-brimstone preacher who condemned the lifestyles of the rich and famous, damned the worldliness of the humanists, and called on the lower classes to make a cultural revolution on behalf of moral reform. The zealot was an eloquent, learned Dominican friar named Girolamo Savonarola. His inflammatory sermons created a frenzy as mobs rioted in the streets and burst into the villas of the rich. Savonarola appeared to encourage the overthrow of the Medici dynasty, preached against all manner of vice, and imagined Florence becoming a veritable kingdom of God destined to reform all of Italy. Under his influence Florentines hurled their sinful possessions—everything from luxurious clothes and perfumes to dice, playing cards, and pornography—into the flames, which Savonarola called the "bonfire of the vanities."

It did not take long for the papacy, rival religious orders, and the social elites of Florence to make all manner of false accusations against the preacher, culminating in his trial and condemnation as a heretic. In the end, the same Florentine citizens who had wept and cheered when Savonarola gained power wept and cheered again when he was burned at the stake.

The contretemps is instructive. Savonarola condemned the values of the Italian Renaissance, but his own rise to prominence mirrored the rhetoric, ambition, and demagogy celebrated by the proponents of *virtù*. Moreover, while Savonarola's definition of the good could not have clashed more with that of the humanists, he too was convinced that he willed the good, which Plutarch— and Pico della Mirandola—had said was all that really mattered. So while it is tempting to see the Florentine revival as a popular reaction against the century's excesses, it was also a product of that age and a dangerous example of the breakdown of authority characteristic of the modern era of history. Finally, inasmuch as Savonarola attacked the corrupt papacy, his revolt can be seen as a harbinger of the Protestant Reformation, which began just twenty-three years later.

However, there is still more to the story, because Savonarola's drama occurred the very same year as that foreign invasion that submerged the city-states beneath the waves of much larger European rivalries. That was ironic, because many of the grand traditions of European statecraft had been invented by Venice and other Italian states during the 1400s. First, the Italians established the practice of opening embassies in foreign capitals to practice diplomacy and to gather political, military, and commercial intelligence. The practice was so valuable that soon the kings of France, Spain, England, and the Holy Roman emperor began to do likewise. Second, the deceptive techniques of Italian statecraft also spread throughout Europe. The first monarch to establish a permanent foreign ministry (staffed and financed mostly by Italians) was Louis XI of France. So poisonous were his intrigues that they earned him the epithet Louis the Spider. Third, the Italian states forged what political scientists call a multipolar balance-of-power system in which states make shifting alliances to prevent any one of them from gaining too much power. The upshot was that Italy as a whole was divided by internal rivalries and unable to unite against foreign invaders.

Already during the late medieval era Germany's Holy Roman emperors had tried to impose their authority over Italy, which forced the city-states to choose between a pro-papal faction called the Guelphs and a pro-imperial faction called the Ghibellines. But in 1494 the Duke of Milan foolishly invited outside intervention, which prompted Louis XI to lead his army into Italy, which prompted Emperor Maximillian to invade as well, which triggered 150 years of endemic warfare, which brought Italy's golden age to an end.

That was the context that molded the personality of Niccolò di Bernardo dei Machiavelli, the founder of modern political science. The adjective "modern" is apt because even though the ancients wrote at length about politics, the purpose of books such as Plato's *Republic* was the moral one of how to design a just society. Medieval scholars had also educated young princes in statecraft, but for the purpose of teaching them to reign justly and wisely. Machiavelli, by contrast, began with the axiom that politics was about power: how to get it, keep it, and increase it, period. His essays—mostly famously *The Prince*—candidly depicted the way rulers really behaved. Machiavelli did not endorse cutthroat politics so much as he said: this is how princes really behave, so you had better do likewise to protect your own—and your own subjects'—interests. He wrote that it is far better to be feared than loved, and he implied that might makes right, which is why he inspired the odious adjective Machiavellian. But the man himself insisted that he, too, willed the good, and that good ends justified devious means. So even though Machiavelli was damned by northern Europeans as the devil's disciple, he was really the first modern realist.

Thus the Renaissance: a rebirth of secular culture; a fascination with science, technology, and exploration; a strong, even hubristic trust in human genius; and a horizontal rather than vertical perspective in art, politics, and religion. Given all that, it is tempting to interpret the Protestant Reformation, which began in 1517, as a religious reaction against the Renaissance. It was indeed a reaction against decadence, greed, and corruption, but otherwise the Reformation was a deafening expression of the humanist spirit. Just consider the invitation issued by Erasmus, the great Dutch humanist, who wrote in *The Philosophy of Christ*: "Only a very few can be learned, but all can be Christian, all can be devout, and—I shall boldly add—all can be theologians."

Those were bold words indeed: words which an obscure monk in Germany would soon take very seriously.

Chapter 5

"A Mighty Fortress Is Our God": The Protestant Reformation

What does the word *revolution* convey to readers today? A radical novelty of some sort? The sudden overthrow of a government? A world-changing development in science, technology, or culture? In fact, the original, literal meaning of *revolution* derives from the Latin verb *revolvere*, meaning "to go around," as the moon revolves around the earth. Hence, to make a revolution once meant to circle back to where you began. It was just that conservative sense of the word in which the sixteenth-century German monk Martin Luther imagined himself a revolutionary. That northern-European humanist meant to purge the Roman Catholic church of the errors he believed had accreted over the centuries, and thus to revolve Christianity back to the simple faith, hope, and charity of the apostolic church.

Indeed, Luther grew up a devout Catholic and, so far as he was concerned, never left the church. But the papacy, in his view, had betrayed the gospel, first by falling away from orthodox doctrine, second by promulgating novel, unbiblical teachings, third by tolerating hypocrisy and corruption in its ranks, and fourth by refusing to repent of its many mistakes. Luther's purpose in protesting was not to found a new church, but rather to goad the Catholic hierarchy into embracing reform and renewal. Only when the pope insisted that Luther recant did the German reluctantly break with the Vatican and inadvertently tear Latin Christendom asunder. Once that happened, Luther's protest created cultural and political space for all manner of other protest movements: religious, but also social, political, and economic, thus reinforcing the tendency of Renaissance humanists to question all received authority.

Luther posed the most existential question of his era. If the church is supposed to be the arbiter of truth about the highest things—the things on which depend both the quality of life in this world and the hope for heaven in the next—then what are believers to do when their own faith and reason persuade them that the church has erred and become incorrigible? Luther's answer was revolutionary in the old sense: the church must revolve back to the purity and simplicity it had displayed in the first centuries following the resurrection of Jesus Christ. But his successful protest enabled other protest movements to arise that soon splintered the original Protestant movement. The ironic result was a diversity of doctrines and institutions that triggered an entire century of quasi-religious warfare and helped to transform Europe into the most restless, dynamic civilization in the world.

Historical perspective—which is to say, hindsight—reveals that the Protestant Reformation was the product of at least seven important factors.

First, the customary deference Europeans had typically paid to the Catholic Church had been gravely weakened by the split between rival popes that lasted until 1417 and caused Renaissance humanists to doubt the church's authority.

Second, that schism was followed by an era of scandalous decadence during which secular rulers attempted to maneuver their own corrupt candidates into the papacy. Hence, pious pilgrims visiting Rome from elsewhere were appalled to witness how the Vatican's popes and archbishops succumbed to bribery, licentious behavior, and criminal intrigues, all the while squandering the tithes of the faithful on lavish art and architecture.

Third, the Italian humanist movement, which celebrated classical texts from ancient Greece and Rome, took a far different turn north of the Alps. In the Netherlands, England, and Germany (where fourteen universities had been founded in the previous century), scholars read the Bible and the works of the early church fathers in Hebrew, Greek, and Latin, and they contrasted their scholarly judgments with the seemingly self-serving theology taught by the Vatican over the centuries. For instance, Christian humanists learned from their historical research that the spiritual authority of the pope had grown gradually over many centuries and that the pontiffs' temporal power over the territorial Papal States was downright fraudulent, in that the Donation of Constantine, which allegedly granted central Italy to the papacy, turned out to be a forgery. Humanists also studied the evolution of Catholic theology over the life of the church and learned that the popes had at various times pronounced doctrines that had no basis in Holy Scripture. Among them were purgatory, the immaculate conception of Mary the mother of Jesus, and clerical celibacy. The Catholic corpus of doctrine known as the *magisterium* had always rested on three sturdy pillars: the Bible, the decisions of ecumenical councils of bishops, and patristics, or the doctrinal teachings and interpretations expressed in the writings of the early church fathers. But humanists asserted that church councils and traditions, being the creations of mortal men, were subject to error, whereas Holy Scripture was inspired by God. Hence they arrived at the principle of *sola scriptura*: scripture alone must be the measure of truth. The greatest of such scholars was Desiderius Erasmus of Rotterdam. He never left the Catholic Church, but he did question papal authority, he did denounce superstition, and he did call Christians back to the authority of scripture. Another innovation of northern humanists was the intense religious devotion their work inspired among literate lay people such as the Dutch Sisters and Brothers of the Common Life, who gathered for Bible study without priests, a practice that anticipated Lutheranism.

Fourth, earnest Christians sought new ways to reform the church because the tried-and-true methods had been stymied. Since antiquity, the church had periodically embraced reforms promoted by ecumenical councils or by new religious orders like the Franciscans and Dominicans. But the three (highly contentious) councils convened in the century before Luther's time dealt only with the papal crisis. Moreover, no new orders had been founded for decades because the corrupt Renaissance popes had no interest in reform.

Fifth, various secular rulers were eager to embrace the Protestant cause, not least because they coveted the vast properties and wealth accumulated by the Catholic Church during the medieval millennium.

Sixth, popular resentment against the wealth and power of the church undermined its prestige and authority, especially north of the Alps. In the late fourteenth century John Wycliffe, an Oxford disciple of philosopher William of Ockham, won a large following by demanding that the clergy renounce worldly goods, distribute monastic lands to the rural poor, and repudiate papal infallibility. Needless to say, Wycliffe was anathematized by the Vatican and might have been burned at the stake if he had not died first. Jan Hus, a Bohemian priest, was less fortunate. When he denounced the worldliness of the church, the Council of Constance ordered him to be burned alive for heresy in the year 1415.

Seventh, national politics were a fertile context for religious protest, especially in Germany. Ever since the so-called Golden Bull of 1346 had made the Holy Roman emperor an elected office, the princes of the House of Habsburg, headquartered in the Austrian capital of Vienna, had been habitually elected. The process tended to limit the emperor's powers because candidates for the throne were obliged to make concessions to the seven prince-electors. Still, the Habsburg dynasty had inherited so many provinces beyond Germany by the early sixteenth century that emperors were tempted to impose their will on the provinces inside the empire. Germany's local princes were keen to resist this imperial intrusion, which made them receptive to Luther's defiance of the pope and empire alike.

These seven important trends shaped the environment in which Luther came of age. He was born in 1483 to a father who began life as a peasant but had gone into iron smelting and grown moderately wealthy, an indication of the growing social mobility that characterized Renaissance Europe. Hans Luther educated his son at the University of Erfurt and expected him to go into the family business. But the pious young Martin suspected he might have a religious calling.

Luther's youthful anxieties about whether such a calling was genuine ended in a literal flash when, at age twenty-one, he and a friend were rushing home through a thunderstorm when a lightning bolt knocked them down and killed his friend. Young man Luther took the tragedy as a clear sign from heaven. At once, he resolved to join the Augustinian order. Soon, however, his anxieties returned. His intensely introspective personality made monastic life an unrelieved torment, for even as he followed the strict regimen of prayer, fasting, and charity, Luther knew that his inner thoughts and desires were far from pristine.

When Luther was ordained as a priest and said his first mass in 1507, he knelt at the altar thinking, "I am dust and ashes and full of sin." But who was not? The great commandment of both Moses and Jesus was to love the Lord thy God with all thy heart, thy soul, and thy mind, and thy neighbor as thyself. That council of perfection was impossible for anyone to follow for five minutes—and no one knew that better than those saints who ardently tried to live holy lives. For Luther, these reflections led to a rediscovery of a core Christian principle: human beings are not sinners because they sin; they sin because they are sinners. It is human nature to deviate from God's perfect path, and the good works people manage to do can never justify them before their Maker, because an omniscient God reads human hearts and counts sins of omission as well as commission.

Then came a day when Luther, while meditating on the Bible in a garden, received an epiphany, a revelation, which caused him to sink to the ground in tears. It was triggered by Paul's Epistle to the Romans, in which the apostle exhorts: "I am not ashamed of the Gospel of Jesus Christ; it is the power of God for salvation given to all who have faith, to the Jew first and also to the Greek. For in the gospel is revealed the righteousness of God: faith for faith. He who is righteous shall live by faith."

Paul's words led Luther to the doctrine known as "justification by faith," which holds that while people can never be justified by their own pathetic efforts, "God so loved the world that he sent his only begotten Son that all who believe in him shall not perish, but have everlasting life" (John 3:16). The fact that souls are redeemed by faith had always been a cardinal Christian doctrine. But during the long medieval era the church had drifted toward the tendency of teaching that salvation hinged more on fulfilling one's duties, which meant avoiding egregious (or "mortal") sins, attending confession and mass, and—more self-servingly—donating money. In short: obey, pray, and pay.

Never did this teaching seem more erroneous, or less effective, than during the Renaissance, when even the upper hierarchy of the clergy blatantly shirked their duties. Luther himself journeyed to Rome in 1510 and was appalled to observe the opulent decadence of the papal court. He returned to take up a professorship at Wittenberg, already persuaded that there was no biblical basis for papal monarchy, no biblical basis for priestly celibacy, no biblical basis for the doctrine of purgatory, and no biblical basis for the latest papal outrage, the sale of indulgences.

It was during these years that Pope Leo X, a scion of the Medicis, was sponsoring the grandest Renaissance project of all: the construction of St. Peter's Basilica. The magnificent cathedral cost a fortune, so Leo raised funds by *commercializing* the forgiveness of sins. It seemed that the church was selling tickets to heaven for cold cash. Leo's reasoning was that the church could tap into Christ's infinite "treasury of merit" and blot out people's sins, even the sins of their deceased ancestors. So the pope's agents went abroad to raise money by exploiting people's guilt. The chief agent peddling indulgences in Germany, a monk name Johann Tetzel, went from town to town reminding people that their dead grandparents were no doubt suffering in purgatory; fortunately, for fifty thalers people could purchase an indulgence that would obtain for them admission to heaven. His sales pitch was: *So bald der Geld in Kasten klingt, wie bald die Seele im Himmel springt* (As soon as the money clinks in the coffer, so fast the souls into heaven spring). Luther abominated indulgences, not least because the money was extorted from pious Germans in order to finance the luxuries of Italians.

Luther petitioned the pope to stop selling indulgences. The pope refused. Luther proposed a church council to debate the issue. The pope refused again. Whereupon Luther fired his decisive arrow: the Bible, the inspired Word of God, which condemned everything about indulgences. From that point on, Luther began to urge all Germans to read the Bible for themselves, to trust in the Holy Spirit to guide them toward the correct interpretation of Scripture, and to act according to their consciences. The implications of these ideas were astoundingly vast. Erasmus imagined every man his own theologian. Luther now called for a priesthood of all believers—and took the first step toward revolution.

In 1517 Luther drafted a bill of particulars and nailed it to the door of the Castle Church in Wittenberg. Soon these "Ninety-Five Theses" were printed and circulated all over Germany. The market for indulgences dried up, and the pope summoned Luther to Rome on charges of heresy. Should he obey and risk imprisonment and possibly death, or refuse and risk excommunication? Luther consulted his secular patron, Frederick III, Elector of Saxony, who said, "Don't trust those slippery Italians. Stay here and be safe in my castle."

The pope then dispatched a famous scholar named Johannes von Eck to try to reason or frighten Luther back to obedience. Still, the stubborn monk insisted that the Bible was the only reliable authority and quoted Scripture to indict the pope. Leo X responded by excommunicating Luther—that is, by denying him the sacraments of the church and thus imperiling his soul. Whereupon the Holy Roman emperor invited Luther to explain himself before the imperial Reichstag, or diet. Luther attended the diet in the city of Worms, and he ended it in dramatic fashion when he cried out words that would ring throughout Europe: "I cannot, I will not, recant. Here I stand. May God help me. Amen."

Luther was allowed to go home because Frederick III (known as Frederick the Wise) shrewdly gave him a sizable bodyguard whose soldiers spirited the monk back to his castle in Wartburg. It was there that he got down to work translating the Bible into German and establishing a breakaway Protestant church.

If but two things come to mind whenever the reader thinks about the Protestant Reformation, let them be these: justification by faith and . . . the printing press. Luther's plea that people read Scripture for themselves would have been absurd a century earlier, because few Europeans knew how to read, Bibles were written only in Latin, and the Bibles that existed had to be hand-copied by monastic scribes. Then came the Renaissance, and with it the expansion of literacy among the urban commercial and professional classes, the expansion of vernacular literature, and most importantly, the invention of the printing press by Johannes Gutenberg in the city of Mainz in 1439.

The printing press was the greatest breakthrough in human communication since the invention of writing itself. The new technology spread quickly to towns all over Germany, then throughout western Europe during the late 1400s. The power of print to spark crises of authority in every human institution was as great as the power of the Internet today. Thanks to the printing press, Luther's tracts and books were distributed throughout the Holy Roman Empire—and his writings were voluminous, including works of theology, collections of sermons, hymnals, and vicious (indeed, scatological) denunciations of the pope. Luther's greatest accomplishment by far, however, was the German Bible, which made possible the scriptural church he believed in and which did more than any other book to standardize the vocabulary, spelling, and grammar of the modern German language.

The Lutheran Church set high educational standards for its clergy, approved a German liturgy for worship services, and urged congregants to purge their buildings of anything it deemed superstitious, such as shrines to saints and holy relics. Luther retained the seven sacraments of the historic church, but he made the sermon the centerpiece of Sunday worship and invited increased congregational participation, especially in the singing of hymns. Among the sublime

One of the numerous portraits of Martin Luther produced by Lucas Cranach the Elder. This one was completed in 1528.

hymns composed by Luther himself, the most famous was "Ein' feste Burg ist unser Gott" (A Mighty Fortress Is Our God). He also denounced priestly celibacy and shut down Catholic monasteries and convents. Legend has it that Luther would storm into convents with a broom and "sweep" the nuns out the door crying, "Gehen Sie weg und finden Sie Männer!" (Go away and find yourselves husbands).

Many German princes rallied to Luther either because they were persuaded by his theology or because they realized his religious revolt was also a political weapon they could use against the Holy Roman emperor. They *all* took the opportunity to seize the Catholic Church's property in their provinces. As a result, most of northern Germany as well as Scandinavia turned Lutheran as early as the 1530s.

Meanwhile, in Switzerland, another Protestant movement arose under a humanist preacher named Huldrych Zwingli, whose idiosyncratic doctrines were more extreme than Luther's. For instance, the Catholic Church's doctrine of transubstantiation taught that a priest's words of consecration over the sacramental elements turned the bread and wine into the actual substance of Christ's body and blood, even though their outward characteristics did not change. Zwingli denied this heretofore central teaching root-and-branch, insisting that the sacraments were merely *symbols* of grace, not the means of *transmitting* grace, and that not only clergy but laypeople should be allowed to perform baptisms, marriages, and the Lord's Supper. Zwingli also abolished the clerical hierarchy, whereas the more conservative Luther retained the traditional hierarchy of bishops, priests, and deacons, eliminating only the bishop of Rome—that is, the pope.

That the Protestant religious movement opened up space for all sorts of challenges to authority was proven in short order. In numerous German towns mobs ransacked churches, elected their own pastors, and fell to quarreling over doctrine and church governance. Luther abhorred such chaos, but he was powerless to stop it until—and this was of monumental importance—he implored the secular princes not only to take over church property but to become the heads of the Lutheran Church in their territories. Thus did the Reformation undo at a stroke the medieval separation of church and state and turn the clergy into public officials serving secular governments.

The delegitimation of authority unleashed by Luther further threatened the social order because poor peasants, upon hearing the New Testament read for the first time in their native tongue, understandably concluded that the gospel of Christ championed the poor and lowly, not the rich and powerful. To be sure, the church had always preached charity toward the poor, but during the medieval era it had also blessed the hierarchical feudal system. So it was, in the year 1525, that many German peasants took up arms against their noble landlords, slaughtered their families, and attempted to seize their farmland. Once again, Luther was appalled. He denounced such rioters as so many swine and appealed to the German princes to suppress the revolt, which they did in bloody fashion during this Peasants' War.

In sum, Luther proved to be conservative in many, perhaps most, respects, and thus not at all revolutionary in the modern sense of that word. He upheld the inherited structure of politics and society and confined his protest to ecclesiastical affairs. Moreover, the Lutheran church flourished thanks to the patronage of secular rulers as heads of the church. The ironic outcome was that Protestantism in Germany, Scandinavia, Switzerland, and later the Netherlands and England abolished separation of church and state and subordinated religious to secular authority.

Within just twenty years the religious protest launched by Luther became subsumed in the international politics of Germany and Europe. That was because, in 1519, just two years after Luther nailed his ninety-five theses to a church door in Wittenberg, the great Habsburg emperor Charles V ascended his throne.

The Habsburg dynasty had begun its rise back in the 1200s, when the family inherited the duchy of Austria. Over the subsequent centuries the Habsburgs became the most powerful dynasty in Europe thanks mostly to strategic marriages and good fortune. As the saying went, *Bella gerunt alii; tu, felix Austria, nubes* (Others make wars, but you, happy Austria, marry). A Habsburg prince married the Burgundian princess and gained the line rule over all the Netherlands when the throne of the Burgundian duchy became vacant in 1477. Next, a Habsburg duke married a Bohemian princess, and when the male line of her native Czech dynasty died out in 1526, the dukes of Austria also became kings of Bohemia. The Habsburgs also married into the Hungarian line, and when—in that very year of 1526—the Hungarian royal family and all its knights were killed fighting a Turkish invasion at the Battle of Mohacs, the Habsburgs inherited the title of kings of Hungary. Finally, when Maximilian von Habsburg married his son to the daughter of King Ferdinand and Queen Isabella, their child Charles became heir to their Iberian kingdoms of Castile and Aragon.

So it was that Charles V inherited from his four grandparents—get ready to gasp—all the Austrian crown lands in Germany plus Bohemia, Hungary, Burgundy (which included the Netherlands), the kingdom of Spain, and all Spain's possessions, including the kingdom of the Two Sicilies in southern Italy and, most notably, the vast New World empire recently claimed for Spain by the explorers who sailed in the wake of Columbus. The rich silver and gold mines of Mexico and Peru made Charles immensely wealthy as well as powerful. Finally, Charles was duly elected to the office of Holy Roman emperor and so was the titular head of all Germany and northern Italy. Save for France, England, and a few minor states, Charles V was the master of Europe. Moreover, he learned all the languages spoken in his many realms and, according to legend, boasted, "I speak Italian to ladies. I speak French to men. I speak German to my soldiers. I speak Spanish only to God."

Charles, a devout Catholic, was personally wounded by the Lutheran defections that occurred during his reign. Latin Christendom had known only one united Christian church since ancient times, and no one believed it possible that the souls of Protestants and Catholics might both be saved. So Charles V hoped to broker a compromise and reunify Christendom. He spied a chance to do so in 1529, when Catholic and Protestant princes rallied in joint defense against Turkish invaders who laid siege to Vienna itself. After the Christian victory Charles convened a diet at the city of Augsburg in the hope that the German princes might come back into the fold. But the Lutherans not only refused, they formed a military alliance called the Schmalkaldic League to resist the emperor. Fifteen years of civil war ensued before Charles gave up and concluded the Peace of Augsburg in 1555.

That treaty established the famous formula *cuius regio, eius religio*: whose regime, his religion. Lutheran princes continued to govern the Protestant churches in their realms, while Catholic princes remained loyal to the papal hierarchy in their realms. The Peace of Augsburg did not establish freedom of religion, but it did recognize—for the first time in European history—a measure of legitimate religious diversity. In the wake of that treaty the heartbroken Charles V divided his enormous empire between two of his heirs and retreated to a monastery, where he fasted and prayed until his death in 1558.

The triumph of the Lutheran church in Germany made thinkable all sorts of other forms of Protestantism, of which the most influential by far was Calvinism. Jean Cauvin—or as the English-speaking world knows him, John Calvin—was born in northern France in 1509 and received a humanist education at the University of Paris. At the age of twenty-four he underwent a profound conversion experience that inspired him, like Martin Luther, to jettison the rituals and nonbiblical dogma that had accumulated in the Catholic Church over a thousand years and to seek a personal relationship with his Lord and Savior. Calvin's first act, again as with Luther, was to codify what he considered to be correct Christian doctrine derived from the Bible alone: *sola scriptura* again. His great book *The Institutes of the Christian Religion*, published in 1536, won thousands of adherents in France, Switzerland, the Netherlands, and England.

Calvin insisted that the God of the Bible is utterly sovereign. He agreed with the medieval philosopher Thomas Aquinas that the very definition of God is "That than which there can be nothing higher," and that to do the will of that omnipotent, omniscient, and omnipresent divinity is the very purpose of life. In other words, for Calvin, to do God's sovereign will as summarized by the Ten Commandments is the duty and happiness of mankind. Alas, the human race had rebelled against God's perfect will, which meant people brought on themselves all the suffering and cruelty of the world. Only by repenting of sin and by saying "yes" to God's unmerited grace could souls be justified and sanctified, or be made holy in this life and be redeemed for eternity.

That sounds like the doctrine of justification by faith as preached by Luther. But Calvin went on to reason that since God, by definition, exists beyond time, he already knows which people will accept, and which will reject, Christ's atonement. In short, some are predestined for heaven, and some for hell. He called such predestination a "terrible decree," because it implied that everyone's fate is already sealed and that human beings do not really possess free will. Indeed, his teaching has over the centuries led many Calvinist denominations to be characteristically fearful, gloomy, or spiritually apathetic (American Presbyterians today are jocularly known as the "frozen chosen"). But Calvin argued that predestination was actually a cheerful doctrine. He reasoned that any person destined for salvation must surely give evidence of that grace in his or her outward behavior. So while good works, a moral life, and worldly success cannot save a person's soul—only faith and grace can do that—they *are* signs that a person is among the elect, that he or she is already under God's grace.

No sooner did Calvin's *Institutes* become a bestselling book than Catholic authorities in France sought his arrest. So he went into exile, planning initially to find refuge in the Protestant haven of Strasbourg. That city was then under siege by a Catholic army, so Calvin turned aside to Geneva, Switzerland, a French-speaking city that had become another haven for Protestants. The civic leaders in Geneva considered it providential when the famous author of the *Institutes* turned up in their city, and they not only persuaded Calvin to settle in Geneva; they placed their municipal government in his hands.

Thus did Calvinism become the established church and polity of the Genevan city-state, but in a very different way than was the case in Lutheran lands. For in northern Germany the secular princes became the heads of the churches, whereas in Geneva the pastors became the heads of the government, which made Calvin's Geneva a sort of theocracy. Exactly that kind of regime would be later established during the seventeenth century by the Puritan settlers of Calvinist New England.

In Geneva (as in Massachusetts after 1630) only church members could be voting citizens, and only the most upstanding could be presbyters (elders), who guided the affairs of church and state alike. Presbyters in turn appointed deacons to care for widows and orphans, the sick and the aged. Presbyters also administered law, promoted business, and disciplined adulterers, gluttons, and drunks. Contrary to myth, Calvin was not himself a prude. He enjoyed wine in moderation and served as a matchmaker for young couples. But under his rule Geneva had no tolerance for egregious sinners or dissenters, especially Catholics.

Theocracy is rather understandably repellent to most people today. But try to imagine how the world looked to seventeenth-century Europeans who were morally certain that the fate of their immortal souls and those of their families and friends depended on correctly interpreting the Bible's requirements for belief and behavior. They were deadly earnest about their theology because they believed it a matter of life and death. Some might even believe the execution of vocal heretics justified, because their false teachings endangered the souls of others. As a result, Calvinists could be just as intolerant and prosecutorial as Catholics in that era. (Let us note that the theocratic regimes of early modern Europe were meek and mild by comparison to the ideological and totalitarian tyrannies that would arise in the twentieth century.)

Calvinism spread rapidly to the Netherlands, England, and Scotland, with momentous political implications. But initially, its biggest impact was felt in Calvin's native France. For during the decades when Calvinism was winning converts, France's Valois royal dynasty became embroiled in a series of wars against Habsburg Spain. No sooner did peace finally break out in 1559 than King Henri II was killed in a jousting accident. At first the Valois dynasty seemed secure, since Henri left behind three sons. But soon it became evident that the boys were not likely to perpetuate the line, given that all three were either sickly or effeminate. None sired children. The most powerful dukes, suspecting the throne would eventually become vacant, began to fight over which of them would occupy it. Their civil wars were over power, but they also had a religious dimension, because Huguenots (as French Calvinists were called) and Catholics both hoped that a duke of their faith would win out.

Thus did the French civil wars mirror events in the Holy Roman Empire. For the nobility they were political contests in which religion played a sizable role, while for the common people they were religious contests in which politics played a sizable role. Either way, they were waged with passion, ferocity, and duplicity. The violence peaked in 1572 when the queen mother, a Machiavellian Italian woman named Catherine de Medici, ordered her soldiers to slaughter

Huguenots indiscriminately. In Paris alone, over three thousand people perished in this St. Bartholomew's Day Massacre. Out of the prolonged chaos rose a new political faction in the 1580s. It was composed of sensible men known simply as *les politiques* (the politicians). They condemned the civil bloodshed and deplored the mixing of politics and religion.

Les politiques urged all sides to rally behind a strong ruler who could impose law and order, reconcile Catholics and Protestants, and unify the nation so it could resume its resistance to the rival Habsburgs abroad. Their preferred royal candidate was Henri de Bourbon. This Henri was married to a daughter of Catherine de Medici, but he was himself a Huguenot. Hence, he had both a claim to the throne and a foot in both religious camps. Henri's opportunity arrived in 1589 when the last of Catherine's sons was assassinated. Collaborating with *les politiques*, Henri declared his intention to assume the throne as Henri IV and return to the Catholic faith—"Paris vaut bien une messe" (Paris is well worth a mass), he supposedly said. He also proclaimed the Edict of Nantes, which extended toleration to Huguenots. That act of statesmanship pacified the country, founded the new Bourbon dynasty, and made possible Europe's first experiment with genuine religious toleration.

Finally, what does one make of the English Reformation? I expect most readers are familiar with Henry VIII, the lusty and powerful king who broke with the Catholic Church in order to obtain a divorce and who ultimately married six wives in the hope one of them might bear a son. A lesser-known fact is that Henry VIII remained a devotee of Catholic faith and liturgy. The "reformation" over which he presided consisted mostly of the rejection of papal authority. In that, he was simply the latest exemplar of English resentment of distant Rome, a feeling that was centuries old. The English had begun to be converted by monks from Ireland in the sixth century, well before the pope sent a monk named Augustine (later to be known as "of Canterbury") to the island, and England's kings often quarreled with the papacy throughout the medieval era. In any event, Henry VIII was greedy to seize Catholic Church property, which by then included a quarter of all the land in England.

Even so, the proximate reason that Henry VIII ran afoul of the pope was a matter of conscience. He had married his widowed sister-in-law, the Spanish princess Catherine of Aragon, a moral lapse for which he received a papal dispensation. When Catherine bore a daughter and then had a series of miscarriages, Henry decided the marriage had been offensive to God and asked the pope to annul it. This time the pope said no, not least because Catherine's nephew—none other than Emperor Charles V—was threatening to occupy Rome with an army. Henry responded by appointing his friend Thomas Cranmer to be Archbishop of Canterbury, on condition that Cranmer grant an annulment and marry the king to his Irish mistress, Anne Boleyn. Parliament made it all official by passing an Act of Supremacy, making the king the head of the Church of England. Then Henry, like Germany's Lutheran princes, proceeded to divest the Catholic Church of its real estate and sell it off to England's landed gentry, which solidified Henry's parliamentary support.

An award-winning Hollywood film, *A Man for All Seasons*, tells the tragic tale of the royal chancellor Sir Thomas More, the only English official who dared denounce Henry's usurpations. More's integrity cost him his head. He died a martyr to his Catholic faith.

The English "game of thrones" continued after Henry's death in 1547. His successor, Edward VI, was Protestant to the core (being the son of Jane Seymour, Henry's third wife). It was he who commissioned Thomas Cranmer to compose the exquisite Anglican Book of Common Prayer. But Edward was a sickly lad and died young in 1553, which brought to the throne the Catholic daughter of Catherine of Aragon. She was the queen who became known as "Bloody Mary," because she not only tried to reestablish Catholicism but also executed some three hundred Protestant leaders, including Cranmer. In 1558 Mary died at age forty-two, whereupon Elizabeth succeeded to the throne. The daughter of Henry VIII and Anne Boleyn, Elizabeth was a Protestant. She practiced a moderate religious policy, making Anglican doctrine and liturgy broad and flexible enough to reconcile most of her subjects.

So it is one arrives at the startling conclusion to this summary of the Protestant Reformation. In the countries of northern Europe various denominations and governments arrived at not one, not two, but *three* plausible solutions to the shattering of religious unity. In Germany the plausible solution was to create many autonomous provinces either Protestant or Catholic depending on the faith of their rulers. In France the plausible solution was to establish a unified kingdom that was Catholic but tolerant of Protestants. In England the plausible solution was an established Protestant state church that embraced a broad and flexible mix of doctrines and liturgies.

All three solutions were ingenious. Alas, as will soon become apparent, none would survive for long.

Chapter 6

"Set All Aflame!"
The Catholic Reformation

In the tragedy he wrote at the beginning of the seventeenth century, Shakespeare has the Scottish thane Macbeth declare that life is a tale told by an idiot. No one appreciates that lament more than historians. It seems to us that the river of time is usually in full flood, complete with crosscurrents, whirlpools, and undertows that either drown human beings trapped in their fury or pitilessly hurl them toward random destinations. Historians are vexed to observe how complex cause-and-effect relationships are in human events, and how often apparently good causes come to some very bad ends.

Words such as *good* and *bad* suggest value judgments, which objective scholars try to avoid. But honest historians know that it is hard to remain objective toward past events about which people remain passionate or which still affect present-day controversies. That is surely the case with the Protestant Reformation, whose five hundredth anniversary was commemorated in 2017. Nearly all progressive and secular historians have applauded the crack-up of the Catholic Church's religious monopoly in Western Christendom and have credited Protestantism for creating the conditions under which Europeans—however gradually and sometimes violently—began to move toward religious toleration. For their part, Catholic historians, a decided minority within Anglo-American faculties, often revile Martin Luther, John Calvin, and Henry VIII for having destroyed the unity of Latin Christendom, even if most of them recognize that the Catholic Church was in desperate need of reform and was unable or unwilling to change until the Protestant challenge arose.

Likewise, progressive historians stress the undeniable fact that the Protestant countries of northern Europe pioneered modern forms of representative government and forged dynamic capitalist societies, whereas the Catholic countries of southern Europe were relatively stagnant. In response, Catholic historians stress the undeniable fact that the formula "Every man his own theologian" undermined spiritual authority and has caused Protestant churches to splinter repeatedly ever since the Reformation. Indeed, the history of Protestantism reflects the truth of the adage coined by philosopher Charles Péguy: "Tout commence en mystique et finit en politique" (Everything begins in mystery and ends in politics).

A sensitivity to such irony and paradox, such truth and illusion, permeated the literature of Renaissance Europe. Thus did Macbeth, tormented by guilt, damn human life as "full of sound and fury, signifying nothing." Thus did the Spanish author Miguel de Cervantes, in what critics consider to be the first modern novel, tell the tale of the mad knight Don Quixote and his simple esquire Sancho Panza in order to illustrate how even—or especially—moral ideals can dissolve into self-defeating caricatures the moment flawed human beings attempt to realize them. Those were characteristic attitudes during the sixteenth and seventeenth centuries, when Renaissance Europeans, who had expanded their consciousness and were busy exploring the natural world during the Age of Exploration (or Discovery), found no haven in their psychic voyage of self-discovery. History rolled over them like a flood.

In the case of the Reformation there is irony not only in its many unintended consequences throughout Protestant northern Europe but also in the new lease on life it gave Catholicism. For once it became clear that Protestantism could not be eradicated, the Catholic hierarchy repented of its decadence and launched its own reform movement. Protestant historians have always given that movement the pejorative name of "Counter-Reformation." But it is more properly thought of as the *Catholic* Reformation, and like the Protestant Reformation it had both spiritual and political aspects. As a spiritual awakening, the Catholic Reformation purified the faith and practice of clergy and inspired saints of a sort not seen since the high medieval era. In its political aspect, the Catholic Reformation motivated popes and Catholic rulers alike to pursue new strategies in their efforts to contain and even roll back the spread of what they considered to be Protestant heresies. No rulers were more eager and able to fight for the Catholic cause than the kings of that Crusader state, Spain.

The Iberian Peninsula, where we find both Spain and Portugal, was the dynamic center of sixteenth-century Catholicism because of four epochal events, all of which occurred during the busy year of 1492. First, it was in that year that the Spaniards, who had been fighting for seven centuries to expel the Muslim Moors who had overrun the peninsula in the early eighth century, finally reconquered the last Moorish stronghold in the province of Granada. That long Reconquista had forged Spaniards into a nation of conquistadors. After the conquest of the Moors, it was only natural for them to redirect their militancy against their new Protestant opponents.

The second epochal event of 1492 was the merger of King Ferdinand's province of Aragon and Queen Isabella's province of Castile to found the unified kingdom of Spain. Ferdinand and Isabella were determined, like other Renaissance monarchs, to build a strong, centralized government. This goal inspired them to undertake some positive initiatives, such as the promulgation of uniform law codes for the entire kingdom. But their state-building also inspired a wrenching act of intolerance, in that Ferdinand and Isabella believed that to be a loyal Spanish subject one must also be Roman Catholic.

Hence, a third epochal event of 1492 was their Alhambra Decree to the effect that any Muslim or Jew who refused to be baptized a Christian must go into exile. In consequence, tens of thousands of Moors and Sephardic Jews fled Spain, mostly to parts of North Africa. Others remained in Spain by pretending to convert, which caused the crown—not the church—to create the Spanish Inquisition as a way of rooting out those people secretly practicing Islam or Judaism. In the long run, those expulsions and persecutions cost Spain thousands of talented, enterprising people who would otherwise have enriched Spain's economy. In the short run, the Inquisition helped the crown mobilize Spaniards for religious war.

Fourth and finally, Ferdinand and Isabella decided in 1492 to gamble on what seemed a preposterous proposition. A certain Genoese geographer and navigator known to us in English as Christopher Columbus believed that if he

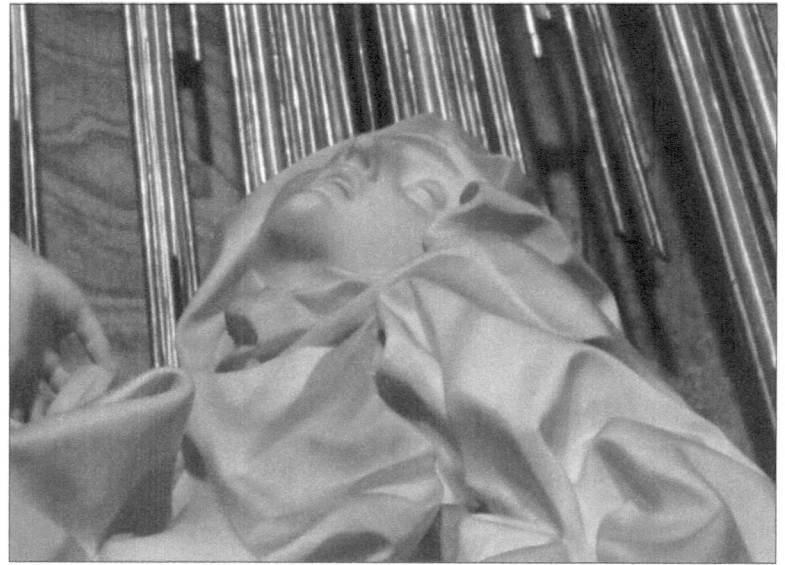

Lorenzo Bernini's sculpture *Ecstasy of St. Teresa* (here in closeup), completed in 1652, shows the saint being pierced by the Holy Spirit.

sailed west across the uncharted Atlantic Ocean, he must eventually reach the East Indies, the Spice Islands of Asia in the Antipodes (a word that literally means the Other Side of the World). Of course, Columbus bumped into an entirely New World instead, whereupon Spanish conquistadors eagerly took ship for the Americas, conquered indigenous peoples such as the Aztecs of Mexico and Incas of Peru, and plundered their bountiful silver and gold. Much of this wealth was confiscated by the crown. These "royalties" were used by the Spanish king, Philip II, to finance his long wars against Protestants and Muslims alike.

The Catholic Reformation's deep spiritual wellsprings were also most evident in Spain. The painter El Greco—he was called "The Greek" because he had been born on the island of Crete—stunningly expressed the mysticism characteristic of the Catholic Reformation in canvases such as *The Holy Trinity* and *The Disrobing of Christ*. Other exemplars of the Catholic Reformation were great saints of the church who imagined their own lives to be works of art dedicated to the glory of God.

"Set All Aflame!"

For instance, San Juan de la Cruz (died 1591) and Santa Teresa de Ávila (died 1582) inspired Iberian Catholics by making a promise similar to those made by Luther and Calvin to northern humanists, which was to purge the church of its worldly accretions and restore Christianity to apostolic simplicity. Protestants had attempted to do that by breaking with Rome. John of the Cross and Teresa of Ávila tried to do that by restoring the austere and mystical practices of the Benedictine monasteries founded in the century following the fall of the Western Roman Empire. In this effort John and Teresa struggled for decades, because their bishops, not to mention the popes, were suspicious of these saintly reformers. At last the pope blessed their petitions to found new orders of Carmelite monks and nuns devoted to poverty, prayer, and meditation. Their lives inspired thousands of young men and women to take holy orders, join monasteries, and practice strenuous devotions, the most famous of which continues to attract tens of thousands of clergy, laypeople, and tourists in the twenty-first century. That is the practice of hiking El Camino de Santiago de Compostela, a five-hundred-mile pilgrimage through northern Spain to the cathedral of St. James, one of Jesus's twelve apostles.

John of the Cross also bequeathed the most influential work of mysticism in Christian history, *The Dark Night of the Soul*. A sort of how-to manual for godly contemplation, it described the stages through which the psyche must pass on its journey to *kenosis*, a Greek word meaning a state of mind in which the self empties the self of self in a sort of out-of-body experience.

Teresa of Ávila was born into a wealthy aristocratic family. Yet she surrendered her life of privilege in favor of a life of poverty, celibacy, service, and mystical prayer. The power of sustained prayer transported Teresa to places few people have gone. To judge by Lorenzo Bernini's famous sculpture of Teresa being pierced by the Holy Spirit, her sustained prayer life caused her to experience a kind of heavenly ecstasy that can only be likened to spiritual orgasm.

Two more representative saints of the Catholic Reformation were decidedly much more worldly, for they meant to wield political weapons against Protestantism and did so by founding a new religious order utterly devoted to the pope. That order was the Society of Jesus, whose members were known as Jesuits.

The Society's founder was the Basque Ignatius of Loyola (died 1556). He was raised in the church, but took religion more or less for granted until, like Luther, he had a brush with death that sparked a radical adult conversion. God had gotten Luther's attention with a storm. For Ignatius, it was a cannonball that shattered his leg while he was serving as a soldier in Spain's wars against France. He emerged from a prolonged, painful convalescence convinced that his calling was to train soldiers for Christ and arm them with all the weapons that spiritual and worldly knowledge could forge. Hence his great emphasis on education, which explains why more Catholic schools and universities are named after Ignatius Loyola than anyone else. Skilled in languages, rhetoric, and debate, the Jesuits recruited by Ignatius became spies, strategists, propagandists, and shock troops for the Catholic Reformation.

Protestants hated and feared the Jesuits and made "Jesuitical" another dirty word like "Machiavellian." Did not Ignatius's *Spiritual Exercises* teach Jesuits to "believe the white that I see is black, if the church so defines it"? Yes, it did. But Loyola's goal was not to brainwash or coerce anyone, but rather to inspire humility in light of human limitations. Because a man's own eyes may deceive him, he must trust in the church's magisterium. Protestants cried humbug. The Catholic Church had repeatedly erred, they retorted, and the only trustworthy authority was the Bible: *sola scriptura*. Yes, the Jesuits rebutted, but who had canonized Holy Scripture? Who had decided which books belonged in the New Testament in the first place? The church had done so through a series of ecumenical councils of bishops inspired by the Holy Spirit. In other words, the church predated Scripture and alone had the authority to interpret the Bible for the masses.

Jesuits interpreted their struggle against Protestant heresy as the latest round in the old fight between people who trusted in God and people who wanted to *play* God, which is what Erasmus's "every man his own theologian" and Luther's "priesthood of all believers" sounded like to Catholic ears. Throughout the sixteenth and seventeenth centuries Jesuit spies infiltrated Protestant countries, even royal courts, in disguise, said masses secretly, and smuggled in tracts from the Vatican's Office for the Propagation of the Faith (*propaganda* in Latin) in order to advance the Catholic cause in the politics of France, the Netherlands, and especially England.

Jesuits also took their spiritual crusade overseas. Their missionaries labored to replace the European souls lost to Protestant heresy with American and Asian converts to Catholicism. Jesuits shrewdly accommodated Catholicism to non-European customs, rituals, and holidays in order to make Christianity more acceptable to alien cultures. They took pains to learn languages ranging from Chinese to Sanskrit to Iroquois. One of the best examples of Jesuit wisdom in this regard was provided by the work of St. Francis Xavier, whom Ignatius chose to send to China, and who also became the first European since Marco Polo to be admitted to Beijing's Forbidden City. Francis Xavier translated parts of the Bible into Chinese, served as interpreter for the Chinese emperor, and planted the first churches in Japan. Thus did he fulfill the instructions given him by Ignatius when he took ship at the Spanish port of Seville: "My son," said Loyola, "set all aflame!"

Finally, and most importantly for Europe at large, the Catholic Church responded to the Protestant challenge by purging the Vatican of its Renaissance corruption. In 1534 Pope Paul III was elected by the College of Cardinals and served as the first in a series of strong, reforming pontiffs. Paul III's principal vehicle for reform was the Council of Trent, which met in three sessions between 1545 and 1563. The assembled bishops abolished simony (the selling of offices). They abolished indulgences. They obliged bishops to leave their splendid cathedrals and visit all the parishes in their dioceses every year. They raised educational and moral standards for clergy. Above all, the Council of Trent endorsed justification by faith, defined faith and works as two sides of the same coin, and declared that all doctrine must rest on the authority of Scripture as well as tradition. So it was that the Council of Trent addressed the very complaints that had upset Martin Luther in the first place. So it was that Spain's Crusader culture, a revived monastic spirituality, the Jesuits' worldly militancy, and the reforms of the Council of Trent served, by the latter half of the sixteenth century, to restore the confidence of Catholic Europe.

Recall the Habsburg emperor Charles V, who was forced to accept the Peace of Augsburg with Germany's Lutheran princes in 1555. A few years after Augsburg, Charles divided his empire into Austrian and Spanish branches and abdicated his throne. His son Felipe—King Philip II of Spain—took up the Catholic cause. Felipe had inherited from his father a vast realm including Spain, Spain's New World empire, and most of southern Italy and the Netherlands. Moreover, due to another lucky Habsburg marriage, Philip came also to rule Portugal and Portugal's overseas empires in Brazil and the East Indies.

Philip II was no warrior. He preferred to serve as his kingdom's chief bureaucrat, diligently pushing paper at a desk in the Escorial palace in Madrid. Throughout his long reign from 1556 to 1598, Philip believed God had given him stupendous power and wealth for the purpose of defending the Catholic faith.

The Mediterranean Sea was the first theater of war to draw Philip's attention. There the Ottoman Turks, having conquered southeastern Europe during the previous centuries, were now building a navy in hopes of monopolizing trade routes. Philip responded by spending large sums on his own navy and allying with the powerful Venetian Republic and other Italian states in what was called the Holy League. In 1571, the League's combined fleets, numbering more than two hundred galleys, engaged the Turks in a mighty battle off Lepanto on the coast of Greece. The Christian victory at Lepanto was a turning point in history, for even though the Sultan rebuilt his navy and continued to control the waters of the Levant, the Turks never again threatened the western Mediterranean.

Meanwhile, Spanish spies and Jesuits insinuated themselves into the convoluted politics of the French civil wars. Naturally they backed Catholic claimants to the throne and got half a loaf when Henri IV reconverted to Catholicism but granted toleration to Huguenots. The Jesuits were vexed by events in England when the Catholic Queen "Bloody Mary" died without heirs and the throne passed to the Protestant Elizabeth I. But Elizabeth never married and thus had no heir, while another claimant to the throne, Mary Queen of Scots, was Catholic. So Jesuits engaged in intrigues hoping to depose Elizabeth in favor of Mary. During these same years, Philip II was thrown on the defensive when the Calvinist Dutch rose up in revolt against Spanish rule.

The Netherlands—or the Low Countries—were part of the Burgundian inheritance that Charles V had bequeathed to Philip. Unfortunately for him, the Dutch bitterly resented Spanish rule: first, because they were heavily taxed; second, because their merchants yearned to break the Spanish and Portuguese monopolies on trade in America and Asia; and third, because Calvinism had made deep inroads in the Low Countries' northern province, called Holland. When the Dutch took up arms in 1568, Philip II dispatched a powerful army commanded by the Duke of Alba in an effort to suppress the rebellion. Alba waged a campaign of terror that included a massacre, in 1576, of seven thousand people in Antwerp, an event that became known as the Spanish Fury.

"Set All Aflame!"

Such cruelty only steeled the Dutch people's will to resist until, in the year 1580, they declared independence under their leader, Prince William of Orange. That was another novelty in European history. Here was a people who claimed the right to rebel against a foreign king—a king whose oppression, they said, forfeited his right to govern. Two centuries later, Britain's thirteen American colonies would follow that example. But the Americans had to fight a mere eight years, whereas the Dutch had to fight for *eighty years* before their independence was recognized in 1648.

During the many phases of that war the Dutch navy embarrassed larger Spanish fleets through superior seamanship, the Dutch militias frustrated the vaunted Spanish infantry by defending well-engineered forts, and Dutch diplomats begged for help from their Protestant neighbors in England. Thus did the Netherlands' revolt intertwine with intrigues over the English throne. Those intrigues climaxed in 1587, when Queen Elizabeth's spies reported that Jesuit agents were plotting to assassinate her. Elizabeth reluctantly decided to end the threat once and for all by having Mary Queen of Scots (her own cousin) beheaded.

The irate Spanish King Philip II now vowed to crush England for good, which in turn would outflank and isolate the rebellious Dutch. In 1588, therefore, the infamous Spanish Armada, numbering more than a hundred ships, sailed into the English Channel. They were met by England's smaller, more seaworthy ships, commanded by officers such as Vice Admiral Francis Drake, which managed to scatter the Armada, after which a torrential storm completed the fleet's destruction. Some Spanish ships were blown so far off course that they circled north around Scotland and were shipwrecked on the coast of Ireland. The so-called Black Irish—people whose hair is black and straight instead of red and curly—are said to be descendants of those Spanish sailors.

In retrospect, 1588 was the point at which Spanish power began its long, languid decline. But the Catholic Reformation and wars of religion continued for another half-century, during which Spain's metallic wealth from the New World was drained away. Instead of stimulating economic growth in Spain, all that silver and gold ended up in the hands of bankers and merchants elsewhere in Europe. Indeed, by the early 1600s the little Netherlands had surpassed Spain in the design of ships for commerce and war. The Dutch even managed to capture most of the Portuguese forts that stretched from India to the East Indies, and came to dominate the lucrative spice trade.

The Spaniards, having lost their advantage at sea, tried to prevail over the Dutch through land warfare, which required that they transport soldiers from Genoa, over the Alps, and down the entire length of the River Rhine. That Spanish Road, as the supply line was called, proved to be insecure and expensive as well as lengthy. Nevertheless, Spain continued to sink armies into that quagmire during the long reigns of Philip III and Philip IV, until at last the Spanish recognized the independence of the Dutch portion of the Netherlands in 1648. Those United Provinces, led by the Presbyterian House of Orange, declared religious toleration for all, much to their economic benefit.

The final act in this Dutch drama played out against a much bloodier conflict across the Rhine in the Holy Roman Empire.

The climactic Thirty Years' War was the most destructive and futile conflict of the Reformation. Like the other religious wars, it was about politics as much as religion. The Germans, recall, had concluded the 1555 Peace of Augsburg based on the principle *cuius regio, eius religio*. That compromise lasted sixty-three years, until in the year 1618 it was challenged by events in the Habsburgs' own kingdom of Bohemia. The nobility in that mostly Czech-speaking province, plus many commoners, had converted to Calvinism and begun to bristle under Catholic rule, especially when Emperor Ferdinand II invoked *cuius regio, eius religio* and attempted to suppress Protestantism in the province.

The Bohemian estates, which represented the nobles and wealthy commoners, pledged to resist. Indeed, when Ferdinand's ambassador arrived in Prague, the Czech leaders literally threw him out of a second-story window in what became known as the Defenestration of Prague. The Bohemians then declared independence and elected a Protestant, Frederick V of the Palatinate, to be their new king. Emperor Ferdinand could not permit that. For not only was Bohemia a large and prosperous kingdom next door to his native Austria; the ruler of Bohemia was one of the seven electors, the princes empowered to elect the Holy Roman emperor. Indeed, Bohemia had become the swing vote, because three of the electorates were now Lutheran (Brandenburg, Saxony, and the Rhineland Palatinate), balancing the three Catholic electorates (Archbishoprics of Trier, Mainz, and Cologne). If Bohemia flipped Protestant, both the Habsburg dynasty and the Catholic church would lose control over much of the Holy Roman Empire.

So Ferdinand dispatched an army to invade Bohemia, inadvertently triggering three decades of withering warfare that would devastate whole provinces and kill a quarter of the entire German population. During the Thirty Years' War, Europeans came as close to realizing a total breakdown of civilization as they would know until the terrible twentieth century.

It all began when Frederick V, known as the Winter King because his reign lasted only a few months, traveled to Bohemia to take up the throne, only to find his realm was threatened by the imperial army. The courageous Bohemians fought to the last man until nearly all their nobles and knights were slain in the Battle of the White Mountain in 1620. Ferdinand promptly created a Catholic aristocracy to lord it over the province.

Other German princes now feared that the emperor might try to impose his authority and religion everywhere and forge a truly centralized Holy Roman Empire. The northern German princes therefore renewed their Lutheran alliance dating from the previous century. They also called on foreign Protestant princes for help, just as the Dutch had done in their own religious war. The first monarch to respond was the king of Denmark, but his soldiers were quickly defeated. That emboldened the imperial field general, the brilliant but unscrupulous Albrecht von Wallenstein, to declare that Lutheran rulers must restore all the real estate they had confiscated from the Catholic Church in the years since 1552. Needless to say, the Protestant rulers refused, whereupon Wallenstein marched his army north and spread civil war throughout most of Germany.

The next monarch to intervene was Gustavus Adolphus, the Lutheran king of Sweden. He styled himself a hero of Protestant liberties and has been celebrated as such ever since. But he also harbored the ambition of annexing Germany's northern coast, thereby making Sweden master of the whole Baltic Sea. The Protestant armies won a series of battles under the leadership of Gustavus Adolphus, which earned him a reputation as one of the greatest military commanders of the century, but his luck ran out at the Battle of Lützen, for while the Swedes were victorious in that engagement, the charismatic king was killed in action.

As the years had passed, the Emperor Ferdinand had grown distrustful of Wallenstein, and for good reason. The mercenary was himself a Bohemian of dubious loyalties, and his military victories tempted him to betray the emperor and rule Germany himself. Ferdinand put the word out that he would not be displeased if Wallenstein were removed. Sure enough, he was assassinated by some of his own officers in 1634.

Alas, neither Wallenstein's death nor Ferdinand's death three years later ended the devastation. Indeed, the war escalated in 1635 when Catholic France intervened . . . on the Protestant side! That was another critical turning point in European international relations, for it proved that the French crown's strategic goal of opposing Habsburg power outweighed its religious loyalties, and thus foreshadowed the end of the era of so-called religious wars. Indeed, no sooner did Catholic France declare war on Catholic Austria than Catholic Spain declared war on Catholic France.

By 1643, one French army had turned back the Spaniards in the Pyrenees, and another had invaded southern Germany. At that point, a new emperor, Ferdinand III, decided to end the bloody stalemate. Thirty years of slaughter had changed nothing except that Bohemia fell back into Habsburg control—and that had been a fait accompli as early as 1620.

At length the belligerent governments hammered out the Peace of Westphalia, which contemporaries called the Peace of Exhaustion. The negotiations lasted for several years because all the Great Powers and the lesser German states haggled over the details. In 1648 a series of treaties was concluded that reaffirmed *cuius regio, eius religio*, extended to Calvinist princes in the Rhineland equal standing with Catholics and Lutherans, enjoined all German princes to permit limited freedom of worship to minorities, and elevated the Catholic duke of Bavaria to the status of an elector. Most importantly, the Peace of Westphalia confirmed the rise of a balance-of-power system in Europe. Germany remained a loose confederation of more than three hundred principalities that emerged devastated from the Thirty Years' War. A century would pass before the human and material losses were made good. Indeed, many German towns never recovered their prosperity, as trade routes shifted to Atlantic ports with maritime access to the Americas and Asia. One can only imagine the anguish Martin Luther would have felt had he witnessed the carnage that befell his beloved fatherland as an indirect result of the movement he sparked in 1517.

Yet this chapter must conclude on a more cheerful note, because one aspect of central European life recovered quickly: its expressions of *themis* rather than *techne*. The late seventeenth and early eighteenth centuries were the heyday of the era known as the Baroque, when elaborate, uplifting art, architecture, and music adorned central Europe, especially the Catholic regions of northern Italy, Austria, and southern Germany. The Baroque cathedrals constructed in those provinces still dazzle the eyes of visitors with their white, gold, and blue interiors. Baroque architecture featured domes, colonnades, mirrors, statues, and busy decoration, all invariably light, airy, grand, and triumphal.

Likewise, the music of the Baroque era was invariably lilting, trilling, and joyous, especially the orchestral and choral compositions, both sacred and secular, of such giants as Johann Sebastian Bach, Antonio Vivaldi, George Frideric Handel, and Georg Telemann. Likewise the painting of the Baroque era, which blossomed especially in Protestant Europe. Consider the work of famous Dutch Masters such as Rembrandt van Rijn and Johannes Vermeer, and marvel at their exquisite portraits, still-lifes, and landscapes, which teased beauty, meaning, and magic from scenes of everyday life, whether ships lying at anchor, children ice-skating on a village pond, or fruit resting in a bowl. The Dutch specialized in depicting the literal "play" of sunlight, the mysteries of which their scientists were discovering through the study of optics. Suffice it to say that the finest mirrors, prisms, and telescopes of that era were the creations of Dutch craftsmen.

Although it had just passed through a cruel century of bitter religious and political strife, European culture not only survived but thrived. One might even say that the life-affirming, ever-creative spirit of early modern Europe was expressed to the utmost in the glorious culture of the Baroque.

Chapter 7

Spices, Specie, and Souls:
Europe Goes Global

In 1998 *The Economist* published a commemoration of the five-hundredth anniversary of Vasco da Gama's voyage from Portugal around Africa and across the Indian Ocean to Calicut, a port city on the west coast of India. Here is how that article began.

> Soon after dawn on May the 21st, 1498, Vasco da Gama and his crew arrived at Calicut after the first direct sea voyage from Europe to Asia. If history's modern age has a beginning, this is it. Europe's ignorance of, and isolation from, the cosmopolitan intellectual and commercial life of Asia were ended forever. With ships, weaponry and a willingness to use them both, the countries of Europe were about to colonise the rest of the world. To support this expansion, its merchant classes would invent new forms of commercial credit and the first great corporations, vital parts of capitalism's operating system, and spread their trading networks across the seven seas. And what did the men shout as they came ashore? "For Christ and spices! [*¡Por Cristo y especias!*]"

Toward the end of the fifteenth century, at the height of the Renaissance and just twenty years before Martin Luther inspired the Reformation, Europeans began to sail all over the globe. So it was—in yet another way—that what historians call early modern history began.

The relative isolation of the world's civilizations from each other could not last forever. Sooner or later, one of them was certain to learn the techniques of oceanic navigation and spill their explorers, merchants, soldiers, and missionaries onto other continents, each with their own cultures. The ensuing clashes of civilizations were bound to have a traumatic impact.

Nowadays political correctness requires people of European descent to display shame over their ancestors' treatment of the non-Western peoples they encountered. But the interesting question about the Age of Discovery is not whether da Gama, Columbus, and other European explorers were audacious, brutal, or greedy. Being human, they were all the above. No, the truly interesting questions are these: Why was it Europeans who began ceaselessly to explore every corner of the world? And why did that explosive era of exploration occur when it did?

That it would be Europeans who took the lead in global exploration was not inevitable. For instance, did Europeans command more sophisticated technology than other cultures around the year 1500? No! Europe was then catching up with the science and technology of some Asian civilizations, and many of the inventions that propelled European expansion—such as the magnetic compass, gunpowder, mathematics, and celestial navigation—were imported from the Chinese, Turks, Arabs, and Hindus. Had Europeans forged stronger, more unified empires than people elsewhere in the world? No! The kingdoms of Renaissance Europe were constantly at war with each other.

Were Europeans even the first to venture onto the high seas in search of new worlds? No again! Between 1405 and 1433, Chinese Admiral Zheng He led majestic fleets of treasure ships on voyages through the Strait of Malacca and Indian Ocean, and perhaps as far as the coast of Africa, to trade and collect tribute. Had these "Ming Voyages" continued, Asians might have discovered sea routes to Europe instead of the other way around. But the Ming dynasty's all-powerful emperors ordered the voyages stopped for three reasons: first, because Confucian ethics denigrated commerce as a legitimate human pursuit; second, because the merchants of southern China were of dubious loyalty to the emperor, who was based far to the north in Beijing; and third, because the principal threat to Chinese security was posed by barbarians on the northern frontier, making it more strategic for the empire to invest in land rather than sea power. Then, too, the Chinese considered their Middle Kingdom the only true civilization on earth and had little curiosity about distant barbarians.

Things were different in Europe. For one thing, no one there—no pope, no king, no emperor—possessed the power or authority to shut down exploration. If there was advantage to be had in seeking out new trading routes, some state or private company was sure to pursue it, and once exploration proved to be profitable, rival rulers and companies were sure to follow. In short, Europe's very disunity was a great source of strength. It bestowed a competitive freedom virtually unknown elsewhere.

Consider the Arabs, who were also avid traders, and whose Muslim religion was also evangelical. By 1400 the Arabs were ruled by the Ottoman Turkish Sultan, who gathered all political and religious authority to himself. Moreover, the Ottoman Turks were a caste of warlike people who, like the Chinese mandarins, considered money-grubbing commerce beneath them. None of that was the case in Europe, where divided authority and competition encouraged quests for new knowledge and opportunity, and where the Renaissance faith in progress validated the pursuit of power and wealth.

Finally, Europeans displayed a unique curiosity about other cultures. While they believed in the truth of their Christian religion, they did not conclude from that conviction that they had nothing to learn from encounters with other places and peoples. On the contrary, Europeans were voraciously interested in any practical knowledge that would serve their material interests.

That Europeans' motives were various and, morally speaking, less than pristine hardly made them exceptional. Why else do peoples seek contact with alien others except to plunder them, trade with them, study them, conquer them, or convert them? What made Europe exceptional lay in its means, not its motives, which brings us back to *techne*. Fascination with the physical world and its laws of nature; eagerness to borrow and improve on the tools and ideas developed by others; boundless self-confidence and willingness to take outrageous risks in hopes of acquiring honor, glory, power, and wealth in the service of church, state, and self—during the late medieval and Renaissance eras such qualities were on bold display in Europeans' innovative shipbuilding, sail rigging, rudders, navigation, mapping, cannons, and muskets. Most striking, perhaps, was the sheer fortitude of the Portuguese and Spanish captains and sailors, plus the Italians in their service, who dared to sail beyond the sight of land in faith that their skill, good fortune, and divine protection would bring them to safe harbors somewhere out there in the vast unknown.

No ocean-plying ships—no Portuguese caravels, Spanish galleons, or Dutch fluyts—would have been built at all unless people had been willing to finance expensive and risky voyages. Two sorts of Europeans were willing to do so by the late 1400s: rich merchants who pooled their money to spread and mitigate risk and state-building monarchs able to acquire the necessary capital via taxation or borrowing, and thus able to fund what amounted to the research and development of that era.

The first monarch to promote exploration was Portugal's Prince Henry the Navigator (1394–1460). At his court he assembled the best astronomers, navigators, and shipwrights and dispatched expeditions that discovered the Azores and Madeira Islands and planted forts on the west African coast to protect trade with the Arabs. Henry reinvested his profits in such efforts. He also borrowed large sums (he would die deep in debt) to finance more ambitious voyages aimed at finding a sea route around Africa. If he was successful, the Portuguese could outflank the Arab, Turkish, and Venetian middlemen who dominated the overland spice trade and capture immense profits for themselves.

Further and further down the torrid, disease-ridden west African coast Henry's caravels sailed. Only sixty feet or so in length, these ships carried two or three masts and lateen-rigged sails. They were equipped with crude but effective rudders for steering. They were also the first European ships that did not require galley slaves to pull oars below deck in order to make headway whenever the wind was contrary. Although these vessels were sturdier than their predecessors, it was still frightening to sail into unknown waters beyond sight of land, often in stormy weather. One 1487 torrent blew a ship captained by Bartolomeu Dias clear around what he named the Cape of Storms at the African continent's southern tip. When the skies cleared he saw, to his amazement, that the coastline now lay to the west, rather than the east! He had entered a new sea: the Indian Ocean.

A decade later Vasco da Gama's expedition crossed that ocean to Calicut on the Malabar Coast of India. That was the encounter celebrated in *The Economist*. The local authorities and merchants were hostile. One false move and the

Europeans might never have made it home. But da Gama found a Jewish interpreter who knew both Arabic and Italian, and through him he negotiated for a cargo of spices that would yield a profit of six thousand percent back in Lisbon. That achievement bestowed on Portugal's king a new epithet: Manuel Fortunado (Manuel the Lucky). It also changed Portugal's name for Africa's southern coast from the Cape of Storms to the Cape of Good Hope.

The next time da Gama sailed for India, in 1502, he commanded a fleet of twenty-one ships. Soon thereafter the Duke of Albuquerque arrived with an even stronger fleet bearing soldiers who attacked strategic ports such as Goa. In a series of ferocious campaigns Albuquerque succeeded in capturing and fortifying the key choke points that controlled access to the Red Sea, Persian Gulf, and Straits of Malacca in the Spice Islands. From there Portuguese merchants and Jesuit missionaries such as St. Francis Xavier reconnoitered Asian coasts as far afield as China and the mysterious islands that they called Cipangu but that inhabitants called Nippon: Japan.

By 1515, the year of Albuquerque's death, little Portugal had forged a thalassocracy—a maritime empire—that began to transform the global economy. Previously, the Arabs, Turks, and Venetians had served as middlemen for the spice trade, but now the Portuguese had outflanked them. For the city-states of Renaissance Italy, the result was a financial calamity as devastating as the military invasions that had begun in 1494. Henceforth, profits from spices, silks, tea, and porcelain flowed through Atlantic ports such as Lisbon, Seville, and, later on, Amsterdam, Antwerp, and London.

Meanwhile, in the year 1492 another expedition set out in search of a maritime route to Asia. How much did the Genoese captain Christopher Colombus know about the western sea he proposed to cross? More than we used to think. Of course, no one at the time believed the world was flat—that canard was concocted much later by smug Enlightenment intellectuals. Indeed, in 1490 the German geographer Martin Behaim crafted the first globe, which he called his *Erdapfel* (earth apple). The globe, being round, obviously suggested the possibility of sailing westward to Asia, especially since Behaim grossly underestimated the distance. The ancient Greeks had made reasonably accurate estimates of the earth's circumference. But Behaim based his calculations on Marco Polo's distorted geography; hence his globe showed Asia stretching far eastward toward Europe.

That notion persuaded Columbus that he could cross the Atlantic to Asia in a matter of weeks. Accordingly, he presented Ferdinand and Isabella with a wildly optimistic business prospectus that projected a trip of just 2,500 miles, not 11,000. Since 2,500 miles just happened to be the rough distance from Spain to the Caribbean Sea, Columbus naturally assumed that the islands he discovered there were the East Indies, which is why he named their inhabitants Indians. His own name was not planted on the New World, because he never realized it *was* a New World. Word that a new continent had been discovered was publicized in 1507 when the geographer Martin Waldseemüller printed a magnificent and mysteriously accurate map of the coastline of a continent he christened America, after the Florentine explorer Amerigo Vespucci.

By 1513, it was clear that another vast ocean must lie beyond America, and the first to lay eyes on it was a Spanish conquistador named Vasco de Balboa. His expedition scaled the mountainous spine of Central America from the east, and upon traversing the crest he gazed upon the ocean Spaniards would call the South Sea or Pacific Ocean. That body of water covers half the planet—if you doubt that, just look at a globe—and if Balboa had any inkling of that fact, he must have gasped, "Santa María! Columbus was lucky he didn't try to cross this!"

The exploits of the Iberians are simply mind-boggling. They sailed into uncharted seas in small ships with only rude navigational instruments and meager rations on voyages that might last for months. High risk, high reward. Not only were the stakes for which the Spanish and Portuguese gambled enormous; they also embarked on their maritime conquests imbued with the crusading spirit bred in them by the long Reconquista of their homeland.

In 1519 the conquistador Hernán Cortés led soldiers to the North American mainland, where they heard tales of a fierce warrior race called the Aztecs. They were told of a great imperial city called Tenochtitlán, where pyramids ran red with the blood of human sacrifices, and palaces gleamed with silver, gold, and emeralds. At the harbor known today as Vera Cruz, Cortés ordered his soldiers to burn their ships so they would not be tempted to retreat. With just six hundred men, he meant to conquer the mighty Aztecs.

Along his way to today's Mexico City, Cortés made alliances with Mesoamerican tribes who feared the bloodthirsty Aztecs. At length he and his fellow conquistadors reached the capital of King Montezuma, whereupon an unparalleled clash of civilizations played out. At first, the Aztecs were in awe of these

Spices, Specie, and Souls

Catholic Spaniards, witnessing Aztec priests garbed in feathers, worshiping hideous deities, and carving the living hearts out of hundreds of victims to appease their gods, had no doubt they had stumbled across the devil's own children.

pale-skinned invaders who seemed to have metallic skin (their armor), wielded fiery weapons (their muskets), and rode great beasts (their horses) unknown in the New World. The beasts in turn pulled wagons that rolled on something else no Native American had ever laid eyes on: wheels. Understandably, the Aztecs suspected the Spaniards might be gods. They imagined Cortés himself might be Quetzalcoatl . . . until they witnessed some of his men get sick, suffer wounds, bleed, and even die. Whereupon they turned on the aliens. Cortés and his greatly outnumbered men found themselves in mortal peril. But the alliances Cortés had made with other tribes allowed him to beat a hasty retreat before regrouping, reoccupying Tenochtitlán, and seizing the Aztecs' treasure.

The Spaniards' original goal, the Asian Spice Islands, remained out of reach. So King Charles V commissioned Ferdinand Magellan to find a sea route around America. In 1520 Magellan's squadron sailed to frigid Patagonia at the southern tip of South America, braved the rocks, storms, icebergs, and volcanoes they called Tierra del Fuego (Land of Fire), and plunged into the Pacific Ocean. As the months passed, many of Magellan's crewmen perished from scurvy caused by vitamin C deficiency. The survivors were reduced to eating rats, leather, and sawdust, while praying daily for rainwater to drink. At last the trade winds bore them ten thousand miles west to the Philippine Islands, where Magellan was killed in a skirmish with natives. One of his ships, however, made it back to Spain, having circled the globe using primitive sixteenth-century technology. In many respects, the expedition's achievement can be considered greater even than the Apollo moon landings that lay 450 years in the future.

One more amazing Spanish achievement of this era must be mentioned. In 1532, the conquistador Francisco Pizarro led a terrestrial expedition into South America and stumbled upon the mysterious Inca civilization, based high in the Andes mountain range. Thanks to a civil war then raging among the Incas, Pizarro's small army managed to conquer Peru and seize the richest silver mines in the world.

So it was that just forty years after Columbus first sailed west for Asia, the kingdom of Spain, numbering just 6.5 million people, had subdued all of Mexico, the Caribbean, and Peru; had laid claim to the rest of South America except for Portuguese Brazil (first claimed by Pedro Cabral in 1500); and had discovered a backdoor to Asia across the Pacific.

The Spaniards' courage, ferocity, and indomitable will were remarkable. But the results of their efforts, for the Americas' native peoples, were calamitous. The Spaniards generally felt no sympathy for—and gave no quarter to—the alien pagans they discovered. But do we have any reason to expect that they would have? Europeans in that era knew only five categories of people: Catholic Christians, Protestant Christians (beginning in 1517), Muslims, Jews, and pagans. For Spanish Catholics, Protestant "heretics" and Muslims were enemies who must be resisted. Anomalous Jews, who were God's people but had rejected the Messiah, were variously tolerated or persecuted depending on their utility to local Christian rulers. And pagans, especially savage ones, existed only to be converted and their idols destroyed. The Spaniards felt especially justified in destroying Aztec civilization because of its unspeakable cruelty. Cortés's men were horrified to witness priests in great feathered cloaks and hideous masks ritually carving the living hearts out of hundreds of victims in stone temples whose elaborate drainage systems channeled blood into the maws of idols—idols that looked to them like nightmarish demons from hell.

Spices, Specie, and Souls

Over the course of the sixteenth century Spain's royal government gradually replicated its political, social, and religious systems in Nueva España (New Spain). The kings divided the New World into the viceroyalties of Mexico and Peru, and soon there were twenty-two dioceses headed by resident bishops. The crown transplanted the feudal system by awarding huge land grants to favored noblemen, who thereby became *hidalgos* presiding over great plantations called *encomiendas*. The Spaniards coerced the Mesoamericans to labor as peons raising corn, cattle, and horses. Neither did the church neglect to transplant the Catholic Reformation in the New World colonies. As early as the 1550s, clergy oversaw the construction of cathedrals and universities in Mexico City and Lima. That was eighty years before the founding of Harvard College by the Puritans of New England. The Spaniards also defended their commercial monopoly by erecting impregnable stone fortresses in critical ports such as Cartagena, in what is now Colombia, and in San Juan, in what is now Puerto Rico. The latter city's forts of El Morro and San Cristóbal remain tourist attractions to this day and fly the battle flag of the sixteenth-century Habsburgs.

The fate of most Mesoamericans was death. Historians estimate that between 60 and 90 percent perished due to war, forced labor, and especially disease. For just as the bodies of medieval Europeans had no antibodies enabling them to resist the bubonic plague imported from Asia, so Native Americans had no immunity against European diseases like smallpox, yellow fever, measles, and chicken pox. The genes of the 10 to 40 percent of Amerindians who survived, however, mixed over the course of two centuries with the genes of Spaniards and enslaved Africans to produce *la raza grande* collectively known as Latin Americans.

Did no Spaniards sympathize with the original inhabitants of America? Many clergymen did, and their protests against the conquistadors' greed and brutality sparked much legal debate back in Spain. With respect to the indigenous people, the *encomienderos* argued: "These people are not really human at all. They are natural beasts of burden and certainly possess no standing or rights under the king's justice." On the contrary, replied many missionary friars, led by a penitent colonist-turned-Dominican named Bartolomé de Las Casas: "God surely guided Spaniards to the New World for the mission of saving these souls from paganism; hence our duty is to convert and civilize them. Moreover, baptized Indians should enjoy the same rights as any other subject of Your Majesty."

Convinced by the friars' arguments, Charles V and Philip II, both men of faith and conscience, founded missions to minister to and protect Amerindians and established courts of law to dispense the king's justice in the New World. But the distances were too great, travel too slow and uncertain, and colonial officials too prone to bribery or intimidation to effectively enforce the crown's edicts. It might take two years for a petition to reach Madrid and a royal decree to find its way back to a local viceroy, governor, judge, or bishop. Moreover, the royal government had a powerful incentive to look the other way when it came to native rights, because it received royalties from the precious metals and gemstones extracted from American mines. The richest mines of all were discovered at Potosí in what is now Bolivia, where tens of thousands of peons slaved at sword point to extract silver oxide and refine the ore with toxic mercury.

Only in the rawest, remotest regions, such as the Rio Grande region on New Spain's far northern frontier, or in the South American jungle, were Indians humanely served by missionaries functioning not only as priests but as agronomists, doctors, and, when necessary, advocates. Some missions in today's northern Mexico, New Mexico, Arizona, and Texas were destroyed by the fierce Apache and Comanche tribes, as well as rebellious Pueblos and Pimas, while some in the South American jungles were wrecked by turf wars between rival religious orders. (The Oscar-winning Hollywood film *The Mission* depicts one such episode in dramatic fashion.)

The European discoveries and conflicts in the Americas and Indian subcontinent during the 1500s are one of the great epics of modern history. Imagine a time when a handful of ships, a few hundred men, or a dozen cannons in the right place and time could win half a continent for king and country. It is also a story familiar to most people, so instead of telling it in more detail, the rest of this chapter will simply summarize four major patterns that shaped Europeans' encounter with the overseas world their explorers discovered.

The first pattern was ever more strenuous competition among European states and chartered companies for geographical knowledge, colonial bases, and commercial opportunities. Because the initial Iberian colonies proved immensely profitable, the Spaniards and Portuguese tried to maintain absolute secrecy about the seas and lands they discovered. They not only forbade foreigners to visit and trade with their ports in America and Asia; they even forbade their own subjects to do so without official permission. After all, information about ocean currents, tides, trade winds, coastal surveys, passages through narrow straits, and the exact latitudes and approximate longitudes of islands and mainland shores constituted priceless intelligence. Not only did governments guard such information closely; pirates from foreign countries craved it—and pirates there were. By the late 1500s French, Dutch, and English freebooters were sailing the Atlantic and Indian oceans hoping to capture Spanish or Portuguese ships, not only for their cargoes but also for their priceless maps, charts, and captains' logs.

International competition began as early as 1498, when Henry VII of England hired the Venetian brothers Giovanni and Sebastiano Caboto (John and Sebastian Cabot) to explore the coastline of North America in hopes of finding a Northwest Passage to the Pacific Ocean. None existed, but the Cabots discovered the rich Grand Banks fisheries off Newfoundland, prompting fishermen from Cornwall and Brittany to begin sailing across the Atlantic in order to gorge their holds with codfish. The English crown also commissioned the mariner Henry Hudson, whose expeditions discovered the eponymous river and bay. Queen Elizabeth's dashing captain Sir Francis Drake sailed around South America and stunned the Spaniards by capturing treasure ships off the coast of Peru. Drake traveled as far north as San Francisco Bay before crossing the Pacific and completing the second circumnavigation of the world.

The French were distracted during the late 1500s by their civil wars at home, but as early as 1534 Jacques Cartier sailed up the St. Lawrence River and claimed for France what the local Iroquois called the Canadas and the French later named Québec. The region was colonized by Samuel de Champlain in 1608. Meanwhile, the Dutch expanded overseas during their eighty-year war of independence by conquering Portugal's fortresses around the Indian Ocean, their efforts climaxing in 1641 when they forced the surrender of the supposedly impregnable Portuguese fortress at Malacca. For decades thereafter the Netherlands controlled most of the precious trade in spices.

The second pattern of overseas expansion was the economic theory and practice inspired by that competition. Under mercantilism, as it was called, the royal governments of Spain, Portugal, England, France, and the Netherlands mobilized private capital for exploration, colonization, and world trade through chartered companies to which they granted special privileges and monopolies. Needless to say, the royal governments forbade their chartered companies from trading with any rival country and considered any gains made by opponents as losses for their own country's merchants. The distinctions between commerce, smuggling, and piracy were therefore often blurry. The monarchical governments tried to impose order through such mercantilist measures as the prohibition of foreign merchants in their overseas spheres of influence. Thus did the British East India Company emerge in the year 1600 and the Dutch East India Company in 1602, both of which proved so successful that France and Sweden soon founded copycat companies.

During the early seventeenth century, mercantilist institutions inspired mercantilist theories of economics and administration. They were certainly capitalist, but of a sort that was highly regulated and protectionist and pursued competition among nations as much as among private firms. The basic assumption of mercantilism seemed to be common sense: countries that export goods more valuable than the goods they import must grow richer, while countries that import more than they export must make up the difference in precious metals and therefore grow poorer. Of course, tropical commodities such as spices, tea, sugar, tobacco, and silk had to be imported because they could not be grown in Europe's northern climate. But if those tropical goods were produced on plantations in one's own colonies and shipped by one's own chartered company, they did not really count as imports at all. Mercantilism was thus a powerful impetus for colonization by all seafaring Europeans.

Of course, acquiring, maintaining, and defending an overseas empire was expensive, which is why chartered companies that were granted monopoly rights and military protection compensated the state with payments of royalties. Chartered companies, in turn, raised capital by selling shares to private investors. They also pioneered marine insurance, paying premiums to financial syndicates in exchange for compensation in the event one of their voyages ended in shipwreck or capture.

As a macroeconomic theory, mercantilism was primitive and based on fallacies, not least the notion that commerce is a zero-sum game. But mercantilism made sense during an era when European monarchs were obsessed with centralized state-building and administrative control over the activities of their subjects, and when Europeans had just begun the risky business of exploring and subduing the world. What was more, the maturation of capitalist techniques of all sorts gradually widened the gap between Europe's economic growth rates and those of other civilizations. Indeed, a fitting benchmark for that growing gap is provided by the founding, in 1694, of the Bank of England, soon to become the richest, most powerful financial institution in the world.

By the year 1700, some two centuries after Vasco da Gama sailed to India, Spain was ruling a massive empire in the Americas and Philippine Islands. Portugal had lost most of its Asian empire to the Dutch but was still clinging to Goa on the Malabar Coast of India, Macao on the China coast, and enormous Brazil in South America. The British and French East India Companies were competing against each other on the Malabar, Coromandel, and Bengali shores of India. And the British, French, Dutch, and Spaniards were all planting lush sugar colonies on the islands of the Caribbean.

What about the thirteen British colonies in North America and other colonies such as the ones in French Québec, Spanish Argentina, and Dutch South Africa? They constitute a separate category, which amounts to our third pattern of European expansion during the early modern era: promotion by governments of white settler colonies that might or might not serve mercantilist goals but that spread European people as well as trade and technology around the world.

This third pattern began in the first three decades of the seventeenth century with the creation of the Virginia Company, which founded Jamestown in 1607; the Compagnie de Nouvelle-France, which founded Québec in 1608; the Spaniards of New Spain who founded Santa Fe in 1609; and the Dutch West India Company, which founded New Amsterdam at the mouth of the Hudson River in 1614. This pattern also includes the English Pilgrims who landed at Plymouth Rock in Massachusetts Bay in 1620 and the great migration of Puritans to Massachusetts Bay that began in 1630.

During their early years, nearly all these settler colonies suffered traumatic die-offs caused by malnutrition, disease, or Indian assault. But by the middle of the seventeenth century these European beachheads in America had survived. The English colonies, especially, began to grow rapidly in population and economic self-sufficiency, while also providing a haven for political and religious refugees from England, Scotland, Wales, and Ireland. England's North American colonies—the last of which, Georgia, was founded in the 1730s—rapidly filled with people eager to exploit a virgin continent teeming with land, timber, and water and brimming with natural resources. By the time of the American Revolution, in fact, the free white people of the thirteen British colonies would already boast the highest standard of living in the world, thanks to their diversified agriculture, animal husbandry, fishing, mining, craftsmanship, manufactures, shipbuilding, and commerce. French Québec failed to replicate that success, both because it suffered from an extremely cold climate and because the royal government foolishly prohibited Huguenots from participating in the colonial endeavor. But that is a story for another chapter. For now, the important point is that settler colonies literally transplanted European cultures and societies to other parts of the world.

Tragically, one of the sources of wealth in the Americas was chattel slave labor. Beginning in the 1500s, Europe's mercantilist shipping companies had begun to transport enslaved Africans to the New World. The vast majority of these men, women, and children were sold in the plantations of Brazil and the sugar islands of the Caribbean. The colonists of North America mostly refrained from engaging in the slave trade; indentured servants from England more than satisfied their demand for cheap labor. But by the end of the seventeenth century the simultaneous spread of plantations and a shortage of indentured servants caused North American planters to begin using African labor as well. That story will get a full treatment in due course. For the moment it is sufficient to observe that the American production and exportation of sugar, tobacco, timber, and other commodities were indicative of the fourth great pattern of European expansion: globalization.

European ships plying the Atlantic traded manufactures, firearms, and rum to West African chieftains in return for slaves, most of whom had been members of rival tribes captured in indigenous wars. These ships crossed the Atlantic to sell the Africans in New World ports, while other European ships took on cargoes of colonial goods. The slavers and merchant ships then returned to European ports, where the cycle would begin anew. All the voyages were financed by bills of exchange issued in the counting houses of the major ports. This flourishing four-continent network had already begun to mature by around 1700. But consider also this extraordinary if little-known fact. The Spaniards in South America were extracting large quantities of silver at mines such as Potosí. Where did that bullion go? Much of it, of course, was shipped to Spain. But a substantial chunk of it went the other direction. Each year the Spaniards sailed a treasure ship simply known as The Galleon across the Pacific to Manila in the Philippines. The silver was then trans-shipped to mainland China in order to purchase luxury goods. Much of the silver gleaned by the Chinese merchant guilds was then carted north to Beijing and stamped into coinage. Can you guess what the Ming Dynasty's imperial treasury used that money for? To finance construction of the Great Wall of China, thousands of miles of fortifications designed to keep out Mongol invaders.

Interconnections. Interdependence. Events, systems, and patterns in one part of the world affecting events, systems, and patterns prevailing in other parts of the world. Over short spans of time the consequences of far-off events could be enriching or disastrous, depending on war and peace, market prices, weather, piracy, shipwreck, and numerous other factors. But the consequences over long spans of time were truly transformative. Historians write of the so-called Columbian exchange, by which they mean the exchanges of culture, goods, and even disease vectors between the Old and New Worlds that began with the voyages of Columbus. Over time America received from Europe the written word, Arabic numerals, the wheel, the horse, firearms, Christianity, and the diseases that killed off most of the Amerindian population. Meanwhile, Europe received from America potatoes, tomatoes, coffee, sugar, chocolate, tobacco, and two noxious scourges: syphilis and financial inflation.

Inflation occurred because the flood of silver and gold from the New World sharply increased the money supply in Europe, which in turn caused prices to spike. During those same decades Europe's royal governments, forever waging costly wars, began to pay off their debts in debased coinage, causing more inflation. Indeed, economic dislocations became so severe during the seventeenth century that political crises erupted from one end of Europe to the other. Kings and their finance ministers and merchants were obliged to confront these crises. The contrasting solutions upon which they landed will be described over four of the next five chapters, because the methods of public finance variously chosen by the European nations go far toward explaining their distinctive national traits. Thus, even as Europeans during the Age of Discovery came to dramatically influence the fate of other peoples, so did globalization reshape the futures of European states.

Chapter 8

Two Cardinals and a Sun King: Absolutism in France

The end of the last chapter described the so-called Columbian exchange of crops, animals, and diseases between Europe and America and concluded with a teaser about an especially unwelcome import: monetary inflation. The enormous influx into Europe of silver and gold caused a sharp rise in prices that destabilized nearly all sectors of the seventeenth-century economy. It also engendered a crisis for royal governments, whose revenue streams were invariably fixed. To make matters worse, Europe's great powers frequently waged wars, which meant their governments were desperate for money. The upshot was a continent-wide phenomenon that historians label early modern state-building, which is to say focused efforts by monarchs to build stronger, more centralized governments placed on a firm fiscal footing. Such efforts were of surpassing importance, because the solutions concocted by the rulers of the leading nations went far toward defining those nations' characters.

By way of prelude to the stories of those state-building kings, we do well to pose a question that might already have occurred to readers: Why were there kings at all? Why was monarchy the most prevalent political model in Europe from the Roman Empire all the way into the twentieth century? There were a few exceptions to this rule. The Venetian Republic's head of state, the doge, functioned as a combined minister of commerce and lord of the admiralty for the merchant oligarchy. Other Italian city-states, such as Florence under the Medici family, were republics. The Netherlands, which gained its independence in that eighty-year war against Habsburg Spain, was a republic governed by a *stadtholder* (state-holder) and an executive council known as *De Hooge Mogende* (Their High Mightinesses). The Swiss cantons were also self-governing. But note that all these republics were small and that every other polity in early modern Europe was a monarchy.

Why monarchies? One response is to ask, Why not? Monarchy was the only form of government in nearly all the ancient civilizations of China, Japan, the Middle East, Africa, and pre-Columbian America. In fact, only in the Mediterranean world was monarchy sometimes absent, as in the ancient Greek city-states, Israel under the judges, Rome before the Caesars, and the modern examples just cited. What is strange about Europe, therefore, is not its autocratic tradition, but its occasional departures from it.

Monarchy is apparently natural for several sensible reasons. First, it has been a common practice throughout global history for a warlord to found a realm or empire. The conqueror made himself ruler and, since he naturally wanted his kingdom to outlive himself, established a hereditary dynasty. Second, in many cultures, monarchs possessed religious validation, a sort of mandate from heaven, either because they were worshiped as divinities themselves or because they served as high priests of the official cult. Third, monarchy can be extremely efficient, especially for imposing law and order at home and mobilizing people against enemies abroad. Indeed, even the ancient Greek and Roman republics appointed temporary dictators in times of war. Fourth, in most civilizations no alternative theory of legitimacy, such as popular sovereignty, contested the "might makes right" claim of monarchs. To be sure, monarchy need not be hereditary. Several of the Germanic tribes who migrated to Europe in late antiquity elected their kings on the basis of prowess and popularity. But elected or not, they were still kings.

Memories of the Greek and Roman republics were part of medieval Europeans' cultural inheritance, but those memories emphasized the republics' collapse, whether from demagogy, corruption, or civil war. What was more, Christianity did not prescribe any particular form of government. So once the late Roman emperors became Christian, it was natural for the church to bless emperors or kings so long as they did not trespass on the church's domain. Europeans also accepted monarchy because they assumed that this world ought to reflect heaven to the degree such was possible, and heaven, after all, was the *kingdom* of God. To be sure, Augustine of Hippo, who observed the Western Roman Empire's collapse, had distinguished the City of God from the City of Man. But he also endorsed the assumption—derived from Platonic philosophy, the Old Testament history of the Jews, and Roman history—that the best government was a monarchy under a just and pious prince, even as the church was an elective monarchy under the pope. Biblical paragons of the just and pious monarch included Israel's David and Solomon.

Medieval monarchy was reinforced by the example of Charlemagne, who not only revived the imperial dream for a season but also bequeathed to his vassals the dynastic right to govern their own local realms under Roman and/or Germanic law. Medieval monarchy thus rested on a firm if unwritten constitutional basis. Kings, dukes, and lesser princes ruled by law, and while their succession was sometimes contested, no one questioned the legality of the throne itself. But what might occur if a given ruler was not just and pious? What if kings became tyrants, trampling on the legal rights of nobles, parliaments, clergy, or peasantry?

If a cruel monarch was too powerful to resist—such as Tsar Ivan the Terrible of Russia—subjects tended to bow and scrape even more than they would to a beloved king. That was why the Renaissance political philosopher Niccolò Machiavelli wrote in *The Prince* that it is better to be feared than loved. But if a monarch was both wicked and vulnerable, then his subjects might rein him in or even depose him. English history provides numerous examples of both contingencies, from King John, whom the nobility and clergy humbled by obliging him to sign Magna Carta (Great Charter) in the year 1215, to Charles I and James II, ousted in coups d'état in 1642 and 1688. But to attempt to depose a rightful king, whether wicked or not, risked provoking civil war, not to mention the lives of the rebels. Hence the old saying: "If you shoot at a king, be sure not to miss!" During succession crises—for instance, when a monarch died without leaving a recognized heir—violence might erupt, as it did in France during the 1500s. But sometimes even civil wars might strengthen monarchical institutions. In the French case, the new Bourbon kings whose dynasty began in 1589 were determined to buttress their royal authority, reassert law and order, and ensure that civil strife would never recur. So they built centralized bureaucracies, suppressed the power of the nobility and the church, and aspired to a pure form of monarchy they called absolutism. That is the achievement which this chapter describes.

Europeans and Americans of the twenty-first century who take for granted their nations' democratic traditions may recoil against the notion of absolute monarchy. They may imagine that those kings and their ministers who extolled absolutism are history's bad guys. But that would be bad history: first, because such an attitude seeks to judge rather than to understand; and second, because it is simply incorrect. In the context of seventeenth-century Europe, emerging as it was from terrible religious and civil wars and saddled as it was with monetary inflation that threatened to bankrupt governments altogether, the proponents of royal absolutism were in fact the *progressives* of their era and agents of modernization. They were the ones who tried to purge their societies of the remaining vestiges of the Middle Ages and to demonstrate—as philosophers Jacques-Bénigne Bossuet and Thomas Hobbes would argue—that absolute monarchy was not only the most natural form of government but also the best.

When we last looked in on the French, they were just emerging from what they called their "cruel century." The Valois dynasty had gone extinct when Queen Catherine de Medici's three sickly sons died without heirs. The civil wars that followed over the royal succession were exacerbated by religious strife between Roman Catholics and Calvinist Huguenots. The private armies of the contesting dukes ravaged the countryside, disrupted economic activity, and prevented France from playing its accustomed role at the center of European diplomacy. But the 1589 accession of the new Bourbon dynasty in the person of Henri Quatre (Henri IV) abruptly ended the turmoil. Henri restored order, decreed religious toleration in the Edict of Nantes, and began to rebuild the strength of *la grande nation*, a nation whose fertile soil and mild climate yielded—in time of peace—abundant crops, fat herds of livestock, and flourishing vineyards. Under Henri IV the market revived for those luxury goods for which France had long been famous: wine, perfume, furniture, carriages, linen, lace. The recovery of trade in turn enriched merchants and bankers while providing livelihoods for craftsmen, farmers, and fishermen. Many sailors populated France's long coastlines, from the English Channel to the Atlantic Ocean to the Bay of Biscay to the Mediterranean Sea.

Indeed, the bourgeoisie—or townspeople—in cities and villages all over France were especially supportive of Henri IV's effective monarchy because the king stood for law and order, the enforcement of contracts, property rights, the expansion of commerce, and opportunities for employment in the expanding royal bureaucracy for educated sons of the middle classes. By contrast, the opponents of Henri's centralizing royal government were those who had held more power in the medieval era, including the landowning nobility, the Catholic church, the provincial law courts (called *parlements*), and the Estates General, France's representative assembly in which the clergy, nobility, and common people were empowered to ratify taxes. The authority to ratify taxes was important, because under French law kings had only two sources of revenue: first, whatever profits they might glean from their personal domains; and second, whatever revenues they might collect from taxes approved by the Estates General. The power of taxation was further limited by the church's exemption from taxation and by nobles hardly being likely to tax their own wealth unless the king made political concessions in return. The provincial *parlements* further limited royal authority, since they were empowered to strike down royal decrees their judges deemed unconstitutional.

Now, during the Hundred Years' War between France and England, which had ended in 1453, the Estates General had granted the crown two principal taxes: the *taille*, a sort of head-tax on all commoners, and the *gabelle*, a sales tax on precious salt. However, the collection of these taxes was hit-and-miss, for royal administration did not reach down to the local level. Accordingly, French kings relied on private tax-farmers, who paid for the right to collect taxes in a given territory in exchange for a percentage of the take. That system all but ensured graft, bribery, and false accounting.

Thus, when Henri IV set out to strengthen the monarchy, he wisely began with public finance, the most important feature of any government in any era of history. Indeed, the power of monarchies was directly proportional to their ability to raise revenue, since kings could not defend their realms or enforce the law without permanent soldiers, gendarmes, and officials, and they could not afford soldiers, gendarmes, and officials without sizable sources of regular income. So it was that the efforts of kings to expand and regularize tax collection created the modern state.

Henri IV's prime minister and treasurer, Maximilien de Béthune, duc de

Sully, began by cracking down on fraud among tax-farmers. He had several of them arrested *pour encourager les autres* (to serve as an example to others). Then Sully lowered the *taille*—the head-tax—imposed on commoners by 25 percent, expecting that the reduction would help to eliminate fraud. It did: revenues rose as a result. He also tapped the wealth of the bourgeoisie by selling government offices that bestowed titles of nobility on their recipients. That practice not only raised revenue; it gave the bourgeoisie another incentive to support the king, since he was offering them opportunities to raise their social status. Needless to say, the traditional *noblesse d'épée* (nobility of the sword) held such bourgeois social climbers or *noblesse de la robe* (nobility of the robe) in contempt. The famous playwright Jean-Baptiste Molière parodied those social tensions in his seventeenth-century comedy *Le bourgeois gentilhomme*.

Whatever his subjects thought of the means used to raise revenue, very few criticized the use Henri IV and Sully made of it, for their program included ambitious infrastructure projects—including roads, bridges, and canals— that stimulated economic growth. The Edict of Nantes had a major economic impact, too, because the now-tolerated Huguenots, true to the stereotypical Protestant work ethic, quickly became leaders in commerce and the professions. Sadly, Henri's religious toleration cost him his life in 1610 when a zealous Catholic charged his royal carriage in the streets of Paris and stabbed the king to death.

Fortunately, no succession crisis followed this assassination, because Henri IV left behind a legitimate heir born to his wife Marie de Medici. Yes, the French monarch had formed a union with that Florentine banking family. Why? Because Henri de Bourbon had run up massive debts during the long civil wars that won him his crown. In 1600 he repaid his principal creditor, Francesco de Medici, by marrying his daughter, thus making her queen. Her little boy, Louis XIII, was only eight years old in 1610, so Marie de Medici governed as regent, just as Catherine de Medici had done during the minority of her own little boys in the previous century.

Unfortunately, the Italian Marie was universally unpopular among her French subjects, not least for promoting a pro-Spanish foreign policy. Accordingly, the Estates General that convened in 1614 refused to grant the crown

Portraitist Philippe de Champaigne brilliantly captured his subject's character and intelligence (*Triple Portrait of Cardinal de Richelieu*, ca. 1642).

new taxes so long as the queen mother was regent. Marie refused to step down, trying instead to rule in defiance of the Estates and nearly everyone else. She even dismissed Sully and replaced him with another slippery Italian, Concino Concini. By 1617, a crisis atmosphere hovered over the city of Paris.

Then, to Marie's surprise, her own son turned against her. For no sooner did Louis XIII turn sixteen than he insisted his mother dismiss Concini, end the regency, and bow her knee to him! When Marie refused, the royal teenager secretly ordered the palace guard to arrest Concini and kill him should he resist. He did resist—and the guards killed him. When that welcome news spread through the streets, ecstatic Parisians shouted "Vive le roi!" while Louis proclaimed, "Enfin, je suis le roi!" (Finally, I am the king!).

However joyful the Parisians, the young monarch faced powerful resistance from the nobility and church prelates until, in the year 1624, he found his own mentor: a brilliant, ruthless, ambitious man named Armand Jean du Plessis, Duc de Richelieu and a cardinal of the church. Study the famous triple portrait of Cardinal Richelieu by the artist Philippe de Champaigne, a portrait executed in that evocative Renaissance style that probes its subject's personality, and you will appreciate Richelieu's power of mind and strength of will. He was possibly the seventeenth century's most astute observer of human behavior, and in the fashion of Machiavelli he knew how to employ force, threats, bribes, alliances, flattery, and deceit to advance his goals and those of his patron. Richelieu might have been a high-ranking nobleman who doubled as a high-ranking cleric. But his highest loyalties were to himself, to the king, and to *raison d'état*: the reason, or rational interests, of the state. To contemporaries it seemed that Richelieu was a traitor to the nobility and clergy. To posterity he has seemed like an amoral statesman for whom the ends justified the means. To students of history Richelieu is the architect of the modern French state and the godfather of what became known as absolute monarchy.

Richelieu discovered his calling in 1614 when he attended the Estates General as a member of the first estate, the clergy. He watched in disgust as Marie, the royal ministers, and the leaders of the Estates fell into quarrels that paralyzed the government. He concluded that the only way to tame the many factions among the French population was to make the king supreme. In 1624 he got his chance when Louis XIII, then twenty-two years of age, named Richelieu, then thirty-nine, his prime minister. The king was smitten by his mentor's program for enhancing royal power, but fearful of the resistance it was bound to provoke. Yet Louis feared civil strife even more—his father had been murdered, after all—as well as the dissent that had incapacitated his mother's regency. So he gave Richelieu authority to move boldly against all those interest groups whose medieval rights and privileges checked the power of the crown.

Richelieu picked off the easiest target first: the religious minority. The Edict of Nantes had promised Huguenots freedom to practice their faith, but the Huguenots had prudently hedged their bets by forming strong communities around the castles of Protestant nobles and by fortifying the coastal towns under their control. The fortifications suggested that the loyalty of French Protestants was something less than absolute, which persuaded Richelieu that their freedom of action must be destroyed. His scheme was to goad the Huguenots into an act of rebellion that would give the crown a pretext to suppress them. So he bade the king issue a decree to the effect that local fortifications were now forbidden unless needed against foreign attack. The suspicious Huguenots refused to dismantle their castles and forts and in 1626 rebelled against royal authority under the leadership of the duc de Rohan. That played into Richelieu's hands. Taking personal command of a royal army, he besieged the Huguenot port of La Rochelle and bombarded the town into surrender. Bear in mind that his purpose was not religious persecution. Louis XIII continued to honor the Edict of Nantes. Rather, Richelieu was sending a strong signal about the consequences of defying the crown.

Next he turned to the Catholic nobility, whom Richelieu purposely insulted by outlawing the *code duello*: dueling, the venerable tradition by which noblemen settled affairs of honor between themselves. Richelieu insisted that henceforth noblemen litigate their disputes in royal courts and bow to the king's justice. Then he added injury to insult by ordering nobles, both Protestant and Catholic, to demolish their castles unless they were needed for national defense, in which case they would be garrisoned by the king's soldiers. Finally, he stunned the proud dukes by banning them from the Louvre, the king's royal palace in Paris. Any nobleman who wished to speak to the king must first ask permission from Richelieu himself. That was more than the king's brother, the duc de Gaston, could tolerate. He secretly plotted with other aristocrats to resist these decrees—unaware that Richelieu's spies and double-agents had infiltrated their conspiracy. Richelieu waited until he had undeniable evidence of the duke's treason, then ordered the palace guards to arrest the cabal. Gaston begged for mercy. His brother the king pardoned him, but his coconspirators were executed.

Richelieu did not inform Louis XIII at the time, but his spies had also learned that Marie, the king's aging mother, had been part of the plot. So he continued to spy on her until Marie showed her cards. In 1630 she urged her son to dismiss Richelieu and conspired with spiteful nobles who meant to assassinate the prime minister. The climax arrived when the plotters held a secret nighttime meeting. Richelieu, informed by his spies of the time and place of their gathering, burst into the building with soldiers and the king himself, a move that forced Louis to realize the extent of his mother's treason. The horrified king fled from the scene. Richelieu's musketeers followed in hot pursuit. They found Louis sulking at Versailles (which, under Louis XIII, was a modest summer house), where Richelieu lectured him: "Sire, if you oppose me you oppose yourself, and if you oppose yourself, you oppose France!"

The king spared the lives of his brother and mother, after which both fled the country for Brussels in the Spanish Netherlands. So ended November 11, 1630, known in French historiography as the infamous Day of Dupes.

The exiles conjured one final plot in league with Spanish agents and a grand French nobleman, the duc de Montmorency. Once again Richelieu's spies enabled him to frustrate their plans. The fact that foreign agents were implicated gave Louis XIII no choice but to condemn the captives for treason. By then the lesson was clear: no matter who you were, opposition to the king meant death.

Finally, Richelieu confronted the Catholic Church—of which he himself was a cardinal. He advised the king to impose Gallicanism, an echo of the Anglicanism that Henry VIII had embraced when he made himself head of the Church of England. Richelieu and Louis XIII did not go to the extreme of breaking with Rome, but they did inform the papal nuncio (ambassador) that henceforth the royal government would nominate the bishops in France and would expect the clergy to give unconditional loyalty to the crown. Bishops and priests might look to Rome for guidance on spiritual matters, but on all other matters they were to take their orders from the king.

His power secure at last, Richelieu pressed on with reforms begun under Henri IV, while adding many of his own initiatives to strengthen the bureaucracy and the military. He divided France into thirty-two administrative units called *généralités* under officials called intendants who enforced royal decrees and oversaw tax collection. He placed command of the army under marshals and generals appointed by the king and centralized military logistics—the supply services without which no army can function. Since he had already broken the power of the dukes, the army reforms secured for the crown a monopoly of force within the boundaries of France.

Richelieu was just as energetic in economic policy. He knew that the wealth and health of the state depended on the wealth and health of the nation. Indeed, he had been impressed by a man he had met at that Estates General of 1614, a theorist named Antoine de Montchrestien, the most prominent French advocate of that new science called mercantilism. Recall that mercantilists viewed foreign trade as a zero-sum game in which a gain for one country was a loss for another. Hence their goal was to maximize exports and minimize imports in pursuit of a positive balance of payments. Various policies might promote that result, including the placement of high tariffs or quotas on foreign imports, the development of diverse industry and agriculture at home, the founding of plantation colonies to raise sugar, tobacco, and other commodities that could not be grown at home, and the formation of chartered companies to monopolize foreign trade in various markets.

Richelieu embraced all those policies. Following the example of the Dutch and British East India Companies, he chartered a French East India Company to compete in Asia, a West India Company to colonize Guadeloupe, Martinique, and other Caribbean islands, and the Compagnie de Nouvelle-France to colonize Québec. Richelieu also earned the epithet *Père de la Marine Française* (father of the French navy) by authorizing construction of royal fleets on the Atlantic and Mediterranean coastlines. Exploration, colonization, navigation, and industry—each of these areas of human activity required specialized knowledge that French subjects needed to learn or discover for themselves. Richelieu therefore founded the Sorbonne, destined to become the most prestigious university in France, as well as the Académie Française, a scientific institute.

It could be said that Richelieu did more than anyone to bring down the curtain on the era of religious wars in 1642 when he advised Louis XIII to hurl the armies of Catholic France into Germany's Thirty Years' War on the side of the Protestants, lest the Austrian Habsburgs prevail. Richelieu even encouraged the Muslim Turks to harass Austria from the rear. To him, the need to balance power and seek national advantage should dictate France's international politics, not religious loyalties. That was genuine *raison d'état*.

Finally, Richelieu bequeathed what some historians consider to be the most brutally honest political testament ever written by a European. It was not published until the 1690s, but he had penned it in order to instruct Louis XIII after his own death, which came in December 1642. Here are some of its axioms:

1. Absolute monarchy is the only alternative to anarchy.
2. The nobility must be excluded from important offices and devote their lives to arms in the service of the state.
3. A minister must often be prepared to act on conjecture, whereas a private person can usually wait for proof before acting.
4. Better a few should suffer, even unjustly, than for the safety of the state to be endangered.

5. Repression and taxation are, within limits, good for the people, just as mules must be kept fit by constant work.

Or, as Richelieu wrote on another occasion: "Give me six lines written by the most honest man, and I will find something in there to hang him."

This chapter has devoted so much attention to Richelieu because it was he who laid the foundations for the absolutism usually associated with Louis XIV. In truth, the long and glorious reign of the "Sun King," as Louis XIV styled himself, only saw the maturation of policies begun under Louis XIII and his prime minister.

They both left the stage suddenly. Louis XIII died in 1643, just five months after Richelieu's death. His heir, the dauphin, was just five years old, so another regency was required under the queen mother and her adviser, another cardinal named Jules Mazarin, or Giulio Mazzarino in his native Italy. The French nobility, sensing another power vacuum, tried one last time to undo Richelieu's work. They launched a rebellion known as the *Fronde*, the name of a children's game perhaps best translated as Mischief. The rebellion began when the *Parlement de Paris*, the greatest of the provincial law courts, ruled that a royal decree was unconstitutional, whereupon a cabal of noblemen took up arms, demanding the queen mother summon the Estates General into session so that the clergy, nobility, and commoners could advise her on how France should be governed. But the *Fronde* was not popular among the bourgeoisie in the cities and towns throughout France. Merchants, professionals, and many townspeople supported the royal government and feared the civil strife the mischievous noblemen were threatening to unleash. The insurgents also hurt their own cause by appealing for help to the king of Spain, the erstwhile enemy of France. Soon the *Fronde* collapsed. But it was enough to persuade Mazarin and the queen mother to end their regency early. In the year 1651 they declared Louis XIV to be of legal age, even though he was only thirteen. Louis was destined to rule for seventy-two years, the longest reign in European history.

The Sun King presided over Europe's mightiest kingdom during an era when French politics, culture, and fashion dominated half the continent. Louis XIV had been educated for autocratic rule and surrounded himself with flatterers.

Court intellectuals, led by his private confessor Bishop Bossuet, assured Louis—and the world—that his glorious reign was God's will because he ruled by divine right. There was some biblical justification for the doctrine that regal powers were expressions of God's will. But the philosophical justification for the divine right of kings was located in the evident chaos that descended on governments whenever power was contested. Bossuet's theory of the divine right of kings was simply the neatest solution to the messy crises of authority that had tormented Europeans during the Renaissance and Reformation eras. He imagined monarchy to be the political mediator between God and humanity, just as the church was the spiritual mediator. That meant the king's will was God's will—and must therefore be the people's will. Louis XIV allegedly summed it all up in a famous boast: "Qu'est ce que c'est l'état? L'état c'est moi!" (What is the state? I am the state!).

Louis consolidated his already considerable power by demoting the *parlements* to mere courts of appeal and making himself France's supreme court. He enforced the king's law with ubiquitous mounted police empowered to capture, try, and execute outlaws on the motto *pris, pendu*: no sooner taken than hanged. He kept the nobility on a tight leash, but not by forbidding them from the royal presence. On the contrary, he adopted the far more effective tactic of requiring the nobility to spend most of each year in residence at his court so he could keep a close watch on them. The important offices in Louis's administration were nevertheless filled not by *noblesse d'épée* but by bourgeois professionals.

Louis XIV did not rely on cardinals to advise him, because the Sun King was his own prime minister. He did, however, have an important right-hand man, Jean Baptiste Colbert, a disciple of the late Richelieu. Colbert served the king as minister of finance, minister of the navy, and mercantilist minister of economics. He had the most difficult job in France, thanks to the king's penchant for expensive wars, subsidies to foreign allies, grand construction projects, a splendiferous court, and, above all, the enormous, elaborate palace Louis insisted on building in the suburb of Versailles.

To pay Louis's enormous bills Colbert raised tariffs on imports and imposed two indirect taxes; a sort of sales tax on commercial transactions and the *portes et fenêtres*: a property tax levied according to how many doors and windows there were in each building. Colbert also milked the royal monopolies on sales of tobacco and other luxuries. Still, Louis's extravagance and the overall inflation plaguing the century forced the minister of finance to debase the currency, which in the days before paper money meant melting down silver and gold coins, mixing in some copper or nickel, and then restriking the coins. Finally, the royal treasury financed itself through debt, often to foreign bankers, until it gradually became obvious that the royal treasury would never be able to pay back the accumulated debt of the monarchical household through tax revenues.

So far this survey has described absolute monarchy objectively so that readers might understand why it appealed to many seventeenth-century Frenchmen. But objectively speaking, a serious flaw existed in the machinery forged by Richelieu and exploited by Louis XIV. Absolute monarchy absolutely required that the king be wise, just, and frugal. For it might take only one foolish, arbitrary, or wasteful monarch to exhaust and even to wreck the royal institutions . . . as indeed Louis XIV did through his extravagance and self-defeating policies. His most notorious blunder was the revocation of the Edict of Nantes in 1685. The king decided—as the Spanish crown had done nearly two centuries before—that an absolute monarchy was not compatible with religious diversity. Hence, the Huguenots were no longer welcome. The revocation obliged hundreds of thousands of enterprising merchants, sailors, and craftsmen to depart from their native land and relocate in other European countries or their overseas colonies, for Louis also forbade Huguenots from settling in Québec or the French West Indies. That foolish restriction crippled the growth of France's territories abroad and prepared the way for their utter defeat in the eighteenth century's colonial wars against Britain.

Yet another flaw in absolute monarchy derived from the fact that it was partly a pretense: even Louis XIV did not really exercise "absolute" power, because there were limits to what he could do. For instance, he could not impose taxes without the approval of the Estates General, yet the pretense of absolutism by definition prohibited him from summoning the Estates into session. Indeed, after 1614 the Estates General did not meet at all for 175 years.

Yet another flaw of absolute monarchy was the egotism and hubris to which it gave rise. In the case of Louis XIV such character flaws expressed themselves in aggressive foreign policies sure to frighten other European states into forging countervailing alliances. During Louis's long reign France was almost constantly at war, and always against coalitions. At various times the governments of England, Spain, the Low Countries, Austria, and various of the

German states banded together to resist France's armies and navies, especially during the climactic War of the Spanish Succession from 1701 to 1714. That conflict was triggered by the vacancy on the throne of Spain caused by the Spanish Habsburg line dying out. Louis promoted the candidacy of one of his own grandsons, a prospect that alarmed the other crowned heads of Europe. Imagine if Spain and its vast empire in the Americas united with France and its colonial empire under a single ruler! The war climaxed when a coalition commanded in part by John Churchill, the future Duke of Marlborough, defeated the French at the Battle of Blenheim in southern Germany. The Treaty of Utrecht, which followed in 1713, did award the Spanish crown to the Bourbon claimant, but only on condition that the kingdoms of Spain and France remain forever separate. Even more telling was the treaty's explicit preamble, which pronounced that a *balance of power* among nations was in the clear interest of the repose and freedom of Europeans at large.

What, therefore, is the bottom line to this tale of state-building in France? First, absolute monarchy did not really mean truly absolute power on the order of an ancient Roman emperor or twentieth-century dictator; even the kings of France operated within limits. But centralized government did mean that the institutional checks on the crown inherited from medieval times were themselves checked. The Estates General was never summoned. The Catholic Church lost most of its political influence. The nobility relinquished its military autonomy and political power. Even the *parlements*, for the most part, ceased to vet royal edicts. In place of those venerable institutions an altogether new entity appeared: a centralized bureaucratic regime; a machinery of government with distinctly modern features; a concentration of power other monarchs could only envy; and a personal rule that permitted Louis XIV to declare, without the least irony: "L'état c'est moi!"

Chapter 9

Parliaments Triumphant: Absolutism Thwarted in England

Long ago and far away, in a suburban high school near Chicago, a tenth-grade teacher assigned to his students a history textbook authored by Carl Becker. Becker's style seemed charming then, although it would probably sound condescending to teenagers today. For instance, Becker titled his first chapter "How the English Made a Revolution, Were Not Well Pleased with It, and Made Another One More to Their Liking." That pretty much summed up Britain's chaotic seventeenth century, during which a narrow majority of the members of England's Parliament voted to take up arms against their lawful Stuart king because they deemed him a tyrant. During the ensuing conflict the rebellious army captured the king, whereupon Parliament voted to condemn him to death . . . only to succumb to a far worse tyranny imposed by the commander of Parliament's army, Oliver Cromwell. A zealous Presbyterian, Cromwell imposed a militant theocracy that alienated the English so much that upon his death the Parliamentarians decided to restore the monarchy . . . only to be reminded of why they had opposed the Stuarts in the first place. So Parliament ousted a second Stuart king and installed a new dynasty whose powers were strictly limited. Thus did the English found a constitutional monarchy that survives to this day.

The only nit to pick regarding Becker's title is that he refers to "the English" as if they were homogeneous. In fact, the British Isles contained several ethnic groups and political parties who often quarreled among themselves, and when several of them did make common cause they often did so for contrasting motives.

The tumultuous era described in Becker's *Modern History* stretched from 1640 to 1688. In Britain, those decades were characterized by the same kinds of overlapping political, religious, and fiscal crises that tormented other seventeenth-century Europeans and obliged their monarchical governments to forge new institutions in hopes of crafting strong, centralized states able to compete on the world stage and to address the fiscal problems wrought by that century's great inflation. Recall that the outcome of Germany's Thirty Years' War prevented the Habsburg emperors from turning the Holy Roman Empire into a modern, unified state. Recall also that France emerged from its civil, religious wars as a unified kingdom that Cardinal Richelieu and King Louis XIII turned into a *soi-disant* (so called) absolute monarchy that reached its pinnacle of prestige under Louis XIV. This chapter explains how England, Wales, Scotland, and Ireland became a truly United Kingdom, but in a way that frustrated advocates of absolute monarchy. For after all was said and done, the British adopted a system in which power was shared between the crown and the Parliament.

Of course, Britain's fate was not decided all at once in the 1600s. The British Isles had a hoary heritage dating to early medieval times, a heritage shaped by the diversity of peoples who had washed up on its island shores over the centuries. Before the Roman Empire conquered Britannia during the first century of the Christian era, the British Isles were an important part of Europe's Celtic fringe and were populated by primitive Scots, Irish, and Welsh. Following the Roman Empire's collapse in the late fifth century AD, the English heartland was occupied by Germanic tribes called the Angles and Saxons. These tribes established the original kingdom of England. The Celtic, Roman, and Anglo-Saxon gene pools then mixed with those of the Viking Norsemen who periodically raided the English coasts for several centuries. Finally, in 1066, French-speaking Normans led by William the Conqueror sailed across the English Channel and imposed their own rule over England. That ethnic stew explains why the modern English language boasts the richest vocabulary in the world, containing as it does words derived from Gaelic, Old English, Middle German, and Scandinavian tongues, in addition to Latin and Greek.

Throughout the medieval centuries, England's feudal lords and clergy, like those elsewhere, resisted efforts by kings to impose their authority, most famously when they obliged King John to swallow Magna Carta in 1215. That charter obliged the king to recognize a long list of rights and privileges traditionally enjoyed by the nobility, church, and towns, including Parliament's right to make laws for the kingdom. Unlike France's tripartite Estates General, however, England's Parliament was bicameral, with the nobility and bishops represented in a House of Lords, and everyone else represented in a House of Commons presided over mostly by lawyers and merchants.

During the early Renaissance, England's Tudor monarchs sharply increased royal power. Such popular, iron-willed rulers as Henry VIII and Elizabeth I successfully bullied, bribed, or persuaded enough members of Parliament to get their way. Henry, of course, broke with the papacy and made himself the head of the Church of England, after which he confiscated the Catholic church's monasteries and their vast land holdings. Henry also expanded the reach of secret courts such as the infamous Star Chamber, whose judge interrogated subjects suspected of treason and scared the wits out of everyone else. But however bold the initiatives taken by the Tudor monarchs, they were always careful to get Parliament's approval. And whatever Parliament did on behalf of a feared but popular monarch, it might just as easily undo in protest against a bungling and unpopular monarch.

What is more, the long-term effects of royal success in sixteenth-century England contrasted sharply with the long-term effects of the royal collapse in sixteenth-century France. Most Frenchmen emerged from their long civil wars weary and ready to tolerate a so-called absolute monarchy as an antidote to such chaos. But wait! Hadn't the English also suffered from civil and religious strife during that century? Yes, they had, and just like the Bourbon kings of France, the Stuart kings of England tried to establish their own absolute monarchy. But many Englishmen—citing their traditional liberties—resisted the crown, and they were joined in that resistance by the fiercely independent Scots and Irish.

The Scots had been thorns in the side of their English neighbors for centuries. Jealous of their liberties, they had often allied with England's archenemy, France. Moreover, the Scots remained stubbornly Catholic during the decades when Henry VIII was founding the Protestant Anglican Church. Finally, the obstreperous Scots vexed Queen Elizabeth I when a rigid Calvinist preacher named John Knox evangelized the Highlands and converted most Scots to Presbyterianism. But whether Catholic or Protestant, most Scots were determined to govern themselves through their own Parliament, and most Scottish clans had a perennial itch to fight the English.

Ireland was another troublesome outlier in the British Isles. England's kings had laid claim to Ireland as early as the twelfth century, but the only area of effective English control was the so-called Pale on the eastern coast around Dublin—until the Tudor monarchs began a long, cruel struggle to subdue the counties "beyond the Pale." That conquest was still a work in progress as late as 1600, because the Catholic Irish hated the English invaders and looked for assistance to Spain.

Yet another complication arose from Queen Elizabeth's effort to calm religious passions by making the Church of England as big a tent as possible. The sublime Book of Common Prayer and its Thirty-Nine Articles of Religion had established a "broad church" that combined all that seemed true and beautiful in Catholic Christianity with all that seemed true and beautiful in Protestant Christianity. Theoretically, everyone from almost-Catholic "high churchmen" to almost-Calvinist "low churchmen" could feel at home in one or another Anglican parish. In reality, most Catholics in England, not to say Ireland, scorned this Anglican compromise, while many Calvinists rejected any episcopal church—that is, a hierarchical, sacramental church led by bishops. They vowed to purify the English church of its Catholic trappings and thus came to be known as Puritans.

Elizabeth managed to keep this cauldron from boiling over, but she was the last of the Tudor dynasty. Upon her death in 1603 the crown passed to the House of Stuart—in fact, to the son of Elizabeth's martyred cousin Mary Queen of Scots. So it was that King James VI of Scotland now became James I of England, as well. He had been raised by the Scottish lairds (lords, or nobility) to be Calvinist, but since he was now the head of the Church of England—and since he now had to rule in tandem with the English Parliament—James turned a cold shoulder to the Presbyterians and to Puritans in particular. That caused widespread discontent, but the kettle did not boil over during James's reign. It would boil over during the reign of his son.

James I was an intelligent, well-educated man who greatly admired all that the Bourbon dynasty was accomplishing in France. He especially concurred in the wisdom of a strong royal government. But he never understood how his headstrong policies were sure to irritate one group of Englishmen after another. Where Elizabeth had sought to appease dissenting factions such as the Catholics and Calvinists, James went out of his way to persecute them. He even threatened to "harry the Puritans out of the land." Consequently, thousands of English Puritans began to take ship for the New World, where they founded the Massachusetts Bay colony in 1630 and soon settled all New England. Likewise, many Scots Presbyterians crossed the Irish Sea to settle in the northern Irish county of Ulster, where they pushed aside the Catholic Irish and initiated a blood feud that persisted until the late twentieth century.

Most momentous was the king's fiscal policy. Whenever James I needed revenue, he would insist that Parliament impose new taxes, even as he ignored requests from Parliament's members for royal accountability. When Parliament refused the king's bidding, he would dissolve it, which was his prerogative. But at length, instead of calling for new elections, James tried to rule *without* Parliament, just as the Bourbon kings began to rule without the Estates General after 1614. Finally, in foreign policy, James revealed his absolutist tendencies by flirting with a Spanish alliance—just about the most unpopular policy an English king could adopt, given that the war of the Spanish Armada was still fresh in people's memory.

James I was sardonically known as "The Wisest Fool in Christendom." He was deemed wise because he patronized the arts and sciences, sponsored the sublime King James translation of the Bible, and presided over England's colonization of the New World. But he was foolish to think that Britain's future would be defined by absolute monarchy, especially given how his policies alienated the Puritans, Scots, and Irish. He sowed the wind, and after his death in 1625 King Charles I reaped the whirlwind.

Charles was a gentle soul, devout and sincere, but he had learned very little from his father's mistakes. He, too, looked to France for his model of governance and wanted to emulate Cardinal Richelieu and Louis XIII in suppressing all opposition to royal authority. Hence, Charles concluded that absolute monarchy was the wave of the future. What he gradually learned was that England was not France and that his advisers, William Laud and Thomas Wentworth, Earl of Stafford, were pale shadows of Richelieu. Charles's first act was to summon Parliament and to insist that its members raise taxes. Members of Parliament replied with a Petition of Right demanding redress of grievances, insisting (among other things) that the crown cease and desist from collecting illegal taxes, reaffirm the right of prisoners to habeas corpus—that is, due process of law before imprisonment—and stop quartering soldiers in private homes. Charles agreed. But as soon as he got his new taxes, he conveniently forgot about the promises he had made and tried to govern without summoning Parliament into session again.

Charles I also blessed a campaign led by Canterbury's Archbishop Laud to impose on all the parishes of the Anglican Church a beautiful but provocative high church liturgy replete with bells, incense, and choral chants. There is nothing inherently idolatrous about "smells and bells" in a church service. But the English Puritans and Scottish Presbyterians hated this effort to impose a Catholicized liturgy on their churches. When in 1637 Laud began to grant English bishops jurisdiction over the dioceses of the Church of Scotland, riots erupted in Edinburgh and tens of thousands of Scots signed a Solemn Covenant to resist what they considered to be religious tyranny. King Charles stubbornly supported Laud, whereupon the bellicose Scottish clans mustered for war.

That rebellion obliged the king to raise an army to suppress the Scots, which meant that he was going to need more money, which meant that he must call Parliament into session after all. The Parliament that convened in 1640 insisted again that the king accede to a long list of checks on royal power. The king angrily dissolved it after three weeks (it was henceforth known as the Short Parliament). At that point, Charles looked to Wentworth, his principal minister, to manage the crises. As lord deputy of Ireland Wentworth had proven himself to be a tough administrator. He now believed that a similar authoritarian form of rule might be imposed on Scotland and even England itself. He called his policy "thorough," by which he meant thorough control of all legislative, executive, and judicial functions by the crown—just the sort of Richelieu-style absolutism certain to make members of Parliament choke.

Wentworth persuaded the king that an expensive new army would *not* be needed in Scotland because his soldiers, who had succeeded in suppressing the Irish, might be transferred to Scotland. But no sooner had the army arrived than the Highland Scots soundly defeated the English army, after which they invaded England itself and refused to go home until the crown paid them damages. Now the king had really dug himself a hole, for he had to summon Parliament again in order to beg for the money needed to pay off the Scots. Finally, for good measure, the Catholic Irish rose up in arms now that the English garrison had departed their island.

When Parliament reassembled in November 1640, the future of the British Isles hung in the balance. The House of Commons was controlled, just barely, by a majority of angry Puritans, angry taxpayers, and defenders of the "ancient rights of Englishmen." The first thing that majority did was to impeach Wentworth and sentence him to death on charges of treason. Had his "thorough" policies violated the unwritten, common-law constitution of the English kingdom? Perhaps, but there was no evidence of treason and indeed no trial. Parliament simply passed a law declaring Wentworth guilty and demanding the king put his own chief minister to death. Charles pitifully consented, whereupon Wentworth, the would-be English Richelieu, bowed his head before the executioner's axe uttering the biblical proverb, "Put not thy trust in princes."

After that the Puritans and their allies in Parliament really flexed their muscles. They ordered Archbishop Laud to be imprisoned in the Tower of London and drafted a program to pull up the Anglican church "root and branch." Now the Latin root for the word *root* is *radix* (from which we get the word *radish*), so these "root and branch" Calvinists were the first "radicals" in European political history. In 1641 the Parliament passed—by a mere eleven-vote majority—a Grand Remonstrance that asserted a level of parliamentary control every bit as "thorough" as the royal control Wentworth had hoped to impose. That was more than Charles I could abide. He accused Parliament of mutiny, gathered what soldiers remained loyal to him, and took to the field. Parliament steeled its will to resist, raised its own army, and plunged England into a civil war.

What was it all about? Was it another religious war? Not entirely, for even though most Puritans sided with Parliament, some feared the economic damage sure to accompany civil war, not to mention what would happen to them if the king's army should prevail. And while most Anglicans supported the king, some low-church believers sympathized with Parliament. The Presbyterian Scots fought first on one side, then the other, because their principal goal was to resist English rule altogether, while English Catholics just kept their heads down and continued to worship in secret. Was it a class war, then? Not really, because landed gentry, merchants, professionals, craftsmen, and farmers were found on both sides depending on their religious, ethnic, or regional loyalties. In sum, the English Civil War exposed all the cleavages in British society. It amounted to a political conflict fought over a constitutional issue for stakes that were religious, ethnic, social, and economic. It is too bad historical reality is so messy, but there it is.

The king's men, called Cavaliers, were led by traditional Anglican gentry, especially from southwestern England. But the royal ranks also included many farmers and other rural folk from Wessex and Yorkshire who resented the rich merchants and lawyers in Parliament. By contrast, the Parliament's men, called Roundheads because they wore their hair short, were mostly townsmen hailing from Essex, Sussex, and East Anglia. The Cavaliers fought for tradition and privilege and often went unpaid since the king had no war chest. The Roundheads fought for civil and religious liberty, as they understood it, and were regularly paid because of Parliament's power to tax. The Roundheads also fought because they had more to lose. As the Earl of Manchester put it, "If we beat the King ninety and nine times, he is the King still and so will his posterity be after him; but if the King beat us once, we shall all be hanged and our posterity made slaves."

The tide soon turned in Parliament's favor thanks to the Roundheads' superior numbers, superior resources, and superior leadership. Indeed, the commander of Parliament's army was a military genius whose reputation at the time equaled or surpassed those of Albrecht von Wallenstein and Gustavus Adolphus. That leader turned his own regiment, known as the Ironsides, into a model of training, discipline, and morale—and upon assuming command of the parliamentary cause, he expanded it into a "New Model Army." His name was Oliver Cromwell, and he was a crusading Puritan who had no doubt whose side God was on in this civil war. Had not Calvin himself taught that earthly success is a sign of one's membership in God's elect and that such membership implied a great earthly mission? Cromwell's victories soon persuaded his Puritan soldiers that their God-given mission was to cleanse the realm of kings and bishops and make the British Isles a sort of heaven on earth, like Calvin's Geneva writ large.

But recall how narrow the margin for rebellion had been in Parliament. And keep in mind that Parliament was still in session and would remain in session for thirteen years; hence its nickname, The Long Parliament. That was the

Parliament that put Wentworth to death, then did the same to Archbishop Laud in 1645.

As the civil war dragged on, some members of Parliament began to favor a compromise peace, perhaps one based on a constitutional monarchy featuring shared power and religious toleration. But Cromwell wanted no part of any compromise. He believed he was waging a war of good versus evil. In fact the civil war begat all manner of radical social movements amid the moors and hedgerows of England, movements Cromwell damned as wicked. Hence the dynamic was not unlike the Peasants' War in Germany triggered by the Lutheran Reformation. Levelers—so-called because they demanded democracy and equal distribution of wealth—founded the first socialist party in history. Diggers—so-called because they squatted on common lands or else "dug" in the fields of aristocratic landlords—demanded the abolition of private property. Various cults and communes also sprang up, ranging from millenarian sects like the Fifth Monarchy Men, who believed England was fulfilling biblical prophecy, to experimental groups that preached either sexual abstinence or else promiscuity. All these movements arose in the space of just one decade in mid-seventeenth-century England. Needless to say, such aberrations, when added to the death and destruction of war, caused a growing number of people of all persuasions to yearn for a compromise peace.

A chance for that outcome seemed to arrive in 1646 when the Highland clans marched south again and trapped the royalist army between themselves and the Roundheads. Charles I agreed to negotiate with the Scots and the Parliament, but after two years of palaver the three-sided talks achieved nothing save for the fact that the king bribed the Scots with so many promises that they flipped sides. Thus began the so-called Second Civil War in 1648, in which Cromwell's army again defeated the Cavaliers, whereupon Charles and the war-weary Parliament agreed once more to negotiate.

Except Cromwell did not agree . . . and his vote was the only one that counted. He ordered his soldiers to occupy key positions in London while Colonel Thomas Pride marched a regiment into the halls of Parliament to expel more than half its five hundred members. That act, known to history as Pride's Purge, meant that the members left in what became known as the Rump Parliament were nearly all hot-headed Puritans and Cromwell supporters. They wasted no time passing a law that declared Charles I guilty of treason and condemned him

The Execution of Charles I of England, by an unknown Dutch artist, records the regicide of January 30, 1649.

to death. In January 1649 the deposed monarch bowed his head to the executioner's axe with these final words: "I shall go from a corruptible to an incorruptible Crown, where no disturbance can be."

Imagine the brazen finality of that act. The lawful king of England was declared public enemy number one and executed—not assassinated or killed in battle, but subjected to judicial murder—by the representatives of his own subjects. For Cromwell and the regicides there was no turning back. They had begun their military campaign by asserting the historic rights of Englishmen. They ended it by attempting to destroy English history itself and leaping into a brave new world of their own making. For from the moment the royal head rolled into the basket, matters began to go terribly wrong. As one Anglican clergyman put it, "All hell broke loose," thereby enriching our lexicon with another evocative phrase.

While imprisoned in London awaiting his fate, Charles Stuart had written letters to his son, urging him to trust in the Lord whatever should happen, to shun hatred and bitterness whatever should happen, and never to cease hoping whatever should happen. "Keep to the principles of piety, virtue, and honor," he wrote, "and ye shall never want [for] a kingdom." The famous poet John Milton, an avid Cromwellian, later twisted those words for his own propaganda. "People of England," he wrote, "keep ye to those principles and ye shall never want [for] a king."

Parliaments Triumphant

The king was dead, and for the first time ever people did not cry, "Long live the king," as a welcome to his heir. Instead, the Rump Parliament declared England a republic called the Commonwealth. Yet that did not satisfy Cromwell. Declaring himself lord protector of the Commonwealth, he dismissed the Rump Parliament in 1653 and appointed a legislature composed of hardcore disciples. They were nicknamed the Barebones after one vocal member from London whose literal name was Praise-God Barebone. They proceeded to pass what Cromwell called the Instrument of Government, which decreed abolition of the monarchy, abolition of the House of Lords, and abolition of the Anglican Church. It also granted Cromwell total executive power for life. The lord protector, henceforth ruling through his army and puppet legislature, wielded power far more authoritarian than that of Charles I or even Louis XIV. He imposed a religious uniformity stricter than that of Catholic Spain or Calvin's Geneva. He waged war more ferociously than had Emperor Ferdinand during Germany's Thirty Years' War.

Cromwell divided England into military districts, in effect placing his own country under martial law. Next, he launched a quick-and-dirty invasion of Scotland with the purpose of destroying its independence once and for all. Then he invaded Ireland, where his soldiers spread carnage and imposed Protestant rule, thereby making Ireland the most oppressed European country west of Russia.

Unification of the British Isles freed Cromwell to turn his attention abroad. Recall that when Philip II of Spain had attacked the Netherlands years before, the English had supported the Dutch. Now the Calvinist Cromwell turned against the Calvinist Dutch in an effort to destroy their commercial and naval power. His mercantilist Navigation Act of 1651 forbade all other countries from trading with England's overseas colonies, a severe blow to Dutch merchants. When the Dutch dared to object, Cromwell waged a war during which the rising English navy swept the outnumbered Dutch out of the contested sea lanes. The Dutch economy subsequently began to decline, bringing to an end the Netherlands' golden age.

Cromwell's career may be likened to that of Wallenstein, the Habsburg general whose personal ambition overshadowed the cause for which he was fighting. But the best analogy to Cromwell's career is that of Napoléon Bonaparte a century and a half later. Both rose to power during a revolution that killed a king, declared a republic, and degenerated into dictatorship. Both claimed to embody an idealistic creed, and both exploited that creed to seize total power. Both were military paragons whose victories tempted them irresistibly to pursue foreign conquest. Finally, Cromwell, like Napoléon, violated every principle he allegedly stood for by trying to make his regime hereditary.

In 1658 Cromwell died at age fifty-nine, probably of malaria. His son Richard duly succeeded him as lord protector of the Commonwealth. But the youngster was a weak reed, compared to his father, and soon lost control of England's political, ethnic, and social factions. Most tellingly, Richard shrank from the self-righteous violence that had come naturally to Oliver. He also loosened the government's controls over freedom of speech and association, which proved to be his undoing. No sooner did the English realize it was safe to speak up than they said to each other, with surprising unanimity, "We've had rather enough of zeal and tyranny, don't you agree? Rather! Methinks we should bring the monarchy back."

So the Long Parliament, or at least those members of it who were still living, gathered in London for a bizarre reunion for the purpose of simply adjourning. A newly elected Parliament promptly invited Charles II to return from exile and take up the scepter of his martyred father. Members asked only that he tolerate a measure of religious freedom, pension off Cromwell's army, and pardon the regicides in the Long Parliament.

Yet the story still was not over because (as the poet Milton quipped) the people got rid of their king only to want one again—and then only to be reminded again of why they got rid of the king in the first place. To be sure, the Restoration Era, under Charles II, got off to a strong start with some meaningful social reform. Parliament abolished all feudal land tenures, which had constrained a free market in real estate. Parliament abolished all feudal dues, which had constrained a free market in labor. Parliament voted to tax the landed wealth of the gentry—the country squires—so that merchants, artisans, workers, and farmers no longer bore the nation's entire fiscal burden. Parliament expanded the Navigation Act, which pleased English merchants. And Parliament waged two more wars against the Dutch to ensure that Britannia would truly rule the waves. In fact, it was during the reign of Charles II that the English captured a certain colony at the mouth of the Hudson River and renamed what had been New Amsterdam after the king's brother, the Duke of York. Under the Restored Monarchy a new Poor Law was also passed, which obliged every parish in England to care for its destitute. Together, these reforms hastened the triumph of capitalism in the British Isles.

Given all that, the reign of the "Merrie Monarch" Charles II should have been a time of internal peace and contentment. In fact, English politics remained tumultuous to the point of paranoia. The Stuarts were still suspected of harboring Catholic sympathies. Popular fears of a popish plot sparked serial riots, especially in the devilish year of 1666, when most of London burned in a terrible fire. Residents blamed it on Jesuits, revolutionaries, or the Jews whom Cromwell had invited to settle in England after 350 years of exclusion. Charles II exacerbated discontent when he imposed all sorts of restrictions on Calvinists as well as Catholics and Jews. By the time he died in 1685, large portions of the English, Scottish, and Welsh populations were chafing under the restored Stuart dynasty. Perhaps wise, charismatic, or just passive government on the part of his successor might have forestalled a crisis. But Charles's brother, the Duke of York, who reigned as James II, was not wise, charismatic, or passive. Indeed, he brought the crisis to a head by coming out of the closet... *as a Catholic*. He also admired the absolute monarchy of Louis XIV and pursued amicable relations with England's Catholic archenemies, France and Spain.

So after just two years many leaders in Parliament, the army, the commercial classes, and the Anglican Church were keen to get rid of James II. They formed a new political party known as the Whigs. The origins of that word are still vague, but historians suspect that it conveyed a sense of rustic opposition to centralized tyranny, a sort of country party opposed to the court party in London.

In June 1688 seven notable leaders of the Whig Party traveled to the Netherlands and invited the *Stadtholder* William of Orange to accompany his modest Dutch army on an invasion of England, promising that England's army and navy would not resist. They chose William of Orange because he was married to King James II's daughter Mary, who had remained Protestant. So it was that the English elites, having recently waged three wars against the Dutch, now begged a Dutchman to take over their country! Such were the vagaries of dynastic and religious politics in a monarchical era.

William landed on the coast of England that November, promising to maintain the liberties of the English and the Protestant religion. James II tried to resist, but when he summoned his generals, they all turned their backs. James was left with no choice but to go into exile, whereupon a special Parliament was convened whose members proclaimed William and Mary to be the new king and queen in what Whig leaders called the Glorious Revolution. That is the label by which it has been known ever since, only the affair was neither glorious nor revolutionary. It was a coup d'état, pure and simple. At least it was bloodless, and it settled once and for all the question of which form of state-building would prevail in the British Isles.

William and Mary (after whom the college in Virginia was named) swore, on behalf of themselves and their successors, that henceforth all British monarchs would be Anglicans and that all would recognize the supremacy of Parliament according to England's unwritten constitution. The monarchs also issued a Bill of Rights—the "true, ancient, and indubitable rights" of all English subjects—that included the right to due process, the right to a jury trial, the right to sue the government, the right to bear arms, the right to freedom of speech and assembly, and the right to not be taxed without the approval of Parliament.

The Whig majority in Parliament then completed this Glorious Revolution through a series of momentous acts. The Toleration Act of 1689 established free exercise of religion for Calvinists and other Protestants. The Act of Settlement of 1701 banned Catholics from the throne of England. The Act of Union in 1707 united the crowns and parliaments of Scotland and England to create the United Kingdom and complete London's rule over the British Isles, or what was now called Great Britain.

Thus did the British emerge, following fifty years of turmoil, with a constitutional monarchy and a memory of how bad *both* absolute monarchy and republics could be. The philosophical charter of the Glorious Revolution was surely John Locke's *Second Treatise on Government*, published in 1689. Locke declared that the people enjoyed natural rights to life, liberty, and property and that the public possessed the right, indeed duty, to overthrow any government that ceased to defend those rights. As a result, eighteenth-century Britain—always with the exception of oppressed Ireland—became the antithesis of Bourbon France and a model of toleration, representative government, and individual rights. Needless to say, those were the cherished rights carried over the ocean by the British settlers of North America's thirteen colonies, and those were the rights that the colonists themselves would invoke in order to justify their own rebellion against Britain's crown and Parliament in 1776.

Such is the cunning of history.

Chapter 10

To Probe the Mind of God: The Scientific Revolution

The first two chapters traced the roots of European civilization to the brilliant technical and thematic innovations of the ancient Greeks and Hebrews. Those roots intertwined during the imperial era of ancient Rome and later nurtured the medieval European civilization that sprang from the wreckage of the Western Roman Empire. The recovery of much ancient learning during the Crusades and after the fall of the Byzantine Empire then contributed to the creative burst of Renaissance humanism in the fifteenth and sixteenth centuries, which in turn helped inspire the Protestant and Catholic Reformations.

This chapter examines another enormously important aspect of the ancient Greek legacy which helped to spark the material and intellectual dynamism of early modern Europe. That was the impact of *epistemology*, or what the modern world usually thinks of as the Scientific Revolution. In the words of the great early twentieth-century English historian Herbert Butterfield, the Scientific Revolution "overturned the authority in science not only of the Middle Ages but of the ancient world as well.... [It] thus outshines everything since the rise of Christianity, and reduces even the Renaissance and Reformation to the rank of mere episodes, mere internal displacements, within the system of medieval Christendom."

Powerful words, indeed! Butterfield saw the ancient triumph of Christianity and the modern triumph of science as the two fundamental turning points in the history of Western civilization. Each, in its own way, changed the habitual functioning—today we might say the hardwiring—of the European mind, that is, the very lens through which people perceived the outside world, the categories they employed to think about that world, and the values by which they judged that world.

As with the Renaissance, the process leading to the discovery of the scientific method had no distinct starting point. The are clear milestones, such as the year 1453, when the Polish priest Nikołaj Kopernik (Nicolaus Copernicus) published his theory of a heliocentric solar system. And 1609, when the Italian genius Galileo Galilei first trained a telescope on the moon and planets. And 1620, when Francis Bacon published his treatise on method. And 1666, when an apple allegedly fell on the head of a dozing Isaac Newton and inspired his theory of universal gravitation. But the Scientific Revolution was not an *event*. It was a *quest*. Moreover, the people engaged on that quest were not "scientists"; that word had not yet been coined. They were instead thought of, and thought of themselves as, natural philosophers, and they did the same thing when investigating the natural world that religious and political leaders now did in their own arenas of investigation: they questioned existing authority and sought some new authority by which they could declare beyond a reasonable doubt that something was really known, proven, discovered, explained. They groped, by trial and error, by diligent observation, and at last by sheer genius to fashion an immensely powerful tool for the increase of human power over nature and other people: the modern sciences and the technologies that are based on them.

The initial quest for a new authority may be divided into four stages: the medieval veneration of the ancient Greek cosmologist Ptolemy; the Renaissance search for the true Ptolemy; the ensuing search for a new Ptolemy; and the breakthrough that occurred when scholars said "Ptooey on Ptolemy." During the first stage, medieval philosophers, thanks to the obeisance they habitually paid to the ancient Greeks, simply assumed that the Aristotelian and Ptolemaic images of creation were true. During the second stage, the European rediscovery of numerous ancient authors revealed how often they had quarreled with Aristotle and Ptolemy and how even various translations of Ptolemy's works appeared to contradict each other. During the third stage, natural philosophers explored new methodologies, questioning whether ancient Greek science deserved its high reputation, not least because Europeans were by then discovering entire continents unknown to the ancients and were crafting better tools to observe the natural world. Hence the search for a new Ptolemy and a new methodology, which is why European savants dabbled in astrology, alchemy, sorcery, necromancy, and numerology as much as or more than they engaged in observation and experimentation.

During the fourth and final phase, the epistemological revolution was accomplished when natural philosophers jettisoned Ptolemy. Bacon, more than anyone else, pointed the way, and Newton, more than anyone else, followed that way toward a mathematically based, inductive/deductive scientific method.

So far there has been no mention of the Catholic Church. Did not the church persecute Galileo, and did not science triumph only when Europeans came to reject papal authority? That has been the metanarrative dominant in Protestant and secular circles all the way into the twenty-first century, but that metanarrative is almost entirely false. Whatever else readers take away from this book, they must discard the myth that there was some thunderous clash between science and religion in Galileo's day—or, for that matter, that there is one in the present day. In fact, the medieval church was the foremost *preserver* of scientific knowledge and *promoter* of new knowledge, as demonstrated by the technical inventions made by the Cluniac monks, by the papal astronomical observatory at Castel Gandolfo outside Rome, and by the medieval universities where scholars studied everything under the sun. On the infrequent occasions when the papacy did obstruct science, it was usually either in defense of ancient Greek theories that the church had imprudently endowed with religious meaning or in resistance to assertions made on the basis of inference rather than fact. In any event, no one was burned at the stake for pursuing science. Indeed, the harshest punishment Galileo ever received was a comfortable house arrest.

What about the philosophers themselves? Were they not conscious of promoting epistemologies that might contradict the church's faith in revelation? Again, the answer is mostly no. Copernicus was a priest. Bacon believed scientific discovery to be another way mortals could discern the mind of God. Galileo was a devout Catholic who believed science and revelation were compatible means to understand God's Creation. The mathematical genius Blaise Pascal published a lengthy collection of religious insights called *Pensées*. Newton's theological commentaries were more voluminous than his scientific treatises. Far from being antireligious, nearly all the men who contributed to the Scientific Revolution imagined themselves to be "probing the mind of God."

Why Europe? Why were Europeans the first civilization to pioneer the scientific method? To begin with, the Judeo-Christian scriptures uniquely validated human reason and curiosity about the natural world. The biblical book of Genesis states repeatedly that God looked upon his creation and saw "that it was good." The Lord then created man and woman in his image and charged them to people the earth while subduing the natural world. According to the Bible, God clearly designed a material reality subject to natural laws discoverable through observation and reason. In like fashion, the pagan Greeks believed the gods had created an orderly Cosmos, as opposed to a disorderly Chaos, and they explained the nature and behavior of heavenly bodies and life itself through the evidence of their senses and logic. Combine those two heritages and one arrives at the thirteenth-century philosophy of St. Thomas Aquinas, who drew on the Bible to explain spiritual realities and on the Greeks to explain natural ones.

Hold on, some readers may shout. How could anyone claim that the Bible encouraged a scientific worldview when it contains so many accounts of miracles? Think again. Belief in miracles is not at all indicative of superstition or ignorance about nature. Rather, belief in miracles *requires* a strong belief in natural law. The ancient Jews were no dummies: when the Bible relates that Moses was stunned to hear a voice from heaven emanating from a burning bush that was not consumed by the fire, it was precisely because the event was utterly contrary to his commonsense notion of what is normal. Likewise, the disciples of Jesus were flabbergasted by his miracles precisely because they were perceived to be supernatural. By the same token, the medieval church, no less than the ancient Greeks, trusted in sensory evidence and logic. The church simply reasoned that a sovereign God is the Author of nature's laws—the Lawgiver, if you will—and thus is free to suspend those laws for his own purposes.

The church's patronage of science for pragmatic purposes is illustrated by the use to which Gregory XIII put the Vatican's store of astronomical knowledge. His papal bull (decree) of February 24, 1582, replaced the ancient Julian calendar, named for Julius Caesar, with the far more accurate Gregorian calendar, which we still use today and according to which a Leap Day is added to February every four years. No, the mistake of the late medieval church was not to oppose science but rather to identify too closely with several Aristotelian postulates that turned out to be wrong . . . and that mistake is readily explicable.

Recall from the very first chapter that the ancient Greek philosophers debated among themselves about method. Academics such as Plato and Aristotle deduced theories about how the world must work, then assumed facts that fit their theories. Sophists began with observable data from which they induced theories. But nobody had a bona fide means of judging which method was best. Thus, Aristotle simply intuited that all matter was composed of four basic elements—earth, air, water, and fire—and that those elements in turn were composed of atoms arranged in different proportions and patterns. By contrast, empirical research allowed Aristarchus of Samos to invent trigonometry, demonstrate that the earth moved around the sun, and measure the distances to the moon and sun with remarkable accuracy. Those were discoveries no Aristotelian could have "intuited" in a lifetime of staring at the sky.

What happened by the time of the Western Roman Empire's collapse is that Aristotelian method got the upper hand, in part because most of the works that survived into the medieval era were of that philosophical persuasion. In addition, a priori reasoning from first principles mirrored the characteristic method of medieval theology, which applied reason to preexisting principles—that is, revelation. Accordingly, the popes, monastics, and university scholars tended to accept Aristotelian philosophy and method without question and to strengthen its authority by conflating it with Christian dogma.

The dominant astronomical model for medieval Europeans was the treatise written by Claudius Ptolemaius in the second century AD, which came to be known by its Arabic name, the *Almagest*. Ptolemy, being a good Aristotelian, assumed that the universe must be pure, immutable, transparent, and weightless, because those were the qualities the Greeks considered transcendent. He imagined the universe to be composed of a series of concentric spheres, with Earth at the center; the moon, sun, and the five visible planets at various distances away; and a great sphere containing the fixed stars on the outside. The spheres could not exist in a vacuum because of the principle that "nature abhors a vacuum," so Ptolemy imagined the clear, crystal spheres to be filled with transparent ether. The rotation of the heavenly spheres accounted for the celestial movements observed from Earth, including the revolutions of the fixed stars around Polaris, the North Star, and the revolutions of the moon and sun around Earth. The wandering planets (*planet* literally means "wanderer") were a mystery, since they periodically seemed to stop and go backwards for weeks or months before resuming their normal orbits. Ptolemy accounted for that "retrograde motion" with fudge factors. He assumed the planets had variable velocities and added epicycles to their orbital cycles. Finally, he assumed that all these cycles were circular because Aristotelians like him considered the circle to be the perfect geometric shape.

Beneath the sublunary sphere—that is, within Earth's own sphere—everything changed. There Aristotle's four elements held sway. If left to their own devices, the elements would create layers of rock, the heaviest element, at the bottom, then water on the surface of the earth, then a layer of air above both earth and water, then a layer of fire as in the sun. But since that was not always the case in reality, Aristotelians assumed that friction or flux imparted to Earth by the movements of the heavenly spheres caused the elements to mix. Thus did they explain the fire—volcanic activity—that occurred underground.

The same a priori assumptions underpinned Greek speculations about animal and human life. Galen, the greatest physician of ancient Greece, imagined medicine to be a philosophical pursuit. His treatise *On Anatomical Procedure* mixed practical medicine with theories about the nature of life and health. Galen popularized Hippocrates's notion that human moods and physical ailments are caused by an imbalance among the four humors, including the sanguine (hopeful), phlegmatic (stoic), choleric (irascible), and melancholic (pessimistic).

Medieval Europeans had little cause to dispute such ancient speculations. It was a simple matter, for instance, to assume that hell was a place inside the earth. Even pagans believed that departed souls "went down" to what the Greeks called Hades and the Jews called Sheol. It was also a simple matter to assume that heaven was up—somewhere beyond the fixed stars—because that suited Ptolemy's model as well as various passages in the Bible. As for Earth being immovable and at the center of everything, that also seemed obvious, for if Earth were in motion, everything on it would fly off into the ether. Moreover, the movements of the sun and moon across the sky were palpably discernible. Finally, maps based on Ptolemy's geography were serviceable enough for people traveling around Europe and the Mediterranean.

Once a steady stream of ancient manuscripts began to flow into western

Europe, however, scholars discovered discrepancies among copies of the *Almagest*. Had the Byzantines or Arabs made serial errors in translation or interpretation? Scholars visited libraries hoping to discern the true Ptolemy . . . until around 1500, when their antiquarian quest was overtaken by practical challenges posed by the Age of Exploration. The Portuguese and Spaniards, followed by the Dutch, English, and French, began to sail all over the world, and their sea captains and geographers displayed an inexhaustible appetite for accurate data and astronomical charts. Ptolemy's numbers were good, but not good enough. Hence the search for a new Ptolemy, a new synthesis that would bestow a more trustworthy model of the physical universe in the same manner that Luther, Calvin, and Loyola were striving to offer a more trustworthy model of the moral universe.

How do we know stuff? How can human beings be sure about anything? That epistemological question propelled Europeans into modernity. Renaissance Europeans believed that God had endowed human beings with their five senses and brains so they might explore, understand, and glorify his creation. Did not the Latin mass declare, "Heaven and earth are full of thy glory"? But what method might people employ to unlock the secrets of an omniscient God? The late sixteenth-century French essayist Michel de Montaigne asked, "What do I know?" and replied, "En vrai, rien" (In fact, nothing). But the early seventeenth-century English essayist Francis Bacon replied, "Not much yet, but in time we shall know *everything*."

Bacon, who lived from 1561 to 1626, realized from a young age that his brilliant mind perceived reality far more keenly than did other people's. Bacon himself was not a practitioner of science. He did little or no observation, exploration, or experimentation himself. But no one did more to define and promote the modern scientific method. Bacon was the youngest of five sons born to the guardian of the royal seal under Queen Elizabeth I. Schooled at Cambridge University, he began his career as a diplomat posted to the embassy in Paris. When his father died prematurely, he returned to London and opened a law practice. However, his avocation, even obsession, was epistemology. The Elizabethan playwright Christopher Marlowe had recently written a stage play about a certain Dr. Faustus who sells his soul to the devil in return for occult knowledge, but Bacon was no Faustus. He remained a devout Anglican, wrote about biblical subjects, and preached that scientific knowledge was worse than useless unless it was put to the service of God and one's fellow man.

Bacon's greatest treatise was the *Novum Organum*, published in 1620 (incidentally, the same year the Pilgrims sailed in the *Mayflower*). Its curious title was a challenge hurled at English universities, which obliged new students to endure a yearlong methodological course based on Aristotle's *Organum*. Bacon's *New Organum* boldly called on Europeans to cease enslaving their minds by deferring uncritically to ancient authors. Citing the great voyages of navigation, Renaissance technological innovations, and contemporary debates over authority, Bacon argued that Europeans now possessed the power to surpass the ancients and to discover new knowledge without limits, if only they would liberate their minds by worshiping the quest for truth instead of those various idols which blinded them.

Bacon described four sorts of "idols of the mind." The first were the idols of the tribe, the conventional wisdom embraced by families, communities, ethnic groups, religious bodies, and whole nations by way of binding themselves together and acknowledging common authorities. Various myths, superstitions, and bits of folklore were passed down from generation to generation through parents, schools, and other agents of socialization. Idols of the tribe often prevented people from seeing what lay before their eyes, or else they inhibited those who *did* see from speaking up, as in the fable about the emperor's new clothes.

The second sort of idols were those of the cave, by which Bacon meant the blindness people impose on themselves by their narrow personal interests and perspectives and by their vain tendency to value their own ideas more than others'. Human beings, Bacon recognized, have a powerful tendency to reach an opinion, identify with it, then refuse even to consider contrary opinions, thus making themselves the measure of truth.

The third sort were the idols of the marketplace, which tempt people to buy into whatever notions others are peddling because espousing them will advance their careers. In short, people "get with the program" in order to get ahead and thereby cease to think for themselves. Today, we would call this phenomenon groupthink or political correctness.

The fourth sort were the idols of the theater, the products of a corrupt philosophical culture that rewards certain styles of argumentation, such as those characterizing the Socratic or Sophist schools of ancient Athens.

Bacon called on his fellow Englishmen, and indeed all Europeans, to purge themselves of mental idolatry and to plunge into the wilderness like the children of Israel, trusting that the true source of knowledge would lead them to the promised land of scientific certitude. What is more, he laid out a step-by-step plan he called The Great Instauration, or Great Re-Invention, by which to achieve it. In order to echo the Bible's six days of creation, he purposely divided this plan into six stages.

The first stage consisted of scholars performing a thorough and honest survey of the present state of knowledge in all sciences and to expose the idolatries that inhibited correction of errors. The second stage consisted of their developing a sound method for obtaining new knowledge. The third stage consisted of their patiently observing and cataloging new data rather than leaping to hasty conclusions. The fourth stage consisted of scholars meditating on that mass of data, giving the brain the time it needs to make sense of it. The fifth stage consisted of their drafting temporary axioms and theories called hypotheses that seemed plausible in light of the data. The sixth and final stage consisted of scholars' testing those hypotheses by designing experiments to prove or refute them.

Bacon's purpose was to draft a blueprint for others to follow—and to offer a vision of the glory to come if they did. His death in 1626 left that vision incomplete, but not before he published a utopian novel called *The New Atlantis*, in which he imagined an island paradise in the Pacific Ocean where Christians lived in peace and plenty, their security ordered by science and their polity governed by charity.

Sir Francis Bacon did not invent the Scientific Revolution. Indeed, there is little evidence his writings had much direct effect on Galileo, Newton, or any experimental scientist. Bacon interpreted the future more than he influenced the present. He expressed in the most lucid form both the questions floating in the air of seventeenth-century Europe and the answers arrived at by experimenters and theorists. Thus, Bacon's call for a breakdown of natural philosophy into its component subjects was answered by savants who began to specialize in astronomy, physics, chemistry, biology, or geology. These scholars took stock of the inventory of knowledge in their respective fields and identified the problems most in need of solution.

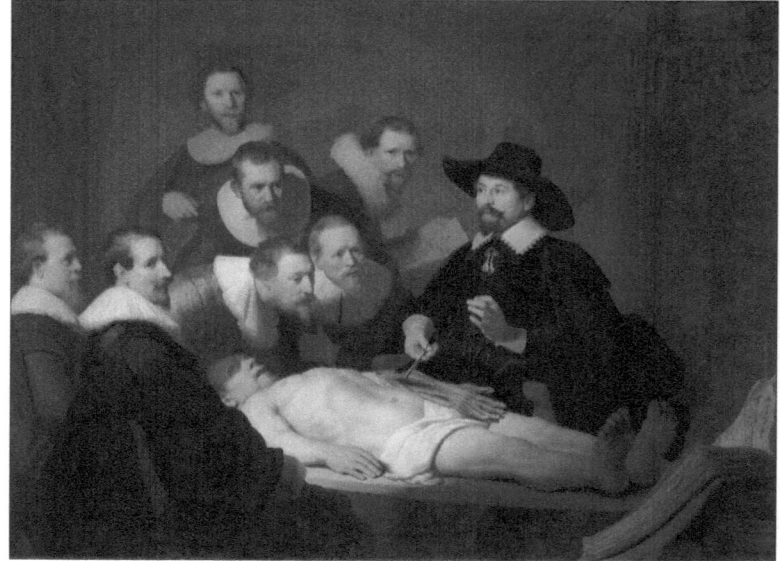

Rembrandt's *The Anatomy Lesson of Dr. Nicolaes Tulp* (1632) dramatizes the transmission of anatomical knowledge by the age's scientists.

Bacon's method for learning emerged over the course of a century, as specialists began to grope toward a fruitful mix of methods that included deduction and induction, mathematical analysis, and repeatable experimentation. These early-modern scientists repaid Bacon's faith that once the old idols were smashed, hard work and ingenuity would do the rest.

The hardest work came in Bacon's fourth stage of the scientific process, during which the scholar engages in serious thought—for nothing is harder than thinking. But the most painstaking work came during Bacon's third step, which called for the meticulous accumulation of new data and its "taxonomy," or the organization of facts into categories, as in the zoologist's identification of animal species and genera. The appetite of Renaissance Europeans for new taxonomies was simply voracious.

Already in fifteenth-century Florence, the genius Leonardo da Vinci had made meticulous sketches of human skeletons and musculature that suggested he was not satisfied with the ideas bequeathed by Galen. That dissatisfaction would become increasingly widespread in the post-Reformation era. In 1543, a Brussels-born surgeon named Andreas van Wesel (Vesalius in Latin) published a seven-volume anatomical masterpiece called *De corporis humani fabrica* (The structure of the human body). Educated at Paris and hired as a professor by the University of Padua, Vesalius was taught to venerate Galen. And he did—to the point of deferring to the ancient physician even when the evidence of Vesalius's own eyes suggested Galen was wrong. Eventually, Vesalius overthrew the idols of blindness by observing and recording accurate anatomical data regardless of what the old authorities had said. What is more, Vesalius came to view the body not as a static assembly of parts, but as a living whole. Indeed, his most famous drawing depicts a skeletal gentleman (or is it a woman?) leaning against a tomb and meditating on the fleeting nature of life.

Another critical feature of the breakthrough to the scientific method exemplified by the career of Vesalius was his training of graduate students who would go on to make discoveries of their own. One of them, Englishman William Harvey, turned the ancient Greeks on their heads when he hypothesized in 1628 that blood circulates through arteries and veins propelled by the pumping heart muscle. (Incidentally, an Arab physician, Ibn al-Nafis, had proposed a similar idea in the thirteenth century, but he was all but unknown in Europe.)

People in the modern and postmodern eras often assume that new science precedes new technology. But if we think historically, it becomes obvious that the opposite is the case at least half the time, either because new instruments are often required to observe and measure the data needed to support new scientific theories or else because new industries and technologies create a demand for new scientific knowledge. During the late medieval and especially the Renaissance eras, new technologies proliferated in shipbuilding and navigation, as inventions such as the compass, sextant, and astrolabe made possible Europe's Age of Exploration.

A similar phenomenon propelled the otherwise mundane science of metallurgy. The engineering difficulties involved in digging structurally sound mine shafts, evacuating underground water, extracting metallic ores, and refining and smelting copper, iron, lead, gold, and silver provided the knowledge that gave birth to inorganic chemistry. The German engineer Georg Bauer (whose last name means farmer; hence his Latin pen name of Agricola) fastidiously compiled the experiences of a lifetime in his 1556 treatise *De Re Metallica*. He modestly called himself a common laborer, but Bauer learned more about mining, geology, metallurgy, and chemistry than any European in the sixteenth century.

Those are just a few examples of the explosion of new knowledge in engineering, medicine, astronomy, geography, topography, climate, botany, and zoology that burst forth during the century when European ships sailed the seven seas—and explorers, merchants, missionaries, and scholars brought home with them notes, artifacts, and specimens from the Americas and Asia.

Naturalists observed the similarities among, and differences between, various forms of life and began to divide them according to genus and species. Astronomers charted previously unknown stars and constellations gracing the night skies of the southern hemisphere (including the mystically Christian Southern Cross). Sea captains and colonial officials recorded reams of information about exotic locales and their inhabitants' customs. During the 1500s and 1600s the first amateurish museums displayed curiosities from overseas, including seashells. insects, quartzes, animal skins, and human artifacts. German princes called these places *Wunderkammer*—chambers of wonders—and proudly displayed them to visitors.

Just as Bacon had prophesied, this acquisition of data led to hypotheses that could be tested and contribute to the discovery of natural laws. During the sixteenth and seventeenth centuries, such theorizing and testing occurred in all scientific fields. It happened first in the most easily numerated fields—physics and astronomy—which is why textbooks so often teach the Scientific Revolution by focusing on the displacement of Ptolemy's terracentric solar system by a new heliocentric paradigm later buttressed by Newton's theory of gravitation.

That story began in Renaissance Poland, where Copernicus began to challenge traditional notions of admissible evidence. In 1543 he published *De Revolutionibus Orbium Coelestium* (On the revolution of the heavenly bodies), in which he revived the heliocentric theory nearly eighteen hundred years after Aristarchus of Samos first proposed it. Copernicus was a priest of conservative temperament. He had no intention of challenging the Aristotelianism blessed by the church. He was simply dissatisfied with Ptolemy's fudge factors, and he realized the planetary orbits all fell into place if the sun was placed at the solar system's center. His theory did not cause a fuss at the time, partly because his heliocentric model was not much more accurate than Ptolemy's model (like Ptolemy, Copernicus also assumed the planets' orbits were circular). But he quietly started a revolution by demonstrating the scientific applicability of Ockham's razor, which held that the simplest explanation of a phenomenon is likely the correct one.

In the decades that followed, the Renaissance appetite for new data caused astronomers to build on Copernican theory and eventually bring about a full-blown paradigm shift. That next stage in "the structure of scientific revolutions" (as historian Thomas Kuhn put it in the title of his famous 1962 book) was pioneered by a Danish nobleman named Tycho Brahe, who built an astronomical observatory on an island in the Baltic Sea. Thanks to precisely calibrated instruments made by Dutch craftsmen, Brahe charted the apparent motions of the planets and stars more accurately than anyone before and amassed a huge database prior to his untimely death in 1601. (Historians suspect that he inadvertently poisoned himself by drinking an alchemical potion during a visit to the Holy Roman emperor.) Theory was not Brahe's strong suit, but he had an imaginative apprentice named Johannes Kepler, and legend has it that as he lay dying he implored Kepler: "Let it not seem to posterity as if I worked in vain."

Kepler was another transitional figure who combined the mathematical scientific approach with mysticism—in his case, a Pythagorean belief in the magic qualities of numbers. He crunched Brahe's statistics and trusted that some magic pattern would appear. Like Copernicus, he put the sun at the center of the solar system, but he also discovered that the length of time the planets take to revolve around the sun varies with their distance from the sun. Hence, a year on Mars is considerably longer than a year on Earth. Furthermore, Kepler found that the planetary orbits—quirky retrograde motion and all—made perfect sense when traced, not as circles, but as *ellipses*, with the sun as their foci.

Following Kepler, the scene shifted to Italy, where the brilliant, curious, and counterintuitive Galileo Galilei was tinkering with telescopes designed by Dutch craftsmen for the use of their country's sea captains. Galileo obtained the most powerful lenses they could grind and aimed them at the heavens, where he discovered, among other things, mountains on the moon, spots on the sun, and the four largest moons of Jupiter. The last discovery was powerful circumstantial evidence for a heliocentric solar system. Did that constitute proof? Galileo insisted that it did—and it was that methodological claim, rather than heliocentrism itself, which got him into trouble with the Catholic Church.

John Heilbron, an eminent historian of science who taught at the University of California, published a biography of Galileo in 2010 that demonstrated beyond any doubt that his dispute with the church was solely about epistemology, or how it is human beings can really know anything. The pope's advisers knew as much astronomy as Galileo. They preferred Ptolemy's system because they assumed it was rational and indeed biblical to believe that God placed man at the center of everything and because certain biblical verses suggested that Earth was motionless. But their main objection to Galileo was his seemingly arrogant claim that one could infer a general law from circumstantial evidence. Moreover—since gravity had not yet been explained—Galileo could not say how everything on his allegedly spinning Earth did not fly off into space. So the pope—who was in fact a friend of Galileo—asked the astronomer to delete the word "proof" from his treatise and insert the word "hypothesis." At first Galileo complied with the pope's wish, but later he succumbed to the temptation to write polemical tracts against Aristotelians in the hope that the resulting notoriety would increase the sales of his own books (for which purpose he published in Italian, not Latin). Only then, in 1633, did the papacy oblige Galileo to recant his belief in terrestrial motion. He did so because he recognized the pope's authority to discipline him, although legend has it that he whispered under his breath, "E pur si muove" (Even so, it moves). That is all. That is the whole truth about the church's alleged persecution of Galileo. He was never put in prison, much less burned at the stake.

The second thing to realize about Galileo is that far and away his most important contributions had nothing to do with stargazing. Rather, he spent many daylight hours rolling balls down inclines, dropping weights from tall buildings like the Leaning Tower of Pisa, timing horse races, and analyzing all those motions mathematically. Thus did Galileo assemble data that suggested formulas, which in turn could be tested by new experiments. The results included the basic laws of mechanics students now learn in ninth grade. The distance traveled by a moving object equals its velocity times elapsed time. Its velocity equals its acceleration times elapsed time. Its acceleration equals the force applied to it divided by its mass. Its momentum equals its mass times velocity. And if acceleration is constant, its distance equals one-half its acceleration times the square of elapsed time. Galileo also proved experimentally that absent wind resistance, objects fall to earth at the same rate regardless of their respective weights.

In 1642, the critical year in which Richelieu plunged France into the Thirty Years' War and Parliament launched the English Civil War, Galileo died in Italy. That very same year Isaac Newton was born, which illustrates another of the important threads that run throughout the history of science—namely, that scientists and their discoveries build on each other. Newton himself, later apotheosized as the world's greatest genius, attested: "I can see far because I stand on the shoulders of giants."

Newton was a polymath and another devout Christian. Like many natural philosophers of the early Scientific Revolution, Newton also dabbled in alchemy and the occult. When he applied his mathematical acumen to the solar system, he could draw on Copernicus's heliocentrism, Brahe's data, Kepler's elliptical orbits, Galileo's mechanics, an accurate calculation of the earth's size made by a Frenchman, Christiaan Huygens's theory of angular momentum, and his own brilliant invention, calculus (an invention made simultaneously by Gottfried Leibniz, in Germany).

Was Newton's universal theory of gravitation inspired by an apple that fell on his head? If so, it was providential, because no one on Earth was better prepared to imagine that all the phenomena described by his predecessors could be explained by the same force and the same laws of universal gravitation. Nobody knew what gravity was. Nobody to this day knows what gravity is. Nevertheless, its effects are universally observable, and Newton's great insight was that the moon and planets, including Earth, were like apples in that they "fell" around each other and around the Sun. They did not fall into each other because they were also moving at a high speed; hence they fell around each other in an elliptical orbit traced by their velocity and the gravitational pull between them. Newton calculated gravitational attraction to be proportional to the product of the masses of two bodies divided by the square of the distance between them. Skeptical scientists objected that Newton was postulating some kind of occult force; they believed that bodies cannot affect each other at a distance. But experiments in the following century proved Newton right—whatever gravity was, it existed—and culminated in Henry Cavendish's discovery of the value of G, the universal gravitational constant; hence the formula that the gravitational force between two objects equals G times the product of the masses of the objects divided by the square of the distance between them.

Newton's *Principia Mathematica*, published in 1687, was so striking that it suggested the possibility of limitless human understanding and progress. As the poet Alexander Pope extolled: "Nature and Nature's laws lay hid in night: / God said, Let Newton be! and all was light."

That was how the scientific method was born in early modern Europe. Notice how the contributions of science were almost exclusively in the realm of *techne*. Could the realm of *themis*—of art, culture, religion, and law—keep up with the march of science? The original masters of scientific method, such as Sir Francis Bacon, very much hoped the answer was yes. But the sheer power of science and technology was already capturing the imaginations of political elites.

Consider René Descartes, the brilliant French mathematician whose *Discourse on Method* (1637) began "Cogito, ergo sum" (I think, therefore I am). Descartes held that there were only two kinds of reality: "thinking substance," which is the subjective human mind, and "extended substance," which is objective matter. From that narrow dichotomy he deduced a devastating philosophy implying that all the things of *themis* were but figments of the imagination, in that objective reality consists only of those things which can be measured. When Newton's formulas then suggested a sort of machine-like universe reducible to impersonal natural laws, government officials began to foster a technocratic mentality that made science itself a sort of religion and its political patrons a sort of new priesthood.

Even before the publication of Newton's *Principia*, the state-building monarchs had gotten into the business of chasing power through organized science. The English crown chartered the Royal Society in 1662 and the Royal Observatory at Greenwich in 1675. Finance Minister Colbert persuaded King Louis XIV to charter the French Academy of Sciences in 1666. Other European monarchies followed suit. At first, these societies were modest and involved mostly in whatever their gentlemen scholars felt like studying. King Charles II, no intellectual he, referred to Newton, the great chemist Robert Boyle, and their colleagues as his fools or jesters, useful only for amusement. But not many years would pass before states mobilized science in the service of power, be it a ship's chronometer to measure the longitude, in the case of England's Royal Society, or a ballistics table for accurate artillery fire, in the case of the French Academy. Indeed, one of the first treatises the academy published was *L'Art de Jetter les Bombes* (The art of hurling bombshells).

The contribution of modern science to the quality of human life is inestimable. But the Dark Side of the Force is undeniable. To perceive the universe solely through the lens of natural science is to strip a sense of the sacred from people's lives and to reduce reality to sheer matter: a process that sociologist Max Weber later called *Entzauberung* (demystification). Worse still, the Dark Side of the Force might, at some point in Europeans' dark, distressing future, tempt scientific and political elites to fill the spiritual void of their increasingly demystified world by trying to play God themselves.

Chapter 11

Soldiers, Serfs, Icons, and Axes: The Rise of Prussia and Russia

This chapter begins with some risky business—namely, ethnic jokes. Since the jokes target only dead, white, European males, they will probably elicit few protests. Nor will they likely elicit chuckles, since the national traits the jokes lampoon have by now been largely eroded by the bland, bureaucratic conformity of the European Union. But if readers can imagine an era when people took it for granted that nations, like individuals, displayed personalities, they may yet make sense.

The first quip contrasts Europeans' attitudes toward law and liberty, and it goes like this. In England everything is permitted unless expressly prohibited. In Germany, everything is prohibited unless expressly permitted. In France, everything is permitted even if expressly prohibited. While in Russia, everything is prohibited even if expressly permitted.

The second quip imagines that in a perfect world all the chefs are French, all the lovers Italian, all the policemen English, all the engineers German, and everything is organized by the Swiss. Whereas, in the worst possible world, all the chefs are English, all the lovers are Swiss, all the policemen are German, all the engineers are French, and everything is organized by the Italians.

Ethnic jokes, with the possible exception of jibes about bodily functions, might be humanity's oldest form of humor. Sometimes they exploit cruel stereotypes, and sometimes benign ones. But behind the humor lurks a question. Is there really such a thing as national character? Is it sometimes valid to generalize about the customs of ethnic or cultural groups, at least in given eras of history? The prima facie evidence would seem to suggest that the answer is yes. For instance, French legal and philosophical traditions have tended to be far more theoretical, rational, and deductive than the traditions of most other nations, whereas English legal and philosophical traditions have tended to be more pragmatic, empirical, and inductive than those of other nations. Simply contrast the bottom-up jurisprudence of English common law, based on centuries of precedents argued by lawyers, with the top-down statutory law of the Napoleonic Code, based on the dictates of magistrates. Likewise, Italians throughout the centuries have tended to be mercurial, charmed more by style than by substance, and gaily disobedient toward authority. Russian religion, literature, and political thought, by contrast, have nearly always been brooding, pessimistic, and authoritarian. You get the idea.

Yet history also provides plenty of evidence that national reputations are subject to radical change. Thus, in the eighteenth and early nineteenth centuries France was considered the most militaristic nation in Europe, whereas Germany was regarded as a nation of poets, philosophers, and musicians. By the late nineteenth century those images had flipped; the Germans came to be seen as militarists and the French as romantic artists. Likewise, Sweden, which had been militantly expansionist in the seventeenth century, had become a neutral and pacifist nation by the nineteenth. The Japanese flipped from being peaceful and isolationist to militant and aggressive, then back to pacifist, in the space of just a hundred and fifty years. Postmodern historians might dismiss all these national stereotypes as mere social constructions. But that raises the question of whether people construct their images of national characters from vague or false impressions, or instead from genuine tendencies born of objective conditions like geography, climate, social structure, culture, religion, and historical trauma.

Charles-Louis de Secondat, the baron de Montesquieu, an eighteenth-century political philosopher, explained national character in terms of climate and topography, contrasting the customs and institutions of people residing in temperate zones such as Europe with those of people living in deserts like the Middle East or tropical regions like Southeast Asia. Leopold von Ranke, a nineteenth-century historian, traced national character to the geopolitical location of a given state. He surmised that the British, an island people who lived by commerce and sea power, did not need a large army, high taxes, and rigid bureaucracy for their defense. Hence the British developed liberal, individualistic institutions, whereas Ranke's native Prussia—a relatively poor country surrounded by land powers—had been obliged to develop disciplined, militant institutions. In the 1890s, historian Frederick Jackson Turner developed a "frontier thesis" to the effect that Americans, being sheltered from invasion by two oceans and enjoying the social safety valve of the Western frontier, naturally embraced limited government, rugged individualism, and a democratic pioneer spirit.

Whatever the truth of such speculations, the fact remains that one of the most significant forces shaping the modern history of European nations has been their method of state-building—the manner by which monarchs either repressed their nobilities, middle classes, parliaments, and churches or else bargained with them, in order to establish permanent, centralized governments. Public finance is a boring subject; there is no getting around it. But the means that monarchs employed, with or without the consent of their people, to pay their bills often go far toward explaining a country's institutions.

We have already seen how royal absolutism—or at least the pretense of absolutism—prevailed in seventeenth-century France. The king suppressed dissent, governed without summoning a legislature, and established a centralized bureaucracy to collect taxes, administer justice, raise a military force, and regulate the economy. As a result, the Bourbon monarchy appeared to be the most streamlined regime in early modern Europe. The price French kings paid for that power was to honor the traditional tax exemptions of the clerical and aristocratic elites, which severely limited the crown's revenue stream. Meanwhile, England's Stuart kings failed in their efforts to establish absolute monarchy in 1642 and again in 1688, when the Glorious Revolution brought to power a new dynasty under William and Mary that accepted a different sort of compromise. In Britain, the crown would henceforth share power with Parliament in a constitutional monarchy, in return for which Britain's wealthy landowners and commercial classes willingly provided the government with new taxes and credits whenever the national interest required. The present chapter chronicles how the rulers of two more rising monarchies solved the problem of how to build efficient centralized states, and how their solutions helped to shape the futures of Germany and Russia.

The plains of northern Europe, which stretch along the Baltic Sea coast from the Netherlands to Russia, would seem an unlikely region to nurture a powerful state. To be sure, several great rivers flow through it, including the Elbe, Weser, Oder, and Vistula, and the port cities at their mouths long boasted a thriving commerce. Many products were exported through them, including cereal grains and naval stores such as timber, pitch, and hemp for rope. In the medieval era, German port cities such as Hamburg, Bremen, and Lübeck even banded together in a Hanseatic League to protect their seaborne commerce. But by the seventeenth century German merchants had lost much of the Baltic Sea trade to their Dutch and English competitors, while the northern swaths of the Holy Roman Empire emerged from the Thirty Years' War devastated, depopulated, and divided.

Nevertheless, one of those north German states was destined for greatness: the Mark of Brandenburg with its capital at Berlin, then a mere town of some fifteen thousand people on the banks of the River Spree. The word *mark* connoted a border province that served as the first line of defense of a larger kingdom or empire. When the Holy Roman emperor first granted the province around Berlin to the Markgraf (margrave) of Brandenburg, the Markgraf became responsible for defending the imperial boundary against the Polish and Baltic tribes to the east. Beginning in the high medieval era, Brandenburg also served as home base for the Teutonic Knights, a crusading order of German knights who went on the offensive in what they called a *Drang nach Osten* (drive to the east). Their crusading mission was to conquer and convert those mostly Slavic tribes which were not yet Christian. Pushing northeast along the coast, the Teutonic Knights carved out a new province they named Preussen, or Prussia in Latin. They also introduced the Teutonic Cross (✠), a Christian symbol that would later become the logo of the nineteenth-century German national state. That Iron Cross, as it is known today, had nothing to do with the swastika invented by the twentieth-century Nazi Party.

Recall that in the year 1356 the imperial diet had issued the Golden Bull, which made the Holy Roman emperor an elected office. That decree appointed seven princes of the empire to be permanent *Kurfürsten* (electors), one of whom was the margrave of Brandenburg. The next milestone in the rise of

Brandenburg occurred in 1417, when the realm fell by inheritance to the House of Hohenzollern, a noble family whose roots were in southwestern Germany. That Hohenzollern dynasty would reign in an unbroken line for five hundred years, during which Berlin became capital of one of the mightiest countries in the world. The rise of that country began in 1525, when the elector of Brandenburg inherited the Duchy of Prussia, and continued in 1618, when Elector Johann Sigismund inherited some scattered fiefs in the Rhineland called Cleves, Jülich, and Mark. By then the inhabitants of Brandenburg, like most northern Germans, had become Lutheran, while the Rhenish provinces (as those in the Rhineland are called) were populated either by Calvinists or by Catholics. Johann Sigismund followed the example of French King Henri IV by extending religious toleration to all. Thus did the ruler of Brandenburg decide not to insist on the principle of *cuius regio, eius religio*. That wise policy made the Hohenzollern realms a haven for dissidents fleeing persecution elsewhere.

Now, 1618, the year of that Rhenish inheritance, was also the year when the Thirty Years' War began. The Hohenzollerns' patchwork realm proved indefensible during the ruinous military campaigns that followed. Its provinces were repeatedly overrun by the plundering armies of Austria, Denmark, Sweden, and France. The helpless elector in Berlin could only wring his hands as reports arrived of his towns being sacked, his peasants being starved, and his subjects being drafted into foreign armies. Fertile fields were overrun by weeds. Wolves and bears returned to parts of Germany where they had not been seen for decades, even centuries. Most of Germany suffered terribly, but it was in Brandenburg that the twig of German history was bent, for in 1640—twenty-two years into the war—an iron-willed prince ascended the throne determined that *never again* would his people suffer such harm and humiliation. His name was Friedrich Wilhelm, and he was acclaimed in his own lifetime as the Great Elector.

How could he realize his ambition, given his small, vulnerable, divided realm? The answer was to forge a permanent, standing army of elite soldiers to deter future enemies from daring to tangle with Brandenburg-Prussia. Friedrich Wilhelm could hope to do that because the inflated cost of warfare in the seventeenth century and the difficulties of transporting troops meant that armies were comparatively small. For instance, during the Thirty Years' War most battles involved armies of fewer than twenty-five thousand soldiers. A medium-sized country, if its regime was frugal and its army disciplined, might therefore play the hedgehog, or, to switch metaphors, might punch above its weight.

All Friedrich Wilhelm needed was money. But his only source of funds, besides tariffs levied on foreign imports, was the taxes paid by burghers and landowners. Taxes, in Brandenburg as elsewhere, had to be approved by the estates, those quasi-parliamentary bodies dating from the Middle Ages that represented the nobility and the commoners. (The church was not represented in the estates of northern German provinces because the rulers of Lutheran countries had in effect nationalized their churches during the Reformation.) In 1653, Friedrich Wilhelm summoned delegations from the nobility and the *Bürgertum*—middle-class urban dwellers—to the *Landtag* (parliament). There he struck a historic bargain with them that fixed the pattern of Prussian state-building. The subjects represented in the Landtag agreed to approve permanent higher taxes, in return for which the elector made lucrative concessions. First, to the landowning nobility the elector granted the power to reduce the peasants who worked their land to abject serfdom, bound to the soil of their landlords for life. That was a valuable concession, because the carnage of the Thirty Years' War had made labor scarce. Next, to middle-class merchants, lawyers, and craftsmen the Great Elector promised law, order, security from invasion, religious liberty, government offices on the basis of merit, and mercantilist policies to stimulate commerce. That was more than enough to please his subjects in Berlin and other towns.

Thus did Friedrich Wilhelm, the Great Elector, acquire the regular, substantial income he needed to forge a rugged army and the centralized bureaucracy he needed to collect taxes and administer law. Furthermore, once he had won the concurrence of the Landtag in Brandenburg-Prussia, the Great Elector never needed to summon the assemblies into session again. The Hohenzollerns began to reign as absolute monarchs, like the kings of France, but unlike the Bourbons they did so with the full cooperation of the nobility and bourgeoisie. No wonder the famous Parliamentary Recess of 1653 is deemed a watershed in the history of Germany. The Hohenzollern rulers, in the wake of the Thirty Years' War, received carte blanche, from their own subjects, to bankroll an efficient modern regime.

The Great Elector's long reign lasted until his death in 1688 (note that his reign from 1640 to 1688 happened to coincide exactly with the dates of the English Civil War and Glorious Revolution). By the time he died, Friedrich Wilhelm had standardized administration in all his possessions, appointed a general commissariat staffed by talented commoners and appointed a *Grosse Generalstab* (great general staff) to oversee the army. The staff officers consisted almost entirely of Junkers (young lords), and their service supplied the famous field marshals and generals with the aristocratic "von" in their names. Their professional successors would mastermind Prussia's, then Germany's, wars for the next three centuries. The Great Elector also founded the *Kommerzkollegium* (commercial college) to make economic policy and a *Geheime Staatskanzlei* (privy council) to advise the elector on politics. Brandenburg-Prussia's officials and soldiers soon achieved a widespread reputation for honesty, efficiency, and lockstep obedience.

Even that was not enough for the state-building Great Elector. He squeezed additional revenues from his personal domains and donated them to the state. He pursued mercantilist policies to slash imports and sponsor new industries. He even attempted to plant a Brandenburg colony on the West African coast. Most importantly, he exploited Louis XIV's foolish decision to revoke the Edict of Nantes and expel the Huguenots from France in 1685. Friedrich Wilhelm loudly announced that all Protestant exiles were more than welcome in Brandenburg-Prussia. The result was such a large influx of Huguenots that by the year 1700 one-sixth of the entire population of Berlin was composed of skilled and industrious French.

The Great Elector's son Friedrich, by contrast, was a dull and pompous man who contributed little to the development of the state. Yet Friedrich I did found the Berlin Academy of Sciences in imitation of the English and French, and when he put his tough little army at the disposal of the Austrian Habsburgs in their wars against Louis XIV, the Holy Roman Empire granted Friedrich the title of king. Thereafter, for the sake of convenience, European diplomats began to refer to the Hohenzollern regime as the Kingdom of Prussia.

When Friedrich I died in 1713, the royal personality abruptly changed again. His son Friedrich Wilhelm I was a whip-cracker known as the Soldier King. He wore his uniform at all times and personally drilled his palace guards, a unit composed of soldiers at least six feet tall (quite tall indeed, in those days). Friedrich Wilhelm I seemed rough and uncouth because he favored the company of his smoking and drinking buddies, the so-called *Tabakkabinette*. But he was no sluggard when it came to governance. In 1722 he folded all the offices of state into a single bureaucracy with the singularly unwieldy name (it contains forty-four letters!) of *Generaloberfinanzkriegsunddomanendirektorium*. The word translates as General Directory for Finance, War, and (Royal) Domains, or General Directory for short.

So it was that in less than a century after the Great Elector cried "never again" during the Thirty Years' War, Brandenburg-Prussia became, through sheer will, a state much tougher than its size would suggest. The Hohenzollerns made absolute monarchy work, in good part because they and their subjects displayed the so-called Protestant virtues of hard work, discipline, and a frugality decidedly not on display at the court of Louis XIV.

Prussian power, far from being squandered, was husbanded all those years until, in 1740, the crown passed to Friedrich II, known to history as King Frederick the Great. He decided the time had come to deploy the excellent army his forebears had built, not only to defend Prussia but to expand it—and to do so by challenging the Habsburg monarchy for leadership in the Holy Roman Empire. Contemporary observers, such as the cynical philosopher Voltaire, liked to quip that Prussia was not a state with an army, but rather an army in search of a state.

The exciting history of the wars of Frederick the Great will be described in chapter 13. For now, in our discussion of state-building, we must note that his most important legacy was to rule as a rational, philosophical ruler in the tradition of his great-grandfather, the Great Elector. Frederick the Great imagined his role as chief executive officer of the enterprise known as the Kingdom of Prussia. To be sure, both he and the kings of France were considered absolute monarchs. But where Louis XIV had boasted, "I am the state," Frederick the Great modestly said, "I am the First Servant of the State."

There was a world of difference between those two statements.

Let us now move much further eastward, where we encounter a vast realm on the periphery of European civilization, an expanse of steppes, forests, and mountains, half-Asiatic and certainly thought of as strange and remote by western and central Europeans. Russia was amorphous, ill-defined, and exposed. Whenever Russia was weak, she could be invaded from the north, south, east, and west. Whenever Russia was strong, she could just as easily expand in all those directions. Russians, therefore, have always been conflicted and ambivalent toward the world outside. Ever insecure, Russia's rulers have always sought to expand, thereby rendering neighboring regions insecure. One historian has called Russia a great amoeba, pushing outward in all directions, less in response to internal stimuli than to a lack of external resistance. But even as Russia grew into the largest polity on the globe, Russians were conscious of their backwardness vis-à-vis Europe, China, or both, and they debated time and again just what it meant to be Russian. Was it their destiny to copy the West or to isolate themselves from the West, to admire Europe for its *techne* or to scorn Europe for its very different version of *themis*?

The late librarian of Congress James Billington titled his epic history of Russian culture *The Icon and the Axe*, thus highlighting the two artifacts sure to hang on the wall of every peasant's hut. One symbolized his Orthodox faith; the other his livelihood in the frigid forested expanse. Russia was one huge frontier, from the granary of the Ukraine, to the oceans of grassland known as the steppes, to the valleys of the Dnepr, Don, and Volga rivers, to the frozen tundra of the Arctic, to the snowy vastness of the Siberian taiga. The earliest inhabitants, from whom the name Rus derives, were foresters, collecting timber, honey, beeswax, and furs. At length they cleared forests to settle down and grow hardy rye and barley. Russia's first polity also came from the North, when Varangians from Scandinavia, led by the legendary Rurik, subdued the lands from the Baltic south to Kiev in Ukraine, then set themselves up as a landed nobility known as the boyars.

The icon, by contrast, came to Russia from the south in the year 988, when the pagan ruler at Kiev invited the Byzantine emperor to send missionaries so that the Rus might learn about the religion called Christianity. Thanks to St. Cyril (who gave his name to Russia's Cyrillic alphabet) and other brave missionaries, a Russian Orthodox Church emerged on the model of the Greek Orthodox. The theology and liturgy of Eastern Orthodoxy are sublime, mystical expressions of a faithful church that holds the holy images known as icons in special reverence. When the Ottoman Turks conquered Constantinople in 1453, Russia's own patriarchs were quick to claim leadership over all Eastern Orthodox believers. "First Rome fell, then Constantinople. But Moscow will be the Third Rome, and there will never be need of a fourth!" Thus did Russians like Tsar Ivan III (died 1505) come to believe they had an exceptional mission that reached far beyond Russia's own boundaries.

But that is getting far ahead of our story. Between the golden age of Kievan

Rus and the golden age of Muscovite Rus lay a yawning chasm. For the Kievan state was brutally conquered by the Mongols, Tatars, or "Golden Horde" ruled by khans, who led their invincible horsemen out of Central Asia in all directions. In 1238, the Golden Horde defeated the Kievan knights. But instead of just stacking skulls, sacking, raping, and pillaging—their modus operandi in other plundered lands—the Tatar khans decided to run an extortion racket through an indirect empire whereby their soldiers collected tribute each year from the boyars and peasants. Russians bowed their necks to that Tatar Yoke for 240 years.

During that lengthy bondage a new force arose. The dukes of Moscow steadily increased their power with the aid of three allies: first, the Tatars themselves, who gave the dukes a franchise to collect taxes and enforce the law in exchange for a share of the take; second, the Russian Orthodox Church, whose patriarchate was based in Moscow and supported its princes; and third, commercial towns such as Novgorod where merchants—like merchants elsewhere in Europe—yearned for a strong central government to impose law and order.

Gradually, the grand dukes of Moscow parlayed these advantages into control over the entire Volga Basin until, in the year 1480, Duke Ivan III felt strong enough to defy the khanate. A single swift war of rebellion sufficed to expel the Tatars forever, at which point Russia's isolated, landlocked remoteness turned into a strength. Muscovy emerged as a strong, unified state surrounded by weak, disorganized neighbors. Hence, Ivan III claimed for himself and his realm the imperial dignity recently lost with the fall of the Byzantine Empire. He began to call himself *Tsar*, which is Caesar in Russian.

Ivan III's grandson, who ascended the throne in 1533, made that imperial boast permanent and respected. Ivan IV, like other centralizing monarchs, met resistance, especially from the boyars, but he brooked no resistance. He was by all accounts deranged, debauched, and demonic, and he assumed that everyone not at his feet would soon be at his throat. It was Ivan IV who founded the *oprichnina*, Russia's first secret state police, and the *streltsy*, an elite military force recruited from the lower social orders to force the tsar's will on the boyars. No wonder, soon after his death in 1584, Russians bestowed on his memory the epithet Ivan the Terrible. But it could be argued that Ivan IV was the principal architect of the tsars' Eurasian empire, for it was he who ordered Cossack

Ivan III tears up the Khan's annual letter of instructions, symbolizing the Russians' revolt.

horsemen and fur-trapping woodsmen called *promyshlenniki* to cross the Ural Mountains and begin the conquest of Siberia. It would take nearly a century, but by the mid-1600s Russians from Europe had reached the remote Pacific coast, having claimed all the lands in between for the tsars.

Following the death of Ivan the Terrible, the boyars found their courage and tried to limit the power of the Muscovite throne. One ploy they adopted was to copy the Holy Roman Empire and declare that the emperor should be elected by a representative assembly called the *zemsky sobor*. Alas, all that move achieved was to condemn Russia to a series of rigged or contested elections that eventuated in civil wars. That era in Russian history became known, by a magnificent understatement, as the Time of Troubles. The troubles ended in 1613, when Michael Romanov emerged as a popular tsar who restored dynastic succession and founded the House of Romanov, which was destined to rule Russia until 1917, or more than three hundred years. Over the course of the seventeenth century, the Romanovs pushed Russia's frontiers eastward and southward to the Caspian Sea. Russia had become a behemoth by European standards. But it was a shockingly primitive one.

Historian R. R. Palmer described just how primitive:

Russia in the seventeenth century reflected its long estrangement from Europe and its long association with Central Asia. Women of the upper classes were secluded and often wore veils. Men wore beards and skirted garments that seemed exotic to Europeans. Customs were crude, wild drunkenness and revelry alternated with spasms of repentance and religious prostration. Dwarves and court jesters, no longer the fashion in the West, still amused the tsar and his retainers. Superstition infected the highest classes of church and state. Life counted for little; murder, kidnapping, torture, and elaborate physical cruelty were common. The Russian church supported no such educational and charitable institutions as did the Catholic and Protestant churches of Europe and had developed no such respect for learning. Indeed, Russians feared the incipient Western influences. Even arithmetic was hardly understood and the Arabic numerals were not used. Merchants computed with an abacus. The calendar was dated from the beginning of the world. . . . In the countryside manors came to resemble slave plantations . . . and peasants were so little regarded that the law authorized anyone killing another man's peasant simply to give him a live peasant in return.

That was the realm inherited by Tsar Peter I in 1682. He was freakishly tall—over seven feet—handsome, virile, vain, and possessed of enormous energy that he expended in drinking, debauchery, work, and especially war. Above all, Peter was a state-builder. He sponsored painstaking surveys of every village, town, rural estate, parish church, and economic institution of any kind. At length he reached the conclusion that the only way to transform the Russian Empire into a state capable of competing with the rest of Europe in the struggle for power, wealth, and security was to westernize his sprawling dominion populated by skirted boyars, bearded priests, wild Cossacks, and ignorant *muzhiks* (peasants). Peter began his campaign by waging wars to gain Russia access to central and western Europe, especially the Baltic Sea coastline, where he built port facilities and an entirely new capital city from scratch. He imported the most talented Italian architects to design St. Petersburg, plus expert engineers and craftsmen from Germany, Denmark, the Netherlands, and England to oversee its construction. Peter called the elegant new city his "window on the West."

Peter himself journeyed twice to western Europe, where he visited shipyards and capital cities to study industry, commerce, armies, navies, and governments.

Western European technology made him salivate, for it equated to power. But Peter had no use for the Dutch or English governments, since they equated to *limits* on power. Peter therefore determined to insulate Russia from Western philosophies while eagerly adopting Western technologies. He founded a Russian Academy of Sciences. He decreed revolutionary changes in Russian culture, the most celebrated being his order to boyars to shave off their beards and adopt Western dress. He created a civil service on the French model and promoted talented commoners, and he copied the Prussian system of obliging noblemen to serve in the army or government. He broke the independence of the Russian Orthodox Church by abolishing the office of patriarch, the Orthodox equivalent of the pope, and substituting a Holy Synod whose members he appointed himself.

Finally, Peter elevated Russia to great-power status over the course of the Great Northern War he waged against King Charles XII of Sweden, a war that climaxed in 1709 when the Russian army routed the Swedes at the Battle of Poltava in Ukraine. The treaty that ended that conflict in 1721 confirmed Russia's hold on the southern shore of the Baltic Sea. Four years later, in 1725, the man now known as Peter the Great died of a painful urinary blockage. He was only fifty-two, but he had successfully dragged Russia a long way toward modernity. He had also defined the love-hate relationship between Russia and the West that persists to this day.

By the mid-eighteenth century, therefore, ambitious, authoritarian regimes based in Berlin and St. Petersburg had claimed the status of major players in the competition among European monarchs for territory, power, and wealth. Prussia and Russia could scarcely have been less alike. One was a small country located in central Europe, ethnically German, culturally Latin, religiously Protestant, and possessed of the advances recently made through the Renaissance and Scientific Revolution. The other was a huge country located on Europe's periphery, ethnically Slavic, culturally Greek, religiously Orthodox, and only just beginning to assimilate western technology. Differences aside, both were the creations of ambitious state-building monarchs determined to increase their power through top-down reforms. It is that last element which is most problematic regarding discussions of national character. Did Brandenburg-Prussia's Great Elector and the kings that followed, or tsars such as Ivan the Terrible and Peter the Great, or for that matter Richelieu and Louis XIII, really reflect their countries' national characters? Or did they themselves shape the characters of their countries for posterity?

Whatever the answer, the contrasts between different methods of state-building may now be clearly discerned. All the monarchical governments faced similar problems in their efforts to forge efficient, sustainable, centralized states. First, they had to achieve a monopoly of force so they could impose uniform law and order and field strong armies to defend or expand their realms. Second, they needed reliable, permanent, and sizable sources of revenue, in addition to a trustworthy, efficient administration to collect taxes and govern. Third, they needed to bribe, cajole, persuade, or force their various aristocracies, clergy, and commoners to pay the requisite taxes. How did that three-step process play out in the major countries of early modern Europe?

In France, Louis XIII and Richelieu bullied the Huguenots and Catholic Church into acceding to royal authority, broke up the private armies and castles of the landed nobility, and ceased to call the Estates General into session, which allowed French kings to rule by decree. That form of state-building was called royal absolutism, even if the king's powers were not really absolute. It meant that the crown earned the right to govern alone, but at the cost of forfeiting the voluntary support of its richest, most powerful subjects.

In England, the Stuarts made feints toward absolutism but got routed twice. At length, Parliament prevailed over the crown, exiled the Stuarts, and agreed to grant William and Mary and their successors whatever new taxes the national interest required, but only in exchange for a package of guarantees that ensured Parliament, not the monarch, would be supreme. Accordingly, Britain's model of state-building was a representative, constitutional monarchy that enjoyed legitimacy in the eyes of its subjects (excepting, as always, the Irish).

In Brandenburg-Prussia the Great Elector and his successors made pragmatic, mutually beneficial bargains with their aristocrats and commoners, by which the people accepted permanent, sizable taxes in exchange for military protection, effective government, economic concessions to the landed aristocracy and burghers, and religious toleration. Thus, the North German state enjoyed a form of absolutism, as in France, but also a measure of popular legitimacy, as in Britain. Finally, in Russia the tsars seized absolute power in a much harsher manner, but through techniques similar to those in Prussia. Peter the Great, especially, won over the merchants and landed gentry by promoting commerce and upholding serfdom, while requiring the nobility to perform military or civil service. Prussia's rulers were the most tolerant in terms of religious liberty, whereas Russia's tsars made no room for religious diversity.

Do these histories of state-building in early modern France, Britain, Prussia, and Russia help us understand why those countries' politics and societies showed distinctively different patterns as they emerged and evolved over the course of the modern era? Do they explain why, for instance, liberalism and overseas empire became the dominant themes of Great Britain's future? Or why absolute monarchy and even more tyrannical revolutionary ideologies became the dominant themes in modern French history? Or why authoritarianism, but also reform from above, became the dominant themes of Germany's future? Or why autocracy and a government-led war against backwardness remained the dominant themes of Russia's history all the way down to the twenty-first century? Such questions are perhaps unanswerable, but it is precisely such questions that make the study of history fascinating.

Chapter 12

Reason Based on Faith: The Competing Enlightenments

Readers might have puzzled over the title to chapter 3, the one that summarized the medieval millennium and called it an era of "faith based on reason." Certainly, Christian Europe took on faith the divine inspiration of Holy Scripture. But for church scholars it was not a *blind* faith. Rather, theologians considered the Bible's depiction of flawed human nature to be piercingly realistic, and its description of the unconditional, indeed sacrificial, love of God for his creatures to be utterly consistent when seen through the eyes of faith. Medieval philosophers such as Thomas Aquinas argued that if God's promises through the prophets and messiah had been false, then the universe was absurd and our brief and troubled lives a bad joke. The medieval mind, in short, began with the Bible, but deduced its theological implications through reason.

This chapter covers the seventeenth and eighteenth centuries, an era that contemporaries as well as historians called the Enlightenment, an era when philosophers embraced reason based on faith. That it was an Age of Reason will become obvious. But by the end of this chapter readers should also appreciate how eighteenth-century rationalism was based on faith in a priori assumptions every bit as bold as those made by theologians.

To write about *the* Enlightenment distorts reality, for there were really several Enlightenments distinguished by the different inquiries made by French, German, English, and Scottish intellectuals. Yet all those *philosophes*, to employ the French term, considered themselves rational theorists who were determined to reform nearly all the institutions their societies had inherited from the past.

The epicenters of the various Enlightenments included Paris, London, Edinburgh, university towns throughout the Holy Roman Empire, and the capital cities of Berlin, Vienna, and St. Petersburg (for the monarchs of Prussia, Austria, and Russia were patrons of the philosophes). One might even include colonial outposts such as Benjamin Franklin's Philadelphia and Thomas Jefferson's Virginia. Moreover, since nearly all the philosophes eagerly read each other's works, they constituted what has been called a transnational Republic of Letters.

The leading figures of the French Enlightenment, or *Éclaircissement*, included François-Marie Arouet, better known by his pen name Voltaire; Denis Diderot, who compiled the first encyclopedia in an effort to accumulate and organize all human knowledge; the Baron de Montesquieu, a political theorist whose writings later influenced the Founding Fathers of the United States; and Jean-Jacques Rousseau, a sentimental theorist whose shocking speculations about what was genuinely natural for human beings, the social contract, and the origins of inequality probably made the most powerful intellectual impact of them all. The leading figures of the German Enlightenment, or *Aufklärung*, included such profound philosophers as Gottfried Leibniz and Immanuel Kant. Finally, the English and Scottish Enlightenments included such intellectual giants as John Locke, the theorist of humanity's natural rights; David Hume, founder of modern skepticism; historian Edward Gibbon, author of *The Decline and Fall of the Roman Empire*; and Adam Smith, the father of modern economics.

Such philosophes—and one could list many more—argued about nearly everything, including the natures of man and God; the possibilities and methodologies of improving the human condition; the origins of society, government, and religion; and whether social, governmental, and religious institutions were necessary to solve human ills or were their cause. But whatever their nationality, philosophy, or specialty, all these *gens de raison* (people of reason) believed in the existence of natural laws, not only in the physical sciences, but in the social sciences as well: laws that ordered—or else ought to order—human behavior.

The philosophes' deep faith in reason as a tool for reforming society derived from four principal sources. First, it expressed the humanist spirit that had first emerged during the Renaissance. Second, it expressed a loss of confidence in religious certainties, a loss that stemmed from the Protestant Reformation and the ensuing religious wars. Third, it expressed the inquisitive spirit of the Age of Discovery, which compelled Europeans to contrast their own civilization with those of the Chinese, Hindus, and Muslims. Fourth and foremost, the Enlightenment was inspired by the Scientific Revolution, which seemed to have provided a trustworthy methodology for discovering those natural laws which governed the universe. The philosophes had faith that the methods of scientific discovery that Francis Bacon had codified and Isaac Newton had practiced could be applied to questions not only about the nonhuman world but also about human society.

Through their application of reason, Enlightenment thinkers meant to strip away—or, better yet, *see through*—the messy complexities of human life to expose the natural laws that governed social, political, and economic existence. If they could achieve that, then presumably they could purge their institutions of the irrational customs they had inherited from the past.

Nothing expressed the Enlightenment's obsession with rationality and order so much as the rigidly geometrical French gardens popular in the 1600s and 1700s, not to mention the stately, predictable harmonies and tempos of eighteenth-century classical music. Simply contrast the orderly metrics and harmonies of composers like Franz Josef Haydn with the complex contrapuntal compositions of Baroque musicians such as Johann Sebastian Bach or the sublime mysticism of later Romantic composers such as Ludwig van Beethoven, and you begin to understand the Enlightenment passion for rational order.

Readers who have paid close attention to what this chapter has described so far might have spied a profound contradiction. If human society is governed by natural laws like those which govern the physical world, then by definition whatever exists is rational, and if whatever exists is rational, how can it be further "rationalized" and reformed? Consider, for instance, those Enlightenment philosophers who were eager to learn why wars happened, in order to prevent them in the future. If, in fact, wars are an unfortunate but natural, indeed common, occurrence between sovereign states, then the only way they can be prevented is through unnatural means. The same would be the case with crime, bigotry, inequality, or any other pathology. If those phenomena are natural, their causes cannot be removed. At best, only their effects can be alleviated. That is why Leibniz concluded that the world, despite its obvious flaws, is nevertheless "the best of all possible worlds." That is also why Voltaire mocked Leibniz's philosophy in his hilarious satire *Candide*, a novella in which all manner of misfortune afflicts the protagonist.

It would appear, therefore, that the eighteenth-century intellectuals were remarkably split-minded. On the one hand, Enlightenment inquiries increased Europeans' knowledge of, and certainly their theorizing about, government, society, and economics. On the other hand, the philosophes' faith in reason tempted them to conclude that they themselves possessed the mental tool kit needed to reform and even perfect society. Did not the framers of the United States Constitution claim to be designing a "more perfect Union"?

Faith in reason encouraged philosophes to adopt a thoroughgoing optimism. They believed in progress, thanks to the malleability and perfectibility of human nature. They believed in the universality of their ideas, for reason and natural law must be just as valid in China or India as they were in France or England. And they believed in the possibility of a truly cosmopolitan, homogeneous human race, for if reason is everywhere identical, then all men and women might theoretically be educated to share the same opinions. The fact that the world was not everywhere harmonious could logically be explained as the product of poor educational systems, oppressive hierarchies, and irrational traditions. Hence the Enlightenment project was to expose and correct such irrationalities.

Philosophes gathered in salons and academies, where they debated and critiqued nearly everything. In France, for instance, the philosophes looked around and saw a hierarchical social order in which a privileged, seemingly useless, aristocracy lived off the sweat of oppressed masses; a fiscal system that exempted the rich while burdening the poor; a mercantilist economy that choked the natural flow of commerce and triggered colonial wars; a judicial and prison system that trampled on human rights and still practiced torture; and an established church that encouraged superstition, guilt, and even fear rather than love for one's neighbors. Voltaire even wrote of the Catholic Church, "Ecrasez l'infame!" (Crush the infamous thing), which not incidentally explains why he was forced to spend most of his life outside France.

Far to the east, in Königsberg, East Prussia, the celebrated philosopher Immanuel Kant pointedly asked, "Was ist die Aufklärung?" (What is the Enlightenment?). He answered, "Enlightenment is the liberation of man from his self-caused state of immaturity.... And self-caused immaturity derives not from a lack of understanding, but a lack of courage to use one's mind without reliance on some other authority. Dare to use your understanding: that is the motto of the Enlightenment!" Kant, like Bacon before him, urged Europeans to reject the idols that prevented them from discerning truths.

The job of the philosophe, therefore, was to denounce irrational traditions and teach people to ask, "Does this law, custom, or institution conform to reason, or not?" Given that a spirit of criticism pervaded Enlightenment thought, you can well understand why historians have always considered that intellectual movement to be one of the principal causes of the French Revolution, which erupted in 1789. Indeed, as the historian Walter Dorn has written, "Great though the contributions of the philosophes were, just as great was the destruction that followed the footsteps of the Army of Reason as closely as its shadow." That would become abundantly clear, as will be shown when we describe the tumultuous revolution in France.

The contributions of the English and Scottish Enlightenments, by contrast, promoted irenic, not violent, doctrines of human rights, liberty, equality under the law, free enterprise, universal education, and public policies informed by the social sciences. Indeed, most of the positive achievements seen in the Anglophone world from the eighteenth through the twentieth century were the fruits of the Enlightenment.

The most fertile ground from which the Enlightenment sprang was the methodological revolution in the natural sciences. Indeed, a pattern began to be traced during the late 1600s that has defined Euro-American intellectual history ever since. That is the tendency for social scientists to follow the latest trends in the natural sciences. Whether it be Antoine Lavoisier's organic chemistry, Charles Darwin's evolutionary biology, Sigmund Freud's psychology, Albert Einstein's physics, or the ecological and cybernetic trends of our own day, social scientists and historians have invariably cried, "Aha! This is the very paradigm we have been looking for in order to explain social, economic, or political change

William Blake's allegory of Isaac Newton expresses, as it also subtly critiques, the Enlightenment notion that all things can be reduced to measurements and laws of nature (*Newton*, 1795).

over time." Read almost any work of history or social science written since the Enlightenment, and you will probably find in it metaphors borrowed from natural science. The philosophes were the first to follow this course, because they were the first generation to experience a culture increasingly shaped by the scientific method. Newton's synthesis of mechanics, gravity, astronomy, and calculus simply astonished educated Europeans. He opened their eyes to an orderly, predictable cosmos governed by immutable natural law, a cosmos that Deistic philosophes likened to a machine designed by a clockmaker God.

One of the earliest philosophers to apply Newton's theories to human affairs was his countryman John Locke. Best known for his *Two Treatises of Government*, Locke was also one of the first social psychologists. In *An Essay on Human Understanding* he pondered the question of how personality is formed. Babies, Locke reasoned, are born *tabulae rasae* (blank slates) to be written upon by society. Children are so many living canvases daubed by the brushes of their parents, nursemaids, siblings, teachers, preachers, friends, and anyone else who influences their environments. Locke was a Christian; as he wrote, he believed in the reasonableness of the Bible. But his radical "nurture over nature" theory of personality formation left little room for what Catholics call original sin and Calvinists call total depravity. Locke overlooked the obvious fact that no human being is more thoroughly selfish than an infant. His theory of personality also implied that a perfect upbringing and education might turn children into perfect adults. In so doing, Locke opened a Pandora's box of dangerous questions, such as, Who should decide what the best environment or education is? (Here it is worth noting that later libertarians, who also trace their philosophical roots back to the Enlightenment, would powerfully rebut the notion that life would be ideal if only the right people were in charge. They would insist that "there are no right people.")

Locke was not alone in believing that traditional notions of sin and grace were difficult to reconcile with a Newtonian model of reality. As early as the 1660s, Baruch Spinoza, a Jewish philosopher in the Netherlands, argued that the natural universe as revealed by science is the only reality and thus must be coterminous with what we call God. In other words, the universe is not God's creation, because creation itself is God. Such pantheism was, for all practical purposes, atheistic, because a God who is everywhere and nowhere, and is material not spiritual, and is subject to the same natural laws as mortals, cannot be concerned with humanity or intervene in human history. Accordingly, Spinoza denied the Bible's veracity and the soul's immortality even as he stoically insisted on a strict moral code that all people should follow. No wonder his synagogue expelled him for heresy.

That some philosophes met resistance from religious and civil authorities goes without saying. They were, after all, exploring entirely new ways of understanding reality. But the Enlightenment project faced three more daunting hurdles. The first concerned how to discover the natural laws philosophes believed must govern collective behavior. The second concerned how to preserve human dignity and morality in a clockwork universe purged of a personal God. The third concerned how to account for the fact that human beings existed at all, and how they existed—as they obviously did, thanks to their consciousness and reason—on a higher plane than the animals.

To clear the first hurdle required relentless faith in reason. That is, enlightened social scientists needed to gather data on human behavior in the same rigorous way that Brahe, Kepler, and Galileo had observed the movements of heavenly bodies, in the hope that sooner or later a genius like Newton would come along to explain how it all connected.

Montesquieu practiced that technique in his *Spirit of the Laws* of 1748. He read European explorers' accounts of the cultures, customs, and traditions of people in Asia, Africa, and Latin America and contrasted them with European civilization. Then he meditated on those data and came up with a theory. Montesquieu decided that forms of government and society evolved over time in ways that conformed to the topographies and climates of the lands on which the various peoples of the world lived. People who lived in temperate climes such as Europe and thrived on agriculture and commerce tended to develop mixed forms of government in which power was shared among kings, parliaments, churches, towns, and landowners. By contrast, people in desert environments such as Egypt and Mesopotamia, where agriculture depended on a centralized system of irrigation, or tropical climates such as rice-growing Asia, where people worked in village communes, tended to develop despotic forms of government.

In similar fashion, Voltaire pioneered the comparative study of religion. He concluded that religion must be a natural human proclivity, since every culture has its peculiar cult. And in his *Universal History* of 1756 Voltaire contended that religion was the glue that held societies together. He went on to scorn the so-called higher religions of Judaism, Christianity, and Islam on the grounds that they made false claims of universality and tended to be intolerant of rivals. It was his expectation that as interactions among people around the world increased, humanity would gravitate toward a "natural religion" derived not from mysticism, tradition, or revelation, but from reason.

Most Enlightenment philosophers in Protestant countries, such as northern Germany and Britain, did not jettison Christianity. But they, too, debated how to interpret the Bible and how to account for such sophisticated Asian religions as Buddhism and Taoism. They also noticed that nearly all the world's religions taught remarkably similar moral codes—for instance, that all condemned perjury, theft, murder, incest, and rape. Was it therefore possible to draft a moral code valid for all peoples?

The quest to articulate a universal theory of morality based on reason rather than Scripture was a veritable obsession of the *Aufklärung*, no doubt because, first, the Reformation had left Germans split between Protestants and Catholics, and, second, no country had suffered more during the wars of religion. The

German quest for a secular morality began with legal scholars such as Samuel Pufendorf during the late seventeenth century and climaxed with Immanuel Kant near the end of the eighteenth century. All these scholars maintained Lutheran identities, but all hoped to reason their way to a natural moral code that all Christians, and indeed all human beings, might apprehend. Thus did Kant arrive at what he called the "categorical imperative," holding that human beings ought to behave as if their every act could exemplify a universal code of behavior. In practice, Kant's categorical imperative closely resembled the Bible's Golden Rule, which in turn closely resembled the Chinese *tao*: "Do unto others as you would have them do unto you." Pufendorf and Kant also wrote treatises on war and diplomacy in the hope that international law might eventually foster perpetual peace among states.

Such Enlightenment inquiries into history, religion, and politics treated humanity itself as if it were a scientific laboratory. They used the mind as a lens through which to observe not only the outside world but the mind itself. Yes, they said, human beings have reason, which elevates them above the animal kingdom. But human beings often behave in unreasonable, not to say cruel and stupid, ways, which sinks them *below* the animal kingdom. Why? That question prompted inquiries into what life must have been like in a "state of nature"—that is, before civilizations and their characteristic institutions emerged.

The implications of these inquiries were either thrilling or chilling, depending on how particular thinkers answered questions like these: What is human nature? Where do our notions of good and bad come from? Are people naturally good or bad, or are they born as blank slates? What is the purpose of life? How can people find happiness in their short and troubled lives? Which social, political, legal, and economic systems best promote life, liberty, and prosperity?

Philosophes answered such questions in ways so multifarious as to fill the political spectrum, which is another reason why it is accurate to speak of competing Enlightenments. For instance, in England Thomas Hobbes wrote in his book *Leviathan* that the natural condition of man was savage and that life in the state of nature was "solitary, poor, nasty, brutish, and short," indeed a *bellum omnium contra omnes* (war of all against all). Hobbes believed that people had formed societies and established governments to escape that chaotic insecurity. They made social contracts under which they agreed to surrender their personal sovereignty to a sovereign ruler. Hobbes, who had endured England's terrible civil war in the 1650s, thought that only absolute monarchy could preserve law and order, in that any system of divided powers was bound to degenerate into either deadlock or anarchy.

Contrast that perspective with the one purveyed by John Locke, who also believed government was based on a social contract, but who in contrast to Hobbes imagined the state of nature as one in which people were reasonable and cooperative and enjoyed an inalienable right to liberty. According to Locke, people formed governments to secure their natural rights. Hence, if their monarch abused people's rights, he made himself an illegitimate tyrant, in which case his subjects had the natural right and indeed duty to overthrow him (precisely what Parliament had done to English kings in 1642 and 1688). Moreover, Locke argued that the most reasonable government was not absolute monarchy, but rather a constitutional monarchy in which executive, legislative, and judicial authorities checked and balanced each other.

In France, Bishop Jacques-Bénigne Bossuet, the personal confessor to King Louis XIV, speculated about the state of nature and social contract from a Catholic perspective. He shared Hobbes's view that human life in a state of nature had been "nasty, brutish, and short"—the biblical account of how Cain killed his brother Abel at the very beginning of history amply proved that—and he shared Hobbes's view that absolute monarchy was the only alternative to anarchy. But he added a doctrine holding that all earthly authorities are given by Providence. Hence, to rebel against them was to rebel against God. This doctrine we call the divine right of kings.

Nearly all the anticlerical French philosophes considered Bossuet's view to be nonsense. But their own a priori assumptions raised the question: What *wasn't* nonsense? What political system *was* reasonable? Prior to 1789, the most popular answer among philosophes was not to abolish monarchy, whether absolute or not, but rather to rationalize monarchy and make it enlightened. After all, the philosophes, being cosmopolitan savants, held ignorant peasants and workers in contempt and therefore had little or no interest in popular government. Instead, most philosophes reasoned that if kings and their officials looked to their intellectuals for policy guidance, they might design reforms for all institutions, be they legal, financial, economic, educational, even religious. Thus did Voltaire and his ilk propagandize in favor of an enlightened absolutism in which a "natural aristocracy" instructed monarchs how to govern.

By 1740 or so, enlightened absolutism (also called enlightened despotism) emerged as the most prevalent and indeed progressive trend on the European continent. King Frederick II of Prussia, Tsarina Catherine II of Russia, Empress Maria Theresa of Austria, plus the kings of Spain, Portugal, and Sweden embraced the philosophes' critiques and made determined efforts to reform their respective realms. Still, enlightened absolutism had three fatal flaws. First, what if a monarch was not enlightened, wise, or progressive? Second, assuming a ruler was enlightened, how was he or she to know which policy proposals to adopt, given that the philosophes themselves disagreed with each other about so many things? Third, what to do if the people pushed back or even rebelled rather than see their age-old institutions overturned from on high? Ordinary people tend to hate change, especially if a given reform is perceived as harming their interests. Indeed, the "enlightened" reforms of Habsburg emperor Josef II proved to be so obnoxious to local noblemen, imperial towns with ancient charters of rights and privileges, craftsmen's guilds, and ordinary workers that the people in various provinces of the empire rose up in protest. Josef II was obliged to rescind most of his decrees.

Lastly, what of Jean-Jacques Rousseau, perhaps the most influential of all the eighteenth-century philosophes? He grappled his whole life with the questions of who should rule and what sorts of rules they should impose on society. But Rousseau was anything but an attractive figure. Born in Switzerland to Calvinist parents, he later became a Catholic, then reconverted to Protestantism, then became disaffected with Christianity altogether. In fact, he ran away from home at age sixteen and by his own confession became a lonely, miserable, maladjusted man. At length he married his housemaid, who bore him five children. But Rousseau deserted his family and fled to France, where he indulged in numerous affairs. There he reinvented himself as a self-styled philosophe and began to sponge off various wealthy patrons. He went on to write a whole series of sentimental, self-pitying books in which he denounced the injustice and cruelty of France's hierarchical society. Yet, Europeans in subsequent generations chose to embrace him—a man one might be forgiven for categorizing as a sheer loser—more than any other Enlightenment philosophe. In fact, such nineteenth- and twentieth-century movements as liberal democracy, social democracy, Marxism, Freudianism, and postmodernism all trace some of their roots to Rousseau.

"Man is born free, but is everywhere in chains." Does that sound like Karl Marx? It was really Rousseau. "Civilization and its discontents are the source of all human pain." Does that sound like Sigmund Freud? It was really Rousseau. He was the first to speculate that human beings in the state of nature were not only free but naturally good and kind. And he certainly was not making reference to the garden of Eden. He meant a state in which families, clans, and tribes lived naturally before the rise of civilizations. For according to Rousseau, what had corrupted and enslaved human beings was society itself. Society had given rise to such wicked inventions as private property, inequality, patriarchy, established churches, and hierarchies of power, wealth, and prestige. The best and most natural human traits, speculated Rousseau, were honesty and charity. But in order to get by in civil society, people were obliged to repress their best instincts and instead to lie, cheat, steal, and covet.

Think about that. It was at that stage of his intellectual journey that Jean-Jacques Rousseau began to exit the Enlightenment. Immanuel Kant, toward the end of his own life, had come to realize the limits of rationality in his book *The Critique of Pure Reason*. Rousseau went much further, employing his reason to conclude that reason was not the defining or even best attribute of humanity, because what really mattered were *people's feelings*. Cruel society could not be rationally reformed from above because feelings mattered far more than ideas. Remember that phrase of Plutarch that was popular during the Renaissance: "It is better to will the good than to know the truth"? Well, most philosophers believed that they "willed the good" by trying to "know the truth." Rousseau claimed that "willing the good" is *identical* to "knowing the truth," because sentimentality trumped knowledge and logic. In other words, Rousseau tempted his disciples to reject all authority, whether that of the church, the judiciary, the royal government, even of reason itself, and decide right and wrong for themselves.

Rousseau did not deny the notion of the social contract, about which he penned a two-volume treatise. But instead of a contract between the people and their ruler, he imagined a primordial contract among the people themselves. Society, he wrote, is formed when individuals subsume their wills into a general will, which is where true sovereignty lies. Properly understood, governments exist for the sole purpose of executing that general will, and by doing so, governments empower people rather than oppress them. To our ears, it may sound like Rousseau's social contract pointed the way toward democracy. But not to Rousseau, because he also granted that majorities could be wrong. Indeed, he wrote that "what generalizes the will is not the number of voices but the common interest that unites them." Somehow, in some mystical way, the real interests and feelings of "the people" bubble to the surface and become sovereign. Rousseau gave no hint of just how this mystical general will might be revealed. Rather, this tormented narcissist evidently craved a feeling of community and acceptance. So he bequeathed a vague doctrine that could theoretically validate majoritarian tyranny over minorities, or the tyranny of minorities, or even the tyranny of one person, so long as they or he claimed to embody the general will.

In the end we are led to ask how reasonable Enlightenment reason really was. The answer depends on which Enlightenment we are talking about. Natural scientists can design repeatable experiments to test their hypotheses, but most students of human behavior cannot run a social experiment over again. That is why most "social sciences" are in fact contradictions in terms. The only laboratory of government, society, law, religion, and economics is history itself, which by definition cannot be repeated. To be sure, scholars may study human behavior in search of patterns and may debate the wisdom or folly of past policies and institutions. But since scholars cannot change variables and replay historical episodes, their reasoning can only be inductive, their evidence circumstantial, and their conclusions tentative.

In 1943 Carl Becker (whom the reader encountered in the introduction and chapter 9) published a book titled *The Heavenly City of the Eighteenth-Century Philosophers*, in which he argued that the philosophy of the Enlightenment was less like a social science than a religion. He showed that the philosophes' faith in reason almost always required assumptions every bit as bold as the assumptions made by people of religious faith. For instance, the church preached a personal, loving God who intervenes in history. Enlightenment Deists preached an impersonal, clockwork God who does not intervene in history. The church quoted the Bible to define human beings as the glory of God's creation but corrupted by sin. Philosophes like Rousseau defined humanity as the glory of nature but corrupted by society. The church considered secular society, the City of Man, to be incorrigibly imperfect. Philosophes like Voltaire considered secular society to be irrational but perfectible through reforms and education. The church assumed, with Shakespeare's Hamlet, "There are more things in heaven and earth, Horatio, than are dreamt of in your philosophy." Philosophes such as Diderot assumed there was nothing in the heavens and earth except what could be sensed and measured. What occurred during the Enlightenment was not an escape from dependence on faith, but rather a displacement of faith in God's love by faith in man's reason.

Judging from their fruits, some eighteenth-century thinkers were to some degree genuinely enlightened. Their ideas would ultimately create considerable cultural space for modern notions of liberty, toleration, human rights, free enterprise, and social mobility. The Anglo-Scottish Enlightenment was especially fruitful in this regard, precisely because of its moderation, empiricism, and pragmatism.

For instance, skeptical commonsense philosophers such as David Hume shrewdly observed that people are creatures of reason, but also of passion. They are capable of moral sentiments but are also self-centered. Hence, the best way to secure liberty is to craft institutions in which no person or faction can acquire exorbitant power and to promote laws such that everyone's private pursuit of happiness might contribute to society as a whole. The genius of Adam Smith applied such common sense to his 1776 treatise *An Inquiry into the Nature and Causes of the Wealth of Nations*, in which he argued that free markets and free trade would maximize wealth and opportunity for all, so long as greed was restrained by conscience. Smith the economist was also Smith the moralist. The message of his book *The Theory of Moral Sentiments* was adumbrated in the University of Pennsylvania's 1755 motto *Sine Moribus Leges Vanae* (Without morals, laws are in vain). Hume, Smith, and other leading figures of the English and Scottish Enlightenments exerted considerable influence over the politics and economics of Great Britain and the United States.

The fruits of the French Enlightenment, by contrast, were bitter, almost as if they were a second apple in a second garden of Eden. For there the play of reason culminated in Rousseau's notion that history itself must be overthrown if the general will is to prevail. The upshot of that teaching could only be anarchy or despotism, according to Rousseau's own prescription to the effect that "men must be forced to be free"—a prescription that became chillingly real in 1789, just eleven years after Rousseau's death.

Chapter 13

Competition for Empire: Britannia Rules the Waves

Every work of history is an exercise in selection, which is to say in deciding what to leave out. An author can never convey all he knows, let alone all there is to say on a given topic. Indeed, to attempt comprehensiveness is to do one's readers no good anyway, for then the author has failed to emphasize what is really important.

Selection is especially pressing in a synthetic history like this one, because each chapter covers a broad subject and a lengthy time period. Hence, the historian's task is typically to highlight dramatic events that move the plot forward and to downplay those periods of time during which most people's lives did not change much. To correct for that tendency, one needs to pause from time to time and describe what French historian Fernand Braudel called *la longue durée*, the long terms over which gradual trends transformed European life without violent upheavals or radical change.

So let us note that during the early modern era most Europeans most of the time still lived on farms or in rural villages. Their lives were measured by the timeless rhythms of planting in the spring and harvesting in the autumn. Seasons of hard labor were relieved only by Sundays, holidays, weddings, childbirth, and (if one were fortunate) semiretirement in old age. Only occasionally was the monotonous life of a rural village disturbed by epidemics, civil unrest, or foreign invasion.

Nevertheless, over the years covered so far, roughly 1450 to 1750, an increasing number of Europeans underwent a transition toward new patterns of life that are conventionally now spoken of as *modern*. In northern and western Europe especially, the decay of the feudal system meant greater independence and a higher standard of living for farmers who owned or leased their own acres. Serfdom still generally prevailed in eastern Europe, where state-building monarchs had made bargains with their landed gentry—the nobility—that allowed them to bind their peasants to the soil. Meanwhile, in the cities and towns of western and central Europe the expansion of commerce and a money economy meant more opportunities for social mobility. That is why historians invariably speak of the "rising bourgeoisie" as if middle-class townspeople were hot air balloons. Likewise, the application of scientific discoveries to agriculture and industry, the spread of literacy among townspeople, and the proliferation of how-to pamphlets instructing people about the best methods to increase production stimulated the growth and diversification of European economies. But none of those developments happened suddenly or completely, and many vestiges of medieval times coexisted with new forms of material culture, just as medieval cathedrals still loomed over bustling marketplaces in towns throughout England, France, the Low Countries, and the German and Italian provinces of the Holy Roman Empire.

Perhaps the most powerful long-term change can be conveyed in the terms of demography and ecology: that is, by noting the sheer number of people inhabiting Europe and their interaction with the environment. Prior to the early modern era, Europe's population grew slowly, if at all. Wars took a drastic toll, but the principal checks on population growth were famines caused by intermittent crop failures and infectious diseases. Moreover, the beneficent global warming characteristic of the high medieval era came to an end during the so-called Little Ice Age of the fifteenth through the seventeenth centuries, when weather in the northern hemisphere turned chilly and damp. That meant shorter growing seasons, smaller harvests, and a higher demand for wood just to heat dwellings. As a result, large swaths of northwestern Europe were deforested by the mid-eighteenth century. Luckily for western Europeans, wood was replaced—and just in time—by the mining of coal: the fossil fuel that would later power the industrial revolution.

In sum, one's mental image of early modern Europe should focus on kings, aristocrats, merchants, and scholars, but only against a vast backdrop filled with rural peasants, herdsmen, and craftsmen. Indeed, many of the people engaged in manufacturing of some kind—such as the roughly four million English cobblers, blacksmiths, and textile workers who existed around 1730—still worked in their own cottages and villages rather than in an urban factory or mill.

Cities were rare during this period, and by later standards quite small. London and Paris, with populations of about 600,000 people in the mid-eighteenth century, were the largest cities in Europe. Few others exceeded 75,000. Many cities had in fact shrunk as their economic fortunes declined, including Venice, Genoa, Lisbon, and Antwerp. Yet eighteenth-century Europe was on the verge of a demographic explosion that would soon make it one of the most crowded regions on earth. Around 1650, Europe's population was just 100 million. Europe's population then grew 40 percent over the subsequent century to reach 140 million by 1750, and then another 90 percent to reach 270 million by 1850. Why?

Europe's demographic boom was the consequence of a green revolution that had five major causes. The first was scientific agronomy, including the use of manure and other organic fertilizers, more sophisticated crop rotation, and improved animal husbandry, which is to say the selective breeding of livestock. The second was the Columbian exchange, which brought new crops from America, especially potatoes, which yielded more calories per acre than any crop except rice. Larger, more nutritious harvests in turn allowed European farmers to set aside more of their fields to grow fruits and vegetables, thereby increasing the vitamins in their diet, and to raise fodder for cattle, pigs, and sheep, thereby increasing the protein in their diet. The third was those enclosure movements, especially in England and the Netherlands, which enabled landlords to consolidate larger farms and promote a more efficient raising of crops for the marketplace. As a result, whereas around 1700 it took the labor of some sixty-five people to feed every hundred, by 1800 in northwestern Europe it took the labor of just thirty-five people to feed one hundred. The fourth was the ending of the Little Ice Age and the beginning of a weather cycle in the northern hemisphere that has made the last two hundred and fifty years the warmest on record. Finally, the fifth reason for the European population explosion consisted of the gradual improvements in medicine, midwifery, and sanitation that reduced both

William Hogarth's *Gin Lane* (1751) is a bitter comment on the evils of alcoholism among the poor in the burgeoning cities.

maternal deaths during childbirth and infant deaths from infectious disease. By the end of the eighteenth century inoculation against diseases like smallpox had begun to spread. The bottom line was that Europe's population took off in the eighteenth century, accelerating economic expansion as never before.

More people meant urbanization, and often more squalid slums rife with crime, vice, and vagrancy. Such pathologies were on poignant display in the maudlin paintings of artists such as William Hogarth. Yet however uneven the distribution of wealth among Europeans, the gap between the productivity of European society and those of the Middle East, India, and China rapidly increased. Marxists and other critics of imperialism would later claim that Europeans' prosperity resulted from their exploitation of overseas empires. Fortunes were certainly made from Spanish American silver and gold, West Indies sugar and tobacco plantations, and the Asian commerce in spices, tea, silk, porcelain, and opium, not to mention the profits gleaned by merchants, shippers, investors, and bankers who serviced global trade networks. But people cannot eat silver and gold, or burn tea to keep warm at night, or sew a new coat from tobacco or sugar. Overseas commerce trafficked mostly in luxury goods, goods that European consumers could afford only thanks to the growth of larger, more prosperous markets for those everyday goods they produced at home. Europe's growing population, more productive agriculture, and better science and technology made its farms, mines, and workshops more efficient, and the entrepreneurial investment of profits gained from one sector of the economy boosted production and profits in other sectors.

Rich profits from commerce with American colonies and Asian countries had three other effects. They spurred momentum toward globalization, gave Europeans an incentive to explore the whole globe in search of new opportunities, and provoked a series of wars among European monarchies for overseas empire.

The initial goal of the first Iberian explorers was to reach Asia, and the first to achieve that goal were the Portuguese. But during the 1600s the Dutch conquered Portugal's network of forts around the southern coast of Asia and founded the Dutch East India Company, which monopolized the lucrative spice trade. Soon the British and French East India Companies challenged the Dutch from their own strongholds on the Malabar, Coromandel, and Bengali coastlines of India. The British, in particular, began to import India's high-quality cotton fabrics, many of whose names are still familiar today, including madras, muslin, calico, chintz, and gingham. Englishmen also imported huge quantities of tea, a beverage that quickly became the national stimulant.

In the early decades of globalization Europeans had to purchase Asian goods with specie (precious metals), which was anathema in mercantilist theory. The British therefore gradually learned to mass produce textiles at home. Eventually they needed only to import the cotton. Likewise, the French built their own porcelain factories in hopes of replicating fine Chinese pottery, which they simply called china. Louis XIV even invested in efforts to transplant mulberry bushes and silkworms in France. That did not work so well.

China was both the largest source of luxury goods in the world and the largest potential market for European exports. Alas, China, unlike Calcutta and Singapore, could not be subdued by a few European warships. China was a gigantic empire and ancient civilization whose emperors severely restricted foreign trade and whose people believed they had no need for anything the white barbarians had to sell. As an English merchant put it, the Chinese already had the most perfect food and clothing in the world, rice and silk. Nevertheless, in the fullness of time the British East India Company began to redress the balance of payments by smuggling into Chinese ports huge quantities of opium, which was extracted from poppies grown in British India. By the 1790s the otherwise respectable East India Company had become the largest, most aggressive narcotics syndicate in the world.

Another theater for predatory European competition was the Americas, where the quest for yellow gold gave way to the quest for white gold, or sugar, and ultimately for black gold, those enslaved Africans imported as labor for the plantations. The tropical Caribbean islands of Cuba, Hispaniola, Jamaica, Barbados, Guadeloupe, Martinique, Trinidad, and Tobago were ideal for the growing of sugar cane. But European planters in those West Indian colonies needed large gangs of laborers. At first the Spaniards used Amerindians, but European diseases had killed off many Amerindians by the seventeenth century. The Spaniards—and later the English, French, and Dutch who colonized the West Indies—found an alternative source of labor in West Africa.

For centuries the enslavement of Africans had been the business of Arabs, who purchased prisoners of war captured by various East African kings and then sold them throughout the Middle East. In Europe, slavery had formed the basis of the ancient Roman economy, but it had all but died out during the medieval era and might have remained extinct if the Ottoman Turks in the fifteenth and sixteenth centuries had not begun buying gangs of Africans from the Arabs to work on their island plantations on Cyprus and Crete. Europeans noticed, so when the Portuguese founded their own plantations on the Azores and Canary Islands in the 1400s, they began to purchase African captives from rulers on the coast of northwestern Africa. Within two centuries the Spaniards in Mexico and Peru, the Portuguese in Brazil, and finally all the colonial masters in the Caribbean began to import enslaved Africans. For the first time in more than a thousand years, to the scandal of Christianity, a large sector of Europe's global economy thrived on the basis of chattel slavery.

There is no excusing this commerce. Indeed, the only argument Europeans could mount was the "everybody's doing it" defense—that is, until the late 1700s, when Protestant clergy and enlightened philosophers began to denounce the slave trade. In other words, for two centuries most Europeans were content to ignore, tolerate, or profit directly or indirectly from the plantation system.

The African trade was overwhelmingly an Iberian enterprise. English ships tried to break in but never captured more than 10 percent of the traffic in human beings. By far the largest market for slaves was the Portuguese plantation colony of Brazil, with the next largest being the Caribbean sugar and tobacco islands.

The planters in the thirteen English colonies of North America, by contrast, imported a mere trickle. But the British and, to a lesser extent, the Dutch and the French, developed elaborate commercial networks in which slavery played an integral role.

The triangular network began in European ports from whence slavers sailed south on the strong Guinea current that flows east past the Ivory Coast (today's Côte d'Ivoire), the Gold Coast (now Ghana), and the Slave Coast (now Dahomey and Benin). There the sailors dropped anchor but rarely ventured inland for fear of the jungle, malaria, and hostile natives. Hence this cautionary doggerel: "Beware, beware the Bight of Benin: one man comes out for each ten that go in." How then did Europeans capture Africans? They did not. They purchased them from African rulers who established slave pens on the coast. The rulers also employed black middlemen called "compradors" who "palavered" in "pidgin lingo" with the European captains and factors and exchanged African captives (usually prisoners of war) for cargoes of jewelry, manufactures, guns, and rum. The captives were then marched in manacles into the stinking holds of the slave ships to endure the so-called Middle Passage. Once at sea, the ships turned south to escape the Guinea current and pick up the westerly trade winds that carried them across the Atlantic Ocean.

In South American and West Indian ports the ships unloaded their human cargoes and picked up raw sugar or molasses (liquid sugar) to ship back to Europe or to North American ports, where they took on cargoes of grain, timber, rice, and tobacco and sailed back to Europe. From these Atlantic trade routes lesser networks branched off—for instance, the Baltic Sea trade in which English, French, or Dutch middlemen shipped sugar, coffee, tobacco, and tea to their home markets as well as to wholesalers in Germany, Scandinavia, and Russia in exchange for timber, pitch, handicrafts such as clocks and cutlery, and rye, oats, and other cereals harvested by serfs on the estates of the landed gentry in Prussia, Poland, and Russia.

Thus, much European commerce in the eighteenth century trafficked in commodities produced by forced labor of one form or another, even in regions where slavery or serfdom did not exist locally, such as England's bustling port of Liverpool. Likewise, the French port cities of Nantes and Bordeaux prospered because of the Atlantic commerce, as did Newport, Rhode Island, home base for American slave traders. Not only planters profited, but also shipowners, bankers, marine insurers like Lloyds of London, brokers, wholesalers, and manufacturers who sold goods in the colonies. Nor were Europeans the only ones to benefit; privileged Indian and Chinese merchants and officials also grew wealthy off their trade with Europeans, while local rulers throughout Asia and Africa received copious payments, bribes, and weapons in exchange for collaborating with European merchants. If one wishes to fix blame for this sordid chapter of modern history, there is plenty to go around.

The question must still be asked: How was it that Europeans betrayed their own biblical theology and Enlightenment philosophy, both of which anathematized the outrage that was chattel slavery?

The facile answer one usually hears today is that Europeans were racist, hypocritical, oppressive, and greedy. But what civilization has not displayed such vices whenever it got the upper hand against some despised "other"? The truly interesting historical question is how Europeans justified their exploitation of Africans. The excuse most people made was to say, in effect, "I'm not a slave-trader, I'm just a sailor, or rum merchant, or clerk in a shipping office. Those slavers are rough, ungodly men. I could never do that myself (even though I make my living off those who do)." Another dodge was simply to shrug that the merchants, shippers, and planters had so much political influence in their governments' councils that the institution of slavery could not be challenged.

But the principal justification for the enslavement of Africans was the one to which most people default when they single out a group for oppression, and that is to claim that their victims are not really human at all. Nor is that an atavism of centuries in our distant past. During the wars of the twentieth century the British called the Germans barbarians and depicted them in their war propaganda as bloodthirsty gorillas. Vladimir Lenin called capitalists insects in need of extermination. Adolf Hitler called Jews vermin and the Slavs *Untermenschen* (subhumans). Americans during the Pacific War called the Japanese a nation of fanatical army ants, while the Japanese called Americans hairy white devils.

Still, ugly war propaganda falls into a different category from the dehumanizing of people for the purpose of slavery. And what made such dehumanization perversely necessary in Europe's culture was precisely its Christian and Enlightened principles. Did pagans in ancient Greece and Rome or modern totalitarian regimes need to rationalize slavery? No, because they possessed no moral code that admonished them to do unto others as they would be done by. Christian

Europe *did* have such a code, and it was Christian doctrine and its implications that gradually quickened European consciences—like the one possessed by the English Methodist preacher John Wilberforce, whose crusade against slavery persuaded Parliament to pass the Abolition Act in 1833.

So much for commerce. What about foreign policy? During the early modern era European wars were so frequent that it seems remarkable that peace sometimes broke out. But wars come in different shapes and sizes. In eras when wars are accompanied by ideological hatreds, destructive weapons, and mass armies, they can be devastating to civilians as well as to soldiers and sailors. In eras when wars are waged by small professional armies with their own supply lines—and are waged for limited, material aims—casualties might be low and civilian populations little affected.

Such was the case during the era of the Enlightenment from 1648 to 1789. For following the Peace of Westphalia, which ended the Thirty Years' War in 1648, European monarchs recoiled from the passions of the so-called Wars of Religion and began to exhibit restraint in their pursuit of their *raison d'état*, their "reason of state" or rational self-interest. First, rulers of great powers saw no advantage in ravaging foreign provinces they hoped to annex. Hence their armies ceased to live off the land at the expense of the civilian populace. Second, the state-building monarchies of that era were very cost conscious and often so strapped for cash that they could not afford to wage war on a large scale lest they drain their treasuries. A third reason was technological. Ever since the late medieval era, Europe had been experiencing a so-called renaissance of infantry. The advent of the longbow followed by the gunpowder revolution rendered mounted knights obsolete and regular cavalry vulnerable. Early modern battlefields were therefore characterized by formations of foot soldiers maneuvering and firing their muskets with strict discipline. Likewise, the advent of artillery cannons and mortars, which had rendered medieval castles obsolete, inspired modern fortifications resistant to cannon fire. Louis XIV's chief engineer, Sebastian de Vauban, perfected the mathematical design of forts with thick, slanted walls for defense and jutting parapets to maximize firepower against attacking soldiers. As a result, the fluid campaigns of the Thirty Years' War gave way to tedious sieges of forts by armies supplied by depots placed along their invasion route.

The point was precisely not to ransack the enemy's countryside, while minimizing the drain on one's own economy. As a result of these trends, the wars of that era were fought for the most part by limited numbers of soldiers at limited costs and for limited ends. Hence that era's wars had limited effects, which was one reason why enlightened philosophes dismissed war as irrational. (In retrospect, it became crystal clear that the mercantilist wars of the eighteenth century had enormous effects whose importance cannot be exaggerated. Among those effects were the rise of the British Empire, the birth of the United States of America, and the outbreak of the French Revolution.)

There is no need to go into detail about those complex eighteenth-century wars, but their gestalt helps explain why the French ended up the big losers and the British the big winners. Recall the many wars of Louis XIV, which finally ended in the Peace of Utrecht of 1713. That treaty formalized—in so many words—a European balance of power and ushered in a rare generation of peace. But in 1739 and 1740 a pair of new conflicts erupted and then merged, hurling Europe's great powers into a global conflict one might as well dub World War Zero.

The first conflict was an indirect result of the British smuggling of goods into Spain's New World empire. The Spanish navy alone could not prevent this smuggling, so the authorities in Cuba gave Spanish freebooters—pirates, essentially—license to capture British ships and confiscate their cargoes. British merchants cried foul and lobbied their government for protection, all to no avail until 1739, when a captain named Robert Jenkins displayed his own severed ear—pickled and preserved in a jar—to the members of Parliament at Westminster. Years before, he testified, wicked Spaniards had boarded his ship. His ear had been cut off in the melee. The outraged members of Parliament promptly declared war. (That may sound silly, but large wars have begun over more trivial matters than that.) The Bourbon king of France came to the aid of the Bourbon king of Spain, and another war, the War of Jenkins' Ear, erupted, during which all parties hoped to capture each other's New World colonies.

The second conflict began the following year, 1740, when the Austrian Habsburg emperor Charles VI died without a male heir. Anticipating his death, Charles VI declared a "pragmatic sanction" whereby his daughter Maria Theresa might reign over the Habsburgs' possessions, and he persuaded the other European monarchs to accept it. By coincidence, Prussia's King Frederick

William I also died in 1740. His heir Frederick II claimed not to be bound by the pragmatic sanction. He dispatched an ultimatum to Vienna insisting that Maria Theresa cede to Prussia the rich province of Silesia, in exchange for which Frederick would agree to recognize her rule over the other Habsburg provinces. Maria Theresa was a self-effacing, pregnant twenty-three-year-old. But her reply to Frederick was "Fahr zur Hölle!" (Go to hell). Whereupon the Prussian king soon to be known as Frederick the Great took command of the excellent army his forefathers had bequeathed to him and invaded Silesia.

During this War of Austrian Succession Britain joined Austria's side and France joined Prussia's side. Battles spread throughout central Europe as the land powers fought over various provinces, even as the sea powers waged war for empire in the Americas and even distant India, where the British and French East India Companies clashed. In 1748, the exhausted governments made peace. The only winner was Frederick of Prussia, who managed to hang on to Silesia.

Frederick II was not only the most driven and effective of all the enlightened despots; he was a military genius, as well. He scorned royal pomp and governed like a miserly shopkeeper. He made numerous administrative reforms in Prussia and subjected his judges, bureaucrats, and officers to rigorous tests of competence. And he hired professional accountants to oversee tax collection and oversee a detailed census of his subjects. That census required, among other things, that all inhabitants of the Kingdom of Prussia adopt, for bureaucratic purposes, surnames. It was then that many Johanns and Ludwigs took surnames after the trades of their fathers, such as Bauer (farmer), Müller (miller), Schuster (shoemaker), and Eisenhower (iron monger), while Jewish families chose surnames such as Kaufman (salesman) and Feldman (real estate agent) or else colors like Weiss, Schwartz, Roth, Gruen, Blau, Gelb, Silber, and Gold.

Frederick was also a great builder of roads and canals and an avid promoter of commerce. However, he did not permit his subjects to import luxury goods such as silks, perfume, coffee, tobacco, and sugar, lest Prussian money flow into the pockets of foreign merchants. (Frederick would no doubt spin in his grave if he were informed that today the largest American shopping mall east of the Mississippi River is located in his namesake town of King of Prussia, Pennsylvania.) Finally, when he was not commanding armies in the field, Frederick made a habit of dropping in, unannounced, on the lowliest government offices just to make sure *dass alles in Ordnung ist* (that everything is in order). Most famous was his ringing claim to be "first servant of the state." That astonishing doctrine elevated the state, the public interest, above all else, including the king himself.

Most of all, Frederick, like any shrewd leader of a central European state, paid close attention to foreign relations and strategy because his realm was susceptible to attack from multiple directions. After the peace of 1748 Frederick suspected it was only a matter of time before Austria resumed the struggle for Silesia. War became imminent when Maria Theresa's foreign minister, Count Wenzel Kaunitz, suggested to French King Louis XV that the old rivalry between the Bourbons and Habsburgs no longer made sense, an argument that became especially cogent after King George II of England—in order to defend his own ancestral German province of Hanover—forged an alliance with Prussia in 1756. The Austrian and French governments, shocked by this reversal, hastened to conclude their own military alliance. The Russian Tsarina Elizabeth joined the Franco-Austrian alliance in hopes of conquering territories in Poland.

These moves placed Prussia in terrible danger, and so, in characteristic fashion, Frederick struck first. He invaded the neighboring state of Saxony, which prompted the rulers of Austria, France, and Russia to declare war on Prussia. This European struggle, later known as the Seven Years' War, soon merged with the conflict between Britain and France, whose respective American colonists had begun fighting in the forests of western Pennsylvania in 1754. That conflict was sparked by the decision of Frenchmen from Québec to construct Fort Duquesne at the headwaters of the Ohio River. The English assemblymen in Virginia contested this affront by ordering a young officer named George Washington to march militiamen to the scene. Washington blundered into a battle that quickly escalated into what the English called King George's War and American colonists called the French and Indian War.

The European struggle stretched Prussia's resources to the limit. Year after year, the armies of the coalition breached Prussia's boundaries, forcing Frederick to maneuver desperately. He would never have been able to survive had it not been for the generous subsidies he received from his British allies. But he was short of manpower and territory to yield, and a Franco-Austrian-Russian offensive planned for 1762 seemed certain to capture Berlin, barring a miracle. The miracle occurred when Tsarina Elizabeth suddenly died. Her successor, Tsar Peter III, himself of German descent, happened greatly to admire Frederick of

Prussia. So he abruptly deserted his allies and pulled Russia out of the Seven Years' War. Within months, Peter's ruthless wife, Catherine, conspired with some patriotic Russian aristocrats to have the incompetent (and possibly dimwitted) Peter assassinated, whereupon she took the throne as Tsarina Catherine II. In the meantime Prussia was saved; Frederick held on to Silesia, and Prussia gained recognition as the fifth great power in Europe.

Pendulous swings of fortune also occurred overseas, where two factors proved decisive. The first explains why the French lost; the other why the British prevailed.

In all the mercantilist wars culminating in World War Zero, French armies and navies had been spread perilously thin, for the government insisted on waging land wars in Europe and naval wars overseas at the same time. The British, by contrast, concentrated their ships and men on the colonial theaters they valued most and left to their continental allies, first Austria and later Prussia, to keep the French busy on land. Prime Minister William Pitt even boasted during the Seven Years' War, "We shall conquer North America in Germany."

They did. The climax of the war in North America came in 1759 at the fortress of Québec City, the capital of Nouvelle France, or what would later become Canada. The English General Thomas Wolfe and French General Louis Montcalm dramatically perished in a battle during which the Redcoats captured both Québec and Montréal while the Royal Navy blockaded the St. Lawrence River so no French reinforcements could arrive. That British victory in the final French and Indian War awarded all North America east of the Mississippi River to Britain in a peace treaty signed in 1763.

Finally, the distant struggle for India also reached a climax in the Seven Years' War. The British East India Company, based at Calcutta, and the French East India Company, based at Pondicherry, fielded armies and made alliances with various Hindu nabobs, rajas, ranis, and maharajas. The soldiers of one princely state hurled forty-six British captives into a dungeon, the infamous Black Hole of Calcutta, where they were suffocated. The Anglo-Indian forces commanded by Robert Clive swore vengeance and got it when they routed French forces at the Battle of Pondicherry. The implications were enormous. The French were expelled from India, while the British East India Company would eventually extend its sway over the entire Indian subcontinent until, by the mid-nineteenth century, India had become the jewel in the crown of the British Empire.

Why did French kings and their ministers pursue the futile course of dividing their forces and fighting on so many fronts? Or rather, why did their political system permit the French crown to do so? The answers to those questions are absolute monarchy and . . . absolute monarchy. Under Louis XIII and Cardinal de Richelieu, and then for a long time under Louis XIV, it seemed that France was so rich and populous, and her kings so mighty, that there was no obvious limit to the expansion of French power, especially after 1713, when the Bourbon dynasty took control of the Spanish throne and seemed to make it highly likely that France and Spain would be allies in future wars.

In addition, France appeared to enjoy unique geographical advantages. The kingdom was located on the continent and blessed to have weak neighbors in Italy, western Germany, and the Low Countries. France also enjoyed long seacoasts on the Atlantic Ocean and Mediterranean Sea. So it was that French strategists were tempted to harbor ambitions everywhere. But in fact the French state could not afford so many simultaneous wars because its absolute monarchy perversely limited the tax revenue the crown could collect to pay for them. Remember: no new taxes without calling the Estates General, which the absolute monarchs refused to do. Thus, not only were French ambitions exorbitant; the crown also could not mobilize the full measure of its national strength. To make matters worse, the Bourbons could drag France into a long series of wasteful wars because no parliament or public opinion existed to prevent or correct foolish policies.

In contrast, the British emerged victorious from the Seven Years' War not because of brilliant strategy—British generals usually suffered ugly initial defeats in all the war's theaters—but because of money. Thanks to its parliamentary system and the Bank of England's floating national debt, the British government could tax or borrow as much money as the wars required with the complicity, even approval, of its own population, because the national interest of all British subjects was at stake.

In short, the very different fiscal outcomes of the state-building process in seventeenth-century France and Britain go far to explain their very different geopolitical outcomes during the wars of the eighteenth century. The French crown not only suffered serial defeats; it also emerged from the Seven Years' War bankrupt, and its credit exhausted. No wonder King Louis XV made the forlorn prophecy "Après moi le déluge" (After me the flood).

Competition for Empire

Finally, the grand British imperial victories that culminated in the 1763 Treaty of Paris had an ironic consequence. The British treasury had run up such a large debt bankrolling its war efforts that King George III, his cabinet ministers, the Parliament, the Bank of England, commercial lobbies, and the general public all agreed it was high time that Britain's thirteen American colonies began to pay their fair share of taxes and duties. The American colonists' reaction to Parliament's impositions was, to say the least, less than cordial. So, well before Louis XVI demanded more revenue from his subjects and inadvertently sparked the French Revolution in 1789, George III demanded more revenue from his subjects and inadvertently sparked the American Revolution in 1776.

As Mark Twain famously observed, history may never repeat itself, but often it rhymes.

Chapter 14

Liberty, Equality, Fraternity Betrayed: The French Revolution

The quarter-century that began in 1789 was a time warp during which history was telescoped and a chain reaction of political and social upheavals gave violent birth to an entirely new era. Over those years the French people witnessed their government evolve from an absolute monarchy to a constitutional monarchy to a republic to a dictatorship and at last to an empire. Their nation's erstwhile leaders launched two revolutions, two conservative reactions, numerous coups d'état, four national assemblies, four constitutions, almost continuous wars, and dozens of radical changes that tore up the old regime by its roots.

At first glance the French Revolution may appear to resemble the English Civil War, which occurred some 150 years earlier. In both cases bitter quarrels erupted between a king and a parliament. In both cases the lords and commoners demanded royal accountability and a share of political power. In both cases the king refused, the assembly rebelled, the king lost his head, and the rebellious leaders declared a republic. In both cases a reign of terror ensued. In both cases the republic succumbed to a military dictator.

Despite those similarities, the French Revolution, not the English one, is heralded as the start of a new era. That is because the English Parliament's struggle against the Stuart kings was an episode in the Protestant Reformation and the early modern state-building efforts of Europe's monarchs, and also because it had no echoes beyond the British Isles. The French Revolution, by contrast, gave birth to ideologies the impact of which would be felt throughout the Atlantic basin for the ensuing two centuries. The events in Paris also marked the appearance of "the masses" as a self-conscious and henceforth permanent force in European politics: a display of people power that shattered the confidence of all ruling classes in the stability of any old regime based on deference to privilege, property, and piety.

The French Revolution thus became the acid test for the politicians and historians who came in its wake. Progressives throughout the nineteenth and twentieth centuries tended to applaud the French Revolution, notwithstanding its violent excesses, while Conservatives tended to damn the French Revolution, not least because of its violent excesses. No Frenchman could be neutral about the events that began in 1789, but neither could Englishmen, Germans, Italians, or Spaniards. Indeed, the entire political spectrum of late modern Europe, from far left to far right, can be traced to that turbulent era.

For historians, the greatest debate concerns the revolution's origins. This was not just another tax revolt gone badly. Deep tensions, even hatreds, must have characterized French society to explain the scale of the violence and turmoil. But what were they? Intellectual historians have held that the revolution was inspired by Enlightenment ideas about popular sovereignty and rational reform. After all, such ideas were ubiquitous throughout the Atlantic basin from 1776 to 1848, a fact that led R. R. Palmer to write *The Age of the Democratic Revolution* and Carl Becker to title his chapter on the Enlightenment "How the French Revolution Was Accomplished in Men's Minds Before They Made It the Work of Their Hands."

Alternatively, social historians—especially those influenced by Marxism—have interpreted the events following the uprising of 1789 as a classic bourgeois revolution made by middle-class people determined to abolish the vestiges of feudalism in favor of free-market capitalism. Finally a third, Conservative school inspired by the Anglo-Irish statesman Edmund Burke has viewed the French Revolution as a presumptuous power grab on the part of ideologues who tried to overturn a whole culture by sheer force of will. Their vain and cruel efforts "to force men to be free," in the words of Jean-Jacques Rousseau, destroyed liberty in the name of liberty while drenching Europe in blood and tyranny.

Members of all three interpretive schools can cite evidence for their perspective, but all three can also be rebutted. So perhaps the best way to try to comprehend the mad rush of events is to ask not why the revolution occurred, but why the old regime broke down. The way to begin doing that is to examine what became of the so-called absolute monarchy that was crafted during the reign of Louis XIII, was apotheosized during the reign of Louis XIV, and became exhausted during the reigns of Louis XV and XVI.

From 1614 to the outset of the revolution, the Bourbon kings denied governmental power to the church, nobility, and commoners, refusing even to summon the Estates General into session. That refusal meant that the crown could not levy new taxes, despite the fact that the wealthy nobility were exempt from most existing taxes. However, that blunt statement obscures the fact that all three legal estates had become increasingly heterogeneous over time.

Consider the clergy, of whom there were some one hundred thousand in 1789. They had no political voice, but since France remained Catholic, the church owned vast possessions, perhaps 10 percent of the kingdom's wealth, and it held a monopoly on education. And who were the clerical leaders—the archbishops, bishops, and abbots? Not surprisingly, they were in most cases younger sons of the aristocracy. Thus, there was significant overlap between the first and second estates. Parish priests, by contrast, tended to be drawn from the common folk. Thus, there was significant overlap between the first and third estates as well.

Next, consider the aristocracy, of whom there were some four hundred thousand in 1789. They, too, lacked political power and wanted very much to recover it. But the French *noblesse* were a hodgepodge ranging from proud dukes with ancient lineage (the nobility of the sword), to petty landlords without much status or wealth, to bourgeois social climbers (the nobility of the robe) who had purchased government offices and the noble titles that went with them. Nor were all large landlords aristocrats, for wealthy merchants had acquired chateaux to the point where some twenty percent of rural estates were owned by commoners. Thus, there was also overlap between the second and third estates.

Finally, the third estate, which numbered some 98 percent of all French subjects, included everyone from merchants, lawyers, and doctors to craftsmen in guilds, to prosperous farmers, to landless peasants, to unskilled urban workers called *sans-culottes*, because they wore simple *pantalons*, or trousers, instead of the fashionable *culottes*, or silk breeches, fancied by the rich. Revolutionary

Political cartoon depicting a chained commoner bearing the burdens of the privileged crown, clergy, and aristocracy.

propaganda cast French society as a simple case of the rich and privileged exploiting the poor. But the confusion of social layers complicated the behavior and perspectives of members of the three estates, and all three played key roles in the revolution at one stage or another.

What about the role of financial crisis in bringing about the revolution? Was the royal government really on the verge of bankruptcy? In fact, the French crown's debt in 1789 was just half the size of Britain's! The difference was that the members of Britain's Parliament represented the people, shared power with the crown, and pledged to tax or borrow as necessary to support the government. Britain therefore had a floating national debt based on interest-bearing government bonds that investors could trust. The French monarchy ruled without a parliament and without a legal mechanism to raise taxes. That was the fatal weakness Louis XV acknowledged when he predicted, "Après moi le déluge." Then Louis XVI unleashed the flood by waging a costly war on behalf of Britain's thirteen rebellious colonies in America. That French alliance secured the independence of the new nation called the United States of America. But the cost of the war emptied the royal treasury to the point that France's own bankers—not to mention its foreign creditors—refused to fund any more royal debt unless and until the crown opened its books and came clean. To make matters worse, because several bad harvests had driven food prices sky high, the peasants and urban poor were in a surly mood during the late 1780s.

Even so, it was not the poor who sparked the initial crisis. Rather, French aristocrats unwittingly took the first step toward revolution when they insisted that King Louis XVI summon the Estates General into session for the first time in 175 years.

All French subjects knew that sweeping reforms were needed, and every town had a plan for those reforms—to judge by the scores of *cahiers de doléances* (petitions of grievances) drafted throughout the country. But no sooner did the Estates General convene than delegates fell into a bitter quarrel over procedure. Bourgeois leaders insisted the third estate be given double the delegates of the clergy and nobles, a demand that a sympathetic clergyman, the Abbé Emmanuel Sieyès, supported in a fiery pamphlet called *Qu'est ce que le Tiers état?* (What is the third estate?). The answer, he wrote, is everything, for the clergy and nobility were but parasites on the nation.

The king agreed to double the number of third estate delegates, but he insisted that each estate vote collectively—that is, he insisted that each estate have one vote, in which case the commoners would remain in the minority. The outraged delegates of the third estate bolted the assembly and reconvened at a nearby club, where they issued the Tennis Court Oath and declared themselves a National Assembly determined not to adjourn before they drafted a written constitution for the Kingdom of France. The confused monarch turned for counsel to his family and courtiers, who advised a show of force. The mere rumor that Louis XVI meant to suppress his rebellious subjects provoked panic and anger among the *sans-culottes*. That was the moment when the mob (if one is a Conservative), the people (if one is a liberal), the crowd (if one is a social historian), or the not-yet-class-conscious proletariat (if one is a Marxist) resorted to violence.

On July 14, 1789, thousands of Parisians charged the Bastille, an old royal prison, with the goal of seizing weapons. When the governor explained there were muskets inside, but no gunpowder, the crowd stormed the bastion anyway. The guards resisted, killing nearly a hundred people, but the dispirited governor of the Bastille surrendered, whereupon the outraged mob murdered him in cold blood. The crowd then proceeded to city hall, where its members murdered the mayor of Paris and his bodyguards, impaled their severed heads on pike staffs, and paraded them all over town. Those were the gruesome events that Frenchmen celebrate to this very day, because the violence that occurred on Bastille

Day chastened Louis XVI and obliged him to order his soldiers to remain in their barracks. In the meantime, the National Assembly rapidly seized control of the government.

During those same weeks, the famine in the countryside and false rumors of soldiers imposing martial law sparked a panic known as the Great Fear. Throughout much of rural France, peasants with pitchforks attacked their landlords' chateaux, often looting, burning, and killing men, women, and children of the aristocracy. That disorder prompted the National Assembly to appease the peasants by abolishing their ancient feudal dues and duties, called *banalités*. In a single dramatic night on August 4, 1789, bourgeois delegates, plus a few sympathetic aristocrats who had joined the assembly, rose one by one to move that each of the feudal privileges be abolished and that peasants be given ownership of the fields they tilled.

That night kicked off three years during which the National Assembly rewrote French law from scratch in the name of a trinitarian motto coined by the bourgeois leader Maximilien Robespierre: *Liberté, Égalité, Fraternité!*

The initial phase of the revolution might indeed be termed that of liberty, in that the National Assembly proceeded to pass laws revoking the privileges of the clergy and aristocracy and declaring the rights of man and the citizen, including rights to liberty, property, security, freedom of thought, freedom of religion, and legal due process. The assembly defined liberty as the freedom to do anything not injurious to others. It also defined law as the general will. Thus did the contradictory language of the two strains of the French Enlightenment—Montesquieu's liberal strain and Rousseau's compulsive strain—jointly inspire the revolutionaries.

The assembly also moved to abolish both mercantilist restrictions on trade and the guild system, thereby forging a free-market economy. The assembly abolished the intendants, those royal administrators established by Richelieu, as well as France's historic provinces, substituting for them artificial *départements* of roughly equal size. Virtually the only political institution left standing was the monarchy. But the revolutionary Constitution of 1791 checked the king's power through a legislature to be chosen by the fifty thousand richest citizens. Was that democratic? Of course not, but liberty does not require equality. Indeed, the prevailing opinion throughout the Atlantic world was that only people of property had a serious stake in good government, and therefore that only people of property should enjoy the right to vote.

Finally, the assembly assaulted the church. The Civil Constitution of the Clergy of 1790 confiscated the Catholic Church's property and turned its clergy into state employees, thereby copying what Europe's Protestant princes and kings had done two and a half centuries before. That was a tipping point for Louis XVI, who decided he could no longer tolerate the revolution without endangering his immortal soul.

In June 1791, King Louis, Queen Marie Antoinette, and other members of the royal court slipped out of the Louvre palace in disguise and fled for the frontier. They were recognized by revolutionary border guards at Varennes, just short of the border, and brought back to Paris under house arrest. Most members of the National Assembly took for granted that Louis was conspiring, and would continue to conspire, against them with foreign courts, especially with the queen's Austrian Habsburg relations. Their fear—and the king's hope—was that the Austrian Habsburg army might invade France and suppress the revolution. Such rumors played into the hands of a belligerent faction known as the Girondins. (They were not the most radical party, however. The most radical was the Jacobins, who took their seats at the extreme left wing of the assembly hall, whence originated our modern terminology of the political left and right.) Girondins were more moderate republicans who imagined that a war against Austria would provide occasion for the National Assembly to abolish the monarchy and—not incidentally—propel their own party to leadership. In April 1792, Girondins stampeded the assembly into declaring war on the Austrian Empire.

Revolution tends to follow a script in which measures become ever more extreme, while wars tend to deepen ideological cleavages, inasmuch as dissenters are easily tarred by accusations of treason. The coming of war in the midst of revolution was thus doubly inflammatory, and conditions were made even worse by the pitiful condition of France's finances. Girondins expected to wage war on the cheap—as war parties always do. Their plan was to issue a paper currency called *assignats* backed by wealth to be accrued from the eventual sale of properties seized from the church. But commoners, especially peasants who had no experience with paper money, refused to sell their crops for this funny money. That didn't stop the National Assembly from issuing increasingly exorbitant quantities of paper. Predictably, prices soared, urban workers went hungry, and social tensions threatened to explode, all while panic spread over the prospect of a foreign invasion. Together, these factors pushed the revolution into a second, even more radical phase stressing not liberty, but equality.

In August 1792, recruits for the army streamed into Paris. One detachment from the Mediterranean port city of Marseilles brought with it a marching song that became the anthem of the revolution (and today's French national anthem): "La Marseillaise." These provincials crowded into working-class districts and soon joined the Parisian crowds in perpetrating more bloody riots, during which they massacred the king's Swiss Guards. The *sans-culottes* then set up neighborhood governments, called sections, and forced the assembly to convene a constitutional convention elected by universal male suffrage. Finally, to stamp out all resistance, the sections established "people's courts" that presided over the infamous September Massacres, in which more than a thousand people suspected of treason were convicted and executed.

In the midst of such violence, the convention met—and guess who had a majority? Not the Girondins, who had outsmarted themselves by pressing for war, but the more radical Jacobins. They tried Louis XVI for treason and voted to condemn him to death. On January 16, 1793, the head of Louis XVI rolled off the guillotine. Nine months later—as if an afterthought—the convention executed Marie Antoinette as well. By now the Jacobins and their *sans-culotte* supporters had seized control of Paris and much of the French nation. To relieve the food shortage they dispatched armed patrols to confiscate crops from peasants. Inside Paris, the workers' sections fixed wages and prices and established a primitive form of socialism. The convention's Committee of Public Safety even began to hunt down anyone suspected of counterrevolutionary thoughts, let alone deeds.

The man chosen to lead this revolutionary inquisition was Robespierre, an enigmatic figure who seemed to be both a visionary idealist and a cold-blooded killer. Like Oliver Cromwell, he was scrupulously pure, even puritanical, in his private life. And like Cromwell he meant to forge a society so pure as to be a republic of virtue. But the French first needed to destroy their foreign foes, something the Jacobins' judicial murder of the king and queen rendered improbable. For the shocking regicide only multiplied France's enemies by causing Prussia and Britain to join with Austria in what would be called the War of the First

Coalition. The Jacobins accepted the challenge, in effect declaring war against monarchies throughout Europe.

To mobilize the nation the convention appointed Lazare Carnot as secretary of war. The Organizer of Victory, as he soon would be known, decreed a *levée en masse*, or compulsory military draft. Almost overnight, the French revolutionary armies became the largest and most fanatical in European history, and they defeated the smaller, plodding royal armies time and again.

Meanwhile, Robespierre's domestic Reign of Terror deepened and spread. His Committee of Public Safety became the first and most glaring example of what has since become an ideological euphemism. For this Committee of Public Safety was essentially a committee of one, and there was nothing at all public or safe about it. The Committee revealed the chilling power of wrathful, self-righteous democracy as its agents arrested several hundred thousand people on suspicion of being insufficiently zealous for the revolution. More than forty thousand men and women—nobles, clerics, and commoners—bowed their heads to the committee's guillotine. Robespierre justified the Reign of Terror with the phrase, "There is no liberty for the assassins of liberty" (a slogan Vladimir Lenin would adopt for Russia 125 years later).

Meanwhile, the national convention went to work designing what its radical members considered to be a perfectly rational society. They abolished the Gregorian calendar and began dating years from the birth of the French Republic. They decided that New Year's Day should be the autumnal equinox. They changed the names of the months to reflect the seasons; hence late July-August became Thermidor, because the weather was hot, and late August-September Fructidor, because that was the time of harvest. They abolished the seven-day week in favor of a ten-day week. They tried to eradicate Christianity by promoting the worship of a goddess of virtue and a Deistic "cult of the supreme being." They outlawed all hierarchical distinctions among people and declared that everyone must address each other as *citoyen*, "citizen"—"Citoyen Jacques," "Citoyenne Marie"—and dress and think exactly alike.

Whatever one thinks of these reforms—and several of them, such as the metric system and the decimal system for money, made sense—the fact remained that the human psyche cannot bear to have its world turned upside down overnight. Nor can people put up for long with the anxiety of living up to ever-changing standards of political correctness. So it was that more and more Parisians quietly began to mutter against Robespierre until a majority in the convention itself decided the terror had gone too far. During the so-called Thermidorian Reaction of the year II (July 1794), the convention voted to abolish the Committee of Public Safety and condemn Robespierre *himself* to the guillotine. Thus was born the axiom that revolutions always devour their own children.

Parisians exhaled in relief following the Thermidorian Reaction, and the national convention finally got to work on what it had been elected to do, which was to design a republican form of government. Its constitution of the year III (1795) established a moderate regime, called the Directory, that reaffirmed civil liberties. Since many of the delegates had begun their tenure by voting to execute the king and launching the Reign of Terror, they protected themselves from future prosecution by requiring that a majority of members in the new legislature be composed of holdovers from the convention. That provoked Conservatives and even some royalists to riot in the streets during Vendémiaire (October). The republican leaders, however, displayed the nerve their monarchical predecessors had lacked. The directors deployed in the streets of Paris soldiers whose forty cannons promptly dispersed a crowd of some seven thousand. That was the famous "whiff of grapeshot" commanded by a young artillery officer named Napoléon Bonaparte.

The waves of liberty and equality had now crested and ebbed, which cleared the beach for the third wave: fraternity, the brotherhood of all French citizens against foreign enemies, which is to say, nationalism. Henceforth, the revolutionaries endeavored to turn France right-side-up by turning Europe upside-down.

Nothing cultivates respect for the achievement of America's Founding Fathers more than a study of the French Revolution. The US Constitution, against all odds, founded a stable, orderly, and (except for the Civil War) united republic. Try and try again, the French revolutionaries never achieved that success. The constitution of the year III set up a five-man executive Directory and a bicameral legislature in the hope of preventing another Robespierre from seizing control. Instead, the system only ensured that no one was in control. Over four years various directors conspired against each other, rigged elections, and made coups d'état, while Parisian society indulged in conspicuous consumption and license in a sort of reaction against Robespierre's joyless republic of virtue. During the same years the invincible armies of the French Republic overran Italy, Switzerland, the Netherlands, and the German Rhineland. That combination of military success abroad and political chaos at home set the stage for some hero, some man-on-horseback, to charge into Paris and seize power.

Napoléon was born into a minor noble family on the island of Corsica. He attended French military schools and was commissioned in the army of Louis XVI. Like thousands of talented, ambitious youth, he spied in the revolution a chance for rapid advancement. Indeed, Napoléon's skill, charisma, and sheer audacity were so evident that he won promotion to the rank of brigadier general at the age of just twenty-four. After he had dispersed the royalist mob in October 1795, the directors rewarded him with command of the republic's armies in Italy, which quickly defeated the Austrian army. He then began to make political contacts and to boost his own image as a hero who stood above politics. In 1798 Napoléon sailed with an army to Egypt to try to cut Britain's imperial lifeline to India. During that romantic campaign the French defeated Arab Mamelukes in the Battle of the Pyramids, and archaeologists accompanying the French army discovered such ancient Egyptian treasures as the Obelisk and Rosetta Stone, whose inscriptions in Demotic, Greek, and ancient Egyptian enabled scholars to begin to decipher the mysterious hieroglyphs of the Pharaohs. Alas, the strategic campaign aborted when a British fleet commanded by Admiral Horatio Nelson either sank or captured all the French warships and transports off the Egyptian coast.

Despite that setback Napoléon remained popular. What catapulted him into power was a devious plot hatched by Abbé Sieyès, the same man who had written "What is the third estate?" back in 1789. The abbé planned to seize power himself, but he figured that he needed a heroic front man. So he sent Napoléon a secret summons that caused him to desert his army and furtively sail back to France. Sieyès persuaded the directors to put Napoléon in command of the Paris army garrison, then gave the general the go-ahead to invade the legislative assembly and expel its members. Sieyès's plan was to establish an authoritarian regime led by three consuls—a triumvirate in imitation of the ancient Roman Republic—and he expected to call the shots himself. Instead, the brash young general played the role of Julius Caesar. Napoléon seized control of the capital on 18 Brumaire (November 9, 1799) and decreed the constitution of the year VIII, already the fourth revolutionary constitution, which made him first consul for life. The Parisian crowds, which had previously cried out for liberty and equality, now cheered the man on horseback who personified fraternity.

How did he do it? Aside from his personal charisma, which certainly helped, Napoléon took and maintained power by elevating nationalism into a sort of civil religion—much needed in a nation whose citizens no longer imagined themselves as members of an estate, or as inhabitants of a province, or as subjects of a king, but rather as citizens of a nation marching against all those other nations which refused to be liberated. (In fact, the word *chauvinist* is derived from the name of Nicolas Chauvin, a zealous French revolutionary whose contempt for foreigners became legendary.) Charisma, nationalism, and Napoléon's policy of championing law and order at home and glorious conquests abroad—that combination is what enabled the general's meteoric rise from a humble, provincial, half-Italian boyhood to the pinnacle of power.

On December 25, 1799—no longer Christmas Day but rather 4 Nivôse, or fourth day of the snowy month—Napoléon became first consul. The captain of the palace guard asked the general to choose the prompt and password for the day. Bonaparte replied, "Frédéric Deux . . . et Dugommier." That exercise in free association spoke volumes. Frédéric Deux was Frederick II, the Prussian king who exercised absolute power but governed according to enlightened principles. Jacques Dugommier was a zealous general in the republican army. Thus in a literal sense did *rational authoritarianism* and *revolutionary militarism* become the watchwords of Napoléon's epoch. Some historians have even suggested that Napoléon ought not to be considered the first modern dictator, but rather the last enlightened despot.

Regardless, the first consul soon went about imposing order—everywhere. He preserved the revolutionary division of France into eighty-three *départements*, placing at the head of each a prefect who took his orders from the minister of the interior, who in turn took his orders from Napoléon. He crushed all dissent, be it royalist, republican, clerical, or regional, while also issuing a general amnesty dating back to 1789. He chose ministers and officers from all social classes and promoted them on the basis of talent. He kept those revolutionary reforms which seemed sensible, such as the calendar and metric system, but made peace with the church through a papal concordat signed in 1801.

His most influential and lasting reform was the Napoleonic Code. Civil, criminal, and commercial law in France had become a shambles, because the old royal legal code plus many revolutionary statutes were simultaneously on the books. Napoléon appointed a battalion of lawyers to sift through them and draft a uniform code, which his armies then spread throughout western and central Europe, regions where Roman or Germanic law codes had prevailed for fifteen hundred years.

The source of Bonaparte's power, and often the object of his reforms, was military efficiency. Eighteenth-century warfare had been characterized by relatively small armies, limited violence, and little disturbance to civilian populations. The French Revolution "revolutionized" warfare through four innovations. The first dated from the last years of the old regime, when French armories experimented to improve the range and accuracy of cannons and devised tactics based on concentrated artillery fire. Bonaparte mastered those tactics. Instead of ordering infantrymen to make costly charges against enemy lines, he would mass his cannons and unleash withering barrages at some weak point in the enemy line. While the stunned enemy was still reeling from the bombardment, Bonaparte would hurl his cavalry through the gap to create havoc in the enemy's rear. Only then would he order columns of foot soldiers forward to crush the demoralized enemy. That devastating combination of shock, mobility, and mass was never effectively countered by France's enemies until very late in the Napoleonic Wars.

The second innovation was Carnot's *levée en masse*, which allowed the French to field not one but several armies as large as or larger than those of its enemies. In addition, the revolutionary élan, or morale, of the French soldiers struck fear in the hearts of their adversaries, not unlike the Confederate rebel yell in the American Civil War.

The third innovation was Napoléon's policy of promotion based on merit, not on accidents of birth or political connections. Napoléon liked to boast that in his army "every private soldier carries a Marshal's baton in his knapsack."

The fourth innovation was a logistical system that enabled the French to supply as many as eight hundred thousand soldiers and sailors at once. Napoléon first mobilized the home front for this purpose. Abroad, his armies lived off the land—but without pillaging it. Instead, Napoléon's logistics officers would requisition what amounted to tribute from captured towns and provinces. Thus, the French might occupy some city in Germany and announce to the *Burgermeister*, "Congratulations, you have just been liberated by the army of the Revolution, in gratitude for which you will deliver by next month a thousand bushels of grain, two hundred cattle, and enough boots for a regiment. I understand your shoemakers are renowned for their craftsmanship." Some economic historians have suggested that this tribute system damaged the long-term economic growth of the continent. They contrast it with the British system of military procurement, which awarded contracts to the lowest bidder and thus incentivized efficiency. Perhaps, but even so, the combination of these four innovations made French armies nearly invincible from 1792 until 1812, during which time they frustrated every coalition the monarchies formed against them.

There is no need to delve into a detailed narrative of the Napoleonic Wars, except to observe that they were the first ideological wars during which no truce, no compromise peace, was possible. Napoléon, a usurper and revolutionary, could not live in peace with Europe's legitimate monarchs any more than the monarchs could tolerate a revolutionary in their midst. In any event, Napoléon achieved law and order at home by giving the French people glory and plunder abroad, so continuous conquest became necessary. As he told the Austrian minister Klemens von Metternich when the latter proposed a compromise peace, "Your monarchs can be defeated a hundred times and still return to their thrones. I cannot do that. I am a self-made soldier."

For that reason, the wars dragged on. They also dragged on for the simple reason that neither side was able to win. Napoléon defeated the land powers—Austria, Prussia, and Russia—time and again, but he could never subdue the sea power, Britain. Finally, the wars continued because Napoléon's ambition grew with his conquests. During the 1790s French officers carried copies of the Declaration of the Rights of Man and the Citizen in their kits in the sincere belief that their soldiers were agents of liberation for people across Europe. German philosopher Georg Wilhelm Friedrich Hegel hailed Napoléon as the embodiment of the *Zeitgeist* (spirit of the age), while Ludwig van Beethoven dedicated a symphony to him. But over time Napoléon came to imagine himself less an enlightened revolutionary than a new Julius Caesar. Whereas the French revolutionary armies had created sister republics in Italy, Switzerland, the Netherlands, and the Rhineland, Napoléon simply annexed those countries to the French Empire or made puppet states of them. For instance, he created an artificial kingdom of Italy and made himself king. He abolished the Holy Roman Empire and fashioned a puppet state called the Confederation of the Rhine.

He put his own brothers and cousins on various thrones as if he were *capo di tutti capi*—the boss of all bosses—of an international mafia. Most disillusioning for his early admirers, Napoléon assumed the title of emperor in May 1804 in imitation of Charlemagne a thousand years earlier . . . except for the fact that Napoléon grabbed the crown from the pope's hand, faced the assembly of notables, and placed it on his own head.

Ultimately, Napoléon's power could not match his expanding ambitions. Like the Bourbon kings before him, he pursued land and sea dominance at the same time. On two occasions he built expensive fleets to invade England, only to see them destroyed by Horatio Nelson's Royal Navy. Thereafter he resorted to economic war against Britain. Following his decisive victories over Austria and Prussia in 1806, and after concluding a truce with Russia in 1807, Napoléon imposed a "continental system" by which the French forbade all continental Europeans from importing British manufactures. He expected the "nation of shopkeepers" to soon beg for peace. Instead, the British imposed a counter-blockade on Napoléon's empire, while Russia—the only land power the emperor had not yet occupied—began to grow restless. The Russian nobility feared that revolutionary ideas might spread among their serfs. Russian merchants resented Napoléon's embargo on foreign trade. Finally, Tsar Alexander I considered Napoléon a parvenu and usurper, and in 1810 he pulled Russia out of the continental system, a defection which gave the British new hope.

At length an angry Napoléon concluded that the only way to persuade the British to give up was to conquer Russia and thus remove Britain's last hope of a continental ally. He spent the next year assembling the largest army Europe had ever seen, and in 1812 he hurled it into the depths of Russia. That fatal decision lowered the curtain on the telescoped time warp that had begun with the outbreak of the French Revolution. And it raised the curtain on an entirely new era, an era known to historians as late modern Europe.

Chapter 15

A World Restored:
The Birth of Conservatism and Liberalism

O pleasant exercise of hope and joy!
For mighty were the auxiliars which then stood
Upon our side, we who were strong in love!
Bliss was it in that dawn to be alive,
But to be young was very Heaven!

Thus did the romantic English poet William Wordsworth recall the ecstasy his youthful cohort felt when first its members heard of the French Revolution's Declaration of the Rights of Man and the Citizen. In the revolution's initial phase the revolutionaries proclaimed liberty, and it seemed for a season as if humanity was soaring—much like the Montgolfier brothers' hot air balloons, whose aerial demonstrations awed Parisian crowds in 1783. But alas, the revolution soon took sick, suffered fevers of terror and war, then died under martial law imposed by a conqueror who plunged Europe into continual war and turned all the continent into his family's personal fief.

By 1812, when Napoléon Bonaparte's *grande armée* invaded Russia, Europeans had endured twenty-three years of revolution and war. *That* must be the starting point for anyone seeking to understand the reaction against the ideas of the French Revolution in favor of some sort of restoration of the old regime. The second fact to be kept in mind is that the era ended only when the armies of the Russian, Prussian, Austrian, and British monarchies prevailed over Napoléon's army and empire. To be sure, those allied powers differed among themselves—simply contrast parliamentary Britain with autocratic Russia—but each of the victorious governments shared a stake in the goals of suppressing radical ideas, restoring a balance of power, and replacing the rule of force with the rule of law.

Revolution and war: the relationship between those two sorts of organized violence was critical to nineteenth-century Europeans, for the train of events after 1789 seemed to have proven both that revolution breeds war and that war spreads revolution. The widespread belief that domestic and international repose had become indivisible inspired the governments of the great powers to convene a grand peace conference at Vienna in 1814 in order to attempt, for the first time in European history, to institutionalize the peaceful resolution of international conflicts. Nor was it anomalous that this experiment was undertaken by Conservative governments. Future historians of a liberal or Marxist persuasion would come to lament the vain efforts of royal and imperial governments to stamp out democratic and nationalist ideas. But to the monarchs, aristocrats, and, for that matter, disillusioned commoners of Europe, the French Revolution had bred chaos, not progress, and must not be permitted to happen again.

In the end, restoration of the old regime could never be thorough or permanent because the ideological genii could not be put back in the bottle. The French Revolutionary trinity lived on to exert decisive influence on European intellectual and political life. From *liberté* sprang liberalism; from *égalité* sprang democracy and socialism; from *fraternité* sprang nationalism; and from opposition to all the above sprang a novel anti-ideology known as Conservatism (with a capital C). This chapter will define those "isms," but its first order of business is to rush Napoléon off the stage and examine what historian and statesman Henry Kissinger (in titling one of his books) would call "a world restored."

The 1812 invasion of Russia was an act of enormous hubris, and hubris, as the ancient Greeks taught, is always followed by nemesis. Napoléon's *grande armée* fought two bloody battles at Smolensk and Borodino and managed to occupy Moscow in September. But contrary to Bonaparte's expectations, neither Tsar Alexander I nor Russia's boyars (the landed nobility) nor even the abject serfs

Austria's foreign minister, the wily Prince Klemens von Metternich (Thomas Lawrence, *Portrait of Prince Metternich*, 1815).

in Russia's army considered surrender. Instead, a mysterious fire erupted in the mostly wooden city of Moscow and burned most of its buildings to the ground. After five weeks, as Russia's brutal winter set in and partisan bands of Cossacks and tsarist cavalry attacked Napoléon's flanks, the French army was obliged to retreat. A cholera epidemic did even more damage. By the time its beleaguered remnants reached Poland, just one-sixth of the six-hundred-thousand-strong *grande armée* had survived.

Prior to his invasion of Russia, Napoléon had obliged his surly allies, Prussia and Austria, to support the war. He deployed their armies to guard the French army's flanks. By December 1812, with the French in full retreat, Prussia's king turned coat and declared a war of German liberation. The moment seemed charmed. If Austria also switched sides, the monarchical coalition might sweep across Europe and invade France before Bonaparte could raise a new army. But the Habsburg Emperor Francis II hesitated for some very good reasons. First, following the latest Austrian military defeat in 1809, Napoléon had bullied Francis into giving him the hand of the Habsburg princess Marie Louise in marriage, which meant Bonaparte was now the emperor's son-in-law. If Francis helped destroy the French Empire he would thereby consign to limbo both his daughter and his grandson (born in 1811). Second, the Austrian court was alarmed by Prussia's call for a *national* war of liberation because the multinational Habsburg empire was just as threatened by German nationalism (not to say Hungarian, Czech, Polish, or Italian nationalism) as it had been by French nationalism. The Austrian Empire's true interest was to suppress national feelings, not encourage them. Third, too sudden a victory over the French would enable the Russian army to occupy much of Europe, thereby threatening to replace a French hegemony with a Russian hegemony.

Thus, Austria's foreign minister, the wily Prince Klemens von Metternich, negotiated with Bonaparte to learn if he would accept peace terms with which the allies could live. Then he negotiated with the Russians and Prussians in order to restrain them to war aims that would restore a conservative balance of power both in Germany and in Europe at large. Napoléon refused to talk peace. He feared that any admission of defeat would break his spell over the French people. Hence the Austrians' delaying tactics gave Bonaparte time to raise a fresh army, with which he halted the Russian and Prussian advance in central Germany. Only after that 1813 campaign ended in deadlock did the rulers of Russia and Prussia accept Metternich's demands for moderate, conservative war objectives. That deal drew Austria into the war in August.

The following spring the allied armies resumed their offensive. In March 1814 they crossed the French border, whereupon Britain's Foreign Secretary Lord Castlereagh crossed the English Channel to engage the continental powers in negotiations over eventual peace terms. The result was the Treaty of Chaumont, which forged a permanent Quadruple Alliance among Prussia, Russia, Austria, and Britain to ensure the French made no mischief in the future. The diplomats also agreed to pursue a peace that would restore the independence of Spain, Switzerland, and various Italian states and to merge Holland and Belgium into a United Netherlands. As for Germany, not even the Austrians tried to restore the defunct Holy Roman Empire, but the great powers did agree that nationalism should not be allowed to triumph there.

The most immediate question was what to do with France after Napoléon abdicated his throne that April. The vengeful Prussians wanted to punish the enemy, but Castlereagh argued for a mild peace in order to placate the French. So the allies agreed to restore France to its 1792 boundaries, to exact no financial indemnity, and to restore the Bourbon pretender King Louis XVIII on condition that henceforth he share power with an elected assembly. Last but not least, they consigned Napoléon to exile on the island of Elba off the Italian coast.

A World Restored

Emperor Francis II then hosted the greatest diplomatic gathering in European history—the Congress of Vienna—in hopes of restoring legitimacy: domestic legitimacy in the sense that most of the dynastic rulers would be restored to their thrones, and international legitimacy in the sense that the five great powers would pledge to act unanimously through treaties rather than force.

The five statesmen who put Humpty-Dumpty together again were Metternich, Castlereagh, Tsar Alexander, Friedrich von Hardenberg (Prussia), and Charles Maurice de Talleyrand (France). Together they solved the German problem by merging most of its three hundred principalities into thirty-four larger ones to be united, for defensive purposes only, into a union called the *Deutscher Bund* (German Confederation). In addition, after some tense debate, they agreed to a territorial settlement that kept Russia from becoming too strong (the tsar had wanted to annex all of Poland) and kept Prussia from becoming too strong in Germany (the king had wanted to annex all of Saxony). The result was a stable balance of power in which none of the great powers would be tempted, much less able, to dominate the continent as the French had done for the past twenty years.

The allied diplomats were still meeting in Vienna when they were reminded why they had sought unanimity in the first place. Napoléon had escaped from Elba, had landed in France, had mobilized his veterans, and was trying to begin all over again. The restored Bourbon king—the feckless, obese Louis XVIII—did not try to resist. He just boarded his oversized royal carriage and fled into exile. Napoléon then drove his resurrected army toward Brussels, where he intended to defeat the Prussians and British before the Austrians and Russians could march across the continent. But a Prussian army commanded by Marshal Leberecht von Blücher and an Anglo-Dutch army commanded by Arthur Wellesley, the Duke of Wellington, withstood the frantic French assaults near the village of Waterloo in June 1815. Napoléon abdicated a second time, after which the allies declared him an enemy of mankind and exiled him to St. Helena, a rocky isle in the South Atlantic Ocean. There Napoléon would die in 1821 despite (or because of) the ministrations of his British doctors.

The Russian army arrived too late for the Battle of Waterloo, but Tsar Alexander took the occasion to add one more stone to the foundations of peace. He called on his brother monarchs to forge a Holy Alliance devoted to Christian love and peace among nations. The British and French governments declined.

Indeed, Castlereagh called the idea "high-minded nonsense," asking how love could be translated into political terms. But the Austrian emperor and Prussian king joined the Holy Alliance, which became in practice a union among the three most autocratic great powers to preserve the status quo.

All told, the Congress of Vienna planted five pillars of peace. The first was legitimacy, the principle by which the great powers unanimously agreed to uphold the monarchical order in Europe and the territorial settlements made in 1814–15. The second was the balance of power. The third was the Quadruple Alliance, meant to deter the French from future mischief. The fourth was the Holy Alliance against godless revolution. And the fifth was a "concert" system of diplomacy called the Concert of Europe, for prior to leaving Vienna the diplomats pledged to reconvene whenever crises arose and to collaborate for peaceful resolutions.

In practice, the Vienna system's overall impact was to retard progressive reforms as well as violent revolutions. Perhaps that wasn't ideal, but the five pillars of peace also permitted the great powers to preserve peace among themselves for nearly four decades—and to prevent another general war for a whole century. Compared to the constant warfare that blighted the old regime, that was a phenomenal record.

So much for international politics. What about those domestic ideologies that were so important to nineteenth-century intellectual, social, and political history? They included such familiar ideologies as Liberalism, socialism, nationalism, and Conservatism in politics, romanticism and realism in culture, and industrial capitalism in economics. The only complication was that some of those "isms" did not mean then what they came to mean in the later nineteenth, let alone twentieth, century. For instance, it would later become de rigueur to describe liberals as people who favor a larger, more interventionist government devoted primarily to social welfare, economic regulation, and peaceful foreign policies. But in the early to mid nineteenth century, classical Liberals (with a capital L) were people who favored small government, self-reliance, and free-market capitalism. Such classical Liberals were opposed by Conservatives, especially elites within the Holy Alliance powers, who abhorred all ideologies and upheld traditional hierarchies and privileges—in other words, the sorts of people who approved of the Congress of Vienna's restoration of aristocracy and monarchy.

That will become less confusing to readers if they keep in mind that during the 1800s Liberal reformers opposed the traditional privileges of their monarchies, aristocracies, and established churches. Over time, through reforms and moderate revolutions, Europeans would succeed in making classical Liberal principles and institutions dominant in Britain and influential in France, Italy, and Germany. That meant that old-fashioned Conservatives gradually became extinct in western and central Europe. Classical Liberals then became the new conservatives. They were in turn challenged by radicals who opposed both aristocracies and liberal capitalists. Put simply, the entire political spectrum would gradually shift to the left over the course of the later nineteenth and early twentieth centuries.

Readers must purge from their minds present-day notions about political ideologies and try instead to visualize the way nineteenth-century Europeans responded to the great engines of change in their era, especially the French and Industrial revolutions. Put yourself in the place of a king, an aristocratic landlord, a clergyman, a middle-class merchant, a craftsman, an unskilled laborer, a farmer, or a wife or daughter whose family belonged to those groups, and try to imagine how you might have reacted to new political notions, social movements, and industrial technologies. Then you may understand how change of any sort could either pose a threat to people's lives or offer the promise of a better life. The next chapter will examine the threats and promises posed by the Industrial Revolution. The remainder of this one will examine how the political ideologies bequeathed by the French Revolution shaped the course of events down to the watershed year of 1848.

Liberty is perhaps both the most used and least understood concept of modern times. Everyone extols liberty or freedom, but what is it, and how can it be established, preserved, and expanded through institutions and laws? Those questions had been major concerns of the enlightened philosophes of the eighteenth century. Were human beings naturally free in the state of nature, but enslaved by society? If human beings were naturally "at liberty," was that a blissful state or a chaotic and insecure one? Were human beings not at all free in the state of nature, but only became free once they banded together to protect their rights? The American Founding Fathers, who drank deeply from the wells of philosophy and history, concluded that all people had natural rights to life, liberty, and the pursuit of happiness, but also that such rights were fragile in the absence of legal and moral order. Hence their design of elaborate checks and balances on government power.

Whereas liberty was a common theme in the writings of eighteenth-century philosophes, the political usage of the word *liberal* derived from a specific, indeed surprising episode: the revolt against Napoléon's occupation of Spain in 1808. Moderate constitutionalists who hoped to found a parliamentary monarchy in Madrid began to call themselves *liberales*, whereupon the term gradually spread throughout northwestern Europe. To be liberal, or a Liberal, meant to be a person who promoted human rights, constitutional government, private property, a free market, the rule of law, and equality before the law. What did classical Liberals oppose? Absolute monarchy, inherited privilege, established churches, and mercantilist economics. Liberals did not have to be full-on libertarians, but they did tend to maximize space for individual choice. The British Liberal Party, founded in the 1830s, was the most famous of Liberal reformist parties, but besides Spain Liberal movements also arose in France, Germany, and Italy.

If one had to choose a single definition of this ideology, a good one might be that of the Frenchman Benjamin Constant: "Liberty is every man's right to be subject to the law alone." That is, no one should be either above the law or beneath it. All persons should be equal in the eyes of the law. Notice that Constant said nothing about what laws should be enacted or how laws should be made. In practice, classical Liberals favored representative government of some sort, but almost none of them favored democracy, fearing that it would invite mob rule, the rise of demagogues, tyrannies of the majority, and legalized theft, should the poor learn to exploit majority rule in order to plunder the rich. Indeed, early nineteenth-century Liberals thought democracy to be as dangerous to liberty as autocracy. In short, liberalism emerged as a revolt against privilege. Liberals thought there should be no special law courts for the clergy or nobility, no tax exemptions for anyone, no religious tests for public office, no jobs or promotions based on birth or connections, no limits to social mobility based on talent and hard work. To nineteenth-century Liberals, a society without those obnoxious features might truly be free.

The proper goal of government, for Liberals, was simply to uphold and enforce the rule of law, using whatever police, judges, and occasional soldiers were deemed necessary to that end. Beyond that, government had little else it must do, because any state that got more than minimally involved in economic and social policy must inevitably treat its citizens unequally. That is, governments might collect taxes from some groups of people in order to spend those funds in ways that benefited other groups. As Thomas Jefferson famously said, "That government is best which governs least." Indeed, classical Liberals needed only to invoke the history of the old regime and French Revolution to justify their fear that activist governments tended to institutionalize privilege and/or violate people's rights.

As political goals, liberty and equality existed in dynamic tension. A Liberal regime implied that people should be free to find their own level in society, even if equality of treatment inevitably yields inequality of results. For the undeniable fact is that all human beings are *not* created equal, that indeed all human beings are individuals demonstrably *different* in appearance, intelligence, strength, health, wealth, talent, ambition, education, and personal qualities such as courage, compassion, and character. Hence the state cannot make people more equal except by treating them *unequally* through taxation and legislation that redistributes wealth, imposes quotas, or legalizes discrimination.

Wait a minute, one might object, what about fairness? Should not the state provide for widows, orphans, and the impoverished, even if that means taxing or otherwise penalizing the privileged? Should not a just society try to expand the freedom of the many, even if it limits somewhat the freedom of the few? Perhaps so. That is a value judgment every electorate must make for itself through its political institutions. But classical Liberals opposed to the aristocratic privileges of the restoration regimes were concerned above all with reducing, not increasing, the impact of government. Moreover, they justified inequality of results in a free-market system by the maxim that people ought ultimately to be judged not on what they achieved, but on what they achieved with what they had—that is, given the advantages or handicaps they inherited from their parents. Liberals believed in equality before the law, not in any intrinsic right to a measure of wealth, power, or prestige.

The so-called restoration era or Metternichian era from 1815 to 1848 is often characterized as a time when Europe's monarchies repressed Liberal ideas. That was certainly true in Russia, and it was largely true in the German Confederation. The so-called Carlsbad Decrees of 1819 imposed strict censorship in the

German states, forbade free speech and association, and granted the Prussian and Austrian monarchies power to intervene against any movements deemed seditious. Even in comparatively Liberal Britain, a mass working-class protest was put down by the army in the infamous 1819 Peterloo massacre, which in turn prompted Parliament to pass the Riot Acts limiting free speech and association. Yet during those same years Prussia's otherwise authoritarian government became a *Rechtstaat*, a state based on the rule of law and equality before the law. The Prussian government also established a system of mass primary education that became a model for other countries. The Prussian ministry of finance even adopted free-market policies to stimulate economic growth, including a *Zollverein*, or customs union, that merged the Prussian economy with those of many other German states.

Nor did the ideas that had inspired the first liberal phase of the French Revolution die out in France, the country where they were born. On the contrary, the French bourgeoisie and working class made another, much more moderate, revolution in 1830 that ousted the Bourbon dynasty once and for all in favor of a constitutional monarchy under the Orleanist King Louis Philippe. He became known as the "bourgeois monarch," because his regime broadened suffrage, expanded the powers of the legislature, and promoted free-market economic policies according to the motto *Enrichissez-vous* (Enrich yourselves).

By far the most striking triumphs of classical Liberalism occurred in Great Britain, where the Reform Bill of 1832 enfranchised most of the middle class and reapportioned parliamentary districts to represent the population more fairly. Then in 1846, the now middle-class-dominated Parliament voted to abolish the Corn Laws, or tariffs imposed on imported foodstuffs, which is to say duties designed to protect the home market for England's gentlemen farmers. Abolition of those tariffs was a signal triumph for manufacturers and merchants, who benefited from free trade with other countries, as well as for the working class, for whom a competitive market meant lower food prices. Yet every Liberal achievement encouraged impatient people among the middle and lower classes to demand further reforms. That impatience waxed for decades until, in 1848, it would explode.

Equality, the second rubric in the French revolutionary trinity, could either mean political equality, as in democracy, or economic equality, as in socialism. At the time, both notions of equality were considered radical, and both were at odds with classical Liberalism. Equality had been given alarming expression in the Jacobin Reign of Terror from 1792 to 1794, when everyone was forced to conform to the French Republic's ideological dictates. Yet even Jacobins shrank from bestowing equal rights upon women, and they absolutely rejected socialism. Needless to say, following the French Revolution nearly all aristocrats, bourgeois liberals, and landowning peasants anathematized socialism as a negation of property rights and a sure path toward tyranny. Nonetheless, *political* democracy survived as an ideal, because it seemed to some intellectuals to be the inevitable outcome of representative government. For once a regime embraced popular sovereignty and granted some of its people the right to vote for their leaders, where might it draw the line? Residents whose wealth did not quite meet the property test for suffrage were certain to agitate for a lowering of the bar, whereupon people just below the new line were certain to call for another lowering of the bar, and so on until all adult males, at least, were granted the vote. That issue would become a major cause of the 1848 revolution in France. It was also an issue that political theorist Alexis de Tocqueville analyzed in his 1835 classic, *Democracy in America*.

Democratic ideas gained traction in England, too, where urban workers launched a prodigious reform movement called Chartism in the 1840s. The Chartists demanded a reform bill that expanded the franchise, plus a written constitution for the United Kingdom. By then a few advanced thinkers such as John Stuart Mill were arguing for women's suffrage as well.

Mill notwithstanding, most classical Liberals, plus all Conservatives, harbored fears that political democracy must eventually lead to demands for social democracy and the forced redistribution of property. Their fears were not groundless. Socialist ideas gained traction during the 1830s and '40s. The first socialists were called utopians. They believed people might be persuaded, out of the goodness of their hearts, to live in communes where all property, work, and profits were held in common. The futility of their dream seemed to be proved when the experimental communities founded by English and Scottish socialists inspired by Robert Owen, by French socialists inspired by Henri de Saint-Simon, and a smattering of others turned out to be embarrassing flops. Nevertheless, during the 1840s two German socialists named Karl Marx and Friedrich Engels devised a philosophy of history which purportedly proved that socialism was not an unrealistic utopian dream but rather the inevitable consequence of social and technological progress. They called their philosophy "scientific socialism." Future chapters will devote ample attention to the impact of Marxist ideology on European social and intellectual history within the context of the Industrial Revolution.

The third and final ideology born in the French Revolution was fraternity—nationalism—which would prove in the middle and long run to be far and away the most powerful. Why that was so is not hard to grasp. Nationalism had enormous appeal because it did not *divide* societies into competing individuals or competing social classes, but instead *united* societies by stressing their common ethnicity, language, and history. The French Republic had declared that sovereignty rested in the nation and that people were now citizens of a nation, not subjects of a king. However, the principle of popular sovereignty did not imply democracy any more than Liberalism implied equality. Compare the title assumed by Louis XVI with the title assumed by Napoléon. Louis was king simply because France was a historic kingdom by law and tradition. But when Napoléon crowned himself, he did not take the title of king of France or even emperor of France. He quite consciously assumed the title "emperor of the French," thereby acknowledging that he reigned in the name of the sovereign French people. Thus did Napoléon claim to embody French nationalism. By contrast, Prussia's King Frederick William II, who summoned all Germans to join a war of liberation, certainly appealed to nationalism in so doing, but being a traditional king, he did *not* believe in popular sovereignty. The Napoleonic Wars stirred the nationalism of the British people, too, but Britain's political system was Liberal, and her people's loyalty was directed to their own royal family.

In other words (and this is important), nineteenth-century nationalism might or might not be compatible with other ideologies. It was a force all to itself. Nationalism might be a threat to monarchy, as in the multiethnic Habsburg Empire, or nationalism might be exploited by monarchy, as in England and Prussia. Nationalism might reinforce popular movements for freedom and equality, or it might be invoked to suppress popular movements. Nationalism was protean, a mighty, unpredictable power.

After 1815, nationalism naturally appealed to those ethnic groups to whom history had denied unity or independence—for instance, the Italians and Germans, whose lands had been divided and fought over by other nations for centuries. Nationalism was also strong among those peoples who had been absorbed by a larger empire, such as the Hungarians and Czechs inside the Habsburg Empire, Poles in the Russian Empire, and Greeks, Serbs, and Romanians in the Ottoman Empire. Sure enough, the lands of all these peoples became hotbeds of revolutionary agitation during the nineteenth century.

Which leads back to where this chapter began: Conservatism, the new political philosophy that opposed all the ideologies born of the French Revolution and thereby really amounted to an anti-ideology. The simplest definition of a Conservative is someone who knows that things could be worse than they are: *period*. The French Revolution provided ample evidence that human efforts to make everything better can perversely make everything worse. Edmund Burke, the Anglo-Irish statesman who damned the presumption of the French revolutionaries, was a Liberal Whig in the context of parliamentary politics. But he earned the epithet "Father of Conservatism" by dint of his 1790 treatise, *Reflections on the Revolution in France*. What the French were attempting, Burke argued therein, was extremely dangerous. For, unlike the English in 1688 or the American colonists in 1776, the French revolutionaries were not invoking their traditional rights against an abusive regime. They were attempting to eradicate all inherited traditions in order to design something entirely new. That attempt, argued Burke, was doomed to fail, for human societies are not artificial constructs like buildings designed by an architect. Human societies are living organisms like trees. They have roots deep in the soil of a nation's past, and they grow and evolve gradually over generations. If you do not fancy a building, you can tear it down and erect a new one. If you tear down a tree you will only manage to kill it.

The belief that living societies are necessarily organic and rooted in history rather than abstract reason is the foundation of all Conservative thought. Conservatism arose when it did for the obvious reason that the status quo was suddenly challenged by the French Revolution. Think about that. It never occurred to anyone to be a Conservative until time-honored, taken-for-granted realities came to be threatened. The very existence of revolutionaries was what conjured Conservatives into existence.

Who were these self-conscious Conservatives? You might think they were the aristocrats who enjoyed wealth, social status, and legal privileges under the old regime. That was indeed so. But Conservatism was also an empirical, intellectual critique of all the phenomena called ideologies, and Conservatism therefore appealed to many middle-class people as well, especially traditional Christians. The Austrian statesman Metternich thought the defining sins of the French revolutionaries were presumption and pride, and he called for a return to humility in European philosophy and politics. His private secretary Adam Müller, the man who translated Burke's writings into German, thought the besetting sin of the Napoleonic era was the arrogant will to power. In France, books such as François de Chateaubriand's *Le Génie du Christianisme* revived the orthodox view of human nature as a combination of body, soul, and spirit, and the soul as a combination of the mind, emotions, and will. Hence, argued Chateaubriand, to attempt to live by the vaunted abstract reason of the philosophes was to ignore most of what it means to be human. Another Catholic, Félicité de Lammenais, wrote of the French Revolution: "The world has fallen prey to opinions. . . . But restore authority, and peace and order will be born again."

Nothing expressed the reaction against the Enlightenment more eloquently—indeed sublimely—than the Romantic cultural movement that flourished from around 1800 to 1850. Romanticism was a powerful reaction against the hyperrationalism of the eighteenth century. Whereas Enlightenment authors had dismissed the medieval era as superstitious and stagnant, Romantic authors such as Sir Walter Scott wrote nostalgically and lyrically about the faith, trust, honor, and authority they imagined had characterized medieval times. Whereas Enlightenment philosophes had considered rural life to be barbaric and wild nature unseemly, nineteenth-century Romantics idealized peasant virtues and favored rustic English gardens over perfectly groomed French gardens.

William Wordsworth, the poet with whom this chapter began, described the Romantic movement as a "spontaneous overflow of powerful feelings." One might call his claim a brave assertion of humanity—as well as an example of literary authenticity that defied the neoclassical verse of the eighteenth century. Wordsworth's fellow Romantic English poets, such as Byron, Coleridge, Keats, Shelley, and Blake, were obsessed with the sublime, the melancholic, the tragic, the transcendent, even death itself. Thus did Keats write in his "Ode to a Nightingale":

I have been half in love with easeful Death,
Call'd him soft names in many a mused rhyme,
To take into the air my quiet breath;
Now more than ever seems it rich to die,
To cease upon the midnight with no pain . . .

Germany's greatest poet, Johann Wolfgang von Goethe, wrote *The Sorrows of Young Werther* in a mystical mode, while his contemporary Friedrich Schiller, a leader of the *Sturm und Drang* (storm and stress) movement, expressed such prevalent Romantic moods as *Lebensmüdigkeit* (weariness with life) and *Weltschmerz* (world-weariness). Yet Schiller's wistful "Ode to Joy" provided Beethoven with the libretto for the fourth movement of his exquisite Ninth Symphony, expressing the wish that all mankind might someday live as brothers.

Romantic novels and short stories of the early nineteenth century told spooky tales of the occult or the wilderness: phenomena beyond the power of reason to explain. That was the era when the Brothers Grimm collected old German fairy tales such as Cinderella, Hansel and Gretel, Little Red Riding Hood, and Rapunzel. That was the era when American writers such as Ralph Waldo Emerson and Henry David Thoreau rhapsodized about the untamed natural world and when American artists of the Hudson River School painted imaginative landscapes.

No artistic medium was better suited to the Romantic mood than music. For music—freed from the strictures of language—is transcendent. It can express pure emotion and pure release. And European music underwent an important shift during and after the French Revolutionary era because the market for classical music became liberalized. In the eighteenth century the patrons of composers and orchestras were exclusively either aristocrats or Lutheran, Anglican, or Catholic clerics. By the first decades of the 1800s, wealthy, bourgeois audiences began to subscribe to orchestras, commission new works from composers, and attend public concerts. Such audiences thrilled to the lyrical, harmonic symphonies, concertos, and string quartets composed by such giants as Beethoven, Franz Schubert, and Felix Mendelssohn.

Romantic art might give eloquent if muted expression to the revolutionary aspirations of liberty, equality, and fraternity, or it might express a nostalgic form of Conservatism. But whatever their politics, Romantic artists' aspirations were infused with a melancholy temperament born of the suspicion that human aspirations must always remain unfulfilled. That is why Wordsworth remembered the "bliss" that it was "in that dawn to be alive" before his generation was disillusioned by the miscarriage of the French Revolution and, ultimately, by the human condition itself.

Sadly, that is what it means to grow up.

Chapter 16

Machines in the Garden: Four Industrial Revolutions

It is hard for people in the twenty-first century to imagine what life was like before modern machines and sources of power. If we found ourselves stranded in a Nevada desert with nothing to rely on except our own muscles, some hand tools, and maybe a mule, we would likely not survive for more than a few days. If we were lost in the woods on a moonless night, we would discover a world that was eerily black and utterly silent. But that was an experience nearly all people used to have, at least after they snuffed out their candles, until some one hundred and eighty years ago. In preindustrial towns—let alone rural villages—what seemed alien to people then were not darkness and silence, but lights, noises, machines. Today, the natural world seems alien to us because we have become alienated from nature.

A twentieth-century historian named Leo Marx once wrote a book titled *The Machine in the Garden.* In it he described the reaction of rural New Englanders to the dawn of industrialization. Marx began with a passage from American author Nathaniel Hawthorne describing a verdant meadow in which the only sounds are the chirping of birds and the buzzing of bees . . . until the idyll is disturbed by a screeching, nerve-wracking whistle. The whistle is soon joined by a rumble, the combined noises become a cacophony, the wildflowers and shrubs are sprayed with steam, soot, and grease. A locomotive on the embankment above, clamoring through the meadow at the once impossible speed of forty miles per hour, is announcing to nature: "Out of my way, I'm coming through!"

The machine in the garden.

Throughout the decades of the Enlightenment, French Revolution, and Napoleonic Wars, England was birthing the age of machines—machines that could perform work a hundred times more efficiently than could people by themselves. But machines were only one part of what historians call the Industrial Revolution. That great transformation really amounted to a great *equation*, in which human work was multiplied by natural resources, and multiplied again by technology. For in addition to machinery, the Industrial Revolution was characterized both by a new way of organizing work called the factory system and by new sources of energy, especially thermal energy released by steam boilers.

Steam boilers needed fuel to burn. For thousands of years *fuel* essentially meant *wood* to heat cottages, cook food, and make charcoal that burned hot enough to enable blacksmiths to smelt metals in their forges. But, thanks to deforestation, by the 1700s wood had become a scarce commodity in western Europe. So Europeans began to dig underground for a previously despised substance: coal.

England and Wales had plenty of coal, but the mines were often flooded with groundwater. Hence, the first use for steam engines was to pump water out of the mines so that coal could be dug up to fuel, among other things, the steam engines themselves. As steam engines were improved, England's iron industry boomed, because metallurgical coke—the coal-based equivalent of charcoal—burned very hot and could smelt high-quality pig iron. Finally, chemists and engineers experimenting with thermodynamics learned how to design safe and efficient steam engines to run many other manufacturing machines. Thus did industrial techniques flourish in symbiotic relationships.

If one had to pick a single year for the rise of the factory system, the exploitation of new forms of energy, and the industrial capitalism which followed, that year would be 1776. First, the rebellion of the thirteen British colonies in North America marked the beginning of the end of colonial mercantilism. Second, in that same year James Watt patented his new and improved steam engine, which soon became the industry standard. Third, 1776 was the year Adam Smith published *The Wealth of Nations*, which founded modern economics by explaining such concepts as comparative advantage, the division of labor, interchangeable parts, how the price mechanism was driven by supply and demand, and how the invisible hand of free-market competition maximized investment decisions and economic growth.

Why was it Englishmen who pioneered the Industrial Revolution, the greatest economic breakthrough since the prehistoric invention of agriculture? On some points historians agree—for instance, about the "necessary conditions" that made the breakthrough of industrialism possible. No less than seven such preconditions favored England above all other countries.

First, thanks to its common law tradition and the Glorious Revolution of 1688, England enjoyed a legal and political system that was far more conducive to innovation than most European countries. Private property rights were absolute, so one did not have to worry about the royal government, local landlords, or some craftsmen's guild forbidding the free use of one's land and its resources. Second, England's tax system was comparatively fair and predictable, so individuals and firms need not fret that the government might confiscate their profits. Third, the British Isles had become an internal free market, which meant that manufacturers could exploit a national market and realize economies of scale. Fourth, population growth provided a growing supply of cheap labor unfettered by serfdom or feudal restrictions, while also increasing domestic demand for affordable food, clothing, and hardware. Fifth, Britain's colonial empire enabled entrepreneurs to exploit overseas markets in America and Asia. Sixth, England was blessed with rich deposits of coal and metals and plenty of water, thanks to its rainy climate. Seventh, the British government promoted manufactures and commerce, not least by encouraging private mobilization of the nation's economic potential during the long Napoleonic Wars.

These necessary conditions were in place during the decades before and after the year 1800. But to explain what made an innovation possible is not the same as to explain why it happened. Hence, the debate among economic historians has centered on the sufficient conditions—or the "spark."

As with the French Revolution, three major theories have competed to explain the Industrial Revolution. Modernization theory, associated above all with a Harvard economist named Walt Whitman Rostow, held that all societies must sooner or later make the transition to modernity, but that each nation modernized at its own pace. The spark, in Rostow's view, was a level of capital reinvestment approaching 10 percent of gross domestic product. Investment at that level generated enough new technology and infrastructure to ensure that the sum of all goods and services in a nation would grow faster than the population. In other words, per capita income would increase, permitting still more reinvestment until the economy took off like a rocket. Rostow figured that Britain had passed that milestone around 1750, the United States around 1830, France and Germany around 1850, and Japan and Russia around 1890.

A second explanation, advanced by Marxist historians such as Eric Hobsbawm, emphasized the demand side of the equation and the critical role played by imperialism. Hobsbawm argued that Britain's success in overseas trade created so many markets for British exports that their manufacturers were driven to innovate new technologies in order to meet that demand. Moreover, they had access to the capital they needed thanks to the large accumulations of wealth that colonial commodities (especially crops raised on slave-worked plantations) delivered into the hands of merchants and their factors and bankers.

Both of those theories were predictable, given the prior commitments of their proponents. The liberal one, modernization theory, stressed the role of increased supply generated by benign entrepreneurship operating in free markets, while the Marxist theory stressed the role of increased demand generated by exploitative imperialism operating in monopolized markets. More interesting is a third theory advanced by historian of technology David Landes, who granted the importance of supply and demand, but was also informed by the understanding that people are not automata acted upon by impersonal forces. Rather, Landes was convinced that the spark for industrial take-off was human inventiveness itself. Moreover, rather than ask "Why England?," he asked why it was that *Europeans* launched the Industrial Revolution. His answer was manifold. First, Europe's idiosyncratic system of nation-states gave its population a competitive vitality without counterpart elsewhere in the world. Second, both Judeo-Christian theology and the Scientific Revolution placed high value on the manipulation of an environment designed by a rational Creator according to natural laws. Third, the Renaissance, the Reformation, the Scientific Revolution, and the Enlightenment all fostered faith in progress, in a future better than the past or present. Finally, as for England, Landes pointed out that its long tradition of independent craftsmen tinkering in their workshops inspired them to advance by trial and error toward more efficient methods of doing and making. What Americans came to call "Yankee know-how" was really born in Britain.

The first economic sector to experience the machine revolution was textiles. England had always had a proud woolen industry, but the mass importation of cotton, initially from India, inspired her craftsmen to design machines to produce cloth cheaply and in large quantities. Their inventions included the flying shuttle, spinning jenny, power loom, carder, mule, and other machines that historians invariably mention but that few of them understand. Suffice to say that those inventions made it possible for a single factory to spin thread or weave cloth that used to require hundreds of individuals working from their cottages with hand tools and raw materials supplied by merchants. Moreover, the shuttles, jennies, and looms were powered by gears, cams, and pullies rather than by women and children stamping their feet on pedals or by horses walking in circles. Power for the machines was generated initially by waterwheels, which had been used since medieval times for grinding flour or sawing timber. But by the late 1700s textile-mill machines were being driven by mechanical sources of power. If one inventor deserves credit for that, it would be Richard Arkwright, whose 1769 water frame became the industry standard for the transfer of power from a river or stream to a building on its banks.

A second breakthrough for industrialization arrived with the steam engine. First conceived by Thomas Newcomen in the early 1700s, steam engines could provide power for nearly any machine. Since steam engines were powered by coal, it made sense to concentrate factories in mill towns located near coal mines, for instance in the English Midlands or Scottish Lowlands. Thanks to steam power, Britain's textile production grew eightfold during the two decades beginning in 1780, and textiles made up nearly half of all British exports by 1820.

The factories that sprang up in new cities such as Manchester and Birmingham needed hundreds, then thousands, of workers. Given that the population of the British Isles was in the process of tripling between 1750 and 1850, the result was rapid urbanization. In 1785 there were only three British cities besides London with more than fifty thousand people. By 1850, there would be thirty-one such cities. Manchester alone grew from twenty-five thousand people in 1775 to five hundred thousand by 1850. The mill towns were initially sinkholes of misery. They lacked sewer systems, garbage disposal, police protection, public transportation, even indoor plumbing (the flush toilet was still just a gleam in the eye of its inventor, Thomas Crapper). Many factory workers fresh off the farm were not accustomed to living in rowhouses or seedy apartments in which their entire families might be crammed into one or two rooms . . . assuming, that is, that their families *survived* the transition to urban life. Teenaged girls frequently became pregnant out of wedlock, homeless waifs begged in the gutters, disease and crime were rife: all the pathologies described in the novels of Charles Dickens were truly present in urban Britain during this period. Those lucky enough to find employment worked twelve-hour shifts for low wages.

Factory labor is tedious even in the best of conditions. But no one could deny its efficiency. Adam Smith had theorized how factories based on a division of labor would be far more productive than the old putting-out system or the handicraft system by which craftsmen made shoes or tools from scratch. Since industrial techniques could produce everything from needles and pins to shirts and shoes far more efficiently than in the past, mass production promised, sooner or later, to raise everyone's standard of living. But the social cost was high. Working in factories driven by power plants was both physically dangerous and profoundly demoralizing, because it turned workers themselves into machines of a sort. Men who once had been proud blacksmiths, weavers, and tailors were now just a pair of hands—factory hands—whose work might just as easily be done by unskilled female or child labor.

By contrast, the exploitation of fossil fuel during the early decades of industrialization created exciting, well-paying jobs for skilled mechanics; they even began to refer to themselves as an "aristocracy of labor." Nowhere was that more true than in the railroad industry. George Stephenson demonstrated his "Rocket," the world's first steam locomotive, in 1829. By 1850, three thousand miles of railroad track had already been laid in England, and the boom was still in its infancy. Railroads sparked a second industrial revolution all their own, for besides triggering an explosion in the demand for iron and coal, they literally transformed human beings' relationship with space and time. Consider that as late as 1820, people, goods, and information could be moved from here to there only as fast as horses could trot. Then, in the twinkling of an eye, a railroad is built from here to there. So instead of hauling, say, four people, six loads of freight, and a couple of mailbags from here to there in three days, now one could haul four *hundred* people, six *hundred* loads of freight, and *scores* of mail bags from here to there in just *three hours*.

In just a few decades the application of steam-powered machinery to other sectors made possible a plethora of labor-saving devices, including the steam drill, steam press, steam roller, steam shovel, steam hammer, and even a steam coach (that one did not catch on). In addition, steam locomotives shipped tons of iron to metallurgical plants that in turn enabled the advent of a modern Iron Age.

Iron rails, iron bridges, iron girders to support large buildings, iron cannons for armies and navies, iron hammers and nails for carpenters, iron ploughshares for farmers, iron needles for housewives, iron shoes for horses. Each new invention or application meant greater markets for other industries. England had indeed "taken off" thanks to the application of scientific technology and management to the production and distribution of goods in a competitive environment.

Which brings up the final sufficient condition for industrial takeoff: the businessman or entrepreneur. Technology and energy can do nothing on their own. A successful industry needs inventors, entrepreneurs, managers, and salesmen who understand the potential of new technologies, have enough faith in their business models to take risks, and have the gumption or pluck (as the English would say) to sell their ideas to investors and their products to consumers.

Consider James Watt, the engineer after whom the electrical unit was later named. A professor of modest means at the University of Glasgow, he tinkered with boilers to study thermodynamics, metallurgy, and the transfer of kinetic energy into mechanical energy until he learned how to streamline the Newcomen engines then in use. He then looked for investors and found one in Matthew Boulton, a toy manufacturer, who bankrolled Watt's experiments and founded their first factory. It took fifteen years for their labors to pay off, but soon the firm of Boulton & Watt was exporting engines around the world.

For all these reasons it was England that became the Workshop of the World and the dominant force in manufacturing and finance for over a century. English, Scottish, and Welsh firms led the world in textiles and steam power, then iron and steel, then all manner of mass-produced products for the home, business, workshop, and farm. Not until the 1840s did Belgium, France, and northern Germany begin to industrialize. Why did the continent lag behind Britain? Partly because during the French revolutionary and Napoleonic wars

Engraving of a Bristol cotton mill in 1837.

the predatory requisitions imposed by the French armies on occupied countries, combined with Napoléon's prohibition of overseas commerce, meant that continental producers had no incentive to invest in new technologies. The British army and navy, by contrast, had dispensed huge sums to their nation's entrepreneurs through the government procurement system. Hence British firms seeking lucrative government contacts were incentivized to install more efficient machinery and to cut costs.

British industrial leadership meant that every other country had to play catchup. But industrialization in other countries could not proceed in exactly the same way as it did in the United Kingdom simply because there already was an industrialized country. That is, Britain's industrial leadership changed the conditions of economic life by rendering every other country comparatively backward. How each country tried to cope with that fact depended on its government policies, economic structures, raw materials, and legal environment. Indeed, those variables are what make comparative economic history so interesting. But little by little the continental entrepreneurs and their governments began to emulate the British as best they could. They begged, borrowed, or stole British machines in order to reverse-engineer them. British industrialists, being no fools, invariably exported machinery that was a bit outmoded. French, Belgian, German, and American industrialists, also no fools, engaged in espionage or else offered high salaries to attract British mechanics and managers to their own firms.

Belgian linen was one of the first industries on the continent to establish the factory system. By the 1840s French industrialists were replicating Britain's sophisticated rolling mill process for casting iron, which the French called *la méthode anglaise*. Rhenish and Silesian entrepreneurs in the kingdom of Prussia began to build factories by the 1850s. But for every worker on the continent who found jobs in the mills a dozen old-fashioned craftsmen were ruined by mass-produced competition. Highly skilled craftsmen such as the silversmiths of Solingen, Germany, might still capture the high-end luxury trade, but the livelihoods of tens of thousands of ordinary weavers, shoemakers, and tinkers were wiped out. Their desperate plight would contribute to the epidemic of social revolutions Europe experienced in 1848.

The industrial revolution was the most powerful engine of social change since human beings first settled down to grow crops. But for everything gained something else is lost. We moderns should remember that adage whenever we smugly take pride in our era's progress. On the plus side, almost everything we consider to be good about modernity stems from the seemingly miraculous march of technology. Yet the power of production became so seductive so quickly that not many decades passed before people became addicted to material consumption and blinded by the idolatrous worship of their own productivity. Industrial societies became virtually enslaved by the clock and dependent on networks of metamachines without which cities could not survive for a week. Thus, as liberating as the Industrial Revolution was in material aspects, it also ensured that human beings would no longer be free from noise, crowding, pollution, and anxiety. The realm of *techne* advanced at a frenetic pace, but the price paid was a rapid retreat in the realm of *themis*.

In *The Wealth of Nations*, Adam Smith explained why free-market capitalism would maximize production. He believed he had discovered the natural laws of the marketplace: the law of supply and demand, the law of diminishing returns, the law of comparative advantage, the division of labor, and the invisible hand that automatically balances supply and demand under free-market conditions. Smith refuted the mercantilist assumption to the effect that economics was a zero-sum game. He argued instead that free trade within and among nations would maximize welfare and liberty for all because people would be dividing a pie that kept growing bigger. As for government, Smith limited its purview to enforcing private contracts, sheltering industries vital to national defense, and retaliating against foreign violations of free trade. Otherwise, he wrote, governments should get out of the way. Curiously, Smith's free-market model got its nickname from the French phrase *laissez faire* (leave to do or to make), popularized by economist Jean-Baptiste Say. That became a sacred principle of England's Manchester School of economics, which dominated the early nineteenth century. Laissez-faire capitalism flourished thanks to the belief, encouraged by Smith, that it was the key to unlocking the door of universal prosperity.

In retrospect, there was reason for that belief. Thanks to industrial capitalism, more economic growth was achieved during the nineteenth century *alone* than in all the centuries that preceded it *combined*. Industry created fortunes for those at the top, enabled the rise of broad and comfortable middle classes, and over a longer time span raised the standard of living among the working classes as well. But that hindsight misses a glaring point. For during the early decades of industrialization and grimy urbanization arose—first in Britain and then in other countries—a veritable crisis caused by the glaring inequality between what Prime Minister Benjamin Disraeli later called the two nations: the rich and the poor. The social realities of urban industrial life also raised such existential questions as what makes life worth living. Many English workers, far from being grateful for their jobs, rebelled against the new organization of labor. Nor were their complaints only about low wages and long hours. Workers deplored the sheer tedium of performing the same, often mindless operations over and over again, alienated from the fruits of their labor. A cobbler working in his shop could take pride in each pair of boots he turned out and profit directly when he sold them. A factory worker took no pride in hammering heels on a hundred soles per day in exchange for a handful of coins meted out at the end of the week.

The first generation of industrial workers, not socialized to monotonous work habits, hated them. That explains why during the 1810s many craftsmen, called Luddites, began to smash their employers' machines. Farmhands thrown out of work by steam-powered threshing machines did likewise. Luddism was a hopeless, romantic protest that soon died away. But by the 1840s, organized protest through the first labor union movements made the problem of how to discipline the working classes a major political challenge.

Liberal, laissez-faire economists such as the Manchester School's Thomas Malthus, David Ricardo, and Jeremy Bentham had no answer. Their understanding of how the laws of supply and demand played out in reality seemed to prove that Adam Smith had been too optimistic. They reasoned that the working class must always be poor in the long run, because labor itself had become a commodity. Thus, when labor was scarce, wages would rise. But rising wages would cause more people to rush into cities seeking jobs, whereupon labor would become abundant again and wages would fall. Workers might even hurt their own cause by having more children when times were good, thus exacerbating the labor glut down the road. No wonder economics came to be known as "the dismal science." No wonder early socialists went to the other extreme, arguing that the only way to improve standards of living was to abolish private property altogether.

We can see now that all camps got it wrong. Economists were wrong to think that the laws of the marketplace condemned the lower social tiers to poverty. Factory owners were wrong to imagine their employees were sullen opponents rather than potential team players in their firm's competition against other firms. Socialists were wrong to think that confiscation of the means of production would improve anyone's lot. Moreover, the social maladies of early industrial cities were not a product of capitalism per se, but rather spoke to the inadequacies of municipal governments unable to cope with the tens of thousands of people who had left the traditional "moral economy" of rural communities to squeeze into urban tenements.

As the twentieth-century social historian E. P. Thompson explained in his seminal book *The Making of the English Working Class*, the rural poor had lived close to the soil and usually knew where their next meal was coming from. Craftsmen in towns and villages belonged to guilds whose members looked out for each other. Parish churches and poorhouses provided charitable safety nets. Rural villagers worked hard for their daily bread, but at least they labored alongside their kinfolk, shared their meals, and went to the church or tavern together. Thompson described how that "moral economy" with its material and psychological support systems ceased to exist in the grimy industrial towns.

Hence the Social Question, as it came to be known in England, commanded attention throughout the burgeoning cities of northwestern Europe. Religious and secular reformers and charities insisted that it be addressed for moral reasons. Middle-class property owners and politicians insisted that it be addressed for prudential reasons. For the concentration in cities of tens of thousands of young malcontents made them susceptible to agitators and demagogues preaching organized resistance. That potential became frighteningly obvious when public outcries inspired Parliament to pass the Factory Act of 1833 and other laws regulating female and child labor. Such reforms did not prevent the outbreak of the massive Chartist movement, whose proponents agitated for constitutional reform in Britain during the 1840s.

Over the middle third of the nineteenth century three principal critiques of the industrial order suggested answers to the question of how to restore security and community to working-class life. The first was Conservative, in that its adherents hoped to conserve what remained of the preindustrial moral economy. For instance, Catholic critics considered the capitalist goal of maximizing profit by any means necessary to be a form of idolatrous greed. They called for a wage system that addressed the needs of workers and their families. For instance, governments might require factory owners to pay higher wages to married men and women, and especially to those who were parents. Government might pass laws abolishing child labor entirely, and it might grant workers ample time off for rest and recreation. Lammenais, the Catholic philosopher who had denounced the politics of the French Revolution, now denounced the social path the Industrial Revolution was taking. But he was not a Romantic reactionary. He named his journal *L'Avenir* (The future), made *Dieu et Liberté* (God and liberty) his motto, and argued that "we should not be afraid of Liberalism, but do need to Catholicize it, and if we do, society will be born again!"

A second critique was leveled by those English Liberals who believed that governments must address the gross inequality bequeathed by industrial capitalism. Calling themselves Philosophical Radicals, people such as John Stuart Mill became the forerunners of twentieth-century progressives insofar as they called on government agencies to regulate businesses and provide social welfare programs. Their philosophy of utilitarianism prescribed policies to promote "the greatest good for the greatest number." Philosophical Radicals sponsored such legislation as the Factory Act of 1833, which reduced working hours and limited child and female labor, and the Poor Law of 1834, which provided relief for the homeless and unemployed.

A third sort of critique was made by utopian socialists, who imagined that industrialism's productive power could lead to perfect societies, if only people could be persuaded to love their neighbors as themselves. Robert Owen, a Welsh textile manufacturer, invested in model communities that provided workers with affordable housing, high wages, schools, and hospitals. Of course, any attempt to generalize this kind of benevolent paternalism required that all businessmen embrace it, lest firms such as Owen's be driven out of business by unscrupulous competitors. Owen's paternalism also required workers to be model citizens who voluntarily adhered to the strict moral code of their benefactor, which in Owen's case included proscription of alcohol and prostitution.

Another utopian socialist, Henri de Saint-Simon, believed that the forces unleashed by the Industrial Revolution could lead to social perfection if all nations adhered to a world religion based on morality without metaphysics and on technology without theology. In other words, Saint-Simon was that sort of atheist who claimed to believe in nothing but was really prepared to believe in anything. Among his weird reveries was the notion that a humanistic revival would soon make the whole human race into a communist brotherhood. He imagined his disciples leading a movement to dig a canal through Egypt's isthmus of Suez and thereby "pierce the membrane of the virgin desert to liberate the universal libido." He imagined a female messiah emerging from Egypt to preach a syncretic religion that fused Eastern mysticism with Western science. Clearly Saint-Simon was more than a little bit daft. Yet he was the man who coined the term *technocracy* and who made *socialism* a household word.

Another Frenchman, Pierre-Joseph Proudhon, famously asked in a pamphlet published in 1840, *Qu'est ce que la propriété?* (What is property?). He answered that property is theft. Proudhon was not, strictly speaking, a utopian socialist, because he did not believe human nature could be improved. Indeed, he prophesied that whereas "capitalism is the exploitation of the weak by the strong, communism would be the exploitation of the strong by the weak."

Proudhon's precocious denunciation of communist ideology made him a target for those who claimed to be "scientific socialists," such as the German intellectuals Karl Marx and Friedrich Engels. In the 1840s, Marx and Engels moved to London, where they studied economic history in the library of the

British Museum. Engels's book *The Condition of the Working Classes in England* described what he took to be the scientific laws of history, which he believed played out through sequential eras of social-class conflict. Marx elaborated on that theory in his three-volume tome *Das Kapital*. He argued that the dominant social class in each era of history was that which controlled the means of production and that the displacement of one ruling class by another through revolution was the engine of historical change. Thus, the slave economy of the ancient world had given way to the feudal economy of medieval times, which had in turn been overthrown by the bourgeois capitalist economy of modern times. At the end of history, Marx predicted, the impoverished working class would overthrow the capitalist class and usher in a communist society through a dictatorship of the proletariat, whose slogan would be "From each according to his abilities, to each according to his needs."

Marx and Engels were not themselves agitators. They were bookish intellectuals from a decidedly bourgeois background. But their ideas began to spread when Marx's first prophecy appeared to come true. He had warned of "a specter haunting Europe" on the eve of a great wave of popular revolution that swept across the continent in 1848. Whereupon Marx and Engels quickly published an inflammatory pamphlet destined to frighten, or perhaps inspire, Europeans in decades to come. They called it *The Communist Manifesto*.

Chapter 17

1848 and After:
Romantic Revolutions and Realistic Reforms

Historians refer to the years 1815 to 1848 as the Metternichian era, Restoration era, or *Vormärz*. As always, such terms remain empty buzzwords unless one knows the facts and trends they are meant to convey. To call that era Metternichian is to adopt the perspective of people who lived during the decades when Klemens von Metternich served as chancellor and foreign minister of the Austrian Empire. Metternich promoted an authoritarian agenda in central Europe and encouraged other European governments to do so as well. To call those years a Restoration is to adopt the perspective of the previous era, because the chaos of the French Revolution and Napoleonic Wars were what inspired the statesmen at the Congress of Vienna to restore the pre-1789 old regime in many respects. Finally, the German historians who refer to those years as the *Vormärz* adopt the perspective of people who experienced the post–March 1848 era, when a wave of revolutionary activity washed away both Metternich and the Restoration.

The most popular metaphor historians use to describe the run-up to 1848 is that of a boiling cauldron of discontent—discontent among peoples inspired by ideologies of liberty, equality, and fraternity and discontent among those made desperate by poverty and unemployment. After the overthrow of Napoléon, for thirty-three years European monarchs and aristocracies managed to keep the lid on the cauldron. Then, in 1848, it boiled over. Why did so many revolutions occur that year in countries whose social, political, and economic conditions were quite different? Given the scale and initial success of those revolutions, why, in the end, did they fail? After all, the Revolution of 1789 had sparked twenty-five years of turmoil, whereas the Revolutions of 1848 fizzled in just twenty-five months.

No single theory accounts for the facts. Social historians once believed that the Revolutions of 1848 were a symptom of rapid social change during the early industrial revolution, as workers across Europe rose up in protest against industrial capitalism. But that theory did not fly. There were still few factory workers in France in 1848, and virtually none in other centers of revolt, such as Vienna, Prague, and Budapest. In any event, if industrialization were the cause of the social unrest, then why was there no revolution in England, the most industrialized country in Europe?

Perhaps, thought other social historians, that was the point. Perhaps it was the relative backwardness of the continental economies that caused widespread discontent. That is, most continental countries were experiencing the same demographic growth that was occurring in Britain, and thousands of people were moving to cities and towns looking for work. But unlike British cities, continental cities had as yet few factory or railroad jobs. Hence, historians speculated that the revolutions of 1848 expressed not the anger of *new* industrial workers but the anger of *pre*-industrial workers whose livelihoods were being destroyed by competition from manufactured goods imported from Britain. That theory was clever. But if economic backwardness were the principal source of discontent, why was there no revolution in Russia, the most populous and most backward country of all?

Still other historians stressed temporary, contingent causes of violence such as the deep economic recession of the 1840s and a series of poor harvests that drove up food prices. But if unemployment and famine were what drove men and women into the streets, why was there no revolution in Ireland, where as many as one million people starved to death between 1845 and 1852, thanks to a catastrophic fungus that ruined their potato crops and ultimately reduced Ireland's population by 20 percent?

Perhaps social historians were asking the wrong questions. Perhaps the revolutions of 1848 were not workers' uprisings so much as bourgeois revolutions seeking to overthrow the monarchical, aristocratic order and to usher in liberalism and capitalism. That would conform to Marxist theory, except for the fact that bourgeois revolutionaries in western and central Europe grew so fearful of popular violence in 1848-49 that they soon rallied behind Conservative forces. Moreover, the agendas of middle-class revolutionaries and reformers focused on issues of nationalism at least as much as on economic or political reforms.

Often the way to confront such confusion in history is just to accept it. What happened in 1848 was that many social groups pursuing different, sometimes contradictory, goals rose up in copycat fashion against their old regimes. The failure of the uprisings can be explained precisely by conflicts among the revolutionaries themselves. Some emphasized *liberté* and called for parliamentary government. Others emphasized *égalité* and called for democracy or even socialism. Still others emphasized *fraternité* and called for the national liberation or unification of their countries.

Assuming that confusion surrounding goals does help to explain the ultimate failure of the 1848 outbreaks, a question remains: How do we explain the initial *success* of the continental revolutions? Here historians are on much firmer ground, because in every case revolutionaries were able to exploit the weakness and demoralization of the monarchies under attack. In Paris, Berlin, Vienna, Budapest, Rome, Milan, and Venice, royal armies could have crushed the middle- and lower-class crowds protesting in the streets. But in every case the rulers lost their nerve and refused to order their soldiers to fire upon their own subjects. Such timidity was characteristic of the French King Louis Philippe, the Prussian King Frederick William IV, and the Austrian Emperor Ferdinand, all of whom were vacillating and sentimental rulers. Their passivity was also due to a certain resignation. There was a growing expectation among the monarchs and their courts that it was only a matter of time before the lid blew off the social cauldron, thanks to the popular ideologies percolating among the masses. So it was that when the expected revolts arrived at last, monarchs simply threw in the towel.

That also helps to explain why no outbreaks occurred in England and Russia. Those countries, located on the peripheries of European civilization, could not have differed more. Yet both regimes had strong, confident rulers in 1848—Queen Victoria and Tsar Nicholas I—and both fielded effective police and military forces which they were not afraid to use. That is what inspired historian William L. Langer to argue that political and social revolutions are often a function of the weakness of Conservative regimes as much as they are a function of the strength of their radical challengers.

Finally, the revolutions of 1848 displayed an undeniably Romantic spirit on the left and right alike. For thirty years the legend of the French Revolution, with its heroic images of "The People" rushing to the barricades to resist tyranny, had intoxicated many commoners in France, Germany, Italy, and the Austrian Empire. That heady myth was evocatively portrayed in Eugene Delacroix's famous 1830 painting *Liberty Leading the People*. Revolutionaries wanted to believe that an aroused populace could overthrow the political status quo even in the face of the king's professional soldiers. At first it appeared they really could do so, because their monarchs were also Romantics who wanted to believe in the mystical bonds of affection between benign rulers and their obedient subjects. So when their subjects rose up against them, the disillusioned rulers chose at first not to resist. But once they recovered their nerve in 1849–50, their armies quickly suppressed the crowds and assemblies, much like antibodies attacking and killing off, one by one, the germs of revolutionary contagion. Those twin disillusionments, first of the Conservatives, then of the revolutionaries, would give rise to a new era in European culture and politics: an era of hardheaded realism, pragmatism, even cynicism.

Why did Parisians overthrow King Louis Philippe in 1848? An old cliché held that *La France s'ennui*—that the French people simply grew bored with the "bourgeois monarchy" and its pursuit of a *juste milieu* (a happy medium of judicious moderation). But in practice the *juste milieu*, in nineteenth-century Liberal fashion, meant the restriction of voting rights based on property qualifications. Only one Frenchman in thirty could vote during Louis Philippe's "July Monarchy." The bourgeoisie, not surprisingly, agitated for a broader franchise. At the same time, Parisian artisans—the descendants of those *sans-culottes* of 1789—and day laborers began to hearken to socialist appeals from agitators such as Louis Blanc and Louis-Auguste Blanqui. Neither the bourgeoisie protesting political conditions nor the working class protesting social conditions could have toppled the monarchy by itself. But for a brief moment middle- and lower-class people joined forces in citywide protests.

The spark was struck in a theater. A popular showman named Frédéric Lemaître was playing to sellout crowds in *The Ragpicker*, a tearjerker, like *Les Misérables*, which depicted the plight of the urban poor. One evening in February

1848 Lemâitre requested that the theater open its doors to people who could not afford tickets. The working-class audience instantly identified with the hero of the play, a beggar who lives on bread crusts picked out of Parisian trash bins. At the climax of the play the beggar discovers a golden crown buried in the garbage. The symbolism was clear: the last shall be first, the meek shall inherit the earth, the lowly shall reign like kings. The rowdy audience spontaneously poured into the streets singing "La Marseillaise" and attracted a swelling mob that careened toward the royal palace, where guards fired a panicky fusillade. When Louis Philippe was told that his troops had killed some of his subjects, he made the same mistake as Louis XVI in 1789: he ordered them back to their barracks. The protests only intensified, until the king abdicated the throne and fled toward the English Channel.

Lawyers led by another Romantic figure, the orator Alphonse de Lamartine, hastened to take control of events at the Hotel de Ville (town hall) in Paris. He and the other bourgeois leaders proclaimed the foundation of a Second French Republic, which would bestow universal male suffrage and be defended by citizen-soldiers in a National Guard.

Working-class revolutionaries were not satisfied. Louis Blanc exhorted the urban day laborers to resist the self-appointed bourgeois leaders and to raise the red flag of social revolution. At first, Lamartine's provisional government tried to appease the poor by offering government-funded workshops for the unemployed. But that first experiment with a welfare state was overwhelmed when some two hundred thousand paupers streamed into Paris from the provinces, demanding wages at government expense. The treasury quickly emptied, prompting more riots. The provisional government deployed the bourgeois National Guard in an effort to restore order, but the workers and paupers raised up barricades in the narrow streets of the working-class districts and waged a literal class war. In just a few weeks of fighting during those infamous June Days more than ten thousand people were killed. In the wake of that slaughter, the French electorate went to the polls to elect a president for the Second Republic. Not surprisingly, both the bourgeoisie and peasantry voted for law and order, but surprisingly the victory went to a candidate with a magical name: Louis Napoléon Bonaparte, grandnephew of the former emperor.

Louis Napoléon had spent his youth kicking around Europe and playing at revolution. He also wrote books. In *Les idées Napoléoniennes* (Napoleonic

In March 1848, lawyers and professors from all over Germany convened the Frankfurt Assembly in the hope of founding a liberal nation-state.

ideas) he argued that his great uncle had been a misunderstood liberator who had simply wanted to reorganize Europe on the basis of nationality. And in *L'extinction du pauperisme* (The extinction of poverty) he advanced the Saint-Simonian notion that technology might enrich everyone if guided by government technocrats rather than greedy capitalists. But those tracts had been published during his radical youth. By 1848 Louis Napoléon sensed the public's fear of the so-called dangerous classes, and he ran for president promising law and order at home and glory abroad.

So it was, as novelist Victor Hugo quipped, that history repeated itself as farce. Louis Napoléon seized control of the Second French Republic as his great uncle had the first republic, and in 1852 imitated him again by taking the title of Napoléon III, Emperor of the French (thereby implying not only that his uncle's deceased son had been Napoléon II, but also that he recognized popular sovereignty; being emperor of the French *people* was different than being the emperor of *France*). What was more, he did all that with the overwhelming support of the French population, who (allegedly) voted *oui* by a twelve-to-one margin in favor of establishing the second French Empire.

1848 and After

Flash back to March 1848, when revolutionary agitation spread from Paris to Berlin. Again crowds gathered in the streets. Again the king refused to order his soldiers to fire on his "dear Berliners," whereupon Prussia's proud army commanders wept in humiliation. The House of Hohenzollern seemed to be paralyzed by these upstart burghers who were occupying government buildings and demanding liberal, democratic, social, or else nationalist reforms. The insurgents called on all Germans to transcend their divisions and elect a national assembly. That assembly convened in the Paulskirche (Church of St. Paul) in the city of Frankfurt-am-Main, its attendees convinced that Germany's age-old divisions were about to give way to a liberal national state.

Far from ending division, however, the delegates, mostly lawyers, in the Frankfurt Assembly argued about everything. They argued over whether to design a constitutional monarchy or a republic. They argued over representation and voting. They argued over what constituted Germany in the first place. Should all the Habsburg Empire be annexed to their notional national state (that was the so-called *grossdeutsch* solution), or just the German-speaking provinces, or indeed none of the Habsburg Empire (that was the *kleindeutsch* solution)? While they argued, two disturbing things happened. First, workers began to riot throughout the Rhineland—some of them inspired by Karl Marx's *Communist Manifesto*—and demanding radical social reforms. Germany's respectable burghers feared such agitation as much as the French bourgeoisie, but lacking any authority or means of coercion, they had nowhere to turn for help except to the king of Prussia, against whom they had rebelled in the first place.

Second, a foreign policy challenge arose when the king of Denmark claimed sovereignty over the contested German provinces of Schleswig and Holstein and occupied them with his army. That threw the Frankfurt Assembly into a nationalist frenzy. But once again, they had no way to resist the Danish claim except by asking the Prussian king if the assembly might "borrow" his army.

In the wake of those events Friedrich Wilhelm IV recovered his nerve. When the Frankfurt Assembly completed its draft of a constitution for a unified Germany in April 1849 and asked the king of Prussia to become *Deutscher Kaiser*, the monarch refused in language that echoed the title of that Parisian play *The Ragpicker*. He would not, he declared, accept a "crown from the gutter"—a crown based on a theory of popular sovereignty in which he did not believe. The Frankfurt Assembly disbanded in May 1849, and Germany's popular revolution sputtered to an end, largely because the causes of liberty, equality, and fraternity clashed with one another.

At least the events in Germany were relatively bloodless. That was not the case in the Habsburg Empire. In its provinces, nationalism could triumph only by smashing the empire to bits. Hence, the imperial armies were bound, sooner or later, to resist popular agitation.

The violence began in March 1848 when a Hungarian patriot named Louis Kossuth made a fiery speech in Budapest demanding independence for his people. The speech was published in Vienna, where workers and students inspired by their radicalized professors seized weapons from government armories, barricaded the emperor's Schönbrunn Palace, and called for Metternich's resignation. Now Emperor Ferdinand was a kindly, dull-witted epileptic. When told that his people were rioting, he asked, "B-b-b-b-ut, are zay allowed to do zat?" Like the rulers of France and Prussia, it took almost no time for Ferdinand to give in. He ordered his soldiers to evacuate Vienna, dismissed Metternich after forty years of service, and promised his people a constitution. *Nicht genug!* (Not enough), cried the students, now drunk with victory and brandishing muskets. So the imperial cabinet and palace guard bustled the royal family into carriages and fled to the Alpine city of Innsbruck, where the heartbroken emperor was persuaded to abdicate in favor of his eighteen-year-old son, Franz Josef. Meanwhile, when news spread that Vienna was in the hands of revolutionaries, ethnic minorities throughout the Habsburg Empire saw their opportunity to rebel.

Hungary, Bohemia, and the Italian provinces of Lombardy and Venetia declared independence, while the Czechs, Poles, and Croats sent representatives to a pan-Slavic assembly in Prague. It seemed a veritable Springtime of Peoples, the hour for national self-determination to triumph. But the armies of the teenaged emperor were still intact and still loyal to the dynasty. Readers may wonder why common soldiers drawn from the people would follow imperial orders to the point of suppressing their own countrymen when they were agitating for freedom. One answer is that disciplined professional soldiers are apolitical and trained to follow orders. Another is that the Habsburgs had long before learned the principle of "divide and conquer"; their commanders habitually stationed soldiers of one ethnicity on the soil of a rival ethnicity.

The Habsburg generals reconquered Franz Josef's empire one town and one province at a time. One Habsburg army under the Bohemian General Josef

Radetzky invaded Italy, where his Czech and German soldiers crushed the Lombards and Venetians, as well as—for good measure—the army of Piedmont-Savoy, whose Italian king had supported the revolt. Another, mostly Austrian army under General Alfred von Windischgrätz bombarded the city of Prague, dispersed the Slavic congress, and put its leaders to death. A third army led by the Croatian general Josip Jelačić invaded Hungary. The warlike Magyars fielded a sizable, well-trained army and successfully defended Hungarian independence for over a year. So Franz Josef was obliged to accept the help offered by Russia's reactionary Tsar Nicholas I, who had been itching to crush the revolutions in central Europe lest they spread eastward. In August 1849, therefore, a Russian army fell on the Hungarian troops from the rear and extinguished their independent republic in the Battle of Temesvár.

Thus did the events of 1848–49 break the heart of Romantics of all political persuasions. The monarchs and aristocrats learned that their dream of restoring the popular deference they had taken for granted prior to 1789 was a wistful folly. The middle classes learned that no matter how idealistic their motives, their nations' populations were divided among themselves, and furthermore that even inspired civilians could not prevail against professional soldiers. The lower classes learned that their demands for social reform would be met with violence from both the aristocrats and the middle classes. By 1850, the revolutionary episodes had ended, with no advance anywhere toward greater liberty, equality, or national unity. In the wake of that disillusionment hundreds of thousands of people abandoned Europe to rekindle their dreams overseas, especially in the United States. Those who remained shed their romanticism in favor of an icy realism, a perspective that would become manifest in European literature, painting, music, and not least in the continent's politics.

History is often described as just "one damned thing after another." Professional historians who try to make sense of the past contest that cynical judgment. But they are often the first to admit that human events are frequently unpredictable and occasionally puzzling. Who would have guessed, given the economic distress of the "Hungry Forties" and the social upheavals of 1848, that the decades of the 1850s and 1860s would be an era of phenomenal economic growth and domestic tranquility? For those were the decades when western and central European countries underwent their industrial take-off. The growth was triggered in part, beginning in 1849, by a huge influx of precious metals from the California Gold Rush, which pumped hundreds of millions of dollars into the world economy. In contrast to what happened when so much gold and silver were imported from New Spain in the seventeenth century, this time there was no inflation, for two very sound reasons. First, the international gold standard had been adopted by the continent's major countries; their currencies were therefore fixed against a particular weight of gold bullion. Second, industrialization was creating an ever-increasing supply of goods such that too much money was *not* chasing too few goods, which is the textbook definition of inflation. To be sure, levels of growth and prosperity varied widely across countries, industries, and social classes. But on the whole, Atlantic civilization boomed during the 1850s and 1860s. That fact, plus the safety valve of emigration, reduced social tensions and made disaffected groups more willing to accept the second great trend of the time, which was the pursuit of moderate adjustments in the status quo through reform from above, not revolution from below.

Thus, when the Crimean War of 1854-56—fought between the British and French empires on the one hand, and the Russian Empire on the other, over foreign influence in the Ottoman Turkish Empire—ended in Russia's defeat, Tsar Alexander II became determined to drag his huge empire into the modern world, just as Peter the Great had done 150 years before. The most stunning of Alexander's reforms from above was the abolition of serfdom in 1861. Meanwhile, war broke out in Italy when Emperor Napoléon III made an alliance with the Italian kingdom of Piedmont-Sardinia in 1859 and secretly plotted to trigger a war against the Austrian Empire. The French imperial and Piedmontese royal armies expelled the Habsburg forces from the Po River valley. That in turn allowed King Victor Emmanuel of Piedmont-Sardinia, his shrewd prime minister, Camillo di Cavour, and a swashbuckling soldier-of-fortune named Giuseppe Garibaldi to persuade or cajole the other Italian states to realize Machiavelli's old dream by merging themselves into a unified Kingdom of Italy in 1860. That same year, Abraham Lincoln was elected president of the United States, which provoked the bloody American Civil War, but which abolished slavery and empowered the federal government to promote national growth, best symbolized by completion of the transcontinental railroad in 1869.

The year 1869 also saw the completion of Egypt's Suez Canal, which was financed and engineered by a jointly owned Anglo-French company. That canal cut in half the length of time needed for ships to reach Asian ports from Europe. Two years before that, Parliament passed the British North America Act, creating the federal Dominion of Canada, as well as the Second Reform Bill, which expanded the franchise in Britain to include nearly all adult males. In 1868, on the other side of the world, rebellious nobles and their armies of samurai overthrew Japan's feudal shogunate and proclaimed the Meiji Restoration in the name of the Emperor Meiji. The new regime imposed a centralized government and promptly launched a crash program of industrialization and military modernization by imitating the institutions of Western countries. All those historic events made the 1850s and 1860s decades of national consolidation and reform-from-above throughout the northern hemisphere.

Finally, economic liberalism triumphed in those decades as France, the German *Zollverein*, and most other countries followed the British lead and adopted free trade by abolishing tariffs on foreign imports. Nationalism and liberalism were thus on the march everywhere, propelled not by revolution, but by the monarchical regimes themselves. The best example of such hard-boiled realism, and the political earthquake that had the most far-reaching effects on European history, was without a doubt the unification of Germany.

During the twentieth century numerous historians made it an article of faith that modern German history had somehow gone wrong and followed a pernicious *Sonderweg* (special path) of its own. It seemed to them that two world wars and a holocaust should not have been provoked by one of the most advanced nations on earth. Were these tragedies the result of no democratic revolution ever succeeding in Germany? Did they come about because national unity came so late to Germany? Or because the stamp of Prussian militarism was so strong in Germany? British historian A. J. P. Taylor singled out the revolution in 1848 as the turning point when Germany did not turn. But such judgments obscured the fact that, while Germany always had one foot in western Europe, it also always had one foot in eastern Europe, where empires thwarted nationalism, serfdom persisted into the nineteenth century, and aristocracy, autocracy, and militarism persisted into the twentieth century. Moreover, the Reformation left Germany divided into a Protestant north led by Prussia and a Catholic south led by Austria. In other words, Germany's geography, history, and culture raised more daunting barriers to the triumph of liberalism and nationalism than did those of, say, Britain, France, or Spain.

After the failure of the Frankfurt Assembly in 1848, Germany remained divided into thirty-four states. But two great movements led by Prussia overcame that disunity with surprising speed. The first was the campaign for economic unity, which dated from 1834. The second was a deft campaign for political unity through war and diplomacy.

The economic movement had been inspired by the free-market theories of Adam Smith. Prussia's ministers of finance recognized in the 1830s that Germany's many states could never prosper or even build a coherent network of railroads unless they liberalized and coordinated their policies. So Prussia negotiated with neighbor states to form the *Zollverein*, the customs union and common market, mentioned in chapter 15, that merged the economy of Prussia with those of central Germany and the southern states of Bavaria, Baden, and Württemberg. When Metternich's Conservative Austria remained aloof, it effectively yielded the economic future to Prussia. That became especially important when Germany's industrial revolution took off in the 1850s.

The political movement toward unification was one of the unintended consequences of the Prussian Constitution of 1850, which the king bestowed from above as a sop to the defeated revolutionaries of 1848. The constitution revived the Landtag, or parliament, but on terms that the monarchical regime and its aristocratic supporters expected would render it harmless. The constitution called for a complicated system of representation whereby the wealthiest group of Prussian subjects received three times the electoral influence, and middle-class subjects twice the influence, of the poorest subjects.

To everyone's surprise, that system did not result in Conservative rule. The economic boom of the 1850s was so enormous that tens of thousands of capitalists and professionals rose to the top rank of wealth, while hundreds of thousands of white-collar workers rose to the middle rank. The comparatively wealthy burghers tended to vote for liberals who promised further reforms. That prompted a crisis when the new king, Wilhelm I, decided to reform and expand his army. The now liberal majority in the Landtag refused to approve the funding the war ministry needed to realize Wilhelm's designs. The king was furious—after all, the army was Prussia's sacred cow—but the long-term stakes were really about who was to run the government: the king and his cabinet, or the parliament?

In 1862 Wilhelm decided to break the stalemate by naming as prime minister a burly, walrus-mustached diplomat named Otto von Bismarck. He would prove to be a ruthless and clever state-builder. Indeed, Bismarck came to personify *Realpolitik*—political realism—the way Richelieu had personified royal absolutism.

Bismarck was a traditional Junker of the Prussian landed gentry. He had little sympathy for the *nouveau riche* industrialists of Prussia's western Rhineland provinces. But being a realist, he had keenly observed the events of 1848-49, and he had judged that liberal and nationalist ideas could not be suppressed forever. He surmised that the supporters of such ideologies could be co-opted in ways that preserved as much royal and aristocratic privilege as possible, and he determined to do that by exploiting the German people's nationalism while frustrating their liberalism, at least in part. He would accomplish these ends by scoring foreign policy successes so popular that even most liberals would rally behind his semiauthoritarian domestic policies. In short, Bismarck was determined to make a revolution from above, which is why he was called a white revolutionary—white being the traditional color of monarchy—as opposed to a red revolutionary, who agitated for revolution from below.

Bismarck's first move was to order the efficient, obedient Prussian bureaucracy to collect the taxes needed to finance the army reforms, this in defiance of the power of the purse supposedly wielded by the Landtag. The Liberal Party howled that such behavior was unconstitutional, but short of inciting another 1848-style insurrection, the Liberals could do nothing about it. Next, Bismarck championed a popular, patriotic cause that all good Germans had to support: the dispute with Denmark over Schleswig-Holstein. In 1864 he petitioned the Diet of the German Confederation to declare a defensive war against the king of Denmark and forcibly add the provinces to the German Confederation. The Austrian and Prussian armies together made quick work of that task. The Liberals in the Landtag cheered.

Next, Bismarck picked a fight with the Habsburg Empire over who would administer Schleswig and Holstein. He knew that if it came to a showdown, the northern German Protestants in the Prussian Landtag would eagerly support a war against the southern German Catholics led by Austria. He also knew that most of the other German states would side with Prussia, if only because of the economic leverage Prussia wielded over them in the *Zollverein*. Finally, the army's general staff, led by a master of military operations named Helmuth von Moltke, assured Bismarck and the king in 1866 that the expanded and improved

Prussian army would soundly defeat the Austrians, not least because Prussian observers had studied the use of railroads and telegraphs in the recently concluded American Civil War.

As it turned out, the Austro-Prussian War of 1866 was a near thing. But when the Prussian army prevailed in the Battle of Königgrätz, Austrian Emperor Franz Josef was obliged to acquiesce in Prussian domination of northern Germany. In 1867 Bismarck replaced the German Confederation with a North German Confederation dominated by Prussia. He even deigned to declare universal male suffrage, with the caveat that ministers were to be appointed by the crown rather than chosen by a majority in the legislature.

Bismarck had gambled by scheduling new Landtag elections for what turned out to be the very day of the Battle of Königgrätz. Such was the patriotic war fever among the electorate that Prussian voters returned a Conservative majority, while many liberals broke off to form a National Liberal Party supportive of Bismarck. The new majority even resolved to legalize retroactively all the taxes, army reforms, and other policies the government had decreed since Bismarck took power in 1862. Thus did the patriotic *Mittelstand* (the middle and upper-middle classes) allow their nationalism to trump their liberalism. Henceforth, the powers of parliament were subordinate to the king, especially in foreign affairs and defense.

The only task left was for Bismarck to lure Bavaria, Baden, and Württemberg into his federation. The populations of those southern German states were mostly Catholic and had no love for Prussia. But Bismarck judged that he could appeal to their patriotism by picking a fight with an enemy all Germans hated and feared: the French. Nor was that hard to do, because French Emperor Napoléon III was a pale shadow of his great uncle and a blundering strategist. Indeed, Napoléon III played himself into Bismarck's hands by demanding German territory as compensation for French neutrality during the Austro-Prussian War. Bismarck publicized that arrogant demand, causing tempers to flare on both sides of the Rhine. Franco-Prussian relations deteriorated further when a Hohenzollern relative of the king of Prussia became a candidate for the throne of Spain, which had fallen vacant. Needless to say, the French were hotly opposed to that possibility. Finally, Louis Napoléon and his ministers foolishly decided that a glorious war was just what they needed to boost the emperor's sagging popularity at home. Bismarck thereby easily maneuvered Napoléon III into declaring war on Prussia in 1870. Von Moltke's finely tuned army, now reinforced by the armies of the south German states, soundly defeated the French. They even captured Louis Napoléon himself at the fortress of Sedan and went on to lay siege to Paris. Napoléon III abdicated the throne, and in 1871 a provisional French government surrendered.

It was during the siege of Paris that the kings and princes of the various German states convened in Louis XIV's palace at Versailles to draw their swords and swear fealty to Wilhelm I as *Deutscher Kaiser* of a now united Reich. This was no crown from the gutter offered by a revolutionary assembly, but a crown offered by the legitimate German princes. Hence it was a crown King Wilhelm I could readily accept.

Thus had Bismarck satisfied the long-frustrated nationalist desires of the German people, but in such a way as to ensure that the Reich was dominated by Prussia and that Prussia was dominated by its king, its army, its Junker aristocracy, and Bismarck himself, who would go on to govern as chancellor for another twenty years. Germany had an all-German parliament, the Reichstag, elected by universal male suffrage, but its powers were limited. Under Bismarck's prudent leadership, moreover, the mighty new Germany did not threaten the other powers on the continent, but instead served as a conservative force for balance and peace.

Finally, Bismarck himself pronounced the epitaph for an era that had begun with futile romantic revolutions but had ended in fruitful realistic reforms, when he lectured the Prussian Landtag in 1862. "The great questions of our time," he intoned, "cannot be solved by speeches and majority votes. That was the mistake of 1848. No, the great questions of our time will be decided by iron and blood."

Chapter 18

"Nothing to Lose but Your Chains": The Rise of Socialism

Long before cable TV, streamers, and YouTube made documentaries a round-the-clock viewing option, the BBC produced a thirteen-episode series on European history since 1871. It was called *The Mighty Continent*—an excellent title, especially because the adjective was never more justified than during the late nineteenth century. Over those decades Europe the Mighty Continent doubled, then redoubled, its power, both in absolute terms and in comparison to most other parts of the world. Moreover, Europe's leap forward occurred during an era of unusual peace, prosperity, reform, and ever-deepening faith in science and technology. Never before or since was European civilization more confident of its progress and superiority than during the years 1871 to 1914.

Consider demography. We have already seen how the green revolution increased Europe's population from 100 million in 1650 to 266 million by 1850. Over those two centuries Europe's share of the human race rose from 18 percent to 25 percent. A mere fifty years later, in 1900, Europeans numbered 400 million (indeed, almost 500 million if one counts emigrants overseas), or fully 30 percent of humanity. Never have white people been more numerous, relative to other races, than around the year 1910.

Why such a phenomenal display of vitality? First, scientific agriculture, including the use of artificial, nitrogen-rich fertilizers developed by organic chemists. Second, the industrial revolution, which enabled mass production of life's essentials, not least mechanized farm implements. Third, medical research, which reduced the mortality rate and yielded vaccines against scourges like cholera and smallpox. Fourth, the willingness of European wives to bear lots of children—and the willingness of their husbands to support large families.

Farm families in Europe had always been large. But the practice of raising more than two children continued even in Europe's late nineteenth-century cities because soaring productivity reduced the price of household staples, and because overseas emigration, especially to North America, offered a relatively cheap solution to overpopulation. Later, during the twentieth century, European birth rates would be sharply reduced by war, economic depression, the spread of birth-control methods, and the entry of women into the work force. But from 1871 to 1914 people of European stock multiplied at a frenetic pace, even as Europe became a modern scientific, industrial powerhouse. Those trends overthrew the rough balance of power that had existed between the West and the Rest. Europe now enjoyed the biggest technological edge any civilization had, or has, ever possessed (which is why Europeans were able to colonize other continents in a process described in the next chapter).

Equally important is the fact that Europe's growth was not at all uniform. Its various countries grew at different paces, and that differential threatened to upset the rough balance of power that existed among the great powers. By 1900, the rapid growth of unified Germany struck fear in the hearts of Frenchmen, whose population mysteriously failed to increase over the course of the nineteenth century, while German industrial and commercial competition worried the British. For their part, the Germans looked eastward and saw in Russia a behemoth that boasted over twice Germany's population—plus, thanks to the industrialization that finally began in the 1890s, a faster economic growth rate. The paranoia born of that uneven growth made for tense foreign relations at the turn of the twentieth century.

Statistics such as coal and steel production and miles of railroad built tell part of the story, but only part. By this time those were mature industries. We must look instead at the host of breakthrough technologies being developed in Europe by the end of the nineteenth century: gas lighting and heating, electricity and the telephone, chemical dyes and paints, the internal combustion engine and the new age of petroleum. The business cycle was still operative, causing periodic recessions, especially during the era from 1873 to 1896. But overall, British exports rose eightfold from 1850 to 1900, Germany raced to surpass Britain in gross domestic product, and world trade as a whole grew at the astounding pace of 3.4 percent per year. That was due largely to the cornucopia of food, raw materials, and manufactures that flooded world markets. But it was also a result of liberal economic policies. The 1840s to 1870s were the heyday of free trade, and even when many governments restored tariffs on foreign competitors during the hard times that followed the financial Panic of 1873, trade barriers never approached the levels of the old mercantilist era.

International cooperation extended to other fields. In 1874, twenty-one nations sent delegates to Geneva to form a Universal Postal Union, creating a cheap, secure system of postal delivery all over Europe. The following year the nations established an international Bureau of Weights and Measures, and in 1883 the Paris Convention standardized laws covering copyrights and patents. The greatest global institution of all was the gold standard. Western governments recognized that ensuring a stable national currency was a sacred responsibility, so they all fixed the value of their paper money and bonds to a weight in gold. That made inflation impossible, since the central banks of that era could not issue new currency without having a safe percentage of their paper money covered by gold reserves. In the United States, because of the Democratic Party's traditional hostility to central banks, the ruinous costs of the Civil War, and Americans' love affair with cheap credit, the federal government was for some time far less responsible. But by the 1880s the US dollar, too, had become "as good as gold." Finally, the rapidly growing global commercial system profited from the leadership of the Bank of England. The Little Old Lady of Threadneedle Street, as the stuffy institution was nicknamed, monitored currency flows and extended credit when some developing economy like the Ottoman or Argentine faced a liquidity crisis. (Incidentally, although paper money had been invented by the Chinese as early as the Han Dynasty, or the second century BC, paper money did not come into fashion in Europe until 1694, when the Bank of England began to issue paper bonds to finance the nation's wars against Louis XIV.)

Trust in money and responsible government encouraged foreign direct investment. By 1850 the British held a stake of some two hundred million pounds in foreign countries. That number became one billion pounds by 1875, then four billion pounds by 1914, the equivalent of twenty billion gold-standard dollars, or about a half trillion dollars today. French foreign investments were also prodigious, numbering by 1914 roughly half the British total. The practice of turning profits by stimulating the growth of another country's economy had been simply unthinkable in the days of mercantilism. By the late 1800s, free-market theorists boasted that global economic interdependence was making war unthinkable.

Still, global industrial capitalism had its tensions. The last half of the nineteenth century was when sheer scale rendered outmoded many firms managed by individual entrepreneurs, families, or partnerships. The times favored the growth of big, impersonal corporations managed by salaried professionals in a pyramidal hierarchy led by a CEO or chairman of the board. Railroads pioneered that executive chain of command, in which authority and responsibility were delegated downward, while information on costs and revenues was passed upward. Railroad management was frankly military. Executives commanded armies of workers, machines, and supply trains dispersed over hundreds of miles. What is more, bigness did not stop at the level of the firm. By the 1870s, in order to share international markets, corporations in mature industries formed oligopolies whose size and scale exceeded the resources of even the richest family firms or partnerships. Thus, firms in need of vast amounts of capital turned themselves into publicly held corporations. This way they could raise capital from the sale of stock and attract investment from banks.

Bigness also extended to marketing. The first department stores and grocery chains opened their doors in the 1870s. They offered shoppers both convenience and, in some cases, lower prices, thanks to their ability to buy in bulk. Mass marketing was a boon to consumers, but it angered small shopkeepers who could not compete.

The upshot of all this dynamic, competitive, sometimes partially rigged big business was mixed and ironic. In one respect, capitalists behaved the way Karl Marx predicted. They swallowed each other up to grow bigger and bigger, or else colluded with other big fish they could not swallow. What French and Germans called industrial cartels and Americans called trusts or rings habitually fixed prices and divvied up market share, in defiance of the laissez-faire capitalism they claimed to support. Sometimes one giant conglomerate controlled what amounted to a national network. Examples include Germany's *Allgemeine*

"Nothing to Lose but Your Chains"

Elektrizitäts Gesellschaft (General Electric Company), British Petroleum, and Royal Dutch Shell. Armaments industries followed this pattern, too. Britain's Vickers, France's Schneider-Creusot, Austria's Skoda Works, and Germany's Krupp virtually monopolized their markets. Yet in another respect, Marx's predictions were confounded by the fact that public stock trading deconcentrated ownership of the means of production and created a large middle class rather than a handful of rich capitalists and a mass of oppressed workers.

A more accurate model of maturing industrial capitalism was provided by sociologist Karl Polanyi, who identified four sturdy foundations of the late nineteenth-century economic order. The first was the self-regulating market or free-enterprise economy. The second was the liberal state, which enforced the law but did not attempt to regulate social and economic outcomes. The third was the gold standard, which stabilized currencies. And the fourth was the European balance of power among nations. Looked at one way, two of these foundations were political and two economic. Looked at another way, two were domestic and two international. Most contemporaries took it for granted that these foundations were not only good but natural. They saw no reason the progress they nourished could not go on forever. Nevertheless, dissenters existed in this bourgeois paradise, and it is to them that this chapter now turns.

What does the term Victorian Age call to mind today? Perhaps sexual prudery, patriarchy, uncomfortable fashions, elegant architecture, or the unabashed exploitation of European workers at home and nonwhite races in colonies overseas. If so, that image says more about contemporary agendas and prejudices than it does about the nineteenth century. In fact, the Victorian Era was a self-assured time when earnest, successful Protestants like British Prime Minister William Gladstone assumed that their prosperity and public morals were signs of God's favor and that their science and industry were sources of continuous progress. It was an era when demure middle-class women were expected to be models of domesticity cared for by their dutiful, striving husbands. It was a point of pride that middle- and upper-class women did not have to work outside the home—except as volunteers serving churches, charities, and the arts. Indeed, Liberal party platforms in the nineteenth century even looked forward to a time when poor women would be freed from the drudgery of labor.

The novelists of the era, such as Charles Dickens and Émile Zola, poignantly recorded the fact that bourgeois propriety and female domesticity rarely extended to the working classes. But what does that term "working classes" even mean? Except for a few aristocratic playboys with inherited money, everyone worked hard during the Victorian Era. Ambitious young clerks, for instance, might work ten- or twelve-hour shifts in the hope of getting ahead, thus working as long and as hard as a factory hand, farmer, or miner. The difference was that white-collar workers did not go home literally soiled, as did the blue-collar workers in the so-called "sweated trades."

The signs of a working-class man were dirty fingernails and body odor that made bourgeois ladies carry scented hankies in the streets. Workers ate cheap meat pies, sausages, and tripe rather than roast beef and lamb. Working-class men drank beer and ale rather than wine and whiskey, and they patronized pubs and taverns rather than restaurants and clubs. Working-class women might augment the family's income by toiling as seamstresses, laundresses, or scullery maids. Working-class neighborhoods had improved significantly since the early decades of the Industrial Revolution, because municipal governments now provided sewers, plumbing, trolley cars, and police and fire protection. Real wages had generally risen, if slowly, during the nineteenth century, and workers' cooperatives now offered mortgages and insurance. Still, lower-class life was anxious. Husbands might be laid off or suffer crippling injuries. Wives might die in childbirth or from infectious diseases. The young and enterprising might take ship for America, Canada, or Australia, or they might save enough money to start a small business. Otherwise, the only hope for advancement was if one's fellows down at the mill could bargain or strike for higher wages, shorter hours, and job security.

Middle-class reformers usually gave moral answers to the social questions raised by working-class existence. Catholic and Protestant evangelists went to the tenements and slums to dispense charity and teach literacy, but also to inveigh against promiscuity, alcohol, tobacco, gambling, and crime. They urged thrift and hard work as the best route out of poverty. But they could not provide the financial benefits needed by workers, such as workman's compensation in case of injury, unemployment insurance, and old-age pensions.

All this must be written to discourage readers from thinking of "the masses," "the workers," or "the proletariat" as some abstract amalgam. Those were labels invoked by Conservatives, Liberals, and radicals who had their own purposes for conjuring fear or sympathy among middle-class people, or else angry solidarity among lower-class people. Unfortunately, most social history has been written by socialists who tend to convey the idea that working-class history is socialist history. A glance at the flag-waving blue-collar workers in today's America should disabuse us of that notion. In the European context, especially, the more workers suffered, the more radical socialists cheered, because *they hoped for* a violent revolution. Alas, for them, that prospect held little appeal for real workers, most of whom simply wanted to improve their own and their families' lives.

Recall that in the 1840s the maturing working-class in England had begun to form trade unions and had launched the great Chartist movement. English workers' ongoing protests finally won the vote for all adult males through the Second Reform Bill of 1867. Meanwhile, Parliament passed legislation to improve conditions in the workplace. Elsewhere in Europe poor people were being driven from farms to towns to find employment. Others were craftsmen whose livelihoods were threatened by competition from factory-made manufactures. Then, following the revolutions of 1848, the continental economy took off. Urban industrial classes formed quickly in France, the Low Countries, and Prussia. As they did, three principal patterns of response gradually developed across Europe. First was the trade union movement. Second was the founding of moderate Socialist parties. Third was the emergence of underground movements, whether Marxist, syndicalist, or anarchist, bent on destroying capitalism altogether.

The labor movement evolved differently in each country. English workers placed their hopes in the trade union movement. The British Labour Party was not founded until the dawn of the twentieth century, and it showed no interest in revolution. German workers also unionized; they founded the Social Democratic Party to compete for votes and press for social reform. In less developed southern Europe, say Spain or Italy, urban workers remained a small minority of the population. They tended to follow movements called syndicalist, movements that exhorted workers in all industries to unite in a general strike that would shut down the entire economy. Labor in France displayed elements of all three patterns: unions, socialist parties, and syndicalists. Finally, workers in Russia, the least industrial economy, were generally represented by underground parties devoted to violent revolution.

Trade unions and (after 1895) the Labour Party were the keynotes of working-class politics in Great Britain in the late nineteenth and early twentieth centuries.

As each country is examined in turn, remember always the distinction that must be drawn between genuine labor organizations and revolutionary intellectuals. For there were always two ways to relate to capitalists, if indeed one blamed them for the ills of society: either destroy them or bargain with them. The first option required that poverty and injustice grow worse and worse until the desperate workers rose in revolution. The second required that class conflict be mollified so that wage workers could share in the wealth created by industrial capitalism. Thus, trade unionists and revolutionaries always worked at cross purposes.

The first generation of socialists, including those weird utopians like Saint-Simon, had been discredited by the failure of the romantic revolutions of 1848–49. They then disappeared completely during the economic boom times of the 1850s and 1860s. What took their place was a revolutionary doctrine that seemed realistic, even scientific, instead of utopian, and promised the working classes real power in the not-so-distant future. That new doctrine was communism.

"Nothing to Lose but Your Chains"

The word *communism* was first popularized by a twenty-year-old English dissident named John Goodwyn Barmby. In 1840, Barmby had traveled to Paris, where he first heard the word. Upon his return to England he founded the Propaganda Society, which declared communism man's true and final religion. "I believe that the divine is communism, that the demoniac is individualism." He wrote communist prayers and hymns and called himself pope of the communist church. Barmby also explained world history in terms of four stages: the pastoral, the feudal, the commercial, and ultimately the communist. "In the holy communist Church," he wrote, "the devil will be converted into God . . . and call all peoples to a communion of works and goods both spiritual and natural, for these latter days . . . when social perfection would be achieved on earth as it is in heaven."

In Germany, a left-wing socialist named Arnold Ruge came to like Barmby's theory of history, but he expressed it in terms derived from the philosopher G. W. F. Hegel's dialectical model of historical progress. Ruge suspected that mankind had been communist in the state of nature and that it would become so again when the proletariat made a revolution that abolished private property. Karl Marx was a protégé of Ruge. Born in 1818 in the Rhineland, the son of a lawyer, Marx was educated in Jewish theology and confessed he was "durch und durch bürgerlich" (bourgeois through and through). He married a tender Gentile woman of some distinction, Jenny von Westphalen, and was a devoted husband and father. Jenny's family money allowed Karl to devote his life to scholarship, which gradually purged him of sentimentality in favor of a hard materialist philosophy.

So it was that Marx's grand synthesis melded Barmby's communism and four stages of history with Ruge's revolutionary proletariat, Hegel's dialectical philosophy of progress, Proudhon's notion of property as theft, Saint-Simon's faith in technology, and the Manchester School's laissez-faire economics. In other words, Marx synthesized the German philosophical tradition with the French revolutionary tradition and the English economic tradition.

He and Friedrich Engels, the rebellious son of a big industrialist, drafted *The Communist Manifesto* in 1848. They spent the next thirty years developing their ideology—most thoroughly in *Das Kapital*—and engaging in polemics against rival socialists who did not accept Marx's theories as gospel. I use the word "gospel" advisedly, for ideologies that purport to explain all mysteries and prophesy the future possess the qualities of a secular religion. As Engels preached, "All religions up to now have merely been the expression of historical stages. . . . Communism is the stage that makes all existing religions superfluous and abolishes them."

Marx and Engels clarified how their communism was unique. First, communism did not mean everyone would share ownership of the means of production (i.e., capital), but rather that nobody would. Second, the communist moral code decreed how wealth was to be distributed: "From each according to his abilities, to each according to his needs." Third, Marx and Engels differed from other socialists in declaring communism a "jealous god," which meant their followers must renounce all bourgeois sentimentality, traditional morality, and interest in other forms of socialism. Like sixteenth-century Jesuits, communists were called to be fanatical, obedient, and disciplined. Fourth, Marxism embraced the violence that utopian socialists had scorned. As early as 1846 Engels said he "refused to recognize any other means to establish communism except by violent, democratic revolution."

Lastly, Marxism purported to explain all history through its analysis of class conflict. History, it claimed, was driven forward by changing technology and struggles for ownership of the means of production. History moved through stages, from slave-based ancient societies that were overthrown by barbaric lords, to feudal societies that were overthrown by bourgeois merchants, to capitalist societies that would in turn be overthrown by proletarians to found communist society. All this was inevitable, not a tale of good and evil, not a tale of heroism, nothing except the iron laws of history playing out over time. This full-blown ideology was internally consistent. Hence it was disprovable on its own terms, so long as one accepted its basic premises. Communism was a sort of secular church, and just like a religious movement the soil of Marxism was fertilized by the blood of its martyrs, the most celebrated of whom were the French Communards of 1871.

That was the year of the Franco-Prussian War when the Germans captured Emperor Napoléon III and laid siege to Paris. The city bravely held out over the winter of 1870–71 despite growing privation. Starving Parisians were in no mood to cheer when their well-fed countrymen staged a national assembly at Versailles to found another republic and talk peace with the Germans. Instead, the working-class districts in Paris raised the red flag of revolution, threw up barricades, and waged a class war against the bourgeois National Guard augmented by prisoners of war whom the Prussian army released for the purpose of suppressing the radical working class. The resulting *semaine saglante*—or bloody week—dwarfed even the violent June Days of 1848. At least twenty thousand people were killed. Needless to say, Marxists throughout Europe celebrated the Communards as martyred saints.

By the 1860s and '70s, Marxism had become an important strain of revolutionary ideology, but it was not the only one. Disciples of Proudhon, who had warned that the dictatorship of the proletariat would prove as oppressive as capitalism, logically concluded that the only way to liberate workers and indeed the whole human race was to abolish governments altogether. Syndicalists believed that might be done through the general strike. But anarchists believed it could be done only by assassinating the leaders of every government. In 1881 Russian anarchists blew up Tsar Alexander II's carriage. Anarchists shot French President Carnot in 1894, Austrian Empress Elisabeth in 1898, Italian King Umberto in 1900, and American President William McKinley in 1901. Anarchists twice narrowly failed to assassinate Kaiser Wilhelm I. Their nihilist spirit was expressed most eloquently by Peter Kropotkin, who called for "permanent revolt, by word of mouth, by writing, by the dagger, the rifle, and dynamite." Marxists considered such fringe groups unscientific and undisciplined: heretics, in effect. But anarchists pioneered modern terrorism as the favored technique by which underground radicals could spread fear and command attention for their cause.

What had all that philosophy and terrorism to do with the ordinary workers of Europe? Very little indeed. To be sure, a Europe-wide Socialist International was formed in 1864. But it was dominated by intellectuals rather than genuine laborers, and it splintered when Marx tried to purge all non-communists from its ranks. It splintered again after the defeat of the Paris Commune.

Real working-class leadership soon passed to the German Social Democratic Party (or SPD), formed in 1869, and to the German Catholic Center Party, formed in 1871. Their leaders, the Marxists Wilhelm Liebknecht and Auguste Bebel, along with the Center Party's Ludwig Windthorst, imagined themselves to be neither ideologues nor revolutionaries, but rather the political voices of Germany's two trade union movements: one secular, the other Catholic. They quickly caught the attention of Germany's Chancellor Otto von Bismarck, who waged a veritable *Kulturkampf* (cultural struggle) against both of them and even persuaded the Reichstag to outlaw the SPD in 1878. The Iron Chancellor's most effective policy, however, was to enact a comprehensive social welfare program providing for state-funded disability and unemployment insurance and old-age pensions: the first such program anywhere. That helps to explain why, after the new Kaiser Wilhelm II allowed the anti-Socialist laws to lapse, the SPD became the largest political party in Germany. Now that it was legal, a party congress promptly adopted Eduard Bernstein's moderate Erfurt Program of 1891, which forswore revolution in favor of gradualism. Henceforth German socialists pledged to work with big business and government to improve workers' standard of living. Communists attacked Bernstein's program as cowardly revisionism.

Britain's labor movement was even less radical. Trade unions had been legal there since 1824, and by 1900 they had organized more than two million workers (there were, by contrast, one million such workers in Germany, and a quarter-million in France). British workers rejected Marxism altogether. They were pleased to let the Liberal and Conservative parties compete for their votes. In 1870 Parliament provided for universal public education and a Public Health Act for state funding of urban sanitation. In 1875, unions were permitted to picket factories to prevent owners from hiring scabs to replace strikers. That same year Parliament voted to subsidize low-income housing. Britain lagged behind Bismarck's Germany in direct social welfare, but clearly the British working class could work within the system. When in 1900 Keir Hardie founded the Labour Party, its platform was socialist but not at all revolutionary.

In France, the constitution that founded the Third Republic in the 1870s legalized trade unions. But the memory of the Paris Commune had a sobering effect. France, more than any country, had experienced bloody class war. Moreover, since France had far less heavy industry than Britain or Germany, her urban workers were a decided minority of the population. Finally, the French labor movement was split; the unions were anarcho-syndicalist, while the leftist political parties were Marxist. So despite occasional paranoia on the part of the French police and factory owners, the French workers' movement was never much of a threat.

All these moderating trends were reflected in the Second Socialist International, founded in 1889. Its platforms were limited to promoting social legislation and protesting militarism and imperialism. Relegated to outcast status, the Marxist delegates argued with each other in the hallways. Marx died in 1883, and Engels's death followed in 1895. By that time their doctrines had already been "socialized" (pardon the pun) into mainstream politics. Only their most fanatical adherents still believed in violent revolution, and most of them were exiles from the country least prepared for an industrial working-class movement: Russia.

Russia was always an enigma for Marxists, for even though the brutality of the tsar's secret police turned many critics into angry revolutionaries, Russia was so underdeveloped that its urban working class was still relatively small. To be sure, radical opposition to the autocracy, aristocracy, and infant capitalist system grew in the mid-nineteenth century. But Alexander Herzen and other sensible radicals imagined a revolution led by peasants eager to dispossess landlords and restore the *mir*, the traditional village commune. In the 1860s Nikolai Chernyshevsky grafted terrorism onto Herzen's populism and inspired radical students to "go to the People" in hopes of stirring up peasant revolt. The only result was that the regime shut down all college campuses for two years, while the police arrested agitators and tsarist judges condemned them to hard labor in Siberian prison camps.

The failure of Chernyshevsky's movement inspired some Russian radicals to become anarchist terrorists. By around 1890, when Russian industrialization began to accelerate, radicals had gravitated toward one or another underground movement. The biggest was the Social Revolutionary Party, or SRs, because it appealed to the peasants. The next largest consisted of the Social Democrats, or SDs, founded in 1898.

The SDs were Marxists who imagined themselves the vanguard of the communist revolution. Orthodox Marxists asked how a communist revolution could take place in a country so retrograde that a bourgeois capitalist revolution had not even overthrown the feudal aristocracy. That was a good question. It caused the SDs' Menshevik faction to conclude that Marxists must wait a long time before Russia would be ripe for a proletarian revolution. But a minority faction, which falsely took the name Bolshevik, or majority, disagreed. They brazenly revised Marxist theory, insisted that Russia could move directly from feudalism to communism, and worked to foment a revolution whenever the right opportunity came along.

In 1903 the SD Party split, whereupon the Bolshevik leader, Vladimir Ilyich Ulyanov, who took the alias Lenin, organized a network of communist cells determined to realize in Russia a Marxist fantasy that events elsewhere had already proven impossible. Urban proletarians—real, live, working-class men and women—did not want to wage a violent insurrection in the name of some future utopia. But thanks to the Bolsheviks' lockstep discipline, plus some unlikely quirks of history, Marxism-Leninism would emerge as one of the mightiest forces on the Mighty Continent throughout the twentieth century.

Chapter 19

Fluttered Folk and Wild: Europe's New Imperialism

In 1946 George Orwell wrote an essay titled "Politics and the English Language." Orwell was an earnest participant in the ideological conflicts of the twentieth century that culminated in World War II. He observed how propaganda and pretense had debased political discourse to the point that words no longer had any real meaning—especially in totalitarian states, yes, but even in democracies like his native Great Britain.

It has long been obvious to post–World War II generations that "imperialism" is just such a word. It has degenerated into a pejorative epithet with no more substance than a curse. During the Cold War the Americans and the Soviets both accused the other of imperialism. Since the end of the Cold War critics at home and abroad have damned what they perceive as America's military, economic, and cultural imperialism masquerading as humanitarian intervention. Critics in the Western democracies likewise accuse the Chinese, Russians, and Iranians of harboring imperialist designs. Even Vladimir Putin accuses the members of the NATO alliance of harboring imperialist designs against Russia.

Imperialism today is simply a dirty word to be hurled at any nation whose foreign policies someone opposes. The more hostility it expresses the less intellectual content it conveys. Historians must nevertheless still use the word, for

Cartoons such as this one either spoofed or celebrated the neocolonial craze in the late nineteenth century.

the simple reason that people in the past employed it and meant something concrete by it. And what was that?

In the late nineteenth century, an era characterized by the so-called New Imperialism, both European governments and their critics took the term to mean formal, political control over non-European lands and peoples in the form of overseas colonies. The phrase New Imperialism was not used by contemporaries. That term was invented by later historians, so it is incumbent on them to explain what was so new about the phenomenon and why many governments and people of the late nineteenth and twentieth centuries imagined imperialism to be a positive good, even a duty, for their states and societies.

By the late 1800s Europeans already possessed a long tradition of overseas empire dating back to the Age of Exploration and the early modern era of mercantilist competition. But by the end of the nineteenth century those mercantilist empires had mostly dissolved. In 1776 Britain's thirteen North American colonies declared independence. That same year Scottish economist Adam Smith debunked mercantilist theory in *The Wealth of Nations*. After 1808 Latin Americans struggled for independence from Spain, and by the 1820s nearly all had achieved it. What followed was an increasingly Liberal era during which free-trade theory persuaded European statesmen and economists that colonies were usually a liability more than an asset.

But there were notable exceptions to this anticolonial consensus. Paradoxically, they occurred in the most liberal countries, including Great Britain and the Netherlands. In India, for example, the British expanded their Raj (rule) to the point that by the 1840s they controlled the Indian subcontinent. However, that conquest was achieved by the privately owned British East India Company. John Company, as it was nicknamed, raised private armies, made private alliances with local rulers, and carried on private commerce. Not until 1857, when the sanguine Sepoy Mutiny erupted among Muslims serving in John Company's army, did the British crown reluctantly take over the Raj. For their part, the Dutch never relinquished their grip on the spice islands. But it was the Dutch East India Company, not the government, that ruled Indonesia. Furthermore, the founding of white settler colonies was, for the most part, a matter of independent pioneers pushing inland and blundering into wars against Australia's Aborigines, New Zealand's Maoris, and South Africa's Zulus. Like the Indian wars in the American West, such conflicts were not planned and indeed were viewed by the European governments as a damnable nuisance.

Then the official mood suddenly changed. After 1876 the European powers, and by the 1890s Japan and the United States as well, engaged in a frenzy of colonial acquisitions that left virtually all the lands and peoples of Africa, Asia, and the Pacific under one or another foreign flag.

It all began when the Khedive (viceroy) of Egypt went broke. Egypt was an autonomous province of the Ottoman Empire, but it had become a vital interest to Europeans when a joint Anglo-French Company completed the Suez Canal in 1869. The Khedive was granted a third of the company's stock in exchange for providing the real estate, but he was such a spendthrift that he soon sold his shares in the company, then borrowed more money from British and French banks, then defaulted on those loans in 1876. Creditors agreed to advance him more money on the condition that European accountants assume control of the Egyptian treasury (a condition that was no more than what the World Bank and International Monetary Fund impose on delinquent countries today). But Egyptian Arabs not only hated the infidels who came to run their country; they also hated the irresponsible Khedive. Their army rebelled and demanded the Europeans go home.

What were the French and British to do? Britain's prime minister at the time was William Gladstone, an outspoken Liberal who despised colonialism, but he could not allow the Egyptian army to defy British banks and officials and perhaps even physically seize the strategic canal. The British and French governments therefore planned a joint occupation. But at the last minute the national assembly in Paris thought better of launching an expensive invasion into a hostile Arab land, so Gladstone reluctantly decided in 1882 that he must go it alone and make Egypt a British protectorate. Whereupon French public opinion succumbed to a nationalist fit of outrage and insisted that the French government compete with the British for empire all over the world.

From Algeria and Senegal in West Africa, French soldiers moved into the Niger River basin, occupied Timbuktu, and by 1890 had claimed the entire Sahara Desert. In Southeast Asia's land of Vietnam, where French missionaries had arrived in the 1860s, French soldiers followed the Red River valley to Hanoi and the Mekong River valley to Saigon. By 1887 they had occupied Cambodia and Laos, as well, and had united all those provinces into a colony called French Indochina. The British, alarmed by all this French colonialist expansion, pushed inland from their own coastal garrisons to annex Burma and Malaysia in Southeast Asia, plus vast African territories like Nigeria, Rhodesia, Kenya, and the Sudan.

Meanwhile, other countries had joined the scramble, the oddest of which was Belgium. For several decades intrepid explorers had been venturing into the heart of what Europeans called the Dark Continent, searching, among other things, for the mysterious source of the Nile River. The most famous explorer was a Scottish missionary and doctor named David Livingstone, who disappeared for years somewhere in Uganda. At length a New York newspaper sponsored journalist Henry Stanley to plunge into the East African bush in a search for the missionary. Finding the good doctor at his clinic deep in the jungle, Stanley uttered a simple greeting that would soon become famous: "Dr. Livingstone, I presume."

Upon Stanley's return from Africa, he was hired by King Leopold I of Belgium to help him realize his dream of claiming a personal empire. Under Leopold's sponsorship Stanley explored the entire length of the Congo River from 1879 to 1884. He either bribed or duped all the African chiefs he encountered into making treaties that placed their realms under the protection of the king of the Belgians.

At the same time, Germany joined the colonialist competition. Chancellor Bismarck had previously had no use for colonies, since Germany was not a naval power and, being sandwiched between France and Russia, it had enough security problems at home. But some German merchants thought colonies might provide markets and raw materials, while nationalists believed the recently unified Reich would not command the respect it deserved until it boasted of overseas empire. Bismarck therefore relented, and in 1884 the German government claimed the present-day countries of Namibia, Togo, Cameroon, and Tanzania, plus Kaiser Wilhelm's Land on the island of New Guinea and the Marshall and Caroline islands in the Pacific. In 1885 Bismarck hosted a conference in Berlin where Europe's diplomats drew up boundaries for existing colonial claims and drafted rules for future ones.

In the 1890s two newcomers joined the scramble. Japan had industrialized rapidly since the Meiji Restoration in 1868 and built a modern navy and army. Japanese strategists realized that if they wished to avoid becoming an object of imperialism they must become empire builders themselves. So in 1894 Japan attacked the decrepit Ch'ing or Manchu Empire of China and conquered Korea, southern Manchuria, and Taiwan. That in turn kicked off a scramble for concessions in China by which France, Russia, and Britain all pressured Peking into granting them spheres of influence, too.

The second rising power, the United States, went to war against Spain in 1898, ostensibly to liberate Cuba. President William McKinley and the Congress took that occasion to annex the Spanish colonies of the Philippines, Guam, and Puerto Rico, as well as the formerly independent Hawaiian islands. Four years later President Theodore Roosevelt engineered a revolution to make Panama independent from Colombia, in exchange for which the new Panamanian government ceded to the United States a zone through which to dig a canal. Finally, British oil companies penetrated the Persian Gulf, while Russian expansionists threatened Persia (modern Iran) from the north.

Thus, in the mere twenty years following Britain's 1882 occupation of Egypt, the imperial powers had divvied up lands and seas covering much of the globe. Why did this New Imperialism occur? Contemporary observers and later historians have advanced no less than six major theories.

First, economic theorists both capitalist and socialist imagined this new burst of imperialism as designed to boost foreign trade and thus to relieve Europe's maturing industries from looming overproduction. Businessmen feared that domestic markets were becoming saturated. Hence, they scoured the world in search of new markets and sources of raw materials. This theory gained plausibility from the fact that some of the colonial promoters were indeed businessmen, and because some government officials justified their colonial policies on economic grounds. Accordingly, English Liberal John Hobson described the New Imperialism as a neo-mercantilist effort to monopolize spheres of influence. Indeed, during the long period of recession or sluggish growth that followed the Panic of 1873, policies of free trade were being rolled back. European governments once again imposed protective tariffs at home while annexing colonies abroad. Germany adopted a tariff in 1879 and five years later became a colonial power. France passed a tariff in 1881 and leapt into the colonial field after the Egyptian affair of 1882. Italy raised tariffs in 1887 and began to seek colonial expansion. Tsarist Russia's high tariff policies in the 1890s coincided with ambitious expansion in Asia. Hobson, writing in 1902, argued that businessmen and officials were wrong to think that occupying faraway deserts and jungles was the stimulus their economies needed. He argued that, in order to increase domestic consumption, industrialists should have focused on raising the standards of living of their own working classes. In any case, Hobson's theory fits much of the evidence.

Second, in 1916, in the midst of the Great War, Vladimir Lenin conceived of a different economic theory to explain imperialism. Being a Marxist, Lenin interpreted overseas empire as a sign of capitalism's terminal weakness rather than strength. His pamphlet *Imperialism, the Highest Stage of Capitalism* argued that industrial capitalism had reached a monopoly stage in which concentrations of wealth became so extreme and opportunities for high profit so scarce that investors began to plunder non-Western countries. Again, being a Marxist, Lenin did not condemn such exploitation on moral or prudential grounds. He even called imperialism a progressive force, in that it helped to destroy feudalism in Asia and Africa. But Lenin considered imperialism to be the final stage of capitalism, and he believed that the world war that imperial rivalries had provoked was preparing the ground for world revolution.

A third and very different theory was offered by sociologist Joseph Schumpeter. He argued that imperialism was not a capitalist phenomenon at all, for he agreed with Hobson that any sensible capitalist would take the position that colonies were wasteful and bad for business. A few investors might strike it rich, such as South African gold magnate Cecil Rhodes. But for the most part, Schumpeter thought, imperialism was a social atavism that reflected the values and interests of the old aristocracies. Those surviving elites from a bygone era had been steadily losing power and wealth in the industrial era, but they found a new calling in empire. Schumpeter noted that many of the civil and military officials who promoted colonial empire were men from the upper crust of European society. The mid-twentieth century brought a variation on this theory called social imperialism. Neo-Marxist historians such as Hans-Ulrich Wehler imagined that Europe's elites self-consciously exploited imperialism to distract their working classes from domestic grievances and rally them around the flag.

Fourth, nearly all historians writing after the First World War interpreted the New Imperialism as an expression of the same competitive nationalism that also gave rise to the militarism of the great powers. Nationalism surely did inspire some of the ideological roots of the New Imperialism, the most striking of which was social Darwinism. Imperial propagandists such as Joseph Chamberlain urged their countrymen to colonize the world because they imagined that territorial and cultural growth was a measure of a nation's virility in the global dog-eat-dog struggle for power, wealth, and security.

More will be said about the impact of Darwinism in chapter 20. Suffice it to say here that despite the cooperation Europeans displayed in matters not touching on their security—such as postal unions, weights and measures, commerce, and the gold standard—the intellectual trends of the era stressed competition and survival of the fittest. The superiority of European over Asian and African societies seemed obvious, while nations within Europe seemed (to themselves) superior or inferior to one another depending on how well they were seeding the world with their people, industry, language, and culture. Hence, the British Empire was the envy of all other nations in part because it provided evidence for the superiority of Britain. The French, Britain's most ubiquitous overseas rivals, took it for granted that their civilization and culture were superior to all others, but their empire certainly helped prove the point. German and Italian imperialists, by contrast, fretted that the millions of their countrymen who had emigrated to the Americas were lost to the nation.

Indeed, a prima facie case to the effect that imperialism was at bottom a virulent nationalist phenomenon can be made by pointing to the fact that only one European power, whether large or small, never showed any interest in it. That was the Habsburg Monarchy, a multinational regime that could not even pretend to be a nation-state.

Another ideology that promoted imperialism was the apparent opposite of social Darwinism. That was the allegedly humanitarian Social Gospel movement derived from the biblical principle "From everyone to whom much is given much will be required." Evangelical preachers of the Social Gospel insisted that wealthy and powerful Christian nations had a God-given duty to uplift inferior races by extending to them paternalistic government, economic assistance, and evangelization. Even many secular-minded Europeans felt called to share the blessings of civilization with backward nations, as they were called. Nowadays the notion that Euro-American Civilization is or ever was superior to others is anathematized as a thought crime. But in the late nineteenth century persons of European descent took European civilizational preeminence for granted. The only question was what duties they owed their inferiors. Their answer was to send missionaries, doctors, engineers, teachers, and administrators abroad to drag their colonial populations into the modern world. Thus did Rudyard Kipling, the poet laureate of the British Empire, famously bestow on his race this exhortation.

> *Take up the white man's burden; send forth the best ye breed—*
> *Go bind your sons to exile to serve your captives' needs;*
> *To wait in heavy harness on fluttered folk and wild—*
> *Your half-caught sullen peoples, half-devil and half-child.*

A fifth explanation for the New Imperialism stressed strategy and diplomacy. The British used to joke that they acquired their empire "in a fit of absence of mind." Two British historians, John Gallagher and Ronald Robinson, even made that quip the hypothesis of their book *Africa and the Victorians*. Gallagher and Robinson researched the actual decision-making processes that led to the claiming of colonies and discovered that in every case British officials had been reluctant to annex new colonies. Only the danger that France, Germany, Russia, or Japan might seize this or that territory and threaten existing British sea lanes—the so-called lifelines of empire—persuaded British officials they must occupy new lands. Egypt came first, then much of East Africa, South Africa, and the Persian Gulf. Then, to secure India from Russian threats from the north, the

British annexed the Punjab (modern Pakistan) and invaded Afghanistan. The British annexed Burma to forestall French threats from Indochina. The British invaded Sudan in 1898 out of fear the French would occupy the upper Nile valley. Meanwhile, the other powers resented Britain and looked for opportunities to challenge British hegemony. Gallagher and Robinson therefore explained the New Imperialism as a phenomenon similar to what Wall Street brokers call "panic buying" and what Germans call *Torschlusspanik* (panic over the closing of a door). That strategic explanation helps to account for the fact that in many and perhaps most cases of colonization the economic motive was expressed only ex post facto.

A sixth and final theory about the motives for the New Imperialism was advanced by historian David K. Fieldhouse in his 1973 book *Economics and Empire, 1830–1914*. His imaginative approach shifted the focus away from Europe's capitals to the colonial world itself. In effect, he invited scholars to look down the barrel of the gun from the perspective of the colonized, rather than gaze over the gunsights from the perspective of the colonizers. Fieldhouse's new perspective showed that, while it was was certainly true that European governments generally shunned colonization during the era before 1873, throughout the nineteenth century European merchants, explorers, missionaries, settlers, prospectors, sailors, and soldiers traveled to Africa, Asia, and the Pacific in sharply increasing numbers. Their very presence caused instability and even crises in traditional African and Asian societies—crises that European governments sooner or later had to confront. For instance, white settlers in South Africa and Australia stumbled into range wars with indigenous peoples. European merchants on the African and Asian coasts enabled the rise of indigenous middlemen or collaborators called compradors, whose growing wealth and influence threatened the authority of Africa's traditional chiefs and religious leaders, or else that of East Asian rulers and their Confucian bureaucrats. Fieldhouse amassed evidence suggesting that by the 1870s and 1880s Europeans' presence abroad was causing a "general crisis on the periphery" that compelled Europeans to impose formal colonization.

It would appear, as in the case of the French Revolution, the Industrial Revolution, and the revolutions of 1848, that historians have confronted a bewildering mix of motives and theories related to the New Imperialism, each of which explains some of the facts, but none of which explains all the facts.

For instance, Hobson's neo-mercantilist theory seemed plausible, except for the glaring fact that Britain, the greatest imperial power, never abandoned free trade and even left its own colonies open to foreign trade and investment. In any event, very few of the colonies acquired during the era of the New Imperialism turned a profit, whether because they lacked raw materials, or because the cost of extracting them was exorbitant, or because they were too primitive to provide markets for European manufactures. How many tons of steel were the nomadic herdsmen of the Kalahari Desert going to import from German factories? Indeed, Bismarck had to twist the arms of bankers and businessmen to get them to invest in Germany's colonies, while the French government sponsored the *Comité de l'Asie française* and *Comité de l'Afrique française* to drum up private investment in the colonies. Trade often followed the flag, not vice versa.

Lenin's theory was also flawed. While it was true that great concentrations of wealth had piled up in Europe, it was not true that Europe was awash in excess capital seeking overseas investment opportunities. The only countries that possessed disposable capital were Britain and France, and while the British certainly invested in their empire, they invested far greater sums in Europe itself and especially in that greatest of all emerging markets, the United States. Likewise, while the French invested some capital in their colonies, they invested far greater sums in another huge emerging market, Russia. The Germans were still net importers of capital because their booming industry sucked up all the available money in their own banks. Finally, to suggest that Belgium, Italy, or Russia was imperialist because of excess capital was absurd.

As for the Schumpeter thesis, there is some evidence for it in Britain, where the colonial and India offices were mostly staffed by younger sons of the peerage, as well as in France and Russia, whose colonial officials and military commanders were often of aristocratic stock. However, Germany's Junker aristocrats were fiercely anti-imperialist; they cared only for agriculture, the army, and continental diplomacy, considering naval and colonial service to be of interest only to middle-class nationalists. As for the social imperialism thesis, there is a certain intuitive appeal to the hypothesis that European elites sought to distract their working classes with flag-waving imperialism. But not a shred of evidence for that motive can be found in the documents. Plus it is hard to believe that the leaders and members of labor unions were so dumb as to forget their work-a-day grievances simply because national honor was at stake in some conflict over a boundary in central Africa.

What of the explanations based on ideology? There is no question that imperialist literature was replete with social Darwinist and Social Gospel themes. Germans spoke of exporting their *Kultur*. Frenchmen boasted of their *mission civilisatrice*. Britons took for granted their "white man's burden." But it is also true, as Gallagher and Robinson showed, that such arguments were often ex post facto justifications, not a priori motives, for annexing this or that colony.

Finally, the Fieldhouse theory about a crisis on the periphery may explain several important colonial decisions. But no "general crisis on the periphery" obliged French premier Jules Ferry to dream of an empire in the sands of the Sahara. No such crisis obliged King Leopold, Bismarck, or Lord Salisbury to claim jungles where no European had ever set foot. To be sure, there was a chain reaction effect stemming from Britain's fear that rivals might pinch their lifelines of empire to India and China. But to say British expansion was reactive only begs the question of why the other powers were proactive.

There is another way to read this riddle, which is to set aside the question of motives altogether and focus instead on the question of means. Historian Daniel Headrick pioneered this approach with his seminal book *The Tools of Empire*, published in 1981. Headrick urged his colleagues to think about means because the answer explained very clearly why the New Imperialism occurred when it did. His query was simply this: How was it that a few thousand Europeans were able to subdue and occupy vast regions of Africa and Asia? The answer, of course, is technology. Magazine-fed infantry rifles, rapid-firing breach-loaded artillery, and the first machine guns, such as the French Maxim (an improved version of the American Gatling gun), bestowed on European soldiers and sailors an immense advantage.

In the Sudanese Battle of Omdurman in 1898, a small British army defeated a fanatical force of Arab dervishes ten times its size. That lopsided victory inspired a young lieutenant named Winston Churchill to pen some doggerel that speaks volumes about Europe's technological dominance in the era of the New Imperialism: "The difference is that we have got / the Maxim gun, and they have not." High-tech weapons in the hands of disciplined soldiers or sailors could destroy the preindustrial armies and fleets of Asian and African empires.

Weapons were only one focus of Headrick's survey. Another of the most powerful tools of empire was the shallow-draft steamboat, which could chug up lazy tropical rivers in Africa and Asia and intimidate villages and forts with a few cannons mounted on deck. The telegraph, too, was a powerful tool, permitting instantaneous communication between coastal towns and outposts in the interior. As for supply and communications, ocean-going steamships freed navigators from thralldom to trade winds, currents, and weather, and they enabled Europeans to transport goods and supplies in bulk quantities. The first steamship ever used in battle sank an entire fleet of Chinese junks during the first Opium War in 1840. Ironclad warships, first constructed in the 1860s, made European navies invulnerable to the weapons possessed by Asian and African militaries.

Finally, medical technology facilitated the New Imperialism because prophylactic drugs such as quinine to ward off malaria and suramin to prevent sleeping sickness, along with insect repellents, protected Europeans against tropical diseases for the first time in history. Armed with such industrial products, Europeans could dwell for years in tropical jungles and emerge with their health intact.

These tools of empire did not appear all at once. But they reached a critical mass around the year 1869. That watershed year also witnessed such engineering feats such as the Suez Canal, the trans-Indian railway, and the American Transcontinental Railroad. Indeed, those feats were what inspired French author Jules Verne to pen his delightful novel *Around the World in Eighty Days*.

The new technologies made it much cheaper in terms of money and manpower to police and develop the interiors of tropical continents and remote islands of the Pacific Ocean. And once Europeans realized that colonization could be pursued on the cheap, with little loss of life, then *any* reason seemed sufficient to do it. In other words, when an exciting enterprise is difficult, dangerous, or expensive, governments need a compelling reason to greenlight it—rocketing astronauts to the moon during the Cold War, for example. But when an exciting enterprise is easy, safe, and cheap, then the only reason *not* to do it is if it seems downright immoral—and nineteenth-century Europeans by no means imagined colonization to be immoral. Perhaps colonies would pay off economically; perhaps not. Perhaps colonies would be strategic assets; perhaps not. Perhaps God had raised Europeans to great power in order to help poor peoples; perhaps not. "But see here: it won't cost us much to find out, so why not go for it?" Thanks to Europe's enormous technological advantage over other civilizations, the temptation to embrace a New Imperialism became irresistible.

Getting in proved to be easy. Getting out proved to be very hard. It would take Europeans eighty to a hundred years to decolonize in a long, bitter retreat that cost them dearly in lives and treasure. In retrospect, therefore, the balance sheet of imperialism is complicated. Third World advocates today accuse the colonial powers of vicious exploitation whose effects still handicap Africa and parts of Asia. Europeans themselves decided by the 1950s, if not before, that their colonies were costing them far more than they were gleaning in profits, while also causing them moral doubt.

Another sort of balance sheet dates from the aftermath of the First World War, when it became conventional wisdom that imperialism had been a principal cause of the slaughter in the trenches. At first glance it might appear that imperialism and war went hand in hand. For instance, between 1871 and 1894 there was only one war involving a European power: the Russo-Turkish War of 1878. But no sooner had the world been carved up into colonial empires than all sorts of wars and crises broke out: the Sino-Japanese War of 1894, the Fashoda Affair between Britain and France on the Nile in 1898, the Spanish-American War in 1898, the Boer War in South Africa in 1899, China's Boxer Rebellion in 1900, the Russo-Japanese War of 1904, the war scares between France and Germany over Morocco in 1905 and 1911, and the Italian-Turkish War over Libya in 1912.

Yet while those were all serious conflicts, none sparked a general European war among two or more great powers. What did spark general war in 1914 would not be colonial rivalry, but an ethnic conflict in Europe itself. That fact even led some historians to speculate that imperialism, far from increasing the tensions leading to World War I, might have served as a safety valve for Europe's internal pressures and helped to postpone a large-scale war. For all the boilerplate about empire, commerce, strategy, and social Darwinism, the fact was that none of the great powers, save perhaps Britain, was willing to risk an existential clash over colonial empire.

Chapter 20

The Snake That Ate Its Tail: The Culture of Modernity

William H. McNeill won the National Book Award in 1964 for *The Rise of the West: A History of the Human Community*. He had decided beforehand to write a history of the world in one volume, to do it in less than a thousand pages, and to divide it into three parts, culminating in the modern era dominated by European civilization. Each part began with a cluster of illustrations that suggested how ideas, artistic styles, and technologies had flowed across civilizations through the ages. One picture in McNeill's final cluster was so troubling as to be unforgettable. It was a photograph of a wooden headboard carved by French artist Georges Lacombe in 1892. The bedstead depicts a great snake twisted into shapes suggesting the eyes and mouth of a human head. At the bottom, the fearsome serpent has curled back on itself and is in the process of devouring its own tail.

Why anyone would want to display that nightmare on his bedstead is unfathomable. But Lacombe's evident purpose was to express the neuroses of a tormented culture in the midst of a slow suicide. Thus did he metaphorically describe those European intellectuals of the late nineteenth century who employed their conscious reason to expose the unconscious psyche in all its primitive savagery.

The symbol-laden Georges Lacombe headboard of 1892.

Even reason itself, they discovered, cannot be trusted; human beings are, in the last analysis, incorrigibly irrational.

This chapter may be the most sobering in this entire book. For we have now reached the frontiers of the appalling twentieth century, the century in which Europeans learned that the progress of science would not give birth to a golden age of peace and prosperity, but instead to an age of illusion, anxiety, and unspeakable violence. It was as if, ever since the Renaissance, Europeans had eaten the fruit of self-knowledge and obtained unlimited access to power in all its forms, only to discover that power is its own punishment. Having eaten the fruit down to the core, Europeans found their appetite for power so quickened that they began to feed on themselves. Perhaps Lacombe sensed that the twentieth century would be an age of idolatry on a Babylonian scale, when governments and ideologies would demand such vast human sacrifice as to amount to cultural cannibalism.

How could that be? Surely the Euro-Atlantic peoples were more advanced, more "civilized," around 1900 than any other region in history. But remember Daniel Bell's dichotomy between *techne* and *themis*. Civilizations comprise a technical realm including science, law, and administration, but also a thematic realm including theology, art, and culture. Modern science and engineering have made human beings so mighty that they would seem like gods to the ancients. But has humanity progressed in the realm of *themis*? Or does modernity fall woefully short of those ideals which the ancient Greeks and Hebrews honored: ideals such as love, joy, beauty, truth, peace, justice, and mercy?

The Snake That Ate Its Tail

The cultural critic Robert Elliot Fitch wrote in a book called *The Odyssey of the Self-Centered Self* that modern humanity has regressed as it has moved away from the worship of God to the worship of science, to the worship of society, to the worship of economics, to the worship of ideologies, and finally to the solipsistic worship of self. Ironically, during the latter stages of that journey Europeans began to conclude that the self is not worthy of worship, for human beings are merely beasts driven by subconscious drives and biochemical reactions. To put it another way, human beings are "nothing but" neurotic apes who have lost most of their hair. What followed from that twin alienation, first from God and then from self, was a century that would be defined by world wars, holocausts, nihilism, and neo-paganism.

The last time this book addressed intellectual history the narrative had reached the mid-nineteenth century. That was a time when utilitarian Liberals such as John Stuart Mill, scientific socialists such as Karl Marx, and scientific positivists such as Benjamin Constant expressed absolute faith in progress. They believed that progress was accelerating, and they expected that progress would lead to social perfection. Alfred, Lord Tennyson's 1842 poem "Locksley Hall" well portrays that age's mood.

> *For I dipp'd into the future, far as human eye could see,*
> *Saw the Vision of the world, and all the wonder that would be;*
> *Saw the heavens fill with commerce, argosies of magic sails,*
> *Pilots of the purple twilight, dropping down with costly bales;*
> *. . . . .*
> *Till the war drum throbbed no longer, and the battle flags were furled*
> *In the Parliament of man, the Federation of the world.*

Why not, given that waves of new technologies were cresting with each passing decade? Indeed, faith in progress became so complete during the middle of the 1800s that many Europeans, who by then took scientific authority on faith, began to embrace a scientism that elevated the laboratory to the status of a church. Natural scientists were becoming a new priesthood dispensing infallible revelations about the heavens, the earth, mankind, and nature, while social scientists pronounced judgments on issues that used to be the domain of religion, including marriage and divorce, child-rearing and education, charity, crime and punishment, social and economic justice, war and peace.

Except for a shrinking number of traditionalists, European intellectuals generally embraced the scientistic mid-Victorian faith. Just consider the messages conveyed by London's Crystal Palace Exhibition in 1851, Paris's Expositions Universelles of 1869, 1878, and 1889, and Philadelphia's Centennial Exhibition of 1876. Religious displays were banned from these world's fairs, not because their sponsors were atheists, but because the exhibitions were an occasion to raise up altars to the scientific and technological miracles wrought by human heads and hands.

After Isaac Newton, European science had for two centuries been led by physicists who made startling breakthroughs in astronomy, mechanics, optics, magnetism, and electricity. Other disciplines, including chemistry, geology, and zoology, lagged behind. To be sure, they also had been busy observing, cataloguing data, and experimenting, when possible. But not until the late eighteenth and nineteenth centuries did they produce great synthesizers and theorists. Antoine Lavoisier discovered the conservation of matter when he learned how to weigh gases and demonstrate oxidation. Lavoisier realized that burning wood did not destroy matter but rather changed the wood's elements into an equivalent mass of ashes and smoke. That discovery revived the ancient Greek notion of the atomic structure of matter, which inspired other chemists to begin isolating the elements, some fifty-six of which had been discovered by 1869, when Dmitri Mendeleev compiled the first periodic table. In 1847 Hermann von Helmholtz theorized that not only matter but also energy is conserved in chemical reactions, and that therefore the total sum of matter and energy in the universe must be constant. That insight inspired scientists to conjecture that such disparate phenomena as heat, light, electricity, and gravity obeyed the same laws, even if those laws were as yet unknown. Finally, thanks to the ubiquitous steam engines of nineteenth-century Europe, chemists made tremendous strides in their studies of thermodynamics.

Meanwhile, biologists and zoologists had been out in the field collecting specimens of plants, animals, fish, and insects from the four corners of the globe. They hoped that some general theory might emerge to explain the planet's profusion of flora and fauna. For a long time, none did. Biologists lacked a vocabulary or paradigm for thinking about how species emerged, changed, or became extinct. The Bible attributed life to the Creator, and no one had cause to dispute that. To be sure, scientists might scoff at the biblical literalism of clerics like the Anglican bishop John Ussher, who calculated from Old Testament genealogies that the Creation described in Genesis must have occurred in exactly 4004 BC. But not until the nineteenth century did geologists begin to study the strata in the earth's crust and paleontologists discover fossils and dinosaur bones. It all suggested that Earth must be far older than a few thousand years, but no one had any other way to account for the mystery of life other than to praise it as heavenly artistry.

Until, that is, a young English naturalist named Charles Darwin risked his father's ire by dropping out of law school in 1831 and putting to sea. He signed on with *H.M.S. Beagle*, a ship dispatched on an expedition to survey the South American coastline. Darwin spent the long voyage pondering specimens he found in Patagonia, Chile, and especially the Galapagos Islands. He noticed how similar birds on neighboring islands displayed different coloring or mating habits, and he asked why. High in the Andes Mountains, Darwin found fossils of marine creatures. How had they gotten there, unless, at some point, the rock in these great mountains had been under the sea? Upon his return to England Darwin pored over treatises on natural history until a hypothesis dawned. In 1859 he published a book that, to many, would become the biological equivalent of Newton's *Principia*. He titled his book *On the Origin of Species by Means of Natural Selection*. Darwin's answer to the mystery of life's variety was evolution.

Evolutionary theories had been kicked around before by geologists, anthropologists, and even historical philosophers such as Hegel and Marx. But Darwin went much further than his predecessors by suggesting that all life on earth could be explained by the evolution of species from simple forms to more complex forms through a process of natural selection. He imagined that biological life did not resemble Newton's harmonious gravitational universe so much as Thomas Hobbes's war of all against all, inasmuch as species of plants and animals—and individual members of each species—competed for ecological niches and either adapted and evolved or died out. Only the fittest survived, with the winners being those whose characteristics best adapted them to their environment by enabling them to dodge predators, find food, and reproduce. In that way, Darwin speculated, all life had evolved from the first amoebas and crustaceans through the fishes, amphibians, reptiles, and mammals.

The initial reception of *On the Origin of Species* was not as contentious as one might expect. For instance, if one concluded, as many Europeans already had, that the biblical account of the six days of creation was meant to be metaphorical and poetic, one could imagine that each "day" was really a geological era lasting millions of years. One could also imagine that evolution was God's natural law for biology, akin to the laws of physics. No wrenching cultural war therefore need result from evolutionary speculations like Darwin's. Moreover, Darwin himself was not hostile to biblical faith. He simply sought "the mind of God" in the same manner as Galileo or Newton. But his theory *did* deliver a shock in 1871 when he carried it to its logical conclusion. In *The Descent of Man, and Selection in Relation to Sex*, Darwin hypothesized that *Homo sapiens* was not God's handiwork, in the garden of Eden or otherwise, but the accidental product of natural selection among the higher primates. The implication was that human beings were not made in the image of God, did not possess immortal souls, and were not really different from animals, but were in fact just apes with big brains.

Christian clergy and lay leaders such as British Prime Minister William Gladstone responded by denouncing Darwinian evolution as a godless doctrine whose effects must surely be pernicious. Was Christendom supposed to jettison three thousand years of faith in divine revelation and the Ten Commandments just because some scholar theorized about the birds and the bees? The champions of a scientific-materialist worldview such as Thomas Henry Huxley (who became known as Darwin's Bulldog) emphatically answered yes, asking in rebuttal whether scientists were supposed to jettison all the physical evidence about natural history just because they appeared to refute ancient Jewish folklore.

However, critics of evolution did not rest their case on the Bible alone. They pointed out that Darwin's theory appeared to raise as many questions as it appeared to answer. For even if natural selection explained which species or members of species came out on top in the struggle to survive and procreate, the theory could not explain how life began in the first place, or how variations within species emerged, or how entirely new species came into existence. Obviously a species of chipmunk that began to dig underground nests would surely survive better than chipmunks that remained exposed to predators. But how could chipmunks learn to do something contrary to their instincts? It was all very well to say that new species began as mutations of existing species, but that begged the question of where mutations came from.

The Snake That Ate Its Tail

It so happened that an obscure Catholic monk in the Habsburg province of Moravia was just then experimenting with the crossbreeding of vegetables. Gregor Mendel learned that if he grafted branches from one sort of pea plant on to another sort of pea plant, the resulting sprouts would resemble one or the other with mathematical precision. Mendel theorized that plant germs contained dominant and recessive genes. Animal breeders had long observed that if you mated white woolly sheep with black woolly sheep, they would produce on average three white lambs for every black one. Mendel, however, made genetics a science. He also unwittingly provided a clue as to how Darwinian evolution might function. If a recessive gene in a plant or animal proved better suited to the environment, then over time the recessive gene would become dominant. Likewise, if climate or topography changed over time, the new environment might favor a different mix of genes. If one further postulated that the earth was millions of years old, as geologists were beginning to do, then it seemed likely that Darwinian evolution could, functioning over eons, account for the emergence of all natural species.

At first, the early Darwinians were ignorant of Mendel's work, so they clung for decades to a bogus theory called the "inheritance of acquired characteristics." But even after Mendelian genetics became universally accepted, some major mysteries remained. Indeed, that is why theories about Intelligent Design have made a comeback in the twenty-first century. How, for instance, could evolution explain sudden leaps in the fossil record known as saltations? Natural selection might plausibly explain gradual changes in the skeleton, musculature, or hair color of squirrels, but where did the *flying* squirrel come from? Why did normal squirrels suddenly decide to try coasting fifty feet through the air, and how come those suicidal squirrels were not "selected" for immediate extinction? Where did the eye come from, and why would its components be selected for before they had (somehow) come together to form a functioning eye? Could the growth of an entirely new organ be the result of some recessive gene? Why did hominids—the presumed ancestors of human beings—suddenly appear with brains much larger than those of any previous hominid? Moreover, was there not something tautological about evolution? It holds that species change and evolve through survival of the fittest. But which species are the fittest? The ones that survive!

Please do not misunderstand. This history survey does not presume to assert a scientific position. Its purpose is simply to suggest that the theory of evolution has never been proven in the same way as the laws of mechanics, thermodynamics, or electrical conduction. What historians *can* say with authority is that most of the intellectual elites in the Atlantic world came to believe in Darwinism by around 1900, and their faith in this particular scientific theory had incalculable consequences for the culture at large. Darwinists purported to explain the biological world without reference to God, creation, or moral purpose. Rather, they depicted the biosphere as a ruthless struggle for survival—or "Nature, red in tooth and claw," as Tennyson put it. But just as Enlightenment philosophers had been quick to apply Newton's scientific model to human society, so did social Darwinists apply Darwin's model to human society.

Darwin is right, they cried, so let us hear no more sentimental talk about the brotherhood of man or the Golden Rule. Life really is a brutal struggle in which big fish eat little fish and human beings compete with each other for money, power, sex, status, and security. Indeed, Darwin's competitive image of life seemed to describe the world most people inhabited far better than the Enlightenment's harmonious image of nature, or the Romantics' idyllic image of nature, or Christianity's sentimental "love thy neighbor" ethic, or socialism's notion of class solidarity. What is more, the real world of social struggle was rendered even more insecure by the dynamic environment of industrial capitalism. Since technologies and markets are forever in flux, the characteristics that make a given person, firm, industry, or nation well adapted to its environment today might doom it to extinction tomorrow. There seemed to be no room for virtue or absolute notions of good and evil in a Darwinian world. In Newton's world natural law had implied regularity, permanence, and balance. In Darwin's world natural law implied chaos, change, and the need for continuous adaptation.

Darwin himself rued such implications, but he could not prevent social Darwinists from flooding the culture with their theories. Social Darwinists judged human history to be like natural history because, well, human beings were animals, and competition among them, both as individuals and members of groups, was an inevitable by-product of progress. Some prominent philosophers, such as Herbert Spencer, even denounced social welfare programs and peace movements, for what did they do but enable the feeble to survive and breed and thus weaken the human gene pool? International politics, in which nations and races competed for survival and growth, seemed an obvious example of Darwinian struggle. Thus did the Frenchman Paul Leroy-Beaulieu, the

German Friedrich Fabri, and the Russian Nikolai Danilevsky, to name a few, advocate colonial expansion to prove that their nations were among the fittest.

In the 1850s, a French count named Arthur de Gobineau had written a precocious work titled *Essay on the Inequality of the Human Races*. No one paid much attention to it. Twenty years later, in a Darwinian world, the book became a bestseller. Gobineau Societies sprang up all over Europe to promote racial awareness. Germans pointed to their victory in the war of 1870-71 as proof that the era of the tired Latin races was over and that of the virile Teutonic races had begun. Englishman Joseph Chamberlain and American Theodore Roosevelt imagined the Anglo-Saxon races to be the fittest—and thus destined to lead the march of civilization. Russian social Darwinists imagined that the youthful Slavic race was poised to assume global leadership. Europeans denigrated other races as well—and not only Africans and Asians. Racial anti-Semitism now emerged alongside perennial religious and economic strains of anti-Semitism.

All the while, traditional religion retreated under this veritable barrage. Scholars practicing the so-called "higher" criticism of the Bible challenged the historicity not only of the creation story in Genesis but of all the miracles portrayed in the Jewish and Christian scriptures. German scholar David Strauss theorized in *The Life of Jesus, Critically Examined* that miracles were "nothing but" mythical wish-fulfillment. He doubted whether the man Jesus had even existed. French scholar Ernst Renan argued that Christianity was "nothing but" a first-century protest movement against the Roman occupation of Judea. Over the same decades, while geologists were studying rock formations millions of years old and paleontologists were excavating dinosaur bones, archaeologists were failing to find material evidence for biblical history.

Churches girded themselves to resist, but the Protestant response was to quarrel and divide yet again. Nearly every denomination split into modernist and fundamentalist factions, depending on whether people chose to embrace the new science or to take their stand on the Bible. Both choices were awkward, because to reinterpret the Bible as myth weakened faith in the biblical God whose commandments were what motivated Jews and Christians to live moral lives. On the other hand, to insist on biblical inerrancy made fundamentalists appear superstitious and stubborn.

The Catholic Church was better equipped to withstand the assaults because it preserved unified authority and based its doctrine on tradition as well as

Scripture. In 1864 Pope Pius IX warned in his Syllabus of Errors against blind faith in reason and science, and he condemned materialism in both its capitalist and socialist variety. In 1870 he convened the first Vatican Council since the Catholic Reformation. The council declared the pope infallible when speaking *ex cathedra* on matters of faith and morals. As a result, the papacy actually grew stronger in response to modern science, but at the cost of persuading non-Catholics that Rome was obscurantist and reactionary. Finally, it was during these decades that Reformed Judaism made its own peace with science and biblical criticism, but at the cost of disunity with Orthodox and Conservative Judaism.

The burden of Darwinism was that *Homo sapiens* is just an ape with a big brain. That was humbling, but at least the big brain—reason and intelligence—elevated human beings above the animals. Unfortunately, that comforting belief didn't last long. In the 1890s, a prolific anthropologist named Gustave Le Bon published a series of books in which he argued that whereas individuals may behave rationally most of the time, masses of people invariably succumbed to irrational fear, panic, and hatred. In 1908 George Sorel's *Reflections on Violence* likewise examined the irrational, paranoid tendency of people living in crowded cities to congeal into riotous mobs.

In short, during the late nineteenth and early twentieth centuries religion and morals were being demystified and denounced as irrational, even as racism and relativism were being heralded as rational and natural. Of course, serious thinkers recognized the need for moral codes to restrain bad behavior. The social Darwinist Herbert Spencer even believed that social evolution had educated humanity to jettison the law of the jungle and embrace human rights. *But* he also believed society should not coddle the weak and unfit, lest they multiply. *But* he granted that charity was one of the traits distinguishing human beings from animals. *But* he thought that charitable traits were "nothing but" a survival mechanism to be obeyed or rejected as the environment required. William James, a philosopher who taught at Harvard University, agreed that religions were either healthy or unhealthy depending on whether their impact on people made society better or worse. *But* the trouble with such pragmatism was that without absolute standards, no basis existed for defining the words *better or worse.*

In other words, the cultural snake was curling back on itself. With the rise of Austrian psychiatrist Sigmund Freud the snake took the first bite from its own tail. Freud was fascinated by hysteria. What made apparently normal men—and especially women—go mad? To answer that question Freud invented a technique he called psychoanalysis. That methodology, with the aid of hypnotism—an old vaudeville trick popularized by Pierre Mesmer—allowed Freud to probe his patients' subconscious minds. Under hypnosis his patients could recall childhood traumas that their conscious minds had repressed. Little by little, Freud explored the dark pit of the human psyche and uncovered those neuroses (as he called them) which made a sorry conceit of the notion that man is a creature of reason.

During those same years the Russian physiologist Ivan Pavlov had been experimenting with dogs. Day after day he rang a bell just before feeding time, until the dogs could be made to salivate just by ringing the bell. Through that and other experiments Pavlov demonstrated that animal behavior was not just a matter of instinct, but also of conditioned responses. Experience conditioned the mind to react in predictable ways, which helped to explain why childhood traumas could lead to adult phobias such as fear of heights, water, spiders, or crowds. For his part, Freud developed a theory of infantile sexuality to the effect that the libido did not emerge during puberty but was already present in the cradle, a time during which children's first objects of sexual desire were their parents or nurses. Healthy children passed through their oral and anal phases to the adolescent genital phase, but neurotic people often suffered from arrested development.

Freud boldly investigated his patients' sex lives, especially through the interpretation of dreams. He strove to be rational, but the burden of his research suggested that rationality was a delusion. It seemed that human beings were pathetic creatures driven by their subconscious hopes and fears. If they seemed to behave normally most of the time, that was because of conditioned responses. Freud concluded, therefore, that the human mind was a combat zone in which the subconscious id (the realm of urges, often sexual), the self-conscious ego (the realm of reason), and the repressive superego (the realm of external socialization) constantly battled one another.

As with Darwinism, the philosophical implications of Freudianism were even more shocking than the science itself. The exposure of the human subconscious made it easy for other thinkers, like William James, to label religion a psychological crutch at best and a psychic oppression at worst. Politics, too, were merely a circus in which bloated egos played out their childhood fantasies and projected them onto the masses. Freud even imagined that the family, previously thought to be a loving refuge against a cruel world, was frequently a dysfunctional prison, a chamber of horrors in which children were driven crazy by their parents or siblings.

So it was that the mid-century Victorian certainties—faith in science and industry, progress and reason, traditional morals and family life—had by the end of the century come under attack from science itself. It was then that Max Weber, a great German sociologist, broke with Karl Marx by asserting the centrality of nonmaterial motivations in history. Man was not *Homo economicus*, a rational actor in pursuit of self-interest. Rather, what made people special was precisely their irrational qualities: they were dreamers, artists, lovers. Weber, who popularized the notion that modern capitalism had been inspired by the Protestant work ethic, was also the first critic of what he called modernization. Ever since the Renaissance, he observed, Europeans had been rationalizing government, economy, and society according to standards of efficiency. Capitalism was part of the process, but so was science, the decline of religion, and the ever-more-expansive bureaucratization of governments, militaries, industries, labor unions, infrastructures, and municipalities. The twentieth century, Weber predicted, would be the age of the "organization man," a time in which individual personalities would be crushed. The British Lord John Dahlberg-Acton had famously said in 1887 that "Power tends to corrupt and absolute power corrupts absolutely." Weber warned that modern society would seduce people into sacrificing their values on the altars of conformity and mass consumption.

Reason proving the absence of reason. Industrial might breeding individual impotence. Human beings reduced to hysterical animals not even in charge of their own minds and behavior, much less their science, technology, and bureaucracy. Religion and ethics debunked, and nothing to take their place except worship of power. Is it any wonder that this era produced the ultimate renegade, a man who anathematized the old religious values *and* the new secular values?

Friedrich Nietzsche, although brilliant, was a mad misanthrope who carried to their logical conclusions his age's speculations about the irrational, degraded nature of man. His books of the 1880s, such as *Thus Spake Zarathustra*, *Beyond Good and Evil*, and *The Genealogy of Morals*, condemned Judaism, Christianity, Liberalism, and Marxism as justifying philosophies for the mediocre. What could be more unnatural in a Darwinian world than to be selfless or to claim that all men are created equal? Christianity, wrote Nietzsche, was a religion fit only for slaves, democracy was the politics of slaves, and capitalism and communism were the pitiful products of a decadent materialism. Nietzsche expressed contempt for everything Europe's establishment stood for.

According to Nietzsche the driving force behind any fully realized man or woman was the will to power, the purpose of which was to create culture. Someone who lacked that radical will could no more create culture than a castrated man could sire children. Nietzsche glorified the genius of titanic rule-breakers such as Julius Caesar, Michelangelo, and Beethoven. He believed that they stood above the pitiful mob as *Übermenschen* (supermen). Fifty years later, Germany's Nazi Party leaders would invoke Nietzschean philosophy to justify their notion of an Aryan master race. But Nietzsche was contemptuous of social Darwinism. He was even contemptuous of himself, which is what makes him the most haunting figure of his time—except, perhaps, for Russian novelist Fyodor Dostoyevsky. Nietzsche even asked why he thought the thoughts that he thought. In the end he went mad. But not before he sketched out, in the quiet of his study in the house he shared with his sister, a "transvaluation of values." To obey the laws imposed by society was to be a worm. To rebel against them was sublime. To pretend to love your neighbor was craven. To indulge your will to power was heroic. "There are no moral phenomena," he wrote, "only moral interpretations of phenomena."

Many years before—in 1817, to be precise—a woman had seen it all coming in a recurring nightmare that inspired her to found a new literary genre: the horror story. Her name was Mary Shelley, and her book was called *Frankenstein, or The Modern Prometheus*. She imagined a future in which men with a will to power would exploit science in a quest to learn the secrets of life and to play God. In her book Dr. Victor Frankenstein knits together a human being from body parts pilfered from graveyards and shocks it back to life with bolts of electricity, only to be horrified by the monster he has created. Predictably, the scientist and the monster destroy each other in the end.

By around 1900 European elites presided over the mightiest civilization in history. Yet they had learned from Weber that individuals were just cogs in their own machines. They had learned from Darwin that people were simply clever apes trapped in a fight for survival. They had learned from Freud, Pavlov, and

Sorel that men and women were but captives of subconscious neuroses, external conditioning, and mass hysteria. Alienated from God, nature, society, and themselves, intelligent Europeans gradually became rudderless.

Artists of the era sensed what was happening around them—that is what good artists do. Hence Georges Lacombe's snake eating its tail, Pablo Picasso's cubist depictions of people and cities cracking up, and Edvard Munch's iconic canvas *The Scream*. But the prophets Nietzsche and Dostoyevsky sounded the keynote for the hideous twentieth century when they both observed—one in cynicism, the other in despair—that God is dead, and everything is permitted.

Chapter 21

"Human, All Too Human": The Descent into World War I

The poignant image that opened chapter 16 describing the early Industrial Revolution was the machine in the garden. Pastoral, agricultural life was still the norm in the first half of the nineteenth century, but dirty, noisy machinery was sprouting up around coal mines and rivers and chugging through pastures on iron rails. By the late nineteenth century, industrialization had become so pervasive that municipal governments set aside real estate for public parks—so that there might at least be a garden in the machine. Modern cities had become complex mechanisms knitted to one another by threads of copper and iron; all were integrated into functionally differentiated national networks.

By the dawn of the twentieth century electric streetcars and subways, telegraphs and telephones, power plants and electrical grids, water works, sewers, and waste treatment plants made city dwellers dependent on a complex infrastructure constituted by machinery. Circa 1815, if people wished to travel, they had to rely on the legs of a horse or the wind in their sails. If they wished to communicate, they or their delegates needed to physically travel to the recipients of their messages. By 1914, both the inconvenience and self-reliance of that era were long gone. Imagine yourself an employee of one of the mammoth Krupp steel mills in Germany's industrial Ruhr Valley. You ride a streetcar from your

Light, flexible, mass-produced steel made possible giant battleships like the *H.M.S. Dreadnought*, launched in 1906.

apartment to your factory or office—a streetcar powered by electricity generated by a power plant powered in turn by steam turbines perhaps manufactured by the great Siemens plant across the Rhine. That factory's forges for smelting iron, plus the furnaces heating the buildings throughout your city, are fired by coal mined nearby by colliers equipped with vein cutters likely imported from England and shipped in barges and railroad cars manufactured by Krupp, your own employer. Hence, in your daily routine you are utterly dependent on several great industries, thousands of people, and dozens of mechanical inventions.

Some historians have referred to the technological and organizational innovations of the 1871–1914 era as the Second Industrial Revolution. But one might better refer to it as the "third wave" of the modern technological revolution, and for three good reasons. The first has to do with the era's inventions, which were based on newly discovered scientific principles. The first wave of the eighteenth century had been mechanical: it was characterized by textile machinery and the factory system. The nineteenth century's second wave had involved energy conversion: think coal, steam engines, and railroads. The third wave of the late nineteenth century introduced a host of products derived from electricity and organic chemistry, including aspirin, fertilizers, paints, and dyes. Alfred Nobel patented his fateful chemical concoction called dynamite in 1867. In 1870, Alexander Parkes and John Hyatt were awarded the patent for celluloid, the first plastic, which transformed photography and inspired Jacques Brandenberger to invent cellophane in 1908. Just as revolutionary were the internal combustion and diesel engines invented by Germans Nikolaus Otto in 1876 and Rudolf Diesel in 1896. By the turn of the twentieth century those inventions made possible the automobile, airplane, submarine, and lowly air compressor, which served as a portable power plant for hundreds of labor-saving machines.

Above all, the third wave was the age of steel. Between 1860 and 1900, chemists and metallurgists in England, Germany, France, and America discovered more efficient ways to blow carbon compounds into molten iron—the Bessemer and Siemens-Martin blast furnace processes—and thereby made possible the mass-produced manufacture of high-quality steel. For centuries, blacksmiths had made steel in their shops, but since steel was rare and expensive, it was used only for cutlery, swords, and surgeon's scalpels. Once it became available in bulk at an affordable price, steel quickly replaced iron in the construction of buildings, bridges, railways, and ocean liners like the *Titanic*. Steel also made possible the gigantic battleships of the early twentieth century, ships like the *H.M.S. Dreadnought* in 1906, as well as huge artillery cannons, machine guns, and tens of millions of rounds of ammunition. Third-wave technology thus made it possible to conduct warfare on a deadlier scale than ever.

A second reason to call this era the third wave of technological revolution has to do with control of the machines—that is, the relationship of machines to their human masters. During the first wave, of the 1700s, machines were based on simple techniques known since antiquity, such as the pulley, lever, sprocket, and pump. Such machines could do plenty of work, but they still needed people to stand by and "man the machine." The second wave produced machines that "ran on their own steam." But engineers still had to monitor the engines, open and shut valves to "let off steam," shift gears, and connect or disconnect drive shafts from the power source. The third wave, by contrast, introduced self-powered and self-regulating machines. An electric heater with a thermostat could turn itself on and off. A timed switch or wheel on the mother board of an assembly line could interrupt or enable the flow of electrical current in order to trigger machines to perform operations and move products on a conveyor belt. The process became automatic, and manufacturing became automated.

A third reason to refer to the innovations of the late nineteenth century as the third wave of technological revolution is that governments and corporations began to found laboratories whose sole purpose was to engage in experimental research and product development. Governments focused on the military applications of steel, chemistry, explosives, electricity, and wireless radio, while private firms such as Germany's Krupp, I. G. Farben, Bayer, and Allgemeine

Elektrizitäts Gesellschaft developed new technologies on command. Technological progress, once the haphazard result of individual tinkerers, became the highly capitalized programmatic goal of the modern industrial megamachine.

A final component of the third wave was the transformation of communications by undersea telegraph cables. Such cables first crossed the English Channel and Atlantic Ocean in the 1860s. By 1914 they linked every continent. News could now travel in minutes, or at most a few hours, around much of the world to land on the front pages of penny newspapers, newspapers nearly everyone could now afford thanks both to linotype machines that set type automatically and the cheap paper manufactured from wood pulp. What is more, by this point most people could *read* newspapers, thanks to the spread of universal primary education. Alas, mass journalism did not necessarily mean a more well-informed public, as benign progressive thinkers had supposed. Instead, journals competed for mass circulation by peddling crime, scandal, violence, and partisan politics. Historian Sidney B. Fay later included such "yellow journalism" and the "jingoist press" among the long-range causes of the First World War.

Given that this third wave of technological innovation overlapped with the economic boom that enriched Europeans beginning in the year 1896, one might suspect that people welcomed the dawn of the twentieth century in the belief that it would bring boundless progress. They did. The French called the turn of the century *La Belle Époque* and celebrated with another Parisian world's fair. German poet Stefan Zweig prophesied an "age of golden security." The *New York World* predicted that the 1900s "will meet and overcome all perils and prove to be the best that this steadily improving planet has ever seen." After all, there had been no major war on the continent since 1871. In fact, war seemed increasingly unlikely, since European powers could expend their excess energy through colonization and their excess people through emigration. As late as 1911, the British liberal Norman Angell could write that war had become impossible, given the economic interdependence of nations and the expense and destructiveness of modern weapons.

Many socialists also believed war was becoming impossible, not because of the virtues of industrial capitalism, but because of the supposed reality of working-class solidarity. The Second Socialist International, labor unions, and working-class political parties believed that governments could not wage war without the forbearance of their industrial workers. Socialists repeatedly warned that workers everywhere would lay down their tools if their governments tried to declare war.

Finally, prior to 1914 middle-class peace movements flourished. Activists lobbied for international congresses to outlaw inhumane weapons, promote disarmament, and resolve disputes among nations. Women's clubs and church groups were especially active in these peace movements, which inspired the first world's first disarmament conferences in 1899 and 1907, as well as the establishment of an international court at The Hague to arbitrate international disputes.

To be sure, a few dissenters peered into the future with foreboding. Prophetic doomsayers, such as the pioneer of science fiction H. G. Wells, sensed the social Darwinist, Freudian, and Nietzschean ghosts haunting their generation and warned that terrible wars fought with diabolical weapons lurked just over the horizon. Socialist August Bebel intuited a desperate mood among the Kaiser's entourage, which led him to predict in 1912 that Europe was on the verge of a wholesale bloodletting. But such voices were drowned out by a generation of shortsighted politicians and prophets of progress. Their complacency increased the danger that hubris would drag Europe's great powers into conflict. The politicians and pundits were especially blind to the tectonic force at work in their midst, the immovable force of nature that would sink their civilization as swiftly as the north Atlantic iceberg that destroyed the "unsinkable" *Titanic* in 1912. That force was nationalism triumphant—and especially nationalism thwarted.

In the 1870s the map of Europe was as simple as it had ever been. At its heart lay the new German Reich of Kaiser Wilhelm I and his Chancellor Bismarck. Once unification was achieved during the Franco-Prussian War, Bismarck declared Germany a satisfied power and deployed his considerable diplomatic acumen in the interest of peace and stability. After all, Germany was surrounded by potential enemies, and Bismarck's nightmare was that France would seek vengeance by teaming up with Russia and/or the Habsburg Empire to attack Germany on two or more fronts. His solution was to forge a defensive alliance of his own. In 1879 Germany concluded an alliance with Habsburg Austria and in 1882 with Italy, thus forming the Triple Alliance. In 1887 Bismarck added a secret nonaggression pact with tsarist Russia. Since his ally Austria had clashes of interests with both Italy and Russia, Bismarck was sorely pressed to keep his alliance system together. But his success in doing so meant that Germany and Europe enjoyed tranquility for two decades.

Bismarck hoped for good relations with all Germany's neighbors, but the ones he could never conciliate lived in France, the nation Germany had humiliated in the war of 1870–71 and which had been forced to cede the strategic, resource-rich province of Alsace-Lorraine in the peace that followed. That disastrous war had also occasioned the abdication of Emperor Napoléon III. By 1875 the French had founded a democratic Third Republic. In domestic affairs the regime was (by French standards) remarkably stable. But the Third Republic's foreign policy was vengeful and restless, since France appeared doomed to permanent inferiority to Germany's land power and Britain's sea power. Hence, the politicians in Paris prioritized two ambitions: first, to compete vigorously with the British in the wide world after the scramble for colonies began, and second, to seek revenge against Germany and recover France's "lost provinces." Yet the French dared not challenge Germany's clearly superior power without first gaining allies.

For the time being no allies could be found. The only other great power not already linked to Bismarck's Germany was Great Britain, and British governments were not interested in alliances. So long as Britannia ruled the waves and a balance of power prevailed on the continent, her empire was secure. British leaders were content to pursue a strategy they called "splendid isolation." Indeed, her late nineteenth-century statesmen, including Benjamin Disraeli, William Ewart Gladstone, and Robert Gascoyne-Cecil, marquess of Salisbury, spent the years 1871 to 1890 casting wary eyes on their traditional rivals in France while generally applauding Bismarck's peaceful leadership in continental affairs. France and Britain remained especially at odds over the future of the Levant, including Egypt, which the British occupied in 1882, and the future of the nations of the Balkan peninsula in southeastern Europe, which periodically rebelled against their Ottoman Turkish overlords.

By this time the Ottoman Empire had been in decline for two hundred years, and the Greeks, Serbs, Romanians, Bulgars, and Albanians had escaped Turkish rule by the end of the 1870s. But each time one or another of them rebelled, it provoked tensions among Europe's great powers, each of whom sought to increase its influence over the Balkans and the strategic Turkish Straits. The British were fearful that Russia might occupy Constantinople, gain naval access to the Mediterranean, and threaten Britain's sea lanes via the Suez Canal. The French and Russians were fearful that Britain would make the Sultan's empire a client state. The Austrians feared Russia's support for the Slavic nations because the Habsburg Empire contained Slavic minorities of its own. Finally, Germany's Bismarck feared that the other powers' fears would provoke a war that would give France the opportunity to find an ally, most likely tsarist Russia. The Ottoman Empire was thus known to other Europeans as "the sick man of Europe," and the question of what was to become of the Ottoman realm was referred to by European diplomats as "the Eastern Question."

What about Russia, the largest, most reactionary, and least economically developed of the European powers? Russia was still ruled by an autocratic tsar and a landed nobility, and the vast majority of Russian subjects remained miserable peasants. But following Russia's dismal showing in the Crimean War of 1854–56, Tsar Alexander II had freed the serfs, begun to build railroads, and pushed armies deep into the Turkic provinces of central Asia. The tsars also pursued their old ambition of capturing a warm-water port, with Constantinople a particularly appealing prize. Finally, Russia's nationalists and social Darwinists embraced a Pan-Slav ideology that conceived of Russia as the big brother and protector of all Orthodox Christian peoples, especially Slavic ones such as the Bulgars and Serbs. The result was that Russia threatened the Ottoman Turks in 1877 and again in 1885. Only Bismarck's diplomacy had restrained his partners and prevented those crises from escalating. Moreover, German fears regarding the future of Russia increased in the years after 1892, when Sergei Witte, Tsar Alexander III's brilliant finance minister, launched a crash industrialization program. A centerpiece of Witte's program was construction of the six-thousand-mile Trans-Siberian Railway, which would enable the Russians to project military, economic, and demographic power all the way to the Pacific Ocean. The prospect of a gigantic Russia economically catching up with central Europe worried the Germans and Austrians, especially, while Russia's ambitions in East Asia caused anxiety among the British and Japanese.

The final great power was the Habsburg Monarchy, also known after 1867 as Austria-Hungary, the Dual Monarchy, and the Danubian Monarchy. Dating from the high medieval era, the imperial and royal House of Habsburg had, after 1815, become the surviving relic of the defunct Holy Roman Empire. To western Europeans, the Habsburg Empire seemed an anomaly, given that it was a multiethnic congeries during a time when nationalism and racialist theories were in the ascendant. It was also, like the Ottoman Empire, a regime in steady decline. In the war of 1859 Austria had lost Lombardy to the new Kingdom of Italy. In the war of 1866 Austria had lost Venice to Italy and lost all her influence in the German states to Prussia. In 1867 the Austrians were obliged to grant Hungarians equal status in the empire. Throughout the century the steady retreat of Ottoman power at the hands of the Balkan peoples increased the threat Slavic nationalism posed to the Habsburg Monarchy. The Serbs in particular dreamed of liberating their Slavic cousins under Austrian rule and of forging a Yugoslav (that is, South Slav) nation. Needless to say, Russians motivated by Pan-Slav ideology were more than eager to support Serbia's ambitions.

Thanks to Bismarck's diplomatic skills, the periodic crises spurred by the Eastern Question during the 1870s and 1880s had been resolved peacefully. But for three reasons, over the years 1890 to 1914 the great powers gradually lost their ability to manage the spread of rival nationalisms in the Balkans. The first reason was a radical shift in German foreign policy. The second was a new alliance system that arose in opposition to Germany's Triple Alliance. And the third was a shocking new specter in international politics: state-sponsored terrorism.

In 1888 both Kaiser Wilhelm I and his fifty-six-year-old Crown Prince Friedrich died within ninety-nine days of each other. Their deaths made Wilhelm's twenty-nine-year-old grandson, Wilhelm II, Germany's emperor. A proud Prussian, Wilhelm II was intelligent, ambitious, and impetuous. He embraced the military tradition of the Junker aristocracy. He was also an enthusiastic proponent of exciting third-wave technologies. The new kaiser thus reflected the mood of Germany's younger generation, whose members did not remember Prussia's wars of unification or the constitutional crisis of the 1860s and who had grown up knowing nothing except German unity, peace, and exciting scientific and industrial progress. These younger Germans did not understand Bismarck's caution.

Wilhelm II pushed Bismarck into retirement in 1890 and chose ministers who seemed more in tune with times. Germany was fast becoming continental Europe's economic locomotive and scientific-technological leader in such fields as electricity, chemicals, steel, and automobiles. The kaiser saw no reason why Germany's political weight should not be as great as her economic weight. Another trend that excited the kaiser was the navalism stimulated by the New Imperialism. An American officer, Captain Alfred Thayer Mahan, had published a bestselling book in 1890 called *The Influence of Sea Power on History*. Mahan argued that throughout history great empires had risen and fallen according to their sea power. The kaiser, who observed that not only Britain and France but every other important nation was building modern steel battleship fleets, saw no reason why Germany should not do likewise.

Finally, Wilhelm II shared many younger Germans' enthusiasm for social Darwinist perspectives on strategy. He and his advisers perceived that the trend toward globalization was quickly transforming Europe's old balance of power into a world balance of power in which only large empires could compete. Britain, Russia, and the United States had achieved the requisite scale, but as yet Germany had not. Somehow, Germany must break out of its central European prison and claim what Wilhelm II called "a place in the sun." Germany no longer needed a cautious continental strategy such as the one Bismarck had followed. Germany needed a *Weltpolitik* (world policy).

The kaiser's first diplomatic gambit was the gratuitous cancellation of Bismarck's Reinsurance Treaty with Russia, since it seemed to him to contradict Germany's alliance with Austria-Hungary. How could Berlin promise to go to war on Austria's behalf while promising Russia to remain neutral? The immediate upshot was to isolate tsarist Russia at the very time when its government needed massive foreign investments in order to finance Count Witte's industrialization program. The French foreign ministry saw its opening. In exchange for millions of francs in loans the tsar concluded a Franco-Russian Alliance in 1894. Just four years after his retirement, Bismarck's nightmare had come to pass.

Three years later the kaiser made an even worse blunder. He pushed through the Reichstag a bill to begin constructing a battleship fleet. The predictable result was that the British began to feel threatened in their home waters. A British admiral, guessing that Germany meant to extort from Great Britain various colonial concessions, said, "The Germans mean to push us into the water and steal our clothes."

The British approached the German government three times between 1899 and 1902 in search of an entente to preserve good bilateral relations. Three times Wilhelm II replied, "If you desire an agreement with Germany, simply join our Triple Alliance: *Schluss, Punkt*" (full stop). Of course, that would have required Britain to fight on Germany's side in case of a continental war against France and Russia—something the British had no intention of doing. A naval arms race therefore ensued, with both Britain and Germany building ever more, larger, and increasingly modern battleships and cruisers.

German military ambitions threatened the viability of Britain's policy of splendid isolation. So did the Franco-Russian alliance, which united Britain's principal competitors in the colonial world. As late as 1898 France and Britain nearly came to blows over which was to control the Upper Nile valley, while Russia aggressively challenged all the other imperial powers, save for France, in East Asia. Completion of the Trans-Siberian Railway in 1904 permitted the tsar's government to ship soldiers and supplies to Korea and Manchuria and to compete for influence in China.

Indeed, the tense competition for the China market and East Asia generally demonstrated how the spread of industrialism was bound to erode Britain's geopolitical security. By 1900 Japan had become a powerful local presence, the United States had annexed the Philippine Islands, and France and Germany had occupied Chinese ports and stationed ships in the South China Sea. Now the Russians were coming. It reached the point where Britain's Royal Navy could no longer rule the waves everywhere at once, especially if it had to keep a sizable fleet in home waters to deter the new German fleet.

In 1902, therefore, the British jettisoned splendid isolation and decided to make an alliance ... with Japan! Whereas Britain's Far Eastern Squadron could no longer dominate Pacific waters, the British and Japanese fleets in combination were more than able to do so. Yet the alliance soon became problematic, for Japan and Russia were poised on the brink of war over which country would dominate China's rich province of Manchuria, not to mention the Korean peninsula. France was an ally of Russia, and Britain was now an ally of Japan, but neither European power had any desire to get sucked into a war on account of these relationships. So, just as the Russo-Japanese War broke out in 1904, Britain and France agreed to settle their own long-standing disputes (over Egypt and Morocco) and to conclude the Entente Cordiale. London and Paris pledged to remain neutral in the event of a war in Asia and to cooperate in future diplomacy.

The Russo-Japanese War, a world-historical watershed whose importance cannot be exaggerated, shocked all observers. It saw the upstart Japanese defeat much larger Russian armies and destroy two Russian fleets. The war so discredited the Tsar's policies that in 1905 revolution erupted in the streets of St. Petersburg, Moscow, Odessa, and Kiev. Nicholas II survived the unrest by promising reforms, but Russia's defeat meant that it was no longer an immediate threat to British interests in Asia. As a result, the British seized the opportunity to settle their colonial feuds with Russia, negotiating an Anglo-Russian Entente in 1907. That meant that a second European alliance system was now complete: the Triple Entente of Britain, France, and Russia, which encircled the Triple Alliance of Germany, Austria-Hungary, and Italy.

By now the air was acrid with the odor of a burning fuse. All the great powers were locked into rival alliance systems. Germany was assertive but thwarted and increasingly paranoid. Wilhelm II naturally interpreted the Triple Entente to be a conspiracy designed to encircle Germany and frustrate the legitimate goals of his *Weltpolitik*. At the same time, the Russians, having been checked in Asia, turned back to the Balkans as the only region where they might throw their weight around and prove to Europeans that the tsarist regime was still vigorous. Even more ominous was the fact that Russian ambitions in the Balkans would now—for the first time in history—be supported by France and Britain. That made the Balkans a powder keg threatening all Europe.

In 1903 Serbia's king and queen had been assassinated in a palace coup d'état that elevated a rival dynasty to power. The new king was a fierce nationalist devoted to expanding little Serbia into a greater Yugoslavia. To achieve that end his regime promoted agitation and propaganda in the Austrian-administered provinces of Bosnia-Herzegovina. The Austrian government tried to choke off the agitation by annexing Bosnia in 1908, whereupon Serbia's intelligence agency gave secret support to a terrorist movement called the Black Hand Society. Its bombs and assassination attempts on Habsburg territory posed a mortal threat to the Austro-Hungarian Empire, for if national self-determination were conceded to the South Slavic provinces under terrorist pressure, then each of the ethnic minorities in the multinational empire might demand independence. The military commanders in Vienna urged the benevolent old Emperor Franz Josef to crush Serbia once and for all. Simultaneously, Nicholas II and his advisers determined that the Russians must stand firm in

Serbia's defense; they feared that the tsarist regime could not survive another humiliation in foreign policy.

The fuse reached the powder on June 28, 1914, when a callow teenager named Gavrilo Princip assassinated the Habsburg heir apparent, Archduke Franz Ferdinand, in the Bosnian capital of Sarajevo. That latest and most shocking outrage gave the Austrians all the pretext they needed to retaliate in force, especially when their German allies gave them a "blank check" to take whatever measures against Serbia they chose. Were the kaiser and German generals *hoping* a big war would break out? They had sometimes talked as if war were inevitable. But in July 1914 the kaiser and his entourage went on a sailing vacation, and the government took no military preparations at all. Hardly what one would expect if the regime were plotting aggressive war. Rather, the Germans hoped they could exploit this crisis—in which their ally had been the victim, after all—to win a diplomatic victory that would enable the German powers to dominate the Balkans and perhaps crack the unity of the Triple Entente partners. Evidently, the kaiser and his ministers believed running the bluff was worth running the risk.

The Austrians certainly did not want a big war. They hoped to minimize the conflict and simply punish Serbia. Nor did sensible Russians want a big war. The chief of the secret police had even warned the tsar's officials that a war against Germany on the heels of the disastrous war against Japan might cause the collapse of the tsarist regime. But the majority of the tsar's advisers feared that to allow the German powers to crush Serbia, dominate the Balkans, and perhaps make the Ottoman Empire another of their spheres of influence would mean to surrender Russia's status as a great power. Foreign Minister Sergei Sazonov, especially, browbeat the vacillating Nicholas II over the need to defend Serbia to the hilt. What is more, a French delegation led by President of the Republic Raymond Poincaré happened to visit St. Petersburg in July 1914 and strongly reassured the Russians they would have the French government's support.

Be it tragedy, farce, or comedy of errors, international politics was fast becoming a Nietzschean nightmare. First, Vienna sent an ultimatum to the Serbian capital Belgrade that, if accepted, would have made Serbia a virtual puppet-state of Austria. The Serbs accepted some of Austria's demands but rejected the most humiliating. The Austrian government judged the reply unacceptable and declared war on July 28, 1914. Next, the belligerent Sazonov leaned on the tsar to mobilize his army in support of the Serbs. Sazonov knew that mustering Russia's gigantic army on the Austrian and German frontiers was bound to trigger mobilizations (or worse) from those regimes. But he pressed for it anyway and was supported by the Russian generals. The tsar, desperately hoping the Austrians would back down now that their bluff was called, signed the order.

The German General Staff was forced to react immediately to Russian mobilization because its own contingency plan put a huge premium on seizing the initiative. In 1894, when the Franco-Russian alliance first threatened Germany with a war on two fronts, General Alfred von Schlieffen had drafted a plan based on hurtling nearly the whole German army westward through Belgium in order to outflank and defeat the French army in a gigantic opening battle. The German army might then ship units by rail to the eastern front in time to block the ponderous Russian advance. But the fact that the Russians mobilized first created anxiety in Berlin. Hence German Chancellor Theobald von Bethmann Hollweg's plaintive telegram to Vienna urging the Austrians not to escalate the crisis by taking punitive measures against Serbia that might provoke Russia's intervention. The Austrians made no such promise, whereupon the German foreign office sent aggressively worded, but in fact forlorn, ultimata to St. Petersburg, insisting the Russian army stand down, and to Paris, insisting the French government remain neutral. When the Russians and French ignored these warnings, Bethmann Hollweg's cabinet, in the name of the kaiser and with the support of the Reichstag, declared war on Russia on the first day of August and declared war on France the third day of August, whereupon the German army invaded Belgium on the fourth day of August 1914.

That unprovoked attack on a small neutral country gave the wavering British cabinet the excuse it needed to go before Parliament and request a declaration of war on Germany. It appeared that everyone's obsession was with the balance of power. For the British reasoned they could not stand aside while Germany defeated its continental rivals. The French reasoned they could not stand aside and permit the Germans and Austrians to defeat their ally Russia. The Germans could not stand aside and let Russia support a terrorist campaign threatening the very existence of their allies the Austrians. The Russians could not stand aside and watch the German powers expand their empires "from Berlin to Baghdad."

Thus did the alliance systems, which had been designed to deter war and to preserve every nation's security, end by sparking a war that threatened every nation's security. Thus did a local dispute escalate by chain reaction into a disastrous general war. Thus did every government claim to be fighting a defensive war and thus did they all accuse each other of aggression. Thus did a century of general European peace and progress reach its irrational, explosive denouement... not because of capitalist greed, not because of imperialism, not because of socialist revolution, and not because anyone plotted a world war. Rather, a century of relative peace and very real progress came to an end because a European security apparatus designed to contain the aggressive impulses of modern imperial powers could not adjust to the terrorist threat a single small country posed to an old-fashioned dynasty that was neither nationalist nor imperialist and just wanted to be left alone. Like the iceberg that sank the *Titanic* two years earlier, nobody saw it coming. Rather, every government ordered "full speed ahead" until it was too late to avoid a catastrophe that would claim ten million lives and shatter the foundations of European civilization.

Two quotes from Nietzsche sum it all up: *menschlich, allzu menschlich*—"human, all too human"—and *Gegen Torheit gibt es kein Mittel*—"Against folly there is no defense."

Chapter 22

Storm of Steel:
The Traumas of War and Peace

The Great War of 1914–18 was the most traumatic event in modern history. It shattered Europe's political, economic, social, and cultural foundations so thoroughly that no restoration like the one following the Napoleonic Wars was even thinkable. Instead, what later came to be known as World War I sowed such seeds of future discord as communism, fascism, World War II, and the Cold War. In numerical terms the Second World War would engulf more countries, last longer, and kill more people. But that conflict at least made some sort of sense. It was clearly a war of aggressors against victims, and the defeat of the Axis powers gave meaning to the suffering. That conflict was also a war of movement in which armies and navies advanced and retreated across vast theaters, making the progress paid for in blood at least discernible. Finally, soldiers and civilians alike were less shocked by the carnage of the Second World War, because the First had been etched in their memory.

None of that was true of the 1914–18 conflict. From the outset, what the war was about was vague, and it quickly became clear that the stakes were not worth the slaughter. Battle fronts were static, as huge conscript armies faced each other along hundreds of miles of muddy, shell-pocked trench lines over four interminable years. Soldiers and citizens in 1914 did not know in advance that an industrial total war of attrition would look like that. Indeed, if they had known, their governments would never have risked such a conflict. Alas, the Great War sprang a technological trap into which political and military leaders unknowingly hurled their nations—in the words of the French president—with "hearty high spirits."

The generation of 1914 felt betrayed. How could this have happened? How could the most advanced nations descend into such suicidal barbarity? Of course, that was the point: *only* the most advanced nations could have waged such total war. A trivial but telling fact is that total war was made possible by the invention of canned food, without which armies could never have fed the millions of hungry men in the trenches. Less trivial is the fact that universal conscription, birthed by the French Revolution, had been adopted by all the continental powers after the Prussian victory over France in 1871. That meant war was no longer a job for professionals only, but the duty of every able-bodied man, woman, and child. Governments waging a total war were obliged to mobilize their home economies in order to churn out weapons, ammunition, boots and helmets, medical supplies, wagons, trucks, railroad cars, horses, and food. Nearly every family included a man in uniform and a woman in war work. Almost every European endured regimentation, rationing, and inflation. No one escaped this democracy of death.

Nations were also capable of waging total war because third-wave technologies and bureaucracies turned people themselves into cogs of the war machine. Indeed, the Great War was the first conflict whose outcome depended almost entirely on machines. Warfare, to be sure, had always been cruel. But in past eras the outcomes of decisive battles might hinge on human virtues like courage, honor, sacrifice, and leadership. Since ancient times war had fascinated poets precisely because it brought out the best in people as well as the worst. By contrast, though they marched off with dreams of glory, the youth of 1914 quickly learned that a twentieth-century army was itself a machine, the soldier an expendable part, the battlefield an amphitheater in which artillery, machine guns, tanks, and poison gas did battle with each other. Human casualties were simply a way to keep score. Max Weber's era of dehumanized social organization came true sooner and more terribly than even he expected as Europeans succumbed to the technology of death.

How did soldiers and civilians put up with four years of slaughter and waste without mutinies in their armies or revolutions at home? In fact, there would be mutinies in the armies of France, Italy, and Russia, and some revolutions as well. But those events occurred only near the end of the war, and only in countries on the verge of defeat. One must conclude that either the nationalistic, industrial war machines were too strong for people to stop even after they came to their senses, or else that they could not come to their senses because the war had driven them mad. The home fronts clung to romantic illusions about their nation's holy cause and its defense by brave boys at the front. The soldiers, trapped in hellish trench warfare, played psychological tricks on themselves to ward off nervous breakdowns amid deafening artillery barrages, bloodcurdling attacks by enemy soldiers brandishing bayonets and grenades, and (worst of all) orders to go "over the top" and attack the enemy in the teeth of machine guns that mowed down soldiers like scythes sweeping through ripe wheat fields. When not engaged in combat, soldiers inhabited noisome dank trenches shared with rats, lice, and decaying human flesh. The Great War was the agony of the snake that ate its tail, the irrationality of mass human behavior that Le Bon and Sorel had described, Freud's monsters of the id breaking free of all restraints, Darwin's struggle for survival in a phantasmagoric psychology of death.

Why did the proud armies that marched to battle with flags waving, crowds singing, and women throwing garlands descend into that nightmare? The short answer is that the elaborate war plans prepared by the generals of the belligerent powers utterly failed. And the reason for *that* was a technological surprise. In 1914 nearly all the chiefs of the military establishments took it for granted that their giant armies and massive firepower would make the next war violent but short. Whichever army arrived at the border soonest with the most infantrymen and artillery tubes must surely defeat the enemy. It was also assumed that war had become too expensive to last very long. The Russo-Japanese War, for example, had ended in just over a year because both governments ran out of money. But in 1914 the generals discovered that firepower in the absence of mobility gave the defense—not offense—a huge advantage. Since the first aircraft and armored tanks were too primitive to destroy fortified positions, soldiers simply dug in, took cover, and mowed down infantrymen attempting to charge their line.

The German Schlieffen Plan probably had the best chance to win a decisive victory. Designed for a war on two fronts, it called for a sweeping assault through neutral Belgium to envelop the French army from the rear, after which the Germans might transfer units eastward to meet the slow-moving "Russian steamroller." But the Schlieffen Plan was itself an artifact of third-wave industrial hubris in that it depended on flesh-and-blood human beings to function as if they were tireless machines. Imagine asking a million soldiers to march on foot from the River Rhine all the way around the city of Paris and then back to the east to attack the French army. Not surprisingly, the German soldiers tasked with carrying out this plan grew weary, and their generals worried about lengthening lines of communication and supply. The result was that German units on the extreme right flank slowed down and pivoted short of Paris. Meanwhile, the French commanders realized the danger just in time and shifted enough divisions westward to check the German advance on the river Marne. After a month of violent combat, both sides ran short of ammunition, broke off the battle, and made a series of leapfrogs to the north in hopes of outflanking each other until they reached the strategic ports on the English Channel.

By the start of 1915 the German army faced the French, British, and Belgian armies over a continuous front stretching from the English Channel to the border of Switzerland. There the armies dug in, building complex networks of trenches with machine gun nests and barbed wire in front and artillery batteries in the rear. Between the trench lines lay the muddy killing field known as "no man's land." Meanwhile, in the east, the Russians' offensive was stopped cold by the meager German forces left to cover the border, while an Austrian offensive was checked in turn by the Russians. The eastern front then bogged down along trench lines running from the Baltic Sea south to the Romanian border.

How could the stalemate be broken? Three ways were tried. The first was to lure new allies into the war. Japan entered at once, citing its alliance with Britain, but the Japanese simply wanted a pretext to seize Germany's colonies in the Pacific. They sent no soldiers or sailors to Europe. In 1915, the British and French enticed Italy into the war with promises of territorial gains. But the Austrians rushed soldiers to their Alpine frontier adjacent to Italy's rugged Dolomite Mountains, so the southern front became deadlocked as well. In 1916 Romania joined the Allies, but the Germans cobbled together an army that quickly defeated the Romanians. The Germans enticed Turkey into the war in 1914 and Bulgaria in 1915, which enabled them finally to overrun Serbia. But the Balkans, over which the war had begun, were now just a sideshow.

A second way to break the deadlock was to pour so much steel on the enemy that he bled to death. That beastly and unimaginative strategy of attrition was tried again and again by commanders on both sides. At the Battle of the Somme in 1916, the British bombarded the German trenches with one and a half million artillery shells, but when their soldiers went over the top no less than thirty-five thousand men from the United Kingdom and Canada perished in the first two hours. Even so, the generals persisted month after month until six hundred thousand Britons and Frenchmen and four hundred and fifty thousand Germans were killed or wounded . . . all for a gain of seven miles. The Germans in turn assaulted the fortress of Verdun for ten months in 1916, in the belief that the French would throw in every last man to defend a symbol of French glory older than Charlemagne. The Germans took three hundred thousand casualties, and the French three hundred fifty thousand, but Verdun held out. On the eastern front a Russian offensive in 1916 cost its army a million casualties over three months. In 1917, Sir Douglas Haig, perhaps the most callous general of all, lost more than a quarter of a million men to death or wounds in the Battle of Passchendaele alone.

A third way to break the stalemate was to employ novel weapons. The German army introduced poison gas, and the Allied forces soon did so as well. But the belligerents quickly issued gas masks to their soldiers, making chemical warfare only an inhumane aberration. The British invented the first armored tracked vehicle, which their engineers code-named the tank. But the tanks employed during the First World War were too few, too clumsy, too slow, and too unsuited to the pockmarked battlefields to make a significant difference. Likewise, airplanes, still in their infancy, were used mostly for artillery spotting and had no direct impact on ground warfare. Germany's dirigibles, those romantic zeppelin airships, conducted random raids that terrorized Londoners but otherwise served no military purpose. Finally, the Germans invented new infantry tactics by elite commandos called *Sturmtruppen* (storm troopers) who pierced through enemy trenches into rear areas, where they raised havoc with supply lines, command posts, and communications. Storm trooper tactics won some major victories on the Italian front in 1917 and the French front in 1918, but commandos were not enough to win a war monopolized by machines, which is to say by economics.

That is why the home fronts became the truly decisive battlefields. Governments fixed wages and prices, deployed labor and raw materials, and restricted consumption in the interest of maximizing war productivity. To pay for it, the Germans and their allies, known as the Central Powers, sold bonds to their patriotic middle classes and otherwise just inflated their currencies by printing paper money. The Allied powers liquidated their foreign assets, sold war bonds at home, and borrowed abroad, especially in the United States. The cost and destruction of the Great War, estimated to have been four hundred billion gold-standard dollars, shattered the financial dominance of Britain and France and in just two and a half years made the United States the world's creditor.

What were Europeans fighting for? The belligerent governments drew up secret war aims and made treaties with their allies on how to divide the spoils of victory. The kaiser's government hoped to annex Belgium and Poland and dominate the Balkans, thereby forging a *Mitteleuropa* empire. Berlin also hoped to forge an empire in *Mittelafrika* by adding the Belgian and French Congo colonies to Germany's existing African empire. For their part, the Entente powers planned to take over Germany's colonies plus the Ottoman Turks' oil-rich Arabian provinces. The French, of course, were determined to regain Alsace-Lorraine and perhaps to annex the German Rhineland, while the Russians lusted after the warm-water port of Constantinople.

As the body counts rose, however, the only war aim that mattered to the home fronts was victory. No province or colony could possibly be worth the lives and treasure being consumed by the war. Only destruction of a hated enemy, demonized by propaganda, could redeem the sacrifice. That was another feature of modern, democratized warfare. In previous centuries monarchies might wage limited wars with their professional armies and navies and maintain some sense of proportion between means and ends. But entire nations will not fight and possibly die unless their people believe they are defending their way of life—or promoting a great ideological cause that turns the war into a crusade.

In the Great War governments perfected the art of vicious propaganda. Why must the killing go on? Why is there no substitute for victory? Because the Germans are barbaric Huns who rape women, kill babies, and mean to conquer the world. Because the English are greedy philistines hoping to strangle Germany and cheat her of her destiny. Because the Russians are half-Asiatic barbarians who mean to spread tsarist despotism and destroy German *Kultur*. Such propaganda motivated civilians to endure total war while destroying any chance for a compromise peace. How could governments justify peace talks with

The Great War's belligerent powers militarized the labor and financial resources of their civilian populations, and whipped up war fever, through vicious propaganda.

an enemy they portrayed as evil incarnate? Nor could domestic dissent survive in the atmosphere of a crusade. The German Social Democratic Party, contrary to the fond hopes of the Second Socialist International, merely abstained when the kaiser asked the political parties in the Reichstag to vote war credits, and throughout the entire war the SPD delegates honored the *Burgfrieden* (fortress peace) declared by the parties in the Reichstag. In France, the political parties swore allegiance to the *Union Sacrée* (sacred union), while Britain's parties formed a National Unity government.

Such unity was precious because civilians also suffered. The British surface fleet blockaded German-occupied Europe for the expressed purpose of starving the enemy's civilian population. The German navy retaliated with a submarine blockade of the British Isles and torpedoed so many merchant ships that Britain's wartime leaders feared their own population might starve. Women and children thus became legitimate targets in a war whose outcome would be determined as much by bread as by bullets and bombs.

By 1917 the belligerents were beginning to crack. In Austria-Hungary, following the death of old Franz Josef in 1916, his heir the Emperor Karl tried in vain to negotiate some sort of truce. Elements of the French army mutinied in 1917 rather than carry out any more suicidal attacks. The British government had to ward off an armed revolt by the Irish Republican Army in 1916, while hiding from its own population the fact that food supplies were dangerously low. In Germany the Reichstag passed an anodyne peace resolution urging the kaiser to declare his war aims and seek a truce.

Finally, 1917 was the year the Great War turned ideological. It was then that two new leaders denounced what they both considered to be an imperialist war. The first was Vladimir Lenin, given an opportunity by the fact that the first belligerent not only to crack but to collapse was tsarist Russia. Her peasant armies had suffered unspeakably, not only from battle, but also from inefficiency and corruption. Russian soldiers lacked rifles, ammunition, and medical supplies, and the country's inadequate railroad system was incapable of shipping food to the army and the cities at home. In March 1917 crowds poured into the streets of Petrograd (as St. Petersburg was renamed during the war) crying for peace and reforms. Tsar Nicholas II finally abdicated the throne. Russia, for a brief flicker, became a liberal democracy under a provisional government led by Alexander Kerensky.

A month later, in April 1917, the United States Congress voted to declare war on Germany. That was when the second new leader appeared. President Woodrow Wilson had declared neutrality in 1914 in the belief that his God-given mission was to mediate a "peace without victory." But his efforts from 1915 to 1917 proved to be fruitless. Meanwhile, most Americans—aside from those of German or Irish descent—came to favor the Allies for any of three reasons. First, Britain, France, and eventually Russia were democracies, whereas Germany and her allies were partly authoritarian. Second, Americans got their war news from Allied sources—the British had severed Germany's trans-Atlantic telegraph cable. Third, German U-boats (submarines) periodically sank ships on which Americans perished, most infamously the *R.M.S. Lusitania* (sister ship of the *Titanic*) in 1915.

That is not to say the American people were eager to get into the war. But in early 1917 their president decided his hand had been forced when the British embassy secretly informed the White House that the British government's treasury and the British people's larders were nearly exhausted. Wilson, a lifelong Anglophile, took the news hard. At length he decided that the United States must enter the war to save Great Britain. But Wilson knew that Congress and the American people were not about to wade into a world war in order to save the widely despised British Empire. The president therefore rhetorically reframed the war as a crusade "to make the world safe for democracy," and it was in light of that goal that he asked Congress for a declaration of war on April 6, 1917.

On the Eastern Front, the Kerensky government soon launched another brave but foolish offensive that only provoked more mutinies in the Russian army. Germany's high command, spying a chance to knock Russia out of the war, gave the incendiary Lenin safe passage from his exile in Switzerland through Finland to Russia, where he was warmly welcomed by many soldiers and urban workers. Lenin did not bother to preach Marxism. He simply promised the people peace and bread. Then, when Kerensky finally decided to schedule national elections, Lenin's Bolsheviks—who knew their fringe party would be swamped by the votes of the peasant masses—rose up in arms and overthrew the provisional government. That was a crushing blow for the Allies. Lenin called on soldiers and workers everywhere to overthrow their imperialist rulers and demand a peace based on "No Annexations! No Indemnities!" His revolution, however, did not spread beyond Russia, so Lenin instead made a separate peace with Germany through the humiliating Treaty of Brest-Litovsk in March 1918. The treaty pulled Russia out of the war, turned western Russia over to German control, and enabled the German high command to transfer a million soldiers to the western front.

Lenin's call for world revolution shocked Wilson into responding with his own liberal internationalist vision for the postwar world. His famous Fourteen Points speech in January 1918 called for open diplomacy, national self-determination, freedom of the seas, free trade, disarmament, and a League of Nations to prevent war in the future. So it was that the last year of the war was really a *four-way* struggle for the soul of Europe in which German militarism, Anglo-French imperialism, American liberalism, and Russian communism each resisted the other three.

The struggle's first climax came in late summer 1918, when Germany's storm trooper attacks failed to break through the western front and the Allies, reinforced by a million American doughboys, counterattacked. The German General Staff at last threw in the towel, urging the kaiser to ask for an armistice on the basis of Wilson's Fourteen Points. The president insisted on regime change; the kaiser must abdicate, which Wilhelm II reluctantly did on November 9. Two days later, at the eleventh hour of the eleventh day of the eleventh month, the Armistice took effect. Peace had arrived at last, a peace that proved as great a shock as war had been fifty-one months before.

When the shooting stopped, celebrations erupted in London, Paris, New York, and Rome. The frontline soldiers, however, did not cheer. They crept out of their trenches, cautious and disbelieving, traded cigarettes and tins of sausage, and felt more comradeship with enemy soldiers than with their own civilians. All wars are alienating, but this one, especially, made its veterans a lonely club of traumatized, bitter survivors. No one back home could fathom what the conflict's fighting men had experienced. They were, in a phrase popularized by author Ernest Hemingway, a lost generation.

What was left of them, that is. Over two million young Germans had been killed, plus three million Russians, one million Frenchmen, one million subjects of Austria-Hungary, three-quarters of a million Brits, and half a million Italians. All told, the Great War claimed twelve million lives and maimed thirty-six million more. To compound these plagues upon mankind, the worst influenza pandemic on record (even worse than the 2020–22 pandemic) caused ten to twenty million more deaths worldwide from 1918 to 1920.

The economic damage was equally severe. The gold standard became but a memory. After wartime controls were removed, inflation ran rampant. The middle classes saw their bank accounts, war bonds, and insurance policies shrink to a fraction of their original value. Thanks to war bonds, European governments owed billions to their own people, and ten billion dollars more to Americans. How could Europe recover with her factories and railroads in shambles, her shipping fleets sunk, her capital squandered, her overseas markets lost to American and Japanese firms, and vast portions of Belgium, France, Poland, and Russia reduced to moonscapes?

The political structure of Europe was also smashed by the collapse of four eastern empires: the Hohenzollern dynasty in Germany; the Habsburg dynasty in Austria-Hungary; the Romanov dynasty in Russia; and the Ottoman dynasty in Turkey. Russia promptly fell into civil war, as Lenin's Bolsheviks confronted various resistance movements. The Habsburg realm disintegrated in 1918, as Czechs, Poles, Romanians, and Yugoslavs proclaimed independence. The

Ottoman Empire collapsed when Arab and Turkish nationalist movements took up arms against the last Sultan. Even the exhausted victors in France, Britain, and Italy feared for the future. Europe's only hope, it appeared, lay in America, personified by her seemingly idealistic president Woodrow Wilson.

After the armistice all eyes turned to Paris, where a great peace conference led by Wilson, British Prime Minister David Lloyd George, French Premier Georges Clemenceau, and Italian Premier Vittorio Orlando gathered in January 1919 to attempt to put Humpty-Dumpty together again. It was the greatest diplomatic gathering since the Congress of Vienna in 1814. But whereas the monarchical victorious states at Vienna had been bent on suppressing democracy and nationalism, the victors of 1919 were democratic states supposedly bent on promoting democracy and national self-determination, at least among European peoples if not their colonial subjects. In one way only did Wilson pursue the same goal as Metternich, Castlereagh, and Tsar Alexander: he meant to institutionalize perpetual peace.

What Wilson failed to anticipate was that democratic statesmen were severely constrained by public opinion in a way monarchies were not. He expected common people everywhere to cheer his liberal-internationalist agenda. But he soon discovered that the Allied publics demanded vengeance against Germany, security against future German attack, and territorial and economic gains for their own countries. To recall Petrarch's quotation, Wilson willed the good, but he did not know the truth. He naïvely asked his advisers, "Tell me what is right, and I'll fight for it," not realizing that the British, French, Italians, and for that matter the Germans all had their own definitions of justice.

Wilson insisted that the first order of business at Paris be the drafting of the League of Nations Covenant. That annoyed Europeans, especially when it became clear that the League magnified their misgivings. The British asked whether sovereign great powers would accept the League's arbitration of international disputes rather than defend their national interest by diplomacy and force. The French asked whether the League would have teeth—that is, real military power behind it. Nearly all delegates asked whether democratic electorates would permit the League of Nations Council to drag them into other nations' wars in which their own countries had no stake.

The barriers to a peace of reconciliation became even more evident once the Big Three leaders—Wilson, Lloyd George, and Clemenceau—began to work on the German peace treaty. The French premier insisted the Germans pay reparations for the physical damage the war had done in France, while the British prime minister insisted Germany compensate his country for the ships sunk by U-boats, for the overseas markets lost by British firms, and for the pensions his government had promised veterans and war widows. The British also insisted that Germany surrender her navy and colonies, while the French demanded the return of Alsace-Lorraine, permanent Allied occupation of the Rhineland, and German disarmament.

Wilson believed it was only just that Germany make amends for what he considered to be their war of aggression. But he opposed dismembering the Rhineland, since that violation of self-determination would make Germans as vengeful as Frenchmen had been after the loss of Alsace-Lorraine. At length, Wilson and Lloyd George sought to appease Clemenceau by offering a guarantee to fight in defense of France in case of a future German attack. Clemenceau nevertheless insisted on a long list of conditions meant to keep Germany disarmed. The bitter debates over the German peace and the disputes over boundaries in eastern Europe were bad omens. Even supporters of Wilson, such as British delegate Harold Nicolson, asked, "Are we making a good peace? I wonder."

A few weeks later the harsh terms of the Treaty of Versailles gave him his answer. Nicolson wrote in his diary: "I returned to my hotel sick of life." Yet the treaty was not harsh enough for France's ranking soldier Marshal Ferdinand Foch. "This is no peace," he bellowed. "It is a truce for twenty years." 1919 . . . 1939 . . . Foch's prophecy was exact—in part because no one was more disillusioned than the Germans. They had made the armistice in exchange for the promise of a treaty based on the Fourteen Points. Instead, the Treaty of Versailles violated the letter or spirit of all Wilson's principles, and it was foisted on the Germans as a sign-it-or-starve proposition, for the Allies vindictively continued their food blockade pending conclusion of a peace treaty. No wonder most Germans called the treaty a punitive *Diktat*.

Nor was that a mere nationalist slogan. Germany's center-left political parties—struggling to found a democratic republic—felt just as betrayed. Not only did the Reich lose Alsace-Lorraine; it also lost territory to Belgium, Denmark, and Poland, including a humiliating land corridor to the Baltic Sea that cut East Prussia off from the rest of Germany. The Rhineland would be occupied for fifteen years, and its rich coal deposits turned over to France. The German army was limited to one hundred thousand men and stripped of all heavy weapons, while the kaiser's battleship fleet, built at such ruinous expense, was scuttled. Germany's colonies were ceded to Britain, France, and Japan under League of Nations mandates. Germany was not permitted to unite with the German-speaking rump state of Austria and would not even be allowed to join the League of Nations. The Germans had to sign a blank check for reparations, later fixed at the impossible sum of 132 billion gold marks. Finally, the treaty added insult to injury through its Article 231, which asserted the war had been caused "by the aggression of Germany and her allies." That infamous "war-guilt clause" not only enraged the Germans; it meant that if historians later argued the Germans had not been more guilty for the outbreak of war than, say, the Russians or Serbs, then the moral foundation for the entire treaty would dissolve.

The perverse results of the peace's terms were immediately evident. First, the democrats in the Reichstag who founded the Weimar Republic (named for the town where its constitution was drafted) were vilified as traitors by right-wing extremists. They insisted the German army had been stabbed in the back by socialists, Jews, and liberal dupes of the hypocrite Wilson. German democracy was therefore hobbled from its inception. Second, United States senators rightly suggested that League of Nations membership would be an unconstitutional infringement on United States sovereignty. Hence, they asked for fourteen reservations to be appended to the Versailles Treaty upon ratification. President Wilson stubbornly refused all compromise and ordered the Democrats in the Senate to vote against the treaty if those reservations were attached. In the end, the US government neither ratified the treaty nor joined the League. Third, the British used that defection as an excuse to withdraw their own commitment to French security, which left the French feeling betrayed and abandoned. Paris's postwar governments became all the more determined to enforce the Versailles Treaty, even if they had to do it alone.

When the Berlin government predictably defaulted on reparations, the French army occupying the Rhineland crossed the river in 1923 to occupy the coal mines and factories of the Ruhr valley, Germany's industrial heartland. That bold bid to seize reparations-in-kind proved to be another disaster. German workers spontaneously went on strike to teach the hated French they could not "mine coal with bayonets." The government in Berlin compensated strikers with paper money it ran off the printing press, which proved to be the immediate cause of the infamous hyperinflation that ruined the *Reichsmark*. By autumn 1923 the chaos throughout Germany had grown so severe that Communists and Nazis were marching and rioting against the republic.

At that point Charles Evans Hughes, the secretary of state in Warren G. Harding's Republican administration, intervened to promote the pacification of Europe. He convened a committee of bankers to draft a plan for Germany's financial reconstruction and persuaded New York bankers to extend credits to the Berlin government that would back a new solid currency and allow Germany to begin to pay reparations. At the London Conference of 1924 the French agreed to evacuate the Ruhr, and German Foreign Minister Gustav Stresemann pledged to fulfill the Versailles Treaty.

By 1925 it seemed the passions of war had finally been leeched. French Foreign Minister Aristide Briand met with Stresemann at the Swiss resort of Locarno, where the French and the Germans voluntarily signed security treaties. Under the Locarno Accords the Germans promised never to remilitarize the Rhineland or use force to change its western boundaries, the French promised never again to violate German territory, and the British and Italian governments promised to guarantee the treaties. When Germany was invited to join the League of Nations the following year, church bells rang all over Europe to herald what everyone hoped would be an era of goodwill, stability, and prosperity.

Alas, that also proved illusory. Three years later the Great Depression would begin. In seven years Adolf Hitler's Nazi Party would take power in Germany and pledge to rip up the Versailles *Diktat*. In retrospect, a more conciliatory peace might have reconciled the German people to their defeat and helped their fledgling democracy survive, while an even harsher peace might have rendered the Germans harmless whatever their internal politics. Instead, the Versailles Treaty, as one delegate lamented bitterly, was the worst of both worlds: "a Napoleonic peace enforced by Wilsonian methods." Once again, Harold Nicolson put it best when he wrote in his diary: "We came to Paris confident a new order was about to be established; we left it convinced the new order had merely fouled the old."

Chapter 23

Class War: Marxism-Leninism Captures Russia

B ackward are beaten! But we do not want to be beaten! No, comrades, we do not want that. History of Old Russia consisted in being constantly beaten for her backwardness. Mongol Khans beat her. Turkish beys beat her. Swedish feudalists beat her. Polish nobles beat her. Anglo-French capitalists beat her. Japanese barons beat her. Prussian imperialists beat her. Everyone beat Russia—for her backwardness!"

Thus spoke Josef Stalin, chairman of the Communist Party of the Soviet Union, in 1931. He exhorted the Soviet people to fulfill his Five Year Plan for crash industrialization, the most ambitious and cruel program of social change ever launched by a European government. His purpose was to ensure that never again would Russia be beaten for her backwardness.

Few global issues are more pressing than underdevelopment. Not only for poor, so-called Third World countries, but also for mature industrial nations that find themselves falling behind their more dynamic competitors. But backwardness is simply the flipside of modernization. For just as it never occurred to anyone to be a Conservative until the French Revolution violently challenged the old regime, so it never occurred to anyone to consider his or her country backward until European countries leaped ahead of the rest of the world on the strength of science, industry, and capitalism. Among Europeans the Russians had always brought up the rear. As late as 1890 tsarist Russia was still locked into a political, social, and religious order that seemed medieval, if not oriental, to western Europeans, and the Russian elites were keenly aware of it. During the early 1700s Tsar Peter the Great began to import European science and technology, and in the late 1700s Catherine the Great practiced enlightened despotism. But their top-down impositions did little to alter the vast hinterlands of the empire. Moreover, the French Revolution alerted the tsars to the threat posed by ideologies from western Europe, which is why throughout the nineteenth century the secret police kept a close watch on Russians attracted to modern ideas. Only after 1856, when Russia was defeated in the Crimean War, did Tsar Alexander II and his successors accept the fact that, unless it wished to lose its status as a great power and sink into stagnation like the Ch'ing and Ottoman empires, Russia could not remain stagnant.

But modernization posed a dilemma. Industrial progress would inevitably create an intelligentsia of scientists, engineers, and managers, plus a business community, a middle class, and an urban working class, all of whom were certain to challenge the autocracy. International competition forced the last tsars to push for progress, but the domestic effects of modernization tended to undermine their regime. The last fifty years of tsarist Russia is therefore the story of the regime's attempts to play economic catchup while somehow preserving the old order. The wars and revolutions of those decades, culminating in 1917, were the death throes of a sclerotic empire struggling to embrace modernity.

The last three tsars tried to modernize both the agricultural and industrial sectors. The first campaign began with emancipation of the serfs in 1861. Since the tsar's power rested on the landed gentry, the government did not redistribute land attached to the nobility's rural estates. The emancipated peasants therefore ended up as tenants or hired hands on those estates. Moreover, since people needed internal passports to travel within Russia—a police measure taken to trace agitators—the condition of rural folk remained scarcely better than it had been under serfdom. Then, in 1906, a farsighted official named Peter Stolypin won the tsar's approval for real land reform. His hope was to create a class of productive and prosperous farmers. Alas, a radical terrorist, fearing such reforms might reconcile peasants to the tsarist regime, assassinated Stolypin in 1911.

Efforts to stimulate industrial progress proved more successful, thanks in great part to a brilliant finance minister named Sergei Witte. Between 1890 and 1904 Witte almost single-handedly made the ruble a solid gold-standard currency. He borrowed billions of French francs to invest in railroads and factories. And he oversaw construction of the Trans-Siberian Railway, stretching from Moscow to Vladivostok on the Pacific. Predictably, however, the technicians and managers employed by these new industries resented the tsarist regime's absolutism, censorship, aristocratic privileges, inefficiency, and corruption. Students at the new engineering schools often became revolutionaries—indeed, Vladimir Lenin formed his first Bolshevik cell at the St. Petersburg Technological Institute—and all educated young men yearned for better career opportunities than the immature economy could provide. Factory and railroad workers were another source of social ferment. Labor conditions in Russia around 1900 resembled those of England seventy years before, with low wages, long hours, and few if any safety standards. Trade unions and strikes were illegal.

Russians knew that serious political and social reforms had to be made, but how? Moderate reformers, a group that included middle-class urban dwellers, progressive gentry, and some state officials, supported the Constitutional Democrat or Kadet Party. They hoped that Russia might evolve into a constitutional monarchy similar to that of Germany. But the Kadets had little to offer workers or peasants, whose mass support was needed to pressure the tsarist regime. The party with the broadest support was the Social Revolutionaries, or SRs, who pleaded the cause of peasants, idealized the *mir*, or traditional village commune, and envisioned the confiscation of the gentry's estates. This rather reactionary, rural version of revolution was anathema to the Marxist Social Democrats, or SDs, who agitated for support among the growing urban proletariat.

Most of the SDs were Mensheviks (which ironically meant Minority) who argued in orthodox Marxist fashion that communist revolution could occur only after a capitalist revolution had transformed the economy. Hence, Mensheviks were resigned to waiting until Russia became a mature industrial society before making their move. Their opponents, called Bolsheviks (which meant Majority), insisted that a violent revolution could establish the dictatorship of the proletariat immediately. Mensheviks accused Bolsheviks of deviationism. Bolsheviks accused Mensheviks of revisionism, a term they applied to the moderate program of social change that Germany's Social Democratic Party had embraced. So the SDs split in 1903, and Vladimir Lenin's Bolshevik party went underground to plot a revolution.

The events of 1905 suggested that Lenin might have been right. Russia's humiliating defeats in the war against Japan undermined confidence in Tsar Nicholas II's military and bureaucracy. Strikes paralyzed Moscow and St. Petersburg. Workers and soldiers spontaneously formed councils called *soviets*. The tsar survived the crisis by granting a constitution and convening a parliament called the Duma. But the parliament proved feckless, especially when the tsar, having recovered his authority, stripped the Duma of most of its powers. After 1906, it seemed like the only way to change old Russia was through revolution.

Vladimir Ilyich Ulyanov, alias Lenin, was determined to trigger that revolution. He had been born in 1870 in a town on the Volga River about four hundred miles southeast of Moscow. His father was a respectable school principal, and Vladimir was expected to become an educator, too—until his radical older brother was implicated in a plot to assassinate the tsar and was sentenced to death in 1886. The teenaged Vladimir then made two decisions. He would devote his life to the revolutionary cause, but he would reject his brother's anarchism in favor of more effective tactics.

Lenin's headmaster called him the "pride of the school." Coincidentally, that headmaster was none other than the father of Alexander Kerensky, whose provisional government Lenin's Bolshevik party would one day destroy. At the age of seventeen Lenin read his brother's copy of *Das Kapital* and joined a Marxist club. In 1893 he moved to Moscow and founded a small club with a very big name: the League of Struggle for the Emancipation of the Working Class. In 1897 he was arrested and exiled to Siberia for three years, where he spent his spare moments playing chess and studying Marxist theory. After his release in 1900, Lenin lived abroad, mostly in Switzerland, for seventeen years. What did he do over those years to prepare for revolution?

Pretty much everything. Lenin's waking moments and, if the legends are true, even his nighttime dreams, were absorbed by revolution. He read and wrote constantly. He attacked his rivals on the left, including Mensheviks and revisionists who hoped, as did labor unions, merely to improve conditions for the working classes. One of his socialist rivals said of Lenin: "There is no one else who for the whole twenty-four hours of every day is busy with the revolution.

What can you do with a man like that?" Lenin was short, hyperactive, and highstrung. He was a merciless debater, and his wife said he would break off relations with his closest friends if he suspected them of hampering the movement. Lenin liked music, but after listening to a Beethoven sonata he grumbled, "I cannot listen to such music often. It affects your nerves, makes you want to say stupid, nice things, and stroke the heads of people who could create such beauty.... You must hit them over the head, without mercy."

Lenin was not mad. He was as calculating a man as ever lived. But he was monomaniacal, willing to sacrifice wealth, comfort, happiness, friends, leisure, beauty, and sleep for the sake of power. His method was to reject alliances with others on the left and to initiate into his vanguard only the most dedicated, disciplined, and merciless comrades. Lenin never sought a mass following, for he had no faith in the fickle, easily duped working class. Indeed, he was opposed to democracy even within his own party, because he believed Bolsheviks could maintain their discipline, ruthlessness, and doctrinal unity only through dictatorship by a central committee chaired by one man. Lenin called that system "democratic centralism."

In any event, the tsar's secret police were everywhere. So Lenin divided his conspiratorial party into small, secret cells whose members did not know the identities of their contacts in other cells. That way any Bolshevik who fell under arrest could not compromise more than a handful of his comrades. From his Swiss exile Lenin stayed in constant contact with informers inside Russia. He wrote ten or more letters per day, probing for intelligence, and by 1917 he understood better than anyone else the state of mind of soldiers, peasants, and urban workers all over Russia. Finally, Lenin had no qualms about revising Marxist doctrine to suit Russian conditions.

Still, there might never have been a revolution, communist or otherwise, if not for the tsar's folly in dragging Russia into the war against Germany in 1914. Russia's huge but technically inferior armies suffered bloody defeats for which Nicholas II bore personal responsibility. Russia's railroad and logistical systems were overtaxed, leaving the country's soldiers short of weapons, ammunition, food, and medicine. The bureaucracy was overburdened, incompetent, and corrupt. The imperial court was poisoned by the infamous Rasputin, a fraudulent monk who gained power behind the throne by persuading the tsarina that he could heal her hemophiliac son. In 1916 outraged nobles at court murdered Rasputin, but it was too late to save the regime. Food riots erupted. Crowds in the streets cried out "down with the tsar!" Soldiers mutinied. Soviets sprang up again. In March 1917 (February by the Orthodox calendar), Nicholas abdicated the throne.

The rickety empire fell into the hands of a provisional government led by Alexander Kerensky. He promised to stage elections, make reforms, and mandate land redistribution, but his cabinet had little authority beyond Petrograd and Moscow. Most local power lay with the workers and soldiers' soviets controlled by peasant SRs or Menshevik SDs. Kerensky also made the patriotic but fatal mistake of continuing to wage war. That was unwelcome news to the German commanders, so they secretly transported Lenin into Finland, whence he crossed the border into Russia. The Germans hoped, of course, that he would seize power and pull Russia out of the war.

Upon his arrival, Lenin hotly denounced the provisional government and other socialists, insisting that only the Bolsheviks could give peace and bread to the people. The party's popularity increased during the late summer, when it led the resistance to an abortive right-wing uprising. All the while the Bolsheviks steadily gained majority support in most local councils, at which point Lenin declared a new slogan: "All Power to the Soviets!" Kerensky, at first slow to appreciate the danger, finally scheduled national elections, which were certain to be won by the peasant parties. Lenin knew that very well, which is why he and his second-in-command Lev Bronstein, alias Leon Trotsky, decided to risk an armed coup d'état in advance of the elections. On October 25, 1917 (November 7 by the Gregorian calendar), Trotsky's commandos seized telephone exchanges, railway terminals, and electrical plants in Petrograd, while Bolshevik sailors on the warship *Aurora* bombarded the Winter Palace, which housed Kerensky's cabinet. The ministers fled, the provisional government dissolved, and the Bolsheviks seized power in the name of the soviets.

Renaming themselves the Communist Party, the Bolsheviks purged the workers' and soldiers' councils of their remaining opponents, outlawed all other political parties, commandeered railroad trains to occupy other cities, and launched the Red Terror, a period of retribution that ultimately dwarfed the French Revolution's Reign of Terror. Among the terror's victims were Tsar

Nicholas, Tsarina Alexandra, the sickly *tsarevich*—their son—and the rest of the imperial family—all shot in cold blood at the Ekaterinburg prison camp.

At first the Communist regime controlled only the Russian core surrounding Petrograd and Moscow, and in fact the regime might not have prevailed had Lenin not extricated Russia from the Great War. His first ploy was to call on Germany's workers and soldiers to overthrow their own imperialist rulers and conclude a peace based on "No Annexations! No Indemnities!" When that revolution failed to materialize, Lenin sent Trotsky to the Byelorussian city of Brest-Litovsk to beg the German warlords for peace. Their terms proved so harsh that Trotsky indignantly stormed out. But Lenin ordered Trotsky to return and swallow whatever surrender terms the Germans demanded. The result was the Treaty of Brest-Litovsk of March 1918, which ceded vast portions of European Russia to Germany. No wonder Russian nationalists deemed the Bolsheviks traitors, and no wonder Woodrow Wilson suspected Lenin of being a German agent.

This first Communist "peace offensive" was designed to trade land for time, time for Trotsky to muster a Red Army to fight against the internal opponents of Bolshevik rule. It turned out perfectly for Lenin, because America's entry into the war in April 1917 not only helped the Allies triumph on the western front; the armistice terms of November 1918 also obliged the German army to cough up its conquests on the eastern front. Ironically, Woodrow Wilson's war, meant to make the world safe for democracy, made the world safe for communism instead.

But wait: Did not the western allies intervene militarily to oppose the Bolshevik regime? Not really. To be sure, in 1918 small contingents of British, French, and American soldiers landed at Russia's Arctic ports of Murmansk and Archangel, and contingents of Japanese and American troops came on shore at Vladivostok. But the mission of those troops was merely to guard the Allied shipments of guns, ammunition, and other supplies that had been piling up in Russian warehouses. French premier Clemenceau even offered to arm the Bolsheviks if they would continue the war against Germany. In any case, a few thousand Allied troops in the Arctic or distant Siberia were scarcely able to influence politics in the core regions of European Russia. After the armistice ended the war against Germany, the French and British governments made half-hearted efforts to help the anti-Bolshevik forces, but their war-weary publics had no stomach for a sizable military intervention in Russia.

The Bolsheviks' Red Army was therefore free to fight it out with the so-called White armies: a congeries of monarchists, Cossacks, and ethnic groups (such as the Ukrainians) who hoped to escape Russian rule entirely. The tide of civil war washed back and forth across the steppe, while the Reds and Whites both engaged in terror and mass executions amid famine and chaos. Millions more Russians would have perished if not for relief operations, led by Herbert Hoover, undertaken by the Red Cross and the United States government in 1921.

The Red Army of the Soviets, as the Bolsheviks now referred to themselves, got off to a chaotic start when Trotsky tried to experiment with an army of equals without ranks or honors, an army in which soldiers in each unit elected their commanders. When those ideas proved to be ludicrous, the Soviets made the first of many compromises with reality. Trotsky ordered military conscription in the regions under Soviet control, reestablished ranks and discipline, and even recruited veterans of the tsarist officer corps. Soon the Red Army became a lethal instrument, and Trotsky, who had been a café intellectual before the war, proved to be a dynamic general. Exploiting interior lines and control of the railroads, he shifted armies from one front to another and defeated the White armies one by one. His biggest crisis loomed in 1920, when the Red Army mistakenly attacked the resurrected nation of Poland and suffered a major defeat. Lenin responded by launching another peace offensive. In 1921 his regime concluded a treaty that, while it ceded to Poland much of Byelorussia and western Ukraine, also freed up Trotsky's Red Army to win more campaigns against the White Russian forces.

By the end of 1921 the Soviets' combination of will, discipline, propaganda, and terror had broken the counterrevolutionary resistance and chased the Anglo-French occupiers from Russia's ports. Against all odds, a small, initially underground conspiracy had captured the world's largest country and founded the world's first socialist state. On what basis would the Soviets rebuild their society? The slogan "All power to the Soviets" implied that Russia would become a workers' democracy realized through decentralized councils in each factory, peasant commune, military unit, town, and city. But the slogan was a lie. The Communist regime proved to be more centralized and dictatorial than the tsarist regime had ever been, and its will was enforced by an even more ruthless secret police.

The first institution established by the Bolshevik Party was the internal security agency led by a Robespierre-like figure named Feliks Dzerzhinsky. That agency was the Cheka, whose name was an acronym standing for Extraordinary, All-Russian Commission of Struggle against Counterrevolution, Speculation, and Sabotage. Over the decades since, the Communists repeatedly changed the name of this infamous agency to the OGPU, then NKVD, then MVD, then KGB. Whatever its name, the agency's purpose was to exterminate anyone who dared oppose the Communist Party's monopoly of power. According to Dzherzinsky, the first question interrogators should ask the accused were "What is your social class and occupation? Those should suffice to decide the fate of the accused. That is the essence of Red Terror."

The second institution founded by the Soviet regime was Trotsky's Red Army, and the third was a relentless economic bureaucracy designed to impose what Lenin called War Communism. All but the smallest businesses were seized by police or soldiers and declared to be property of the people—that is, of the state, which is to say the Communist Party. The Bolsheviks promised land reform, but the civil war and famine required that food be sequestered from peasants and shipped to cities and battle fronts to feed workers and soldiers. Thus did urban Bolsheviks, just like Jacobins during the French Revolution, declare virtual war on peasants. Armed marauders ravaged the countryside, inspecting barns and silos and hauling off crops and livestock. Peasants resisted by hiding their harvests, slaughtering livestock, or enlisting in the White Armies. Still, in the end those three institutions—the Cheka, the Red Army, and War Communism—enabled the Bolsheviks to triumph in the Russian Civil War.

It was then that the true nature of the Bolshevik regime began to emerge. For instance, would Lenin and the Communist Party renounce imperialism and permit the subject nationalities of the old tsarist empire to determine their own fate? The answer to that was delivered by the first Commissar for Nationalities, Josef Stalin. Since Marxist theory defined nationalism as bourgeois false consciousness, any ethnic groups seeking self-government were, by definition, counterrevolutionary "wreckers." A few ethnic groups escaped Russia's grip, including Finland, Latvia, Lithuania, and Estonia on the Baltic Sea. But wherever the Red Army reached, so did Soviet power, until Lenin proclaimed the Union of Soviet Socialist Republics (USSR) in 1922. The USSR included some fifteen constituent republics, but all power within these "republics" was wielded by local Communist parties, whose leaders in turn took their orders from the Central Committee and Politburo in Moscow.

Likewise, Lenin promulgated a constitution filled with references to social equality, human rights, regular elections, and a council of ministers that answered to a legislature called the Supreme Soviet. But the constitution's words were nothing but propaganda, because only one political party was allowed, Communists controlled every level of government, and the secret police ensured that everyone cheered the Kremlin's party line.

Thus did Russians shuck off the tyranny of the tsars only to be captured by a far more efficient tyranny. The one-party state systematically destroyed every institution of civil society. With atheism declared the official Bolshevik creed, churches, synagogues, and mosques were razed or repurposed, while steadfast Christians, Jews, and Muslims were suspected of thought crime. Labor unions became puppets of a regime that otherwise claimed to be the vanguard of the proletariat and to be building a workers' paradise. Law courts became Soviet tribunals. Universities became schools of Marxist indoctrination. Newspapers and radio stations became media for propaganda. Society itself was effaced until nothing remained but atomized individuals standing naked before a monolithic, ideological, one-party state.

What was the purpose of that one-party state? Lenin made the answer clear when he launched Russia's postwar reconstruction under the aegis of the Gosplan, or State Economic Planning Commission. He famously announced that "Communism equals Soviet power plus electrification of the whole country." That was the bold, positive view of the future the Soviet government appeared to offer: the rapid development of science and technology, not for private profit, but for public goods, including the elimination of poverty, inequality, and class conflict and the liberation of humanity from material limits. In other words, the regime's alleged purpose was to build the secular humanist utopia prophesied by Marx and Engels.

The initial program of the Gosplan brought an end to War Communism and even a limited return to free markets. That New Economic Policy, or NEP, prevailed from 1922 to 1927. It was based on the pragmatic conclusion that the best way to boost food production was to permit peasants to grow and sell their own crops. Lenin justified the NEP by claiming that Russia was not ready for socialism all at once; it must take one step back for every two steps forward.

The Gosplan continued to control midsize and large industrial entities. But even there Lenin modulated his class war rhetoric. For instance, he encouraged the Gosplan to hire thousands of "bourgeois experts" who had received their training under the tsarist regime. These experts included nearly all the faculty members at the institutes founded to teach physics, electricity, chemistry, radio, aviation, and civil engineering. All devotees of scientific and technological progress, whether or not they were socialists, rallied to this Second Party Program, because Lenin promised the Gosplan would make Russia technologically equal, if not superior, to western European countries.

Still, three big questions—dilemmas, really—loomed over the future of the Soviet Union. The first was its relations with the outside world. In their initial euphoria of 1917, Lenin and Trotsky hoped revolution would spread to each of the war-torn countries of Europe. It did not spread, because Marxist theory was false. The most mature industrial nations, such as Germany and Great Britain, turned out to be the least prone to social revolution, even in the cauldron of total war, whereas subsequent twentieth-century events would prove that only backward and colonized societies were attracted to Marxist movements. The upshot in the 1920s was that the Soviet Union had to adjust to a situation neither Marx nor Lenin had anticipated: socialism in one country. The Communist Party had triumphed in Russia, but only in Russia. How then should its regime relate to the capitalist, imperialist world outside?

Lenin's answer was to formulate a two-track foreign policy. On the one hand, Moscow would steer a worldwide revolutionary movement comprising the Communist parties in all other nations. Hence, in 1919 Lenin founded the Third Socialist International, the Communist International or Comintern. Moderate socialists need not apply: the Comintern was only for hardcore revolutionaries prepared to take orders from Moscow. Communist parties sprang up quickly in Germany, Italy, France, the United States, and elsewhere in order to agitate, propagandize, promote Soviet interests, and foment revolution.

On the other hand, the USSR functioned both as a territorial state in need of diplomatic recognition and as a developing economy in need of foreign investment, trade, and technology. So even as the Soviets tried to subvert capitalist countries, they also established the Narkomindel (People's Commissariat of Foreign Affairs) to pursue friendly relations with capitalist governments. The Narkomindel made its first breakthrough in 1922, when Europe's other outcast,

This famous photograph, which implied that Stalin (right) was Lenin's (left) handpicked successor, was deceitfully cropped. It was an early example of what became a Soviet specialty: disinformation.

Germany, signed a treaty of friendship and commerce with the Soviet Union. France and Britain recognized the Soviet regime in 1924, and even though the United States government held off doing so until 1933, American corporations began doing business in Russia during the 1920s. Lenin's two-track foreign policy—normal relations with foreign governments combined with espionage and subversion—set a pattern for subsequent Soviet history. For, as Lenin quipped, the greedy capitalists could be counted upon to sell the rope to their own hangmen.

The second problem facing the Soviets was what to do with the peasants. The NEP worked in the short run, but it risked creating a class of *kulaks*—that is, prosperous farmers wedded to markets and private property. Yet how else could the Gosplan acquire the foreign exchange needed to invest in technology and infrastructure except by selling on world markets the bountiful crops grown in the fertile fields of Ukraine and Russia? The Communist regime had begun life by plundering the countryside, and it faced a growing temptation to do so again.

Nobody knows how Lenin would have tackled this problem, because he suffered a cerebral hemorrhage and died in January 1924. That event posed the third dilemma hanging over the USSR: How do you manage the transfer of power in a dictatorial regime? The Communist Party never solved that dilemma. Every time a party boss died, a behind-the-scenes power struggle ensued. In the first power struggle, from 1924 to 1927, Trotsky and Stalin emerged as the main competitors. Trotsky appeared to have every advantage. He was a charismatic military commander, an eloquent orator, a zealous revolutionary, and erstwhile second-in-command below Lenin. Stalin, by contrast, was a sullen *apparatchik* (bureaucrat) who hailed from the obscure Caucasian province of Georgia, where he had been baptized Ioseb Jughashvili and begun adult life as a criminal.

Nevertheless, the "Man of Steel" played office politics with the same single-mindedness that Lenin evinced for the revolution. While Trotsky published essays, delivered speeches, and traveled abroad, Stalin patiently built a power base in the party. When their rivalry climaxed in 1927, Trotsky was shocked to find that nearly all the other Communist leaders sided with Stalin. Once he had seized power, Stalin imprisoned Trotsky for "ideological deviation," drove him into exile, and finally had him murdered in Mexico.

Beginning in 1928, Stalin launched a radical new program justified by the claim that the capitalist-imperialist nations were entering another crisis that would cause them to invade the USSR. Hence his warning to the effect that the "backward are beaten!" Stalin's audacious new program was called the First Five Year Plan for crash industrialization. It established a command economy in which all allocation of resources and labor was dictated from above by the bureaucracy. Stalin declared ambitious production goals for steel, coal, trucks, tanks, airplanes, railroad cars, electric generators, and machinery of all sorts. To meet those goals required large investments that in turn required large reserves of hard currency. Stalin meant to earn foreign currency by selling Soviet grain on world markets. That is why a key element of the Five Year Plan was the brutal transfer of all rural property into collective farms owned by the state. Peasants who resisted were shot, left to starve, or shipped to Siberian slave camps. In Ukraine alone, millions of farmers perished. Likewise, if anyone in the industrial sectors grumbled about their production quotas, bosses, or wages, or if they criticized the Great Stalin's wisdom, the NKVD's spies and informants would arrest them on suspicion of being counterrevolutionary "wreckers," weaklings with false consciousness, or (worst of all) saboteurs in the pay of foreign capitalists.

Likewise, if any Communists questioned the Marxist-Leninist orthodoxy of Stalin's decrees, they risked being liquidated (the Soviet euphemism for tortured and killed). The most fearsome purges lay in the future, but they began as early as 1928. Stalin was a ruthless, bureaucratic tyrant seemingly bereft of all humanity, yet as Stephen Kotkin explained in *Stalin: Paradoxes of Power, 1878–1928*, his dictatorship was the logical consequence of an ideological party-state devoted to material progress and utterly indifferent to its human cost. Stalin meant to solve all three Soviet dilemmas with a single, all-purpose tool: terror. Under his iron hand all institutions in the USSR fell under totalitarian control. Perhaps the best way to summarize Stalin's character and place in history is to observe that Adolf Hitler would come to admire Stalin's methods and, during the 1930s, employ them to forge his own totalitarian state.

Techne devouring *themis*. The will to power unleashed. Nietzsche's dystopia becoming reality. Such were the trends of European history during the terrible twentieth century.

Chapter 24

Race War: Fascism and Nazism Capture Italy and Germany

Read this political party platform carefully.

> We pledge to convene a national assembly to effect a radical transformation of political and economic foundations: abolition of the monarchy; decentralization of administration; abolition of political police; suppression of all titles of nobility; suppression of compulsory military service; freedom of opinion and belief; maximum public health measures; suppression of private banks, shareholding companies, and stock exchanges; taxation or confiscation of unproductive wealth; reorganization of industry to share profits with workers; abolition of secret diplomacy and foreign policy based on international solidarity.

What sort of movement might proclaim such a platform? Surprise! That was the official program of the Italian Fascist Party in March 1919.

Here is another party platform. Read it carefully.

> We insist the chief duty of the State to be provision of the means of livelihood for all citizens and equality for every citizen as regards rights and

duties. The first duty of every citizen should be to work with mind or body in activities that do not clash with the interests of society. We demand abolition of incomes unearned by work and emancipation of all from the slavery of interest charges. We demand confiscation of war profits, nationalization of business trusts, reorganization of heavy industry on a profit-sharing basis for workers, maintenance of a healthy middle class, and a program of land reform for farmers. We demand social security for the elderly, a national system of education for the young, and national standards of health for all citizens.

Those were the domestic policy planks of Germany's Nazi Party in 1928. What do these quotations suggest? Is it not customary to think of fascism as an extreme right-wing movement, the very opposite of communism on the extreme left? Indeed, but the reason it became customary to imagine fascism and communism as opposites was the propaganda of the fascist and communist regimes, which boasted of being the other's bitterest enemy in order to exploit their people's fear and to justify the oppression that both imposed on their people. Indeed, when the historian looks closely at what their movements claimed to support and what their regimes actually did after obtaining power, the similarities between them are at least as striking as the differences.

What was fascism, really? It is hard to provide a satisfactory answer to that question for three reasons. First, no truly fascist regimes exist anymore, so we cannot point to one and say "that's fascism" the way we can still point to North Korea, China, or Cuba and say "that's communism." Second, the word *fascist*, like the word *imperialist*, has degenerated into a slur about any regime whose policies one does not like, even democracies such as Israel or the United States. Third, even if one carefully studies fascism as a phenomenon in its specific historical context, confusion is rampant because of the diverse authoritarian movements that sprang up in the wake of the Great War. Was Francisco Franco's Spain or Antonio Salazar's Portugal truly fascist? Or the Romanian Iron Guard? Or the militaristic government of the Japanese Empire? The only country that actually *called* itself fascist was Benito Mussolini's Italy. So how should historians define the characteristics of fascism and identify regimes that shared them?

In general terms fascism was characterized by a mass movement that exalted the revolutionary role of a political party led by a single charismatic leader. The aim of a fascist party was to seize total power—if necessary, by ruthless methods. Fascists appealed to numerous people largely because of what they opposed. Fascists were antiliberal, antidemocratic, antireligious, antimonarchical, antirational, antiscientific, anticommunist, antipacifist, anti–League of Nations, and anti-world order, if that meant the order created by the Paris Peace Conference of 1919. Indeed, fascism was largely a reactive movement, a frustrated rebellion against the structures of modern life that seemed to oppress or frustrate ordinary people. Fascists exploited disillusionment, fear, and insecurity, and they offered people simple answers and simple enemies. Fascists claimed to "feel the pain" of people who were alienated by urban industrial society, victimized by the death and destruction of the Great War, impoverished by postwar inflation and unemployment, angered by the apparent injustice of the peace treaties, and frightened by the specter of leftist revolutions. Indeed, the evident collapse of capitalism and democracy during the recession that followed 1919, and especially during the Great Depression of the 1930s, allowed fascist movements to present themselves as the wave of the future and the only alternative to communism.

Yet in terms of party organization, tactics, and methods, fascist movements were in fact mirror images of the movement led by the Bolsheviks, whom they despised. Indeed, both would serve as models for the famous dystopian novels of the mid-twentieth century, such as Aldous Huxley's *Brave New World* and George Orwell's *Nineteen Eighty-Four*, and for the evil regimes of Saruman and Sauron in J. R. R. Tolkien's *Lord of the Rings*. Like communists, fascists denounced liberal democracy as weak and decadent. Like communists, fascists organized paramilitary street fighters to intimidate their opponents. Like communists, fascists crushed all dissent, seized total power, and destroyed or subverted the institutions of civil society. Moreover, while fascist regimes did not abolish private property, they did subject big business to strict government controls. In all those ways, fascism and communism were both variations on that ugly twentieth-century theme called totalitarianism. That is why the eminent twentieth-century historian Hannah Arendt argued that the linear political spectrum that places communism on the far left and fascism on the far right should be replaced by a circle with liberal democracy at one pole and both fascism and communism hovering around the opposite pole.

Nevertheless, communism and fascism can be distinguished in important ways. First, communism claimed to be a scientific socialism rooted in Karl

Marx's effort to uncover the natural laws driving modern history relentlessly forward. Fascism, by contrast, was a revolt against some features of modernity in the name of a premodern, even pre-Christian tribalism. Thus, Italian fascists idealized the pagan Roman Empire of antiquity, and German Nazis idealized the ancient Teutonic *Volk*. Indeed, it has been said that atheist communism was totalitarianism with roots in the Enlightenment era, while pagan fascism was totalitarianism with roots in the Romantic era.

A second distinction was the fascists' willingness to make temporary alliances with Conservative elites—the monarchy and church in Italy, big business and the army in Germany—even though the leaders of fascist parties secretly meant to abolish those elites when they were no longer needed. Bolsheviks, by contrast, declared total war against all elites and institutions and rejected alliances with other socialists and leftist parties. A third, obviously ideological distinction was that fascists were fiercely nationalistic, whereas communists denounced nationalism as bourgeois false consciousness and instead promoted international class warfare.

Keep in mind that the European era starting in 1914 had bred unprecedented anxiety born of the carnage of the world war, the botched treaties of peace, and the consequent loss of faith in all prewar beliefs and authorities, beliefs and authorities that were assumed to have caused (or at least failed to prevent) the catastrophe. This anxiety grew during the years of postwar economic distress and the bitter conflict over war reparations that culminated in the French occupation of the Ruhr valley and the German hyperinflation of 1923. Then, beginning in 1929, the Great Depression threw millions out of work and undermined what faith remained in free markets, hard work, and self-reliance. All the while the Soviet Union loomed in the east, a hopeful beacon for some Europeans, but a threatening torch for most. The years 1914 to 1933 were one long era of disillusionment, creating what French poets dubbed *anomie*: an apathetic nihilism and moral vacuum.

Disillusionment soon proved to be itself the last illusion, for into that vacuum marched new ideologies that purported to explain the hardships of common people, blamed them on a wicked enemy, and promised redemption if the advocates of the new ideologies were empowered. According to communism, all human history was a story of class conflict in which the engine of change was revolution and the glorious climax the dictatorship of the proletariat. According to fascism, all history was a story of racial conflict in which the engine of change was war and the glorious climax the dictatorship of a master race. In practice, communists justified extermination, thought control, and virtual slavery as necessary for the realization of natural human equality. Fascists justified the same evils as necessary for the realization of natural human inequality. communists identified the enemy as the ruling classes, who oppressed the "have-not" working classes through their ownership of the means of production. Fascists identified the enemy as the ruling nations, who oppressed the "have-not" nations through the hegemony imposed by their 1919 peace treaties.

Both communism and fascism were revolutionary. But the latter aimed at overthrowing the international system. Mussolini's fascist regime referred to Italy as a proletarian nation oppressed by Britain and France, while Adolf Hitler's Nazi regime considered Germany a nation enslaved by the Versailles Treaty.

That rebellion against the international system offers a good working definition of fascism, because its defining feature can really be found not in domestic agendas but in foreign policies. Where, after all, did fascism thrive? In the countries defeated in the 1914-18 war, such as Germany, Austria, and Hungary, and in countries, such as Italy and Japan, whose people believed they had been cheated at the Paris Peace Conference. Fascist movements triumphed in none of the countries that emerged as winners in the Great War, even though their people also suffered from war and economic depression.

Fascism was thus an ideology of hypernationalism devoted to overthrowing the international order. Fascists exhorted people to reject the class warfare preached by communists and instead to rekindle the spirit of unity and sacrifice they had displayed in the trenches and home fronts during the war. That explains why the regimes of Catholics and military *caudillos* (warlords or strongmen) such as Franco's were not fascist. Spain had clung to neutrality in the war and afterward fostered no expansionist ambitions. But Italy, Germany, and Japan were decidedly fascist and indeed harbored nearly unlimited ambitions.

The first fascist regime took power in 1922, the same year that the Russian Civil War ended in the Bolsheviks' victory. It happened in Italy, thanks to the efforts of Benito Mussolini, pugnacious son of a humble blacksmith and his wife, a devout Catholic school teacher. Before the war, Mussolini, following his father's politics, had been a socialist inspired by the radical syndicalist Georges

Sorel. But his service as a rifleman during the war turned him into a virulent nationalist. Like many bitter veterans, Mussolini could not adjust to the boring, decadent, depressed postwar society. Not only did Italy suffer from war debts, inflation, and unemployment, but her victory also appeared to have been "mutilated" by Woodrow Wilson.

Recall that Italy had entered the war in 1915 when the British and French promised the Italian government territorial gains at the expense of Austria-Hungary. Then, at the 1919 peace conference, President Wilson, who despised the Allies' secret war aims diplomacy, denied Italian Prime Minister Vittorio Orlando several of the territories to which Italians felt entitled. Meanwhile, social unrest was spreading in Italy's cities as communists and syndicalists incited strikes and revolts. Mussolini exploited the unrest by founding a militia composed of war veterans. He called it the *Fascio di Combattimento*. The term derived from the Latin word *fasces*, which connoted the tightly bundled wooden rods and axe that officials in ancient Rome had carried as symbols of their authority. In contrast to the weak, bumbling parliamentary governments of postwar Italy, the rods and axe suggested unity, will, and power. The Fascio di Combattimento, also known as Squadristi and Blackshirts, would march into factories, brawl with communists, and break strikes. Mussolini railed against capitalists, too, especially war profiteers, but to win support from those same elites, he rebranded himself as a patriotic champion of law, order, and property. Even so, the Fascist Party did poorly in elections.

So Mussolini gambled everything in October 1922 by threatening to lead a march on Rome and overthrow the government unless Italy's king, Victor Emmanuel III, named him prime minister. The king lost his nerve. Fearing civil war, he ordered his army not to resist the Blackshirts, whereupon his cabinet resigned in protest and the king appointed Mussolini prime minister. It was a bloodless, putatively legal revolution. Once in power, the fascists bullied opponents and rigged an election that gave them 60 percent of the seats in parliament. That majority proceeded to pass laws abolishing a free press, the labor unions, and other political parties. Secret police and fascist courts enforced obedience, and several outspoken critics were murdered. Thus did Italy succumb to the world's second totalitarian regime and a new, fascist style of politics.

Mussolini gave himself the title of *Il Duce* (The Leader) and whipped Italians into a nationalist frenzy with pompous, breast-beating orations about the need to overthrow the treaties of 1919 and forge a new Roman Empire. Class conflict was over, he boasted, and so were flaccid liberalism and selfish materialism, whether of the bourgeois or Marxist variety. Fascism was to be a third way, mightier than capitalism or communism, not least because it would place futuristic technologies such as aviation, wireless radio, and hydroelectric power at the service of the nation.

Mussolini's chief ideologue, Enrico Rocca, called his government "corporatist," using a term that did not refer to corporations in the business sense, but rather to the word *corporeal* in the organic sense. Rocca imagined the ideal society to be akin to a healthy body, in which the limbs, muscles, and organs worked together in harmony. Thus, all who were involved in making steel for *la patria*, including factory owners, managers, and workers, must act as members of one corporation, cooperate with the government to share profits, fix fair wages and prices, and maximize production. Such corporate bodies would coordinate industry, agriculture, and utilities so that all Italians might contribute to a national effort overseen by a Ministry of Corporations. "Fascism," declared Mussolini, "is the dictatorship of the State over many classes cooperating."

The goal of fascist economics was autarky (self-sufficiency). Consequently, once the Great Depression began and world trade collapsed, many foreign observers were impressed by the accomplishments of the regime—as expressed in the famous quip that Mussolini made Italy's trains run on time. The fascist regime accomplished much. It electrified Italy's rural south, broke the power of the Sicilian and Neapolitan mafia, sponsored grand public works, and leveraged Italians' innate genius for design. Thanks to the famous pilot Italo Balbo and air-power theorist Giulio Douhet, Italians became world leaders in aircraft design during the 1920s and early 1930s.

Mussolini's ultimate purpose, however, was to win power and glory through conquest of a New Roman Empire in the Mediterranean and North Africa. *Il Duce* launched that campaign in 1935 when he ordered his military to invade the independent African empire of Abyssinia, as Ethiopia was then called. Such foreign-policy ambitions were the defining feature of his fascism—and also his fatal flaw. Mussolini's dreams of empire soon steered Italy into a fateful alliance with the other, far more formidable, fascist regime that had recently seized power north of the Alps.

If damning the 1919 peace treaties and offering a third way between democratic capitalism and dictatorial communism proved to be popular in Italy, imagine how much more powerful such appeals were in defeated, depressed, and humiliated Germany. After 1918 Germans not only suffered from wounds inflicted by total war; they also suffered from psychic wounds inflicted by the Versailles treaty, the reparations conflict, and the ravages of hyperinflation. One wounded veteran would invent his own variety of fascism.

Adolf Hitler was born in 1889 in Braunau-am-Inn, a small town in Austria. Orphaned as a child, he went to Vienna, alone and penniless, with the hope of becoming an artist. There, in the cosmopolitan capital of the declining Habsburg Empire, Hitler brooded. Desperate to find some explanation for his failure and loneliness, searching for some cause to believe in, he gradually persuaded himself that the central, defining feature of history was conflict among races. Social Darwinist ideas were prevalent at the time, especially in Vienna, where Czechs, Hungarians, Poles, Yugoslavs, and Jews mixed with the German-speaking Austrians. Hitler yearned to be somebody, to belong somewhere. But there was nothing in Vienna with which to identify except his own Germanness. So Hitler declared himself the enemy of all who opposed the German *Volk* and all who confused and corrupted Germans with false appeals to class conflict and internationalism. Hitler professed to see more clearly than others the sources of modern alienation and corruption. He concluded that what lay behind those phenomena were the secret machinations of a dispersed and stateless race that was subversive of all other races.

Who owned the banks, department stores, and newspapers? asked Hitler. The Jews! Who were the radicals and revolutionaries? More Jews! Who ran the prostitution and gambling rackets, corrupting German youth? Who promoted both international capitalism and international socialism? Who had no nation-state of their own, but were spread throughout the world, polluting the purity of other nation-states? In every case, answered Hitler, the Jews! By 1912, when Hitler moved to the German state of Bavaria out of disgust with the polyglot Austrian Empire, he had become obsessed with the social Darwinian metapolitics of the great struggles among nations and, in the Jewish case, against all other races.

Not surprisingly, no one cheered more loudly than Hitler when, on August 2, 1914, mobilization for the Great War was declared to crowds gathered in the

Odeonsplatz in Munich, capital of the German state of Bavaria. Eager to fight, he enlisted in the German rather than Austrian army, and when the war ended he returned to Bavaria, not Austria. Now, Munich in 1919 was a hotbed of radical agitation. The streets swelled with demobilized soldiers who returned from the trenches only to find defeat, dissent, and unemployment. Germany's wartime unity had dissolved, giving way to the feeble Weimar Republic, which was saddled with the Diktat of Versailles. One rabble-rousing political start-up in Munich was called the *Deutsche Arbeiterpartei* (German Workers Party). Hitler joined up, quickly took it over, and changed its name to the *Nationalsozialistische Deutsche Arbeiterpartei* (National Socialist German Worker Party), nicknamed the Nazi Party from the initial syllables of its first two words.

From 1919 to 1923 Hitler built a following, earning the epithet "Bavarian Mussolini." He even called himself *Der Führer* (The Leader) in imitation of *Il Duce*. He denounced Bolsheviks, Jews, and those democratic defeatists who had allegedly stabbed the German army in the back by concluding the 1918 armistice. On November 7, 1923, at the height of the chaos accompanying the French occupation of the Ruhr, Hitler led his Nazi street fighters in a ridiculous attempt at a coup d'état, later called the Beer Hall Putsch, that aimed to seize power in Bavaria. Instead of seizing power, however, he was arrested by the Munich police and served eight months in prison. It was then that Hitler wrote his political testament, *Mein Kampf* (My struggle). The long, incoherent rant attracted little attention. Those who did read the book could not take it seriously. Hitler seemed harmless enough. He remained harmless enough for another five years.

Then the Great Depression hit, American banks ceased to subsidize the Weimar Republic, Germany's export markets disappeared, banks and businesses failed, and unemployment soared. It seemed the free-market system was on the verge of a total collapse. The feckless coalition governments in Berlin were at a loss for ways to address the emergency, and beginning in 1930 moderate political parties were punished at the polls. Finally, Communists and various right-wing parties were winning so many seats in the Reichstag that no coalition could obtain a governing majority. The Depression also rekindled resentment over the Versailles Treaty shackles under which Germans suffered: reparations, disarmament, lost territories and colonies. The protest movement that benefited the most was the Nazi Party. From just 12 seats in the 1928 Reichstag the party

The German president Paul von Hindenburg appointed Hitler as chancellor on January 20, 1933.

grew to 107 seats in 1930 and to 230 seats in 1932. Another hundred Reichstag seats were won by the Communist Party.

How could German democracy survive when its parliament was dominated by parties hostile to democracy itself? Constitutional government stumbled on under emergency cabinets appointed by the aged president, Paul von Hindenburg. But no government could get legislation enacted. Accordingly, a reactionary schemer named Franz von Papen decided that the only solution was to co-opt the Nazis by persuading them to join a right-wing coalition. Von Papen and his (mostly aristocratic) associates dismissed Hitler as a rabble-rousing demagogue. They expected him to serve as the front man in a regime directed by themselves. In other words, they made the same mistake that the Abbé Sieyès had made when he elevated Napoléon Bonaparte to power in 1799.

President Hindenburg appointed Hitler to the office of Chancellor of the Republic in January 1933, whereupon Hitler seized total control. First, he called for new elections, during which his Nazi Brownshirts, called the *Sturmabteilung* (Storm Division), marched in the streets and intimidated opponents. During the campaign the Reichstag building mysteriously caught fire, which the Nazis blamed on Communist incendiaries. Even so, the Nazis gained just 44 percent of the vote. Hitler then persuaded enough deputies from other authoritarian parties to pass the Enabling Act, which granted the chancellor emergency powers. So it was that the Nazi revolution in Germany, like Mussolini's in Italy, was technically legal. The Weimar Republic had just committed suicide. An ironic footnote to that outcome lies in the fact that the German Communist Party, acting on orders from Stalin, collaborated with the Nazis by attacking Social Democrats and other enemies on the Left. Stalin did not take Hitler seriously either. He expected that the Nazi government would make such a mess of things that Germany's Communist Party would soon get the chance to seize power. Indeed, not until 1936 did Stalin realize his mistake and order Communist parties in western Europe to join popular-front coalitions opposing fascism.

How did Hitler win the support of even 44 percent of the national electorate? No doubt a large part of the answer was his magnetic personality and the Nazis' theatrical skills. Their moonlight marches and mass displays of solidarity were intoxicating, and they made deft use of stirring music, light shows, chanted slogans, and stem-winding speeches, not least speeches by the Führer himself. Otto Strasser, a former Nazi Party member, recalled:

> Hitler responds to the vibration of the human heart with the delicacy of a seismograph, enabling him . . . to act as a loudspeaker proclaiming the most secret desires, the least admissible instincts . . . and the personal revolts of a whole nation. . . . I have been asked many times what was the secret of Hitler's extraordinary power as a speaker. I can only attribute it to his uncanny intuition, which infallibly diagnoses the ills from which his audience is suffering. If he tries to bolster his argument with theories or quotations from books he has only imperfectly understood, he scarcely rises above a very poor mediocrity. But let him throw away his crutches and step out boldly, speaking as the spirit moves him, and he is promptly transformed into one of the greatest speakers of the century. . . . Imagine: Adolf Hitler enters a hall. He sniffs the air. For a minute he gropes, feels his way, senses the atmosphere. Suddenly he bursts forth. His words go like an arrow to their target. He touches every private wound on the raw, liberating the mass unconscious, expressing its innermost aspirations, telling [the audience] what it most wants to hear.

The Nazis appealed promiscuously to nearly all sorts of people, because their party platform was a congeries of nationalist and socialist programs, while their sheer dynamism suggested that they alone could fix the economy, unite Germans, and defy foreign powers. Nazis even posed as the champions of moral revival, calling people back to the duty, honor, family values, and social discipline they had displayed during the war.

Historians used to assume that most Nazi voters were drawn from the lower-middle class, the people whom Marxists called *petit bourgeois*: clerks, shopkeepers, craftsmen, farmers, minor government officials, and the like. Such groups were indeed attracted to Nazism. But Thomas Childers, a renowned historian of Germany who began his career with a study of the Nazi electorate and ended it with a chilling survey of Hitler's tenure in power, proved otherwise. His computer analyses of election returns revealed that the Nazi party had a broad base, including people from all regions, all classes, and both sexes. The only groups that resisted the Nazi appeal were socialists and Catholics, presumably because they possessed transnational loyalties broader than nationalism. Otherwise, the Nazis rightly claimed theirs to be a truly national party. Childers also found that anti-Semitism was not an important source of the Nazi appeal, since few votes could be won by Jew-baiting. Far and away the most important issues were unemployment, national pride, and fear of the Communists.

Once in power, Hitler forged Europe's third totalitarian state. He promised that his regime, which he called the Third Reich, was destined to last a thousand years. The bulwarks of his regime were the secret police—the *Geheime Staatspolizei* or Gestapo—and Nazi brigades such as the *Sturmabteiling* (Storm Division) and the later *Schutzstaffel* (Protection Squad), the brown-shirted German equivalents of Mussolini's black-shirted *Squadristi*.

Hitler also made war on history itself when—like the Jacobins during the French Revolution—he abolished Germany's historic provinces, including Prussia, Saxony, and Bavaria, in favor of administrative units ruled by Nazi bureaucrats called *Gauleiter*. The Nazis' equivalent of fascist Italy's corporatism was *Gleichschaltung* (coordination) of every institution in civil society. German media became propaganda outlets for the Ministry of Propaganda, led by Nazi ideologue Joseph Goebbels. The Lutheran state church was gelded, since any pastor who dared preach against the regime landed in prison. Pope Pius XI made a concordat with the Nazi regime in 1933 in the forlorn hope of protecting

German Catholics' right to worship. But in practice, priests were also forbidden to discuss politics. Finally, to compete with Christianity, Goebbels promoted a civil religion that amounted to a pagan Teutonic cult. It was symbolized by the swastika. Hitler adopted that ancient Hindu symbol because it had Aryan racial connotations. But its subliminal message was that of the *Hakenkreuz*, a hooked or broken cross.

The Nazi regime established a League of German Farmers, a German Labor Front, a League of German Women, and the Hitler Youth, a sort of Nazi Boy Scouts. German industry began to be coordinated by the state in 1936 when *Reichsmarschall* Hermann Göring was put in charge of the Nazi Four Year Plan, a scheme that mimicked Stalin's Five Year Plan and allocated labor and raw materials according to the regime's priorities.

Two venerable Prussian institutions that initially escaped *Gleichschaltung* were the army and foreign ministry. But Hitler did not trust the mostly aristocratic generals and diplomats. Beginning in 1937 he therefore imitated Stalin again, purging the foreign and military establishments, appointing a Nazi crony, Joachim von Ribbentrop, to be foreign minister, and placing the *Wehrmacht*— the Nazi term for Germany's armed forces—under the command of Nazi loyalists.

Despite the rigors of totalitarianism, many Germans later recalled the years from 1933 to 1939 as an era of progress, prosperity, and national pride. For the Nazi regime did achieve full employment and sponsored bold public works such as the *Autobahn* highways. The Nazi regime put an end to social conflicts, tore up the Versailles and Locarno treaties, and undertook crash rearmament. As late as 1967, old folks who had reached adolescence by the mid-1930s candidly confessed, *Vor dem Kriege Hitler hat viel Gut getan. Das war die gute alte Zeit.* (Before the war Hitler did a great deal of good. Those were the good old days.)

How was it that Germany, a thoroughly modern society and culture, surrendered to a gangster regime? Probably the first reason was a desire to restore national pride, disillusionment with democracy, and the widespread belief that only an authoritarian state could pull the country out of Depression. A second reason was the Nazi mystique, which stemmed from the seemingly irresistible force of the movement. A third reason was the futuristic technological achievements of the Nazi regime, which quickly surpassed the depressed economies of Britain and France and amounted to what historian Geoffrey Herf aptly called "reactionary modernism." A fourth reason was the hypnotic attraction of Hitler's personality and the Nazis' Führer principle as expressed in the phrase *Ein Reich, ein Volk, ein Führer* (One realm, one people, one leader). The fifth and by no means least reason was sheer terror: resistance of any sort was extremely risky.

Nevertheless, the truly distinctive feature of fascist parties could be found in their *foreign* policies, their militant revolts against the international distribution of power. Hitler had declared himself a geopolitical revolutionary as early as 1925 when he discussed foreign policy—at tiresome length—in *Mein Kampf.* Indeed, the ultimate purpose of Hitler's dictatorship, propaganda, uniting of all *Volksdeutsche* (ethnic Germans), and dynamic economic program was to prepare the nation to expand through diplomacy and war. He meant to conquer the *Lebensraum* (living space) that Germany's "master race" needed, according to his social Darwinist understanding of history.

Hitler's primary azimuth of expansion was eastward. He imagined the Soviet Union to be Nazism's nemesis, the principal refuge for Germany's Jewish-Bolshevik-Slavic enemies, and the obvious locus of the territory, resources, and labor an expansive Third Reich would soon require. Once in power, Hitler proved flexible and opportunistic in foreign policy, usually willing to follow the path of least resistance. But he was nothing if not impatient.

In 1933 Hitler pulled Germany out of the League of Nations Disarmament Conference and then quit the League entirely. In 1934 he forged an anti-Soviet alliance with Poland and made his first (abortive) attempt to annex Austria. In 1935 he tore up the Versailles Treaty by ordering crash rearmament. In 1936 he tore up the Locarno Treaty by marching soldiers back into the Rhineland and by concluding the Pact of Steel with Fascist Italy. The fact that Britain and France did nothing to resist such provocations—indeed, they granted more concessions to Nazi Germany in three years than they had granted Weimar Germany in thirteen—only whetted Hitler's appetite. It was just a matter of time before he provoked the war that his ideology taught was inevitable, a war he deemed to be the engine of historical progress.

Hitler called his party both nationalist and socialist. Josef Stalin was a radical socialist yet governed as a nationalist as well. Recall his stirring speech to that Communist Party congress to the effect that Old Russia was always beaten because of her backwardness. So Stalin also amassed immense military force while promoting Russian patriotism, and he, too, hoped to expand the territory and ideological sway of the Soviet Union.

It is tempting to conclude, therefore, that the totalitarian responses to the challenges of the twentieth century were similar efforts to maximize national strength in anticipation of another total war. Fascism and communism claimed to be polar opposites, and each exploited fear of the other. But in substance totalitarianism in whatever guise completed the drift of modern society toward total state control in peacetime as well as in wartime, toward total commitment to modern technology, toward total rejection of traditional morals, toward total subjection of the individual to the interests of the party-state. George Orwell called such totalitarianism "the beehive state" because it turned citizens into insects while utterly destroying whatever was left of the balance between *techne* and *themis*, the balance that had nurtured the Greco-Roman, Judeo-Christian, humanist, scientific, and enlightened values that had propelled the ascent of Europe and made it the "mighty continent."

Chapter 25

Years the Locust Hath Eaten: The Great Depression

A plaintive photograph snapped in the early 1930s depicted a man in the street with a sandwich board that read: "Ich suche Arbeit jeder Art" (I seek work of any kind). He was a typical victim of the Great Depression, one of the six million unemployed male heads of households in Germany. But there was more to the picture than that. For this was not some beggar, crippled war veteran, or unskilled laborer. The man's rakish Homburg hat, broadcloth suit, starched white collar, and bow tie constituted the uniform of a prosperous burgher. Perhaps he had owned a small business that went bankrupt. Perhaps he had been an accountant, salesman, or manager whom his stricken employers had been obliged to lay off.

In any event, his desperation was obvious—one could see it in his defiant eyes. He was fearful of becoming a charity case and thus a shameful failure. The same fear was common in the United States, to judge by a file at the Franklin D. Roosevelt Presidential Library, which contains thousands of letters sent to the White House by ordinary Americans. Most were written by middle-class men who had lost their jobs, could not pay their mortgage or rent, and had to line up at soup kitchens. The authors of these pitiful letters invariably felt ashamed of being unable to provide for their wives and children.

Such was the crisis of bourgeois values posed by the Great Depression. Such was the pressure, in all countries, for governments to take drastic measures aimed at restoring a semblance of prosperity. The Depression was not just a serious problem leaders of the 1930s had to address. The Depression was the very matrix of that decade's politics and culture.

That such was the case illuminates a great reversal. The state-building monarchs of the early modern era, under the influence of mercantilist theory, had regarded their domestic economies as a source of wealth for their treasuries, as if their subjects were servants of the state (recall that Prussian King Frederick II had imagined himself the "first servant of the state"). But beginning with Adam Smith, economists throughout much of Europe began to embrace the free-market system. They preached separation of the economy from the state on the grounds that economic growth best occurred in a laissez-faire environment and that growth strengthened a government's tax base. Yet by the turn of the twentieth century European governments had turned interventionist once again, first through protective tariffs, then through mobilization for the Great War, and finally through the measures taken during the Great Depression. By the 1930s the purpose of governments, in democracies at least, was not to enable citizens to enrich the state, but to enable the state to enrich its citizens. Regulatory policies and welfare programs designed to promote social security made the state the servant of society. The political corollary was that political parties came to be held accountable for their nation's economic performance. Whenever downturns occurred, the voters blamed the party in power. In extreme cases, they lost faith in democracy altogether.

The interplay of economics and politics is always and everywhere complex and fluid, but it is safe to say that during the Great Depression economic crisis became the fundamental fact that all Western governments had to confront. All other issues took a back seat. However, the effects of the Depression on democratic governments differed sharply from its effects on totalitarian regimes. Whereas the catastrophe enervated the foreign policies of democracies, it energized the foreign policies of dictatorships. The combination of feeble, divided democracies obsessed with problems at home, on the one hand, and robust, united dictatorships bent on expansion abroad, on the other, hurled Europe once again toward total war.

It is hard for people today to grasp the scale of the economic contraction described by the term Great Depression. Between the Wall Street crash of October 1929 and the end of 1932, the value of stocks and bonds traded on European and American exchanges plummeted more than 75 percent. Gross national incomes tumbled more than 50 percent. Industrial production fell by 38 percent, and world trade by 65 percent. Bankrupt countries in Europe and South America defaulted on their foreign loans, which put the world's reserve currencies, the American dollar and British pound sterling, under intense pressure. When the Bank of England pulled the pound sterling off the gold standard in 1932, and the US Federal Reserve Bank did the same with the dollar in 1933, central banks in dozens of other countries were rendered insolvent overnight.

Prices collapsed. Credit dried up. Businesses went bust. The savings and jobs of millions of families evaporated. Unemployment reached unprecedented levels, especially in Germany, where 44 percent of adult male breadwinners were out of work by 1932. European and American cities teemed with idle men and women begging for work—or food for their children. Governments took emergency measures such as devaluing currencies, raising tariffs even higher to keep out foreign competition, and funding public works to boost employment. Their goal was self-sufficiency, for economic globalization seemed to have failed, at least for the time being. It was now every nation for itself, or *Sauve qui peut*, in the evocative French phrase (Save himself who can). At the same time, highly industrialized countries hungered for foreign markets more than ever, inasmuch as domestic consumer spending had collapsed.

One technique used to boost exports was the bilateral treaty, in which an industrial country agreed to barter with a commodities-producing country without any cash changing hands. For instance, the British might trade their steel for Argentine beef or Chinese tea, and the Americans their automobiles for Central American bananas or Mexican petroleum. Another technique was neo-mercantilist autarky. At a grand imperial conference in Ottawa, Canada, in 1933, the representatives of the United Kingdom and its overseas dominions founded the British Commonwealth of Nations, a preferential commercial bloc based on the pound sterling. The French turned their colonial empire into an exclusive trading bloc based on the franc. The United States pursued a "good neighbor policy" toward Latin America in hopes of boosting hemispheric commerce based on the dollar.

In reality, such economic blocs did little good, but they did make an impression on those industrial states which lacked large-scale spheres of influence, countries like Italy, Germany, and Japan. All three had relied heavily on foreign markets and loans during the 1920s, but now those economic crutches were gone. What was more, all three had gone fascist by 1933, so their apparent need to conquer markets and raw materials helped to justify their regimes' expansionist ideologies. The Depression did not give rise to the ideologies of Italian fascists, German Nazis, and Japanese imperialists. Those ideologies all predated the 1930s. But the Depression did give those nations' governments both the incentive and an opportunity for conquest.

Economic distress caused democratic governments to turn a blind eye to early signs of aggression. The United States succumbed to an isolationist mood during the 1930s for reasons not at all mysterious. Americans had been deeply disillusioned by Woodrow Wilson's utopian crusade. Most now interpreted the Great War as a nationalistic European conflict in which the United States had no business getting involved. The Senate even held hearings to investigate whether American bankers and war profiteers had prodded the Wilson administration into the war. In any event it seemed clear that the Old World, even democracies like Britain and France, had pursued imperialistic agendas, duped Wilson at the Paris Peace Conference, and cheated the United States by refusing to repay their war debts.

Thus, Americans in the 1930s wanted no part of overseas entanglements, and President Roosevelt was an astute enough politician to give voters what they wanted. When he launched the New Deal in 1933, FDR jettisoned President Herbert Hoover's efforts to restore international cooperation. Beginning in 1935 he signed a whole series of "neutrality acts" passed by Congress: laws that made it illegal for American citizens to sell goods, lend money, or even sail on the ships of any foreign country at war. So even as Asia and Europe became threatened with fascist expansion, Americans tried to insulate themselves from foreign chaos.

The British were just as paralyzed. Their political parties formed another national government, as if the Depression were an emergency as dire as the Great War had been. Ramsay MacDonald, the first Labour Party prime minister, tried various measures to jumpstart the economy. But like all democracies of that era, the British clung to orthodox economic theory, which demanded that governments balance their budgets. In 1936 economist John Maynard Keynes would publish his famous treatise arguing that governments should in fact do the opposite. To fight a recession they should deficit-spend to inflate the money supply, stimulate consumption, and encourage investment. (Ironically, Hitler's regime was doing just that in Germany.) But Keynesianism was not widely embraced before World War II. Meanwhile, the British and American treasuries rued wasteful spending, especially on armaments. The democracies therefore disarmed during the same years when Japan, Italy, and Germany rapidly rearmed.

Isolationism was not a possible response to this threat for the far-flung British Empire. But what was? The British were overextended, exhausted from the Great War, and strategically dependent on Canada, South Africa, Australia, and New Zealand, whose people were unwilling to get dragged into another European war. Furthermore, British historians and politicians had decided by the 1930s that Germany had not been especially guilty for the war of 1914 and that the Versailles Treaty had been unduly severe. Accordingly, conventional wisdom suggested that this time around Britain should shun alliance systems, arms races, and secret diplomacy and instead remove Germany's just grievances through negotiations. If Germany had not been ruled by a fanatical dictator, that might have been the prudent approach.

France was the only European democracy that still maintained a strong army. France was the democracy most threatened by a resurgent Germany. And France was the country least harmed by the collapse of world trade. So as late as 1936 it was still within the power of the Third French Republic to call Hitler's bluffs. Alas, Paris suffered from a political palsy even more severe than that of Britain or America. In 1934, Communists and socialists launched a wave of bitter strikes and brawled in the streets with a quasi-fascist movement called the Action Française. In 1936 France's Communist Party allied with other leftists in a "popular front" government that was explicitly antifascist, but socialist Premier Leon Blum's ill-conceived efforts to nationalize industry while simultaneously cutting government budgets angered business and labor alike. Blum resigned, cabinets rose and fell in dizzying succession, and French civil and military leaders thereby became paralyzed during these critical years when Nazi Germany was on the rise. Nor did French leaders think it necessary to take preemptive action against Germany anyway, for the ministry of war had spent millions of francs constructing the Maginot Line, a modern "Chinese

Wall" of elaborate concrete fortresses along the German frontier that presumably rendered France impregnable.

Depression notwithstanding, was no one alert to the dangers posed by Hitler and Mussolini? Some were, most famously a Tory backbencher named Winston Churchill. But far more people made excuses for fascist militancy, or else imagined fascism to be the wave of the future, or else were petrified by the specter of another total war. Indeed, by the 1930s people imagined the next war would be even worse than the last, thanks in part to air-power strategists such as Giulio Douhet, who predicted there would be massive bombing of cities. No wonder the democracies put their faith in isolationism, appeasement, or pacifism.

Accordingly, when the fascist powers went on the march, the British and French shrank from confrontation and looked instead to the League of Nations. In 1931 the Japanese invaded Manchuria, a northeastern Chinese province as large as France and Germany combined and richly endowed with raw materials. The League of Nations Council scolded the Japanese—a loss of face that caused the Tokyo government to quit the League in a huff—but did nothing to resist or punish the aggressors. Mussolini noticed. In 1935 he deployed armies in Italy's colonies in east Africa and ordered their commanders to invade the independent empire of Abyssinia (modern Ethiopia). This time the League of Nations—after much hand-wringing—decided to impose anodyne economic sanctions against Italy. But still the League took no military measures. In fact, the British and French governments offered Mussolini half of Abyssinia if he would agree to help them contain Nazi Germany. When that offer was leaked to the press, the League of Nations became a laughingstock overnight. Mussolini promptly made an alliance with Hitler, the infamous Pact of Steel, and the Italian army went on to conquer Abyssinia.

Finally, in 1936, civil war broke out in Spain between the leftist republican government and Generalissimo Francisco Franco's authoritarian Falange movement. Fascist Italy and Nazi Germany sent weapons and soldiers to Spain in the hope that Franco would emerge victorious and become their ally, while the Soviet Union sent arms and agents to Spain in the hope that the republic would emerge victorious and become its communist satellite. The democracies stood on the sidelines. That decision may have been politically wise, but it also gave the distinct impression that they were paralyzed and that either fascism or communism would dominate Europe's future.

The appeal of communism peaked during the 1930s, largely because of the widespread distress that characterized the capitalist world. Yet in reality the cruelest economic upheaval of all was occurring deep inside the secret Soviet Empire. After Lenin's death in 1924 a three-year struggle for power had ended with Trotsky's exile and Stalin's dictatorship. In 1928, Stalin announced what he meant to achieve with that power: the First Five Year Plan for crash industrialization, to be financed by the export of grain seized from *kulaks*, those independent farmers whom Lenin had tolerated but whom Stalin now subjected to the mass collectivization of agriculture.

At the same time the economic bureaucrats of the Soviets' Gosplan put engineers, slave laborers, and soldiers to work on immense projects, including building dams on Russia's rivers to power hydroelectric plants, establishing new mining fields, and constructing factories and apartment complexes in entirely new cities such as Magnetogorsk. The goals of the Five Year Plan included the doubling or tripling of the production of coal, steel, trucks, tractors, tires, locomotives, freight cars, aircraft, tanks, and artillery. In all sectors Stalin allocated large budgets for research and development and ordered Soviet scientists and engineers either to invent new technologies or else to beg, borrow, or steal machinery from western Europe. European and American corporations, desperate for markets, were pleased to do business with the USSR despite rumors of its tyranny and slave camps.

Last but not least, Stalin's regime sent twenty-five thousand "socially conscious workers"—which is to say, armed militias—into the countryside, where they forced peasants to choose either to surrender their land to collective farms called *kolkhozes* or to starve, go into exile, or worse. On *kolkhozes* peasants received precious, government-supplied equipment like tractors and reapers, but otherwise they were reduced to menial workers, a sort of rural proletariat. Stalin justified the confiscations by claiming that the *kulaks* had become *petit bourgeois* counterrevolutionaries, and hence that they must be liquidated as a class. The fact that many *kulaks* were independence-minded Ukrainians made their persecution politically expedient as well. The Soviet regime systematically murdered Ukrainians, exiled them to Siberian labor camps, or left them to starve. It has been estimated that Stalin's collectivization of agriculture caused between ten and fifteen million deaths in a holocaust known in Ukraine as the *Holodomor*, or Great Starvation.

Few people in western Europe suspected what horrors were occurring on the continent's eastern edge. Most of the Soviet Union was off-limits to foreigners, and Stalin followed the hoary Russian tradition of setting up façades called Potemkin villages for those foreign observers who did visit. Hence, all the visitors saw were model farms and factories where everything was modern and everyone was smiling. American journalist Lincoln Steffens was thoroughly duped. "I have seen the future, and it works!" he reported upon his return. In public, Communist Party members called such Westerners "fellow travelers." In private, they called them "useful idiots."

English journalist Malcolm Muggeridge was another man who wanted to believe in this brave new world. But on a 1932 visit to the USSR he eluded his Soviet keepers and traveled some on his own. His biographer later recorded that Muggeridge

> saw the richest wheat lands of Europe turned into a wilderness. He saw planned and deliberate famine, an administrative famine brought about by the forced collectivization of agriculture. Abandoned villages, absence of livestock, neglected fields, everywhere famished, frightened people. He made a vow to himself: "Whatever else I may do or think in the future, I must never pretend that I haven't seen this. Ideas will come and go, but this is more than an idea. It is peasants kneeling in the snow and begging for bread, or herded into cattle trucks at gunpoint, all so silent and horrible in the half light, like some macabre ballet."

Back in London, Muggeridge's editor refused to publish his reports, on the grounds that British intellectuals would dismiss them as anticommunist hate-speech. That prompted Muggeridge to record in his diary: "If the so-called finest minds of our age, George Bernard Shaw, Aldous Huxley, Harold Laski, can be easily gulled over something so obvious as Stalin's tyranny, why pay attention to their pronouncements on subtler questions?" He could only explain their blindness as willful self-hatred. "So this is how civilization ends, not with a bang or whimper, but a death wish. Why is it the quest for a heaven on earth always ends up in a slave camp?"

The Soviet people paid a terrible price, but under Stalin's Five Year Plan production soared in the metallurgical, electrical, and arms industries, wherein especially hard workers were awarded Stakhonovite medals as if they were war heroes. The Soviets replicated wartime mobilization of the economy in peacetime. Indeed, they claimed to be in a permanent war against saboteurs, spies, imperialists, and fascists bent on strangling the motherland of the revolution. That war mentality justified the iron discipline, thought control, and utter effacement of human rights and the rule of law in Stalin's Soviet Union.

A war mentality also justified Stalin's murderous purges, which spiraled throughout the 1930s. The first targets were those scientists, engineers, and former tsarist officers whom Lenin had rehabilitated after the Russian Civil War. Stalin claimed that such bourgeois technicians were wreckers. Tens of thousands of them were thrown into concentration camps, where they labored under the submachine guns of the secret police. By the mid-1930s purges spread to the Communist Party itself. Under its dreaded chief Lavrentiy Beria, the NKVD arrested thousands of old Bolsheviks, then tortured them and threatened their families until they confessed to trumped-up charges of treason. One by one heroes of the revolution such as Lev Kamenev, Grigory Zinoviev, and Nikolai Bukharin were subjected to public show trials, declared guilty, and shot. The scythe eventually reached down to the lower ranks of the party until every possible rival to Stalin was "liquidated" (to employ the Soviet euphemism). How could such men be made to confess to crimes they did not commit? Read Arthur Koestler's 1940 novel *Darkness at Noon* for a chilling account of the hideous strength of brainwashing and terror.

In 1937 it was the Red Army's turn. Stalin accused Marshal Mikhail Tukhachevsky and other heroes of the Russian Civil War of betraying their "Bonapartist tendencies," which implied they were plotting a coup d'état. The NKVD arrested three-quarters of all the generals and colonels, plus those staff officers who were presumed to be loyal to them. In the case of Tukhachevsky, who had been chief of military research and development, that included many of the best weapons designers. Thus did Stalin purge his own military establishment of its most highly skilled people just a few years before the Soviets would face invasion.

All told, collectivization and the purges claimed some twenty million lives, and millions more vanished into the "gulag archipelago" of concentration camps.

Revolution had devoured her children again, this time on a gigantic scale. Those Soviet citizens who were not victimized idolized (or pretended to idolize) their great helmsman Stalin. His drumbeat propaganda mill used posters and rallies, radio and film, to praise the Great Leader in what the 1950s Soviet Premier Nikita Khrushchev would denounce as a personality cult utterly contrary to Marxism-Leninism. Which it was. But it was not contrary to totalitarianism.

Indeed, during the years when Stalin was imposing a nationalist and socialist dictatorship propped up by a personality cult, and purging his own political party, Adolf Hitler was doing likewise. On the so-called Night of the Long Knives in 1934 the Gestapo arrested or shot the Nazi Party's own *Sturmabteilung* brownshirts and replaced them with the *Schutzstaffel*, the dreaded SS. Joseph Goebbels's Ministry of Propaganda then used the SS men to promote a cult of the Germanic Volk, or Aryan race, invariably depicting them as tall, blond, strong, and militant.

Just as Stalin's propaganda boasted of creating a "new Soviet man," so did Hitler's Nazi propaganda boast of creating the ideal "Nordic man." Just as Soviet scholars claimed that Marxist science—for instance, chemistry and agronomy—were somehow superior to bourgeois science, so did the Nazis condemn such scientific fields as psychology and nuclear physics for being allegedly tainted by Jewish influences. In all things Hitler and Goebbels practiced the technique of the Big Lie: tell lies often enough and loudly enough, and they will sink into people subliminally until they can no longer tell truth from falsehood. Thanks to their propaganda, censorship, and surveillance and the state control of media, schools, and churches, the only news and ideas German citizens could hear were Nazi news and ideas.

Finally, as Hitler grew confident of his control, he revealed his intention of ridding Germany of its large, prosperous, deeply educated, and historically well-assimilated Jewish population. Nazi propaganda called on "pure"-blooded Germans to raise their racial consciousness—just as the Marxists preached class consciousness—and to imagine that Jewish agendas lurked behind international capitalism and socialism alike. The Nuremberg laws of 1935 defined who was a Jew primarily on racial grounds. The Spanish Inquisition had at least given Jews the option of converting to Christianity, but the Nazis' definition, based on genetics, was indelible. If three of one's grandparents were deemed to be Jewish, one was stripped of all civil rights and forbidden to marry a Gentile, hold public office, or practice professions such as law and medicine. The prewar persecutions climaxed in November 1938, when Goebbels incited riots in what amounted to a Russian-style pogrom. On *Kristallnacht* (the night of broken glass), mobs destroyed Jewish properties and beat up Jews caught in the streets. In chapter 11 we saw how the Great Elector had welcomed persecuted minorities, including Jews, to the great benefit of the Brandenburg-Prussian state. Surely Friedrich Wilhelm would have wept to have witnessed events like Kristallnacht in his beloved city of Berlin.

Hitler's anti-Semitic excesses, besides being morally repugnant, were strategically stupid, just as Stalin's purge of Soviet officers and scientists was strategically stupid. Thousands of brilliant, patriotic Jewish Germans—among whom Albert Einstein was the most celebrated—were forced to flee Germany for the western democracies, where many of them would make valuable contributions to the future war efforts of Hitler's enemies.

Hitler knew that war was coming because he wanted war the same way Marxists wanted revolution. That is why his regime's top priority was frenetic rearmament. Between 1933 and 1937 he quit the League of Nations, renounced the Versailles Treaty's disarmament clauses, tore up the Locarno Accords by ordering the Wehrmacht to reoccupy the Rhineland, and purged the aristocrats in charge of the army and foreign office, replacing them with Nazi loyalists. In March 1938 he began to execute the plan he had described fifteen years earlier in *Mein Kampf*, which was to gather all *Volksdeutsche* into the Reich, extinguish those nations in east-central Europe which owed their existence to the Versailles Treaty, and ultimately destroy the Soviet Union in order to conquer the *Lebensraum* the Third Reich needed to become a world power. Since the French and British had done nothing to hinder German rearmament, by 1938 it was too late to stop Nazi Germany except by waging the total war that the democracies had been determined, at nearly all cost, to prevent.

In 1937 the Conservative Party's leader, Neville Chamberlain, became British prime minister. A businessman and former mayor of Birmingham, Chamberlain was skilled at managing municipal services and balancing a budget. He knew next to nothing about foreign affairs. His black suit with tails, top hat, and umbrella oozed respectability in the streets of London but made a ludicrous contrast to the crisp military uniforms sported by Hitler and Mussolini. To the extent Chamberlain had a diplomatic vision, it was the conventional wisdom that the Great War had been a tragic blunder that must never happen again. Had not former Prime Minister David Lloyd George reached the conclusion that "we all stumbled into war" in 1914?

Chamberlain determined that this time the democracies must be willing to meet the Germans halfway. This time Britain and France must not engage in alliance-building or arms-racing. This time they must not permit petty disputes in eastern Europe to escalate. This time they must acknowledge Germany's legitimate foreign-policy goals. That certainly seemed to be the enlightened approach as well as the practical one, and it was overwhelmingly supported by the British public, press, and parliamentarians. After all, the United Kingdom was still economically depressed, and her overextended military was hard-pressed to deter those threats to the British Empire coming from Japan and Italy.

Only a few British statesmen warned that nothing would stop Hitler but force. A Tory in Parliament, Winston Churchill, had repeatedly called for British rearmament. But neither the Conservative majority nor Labour opposition wanted to hear that. So Chamberlain pressed ahead with the policy he proudly called appeasement by literally begging Hitler to name his demands so that Britain and France could accommodate him. Hitler was not interested in being appeased, but he drew the obvious conclusion that Germany could expand without resistance. In March 1938 he ordered the Wehrmacht to effect the *Anschluss* (merger) of his native Austria with his adopted fatherland Germany. That was another violation of the Versailles Treaty, but one that Hitler easily justified on the grounds of national self-determination. Likewise, Hitler insisted that Czechoslovakia cede the Sudetenland region on account of its three million German-speaking residents. Once again Chamberlain was eager to appease him but was frustrated by the feisty Czechs, who prepared to fight and pleaded for help. The issue was critical because Czechoslovakia—the last surviving democracy east of the Rhine—possessed state-of-the-art weaponry and formidable fortifications in the mountainous Sudetenland. If Germany were allowed to annex the Sudetenland, the rest of Czechoslovakia would be defenseless, and all the other countries in eastern Europe might topple into the Nazis' grasp.

That, of course, is what Hitler intended. He was prepared to achieve it through war. But in September 1938 Mussolini, of all people, proposed a summit to resolve the dispute. Chamberlain and French Premier Édouard Daladier eagerly agreed to attend. They flew to the city of Munich to meet with

British Prime Minister Neville Chamberlain proudly brandishes the Munich Agreement of 1938. Alas, it did not mean, as he thought, "peace for our time."

Hitler. There they withdrew their support for the Czechs unless the latter ceded the Sudetenland. People in Prague wept in the streets when they heard of the betrayal. But the greatly relieved British public turned out to greet Chamberlain at London's Heathrow Airport and cheered when he proclaimed to them, "I believe it is peace for our time."

If Bismarck had been governing Germany, or even Kaiser Wilhelm II, Chamberlain's appeasement policy might have laid the basis for a lasting peace. But Hitler's ambitions were unlimited. He had even been privately furious that Mussolini's mediation had cheated him of his war. Just six months later, in March 1939, he tore up the Munich accord and ordered the Wehrmacht to occupy the rest of Czechoslovakia. Again the British and French did nothing but protest.

Hitler was now persuaded that the western democracies had no intention of risking a war over eastern Europe. So was Stalin, who had been watching warily from the sidelines. He took it for granted that the capitalist powers were purposely pushing Hitler eastward so that the Nazi and Communist powers would go to war against each other. Yet when Hitler next insisted upon the return of the Polish corridor carved out of Germany in 1919, Chamberlain abruptly changed tactics, granting to Poland a military guarantee to *resist* a hypothetical German attack. Why? Had Chamberlain abandoned appeasement? Not at all. Rather, he was hoping to send Hitler a loud message to the effect that he must pursue peaceful diplomacy as at Munich, not unilateral force as at Prague. But Chamberlain's military guarantee was in fact foolish. The British and French armies had no practical way to fulfill his commitment . . . unless, that is, they secured the assistance of the only power that might be able to resist a German attack on Poland: the Soviet Union.

All eyes turned to Moscow over the summer of 1939, as British and French diplomats competed with German diplomats to reach a bargain with Josef Stalin. All the democracies could offer the Soviet leader was an alliance that might embroil the USSR in war. The Germans could offer him a peace pact— plus a large chunk of the spoils in eastern Europe. As a result, in August 1939, Nazi Foreign Minister Joachim von Ribbentrop and Soviet Foreign Commissar Vyacheslav Molotov signed the most cynical document imaginable: the Nazi-Soviet Non-Aggression Pact.

Hitler wasted no time cashing in. On September 1, 1939, the Wehrmacht's *panzer* (armored) divisions, covered by the *Luftwaffe*'s dive bombers, launched a *Blitzkrieg* invasion of Poland. When the Red Army also attacked from the east to gobble up Stalin's share of Poland, the country was doomed. The British and French governments, persuaded at last that Hitler understood nothing but force, steeled their nerves. Indeed, the Nazi-Soviet Pact ripped the masks off the dictators. It revealed that all that fascist and Communist propaganda had been a pack of lies perpetrated by gangster-states merely out for plunder. Hence the British and French parliaments, twenty-five years after the outbreak of the Great War, declared a second total war against Germany, a nation that had coalesced only in 1871 and been gravely wounded in the Great War, yet was nevertheless too mighty for the Mighty Continent.

The sullen democratic leaders and their publics could not muster much hope of victory in 1939. They waded in anyway, with the faith of free peoples, to defend whatever decency still remained in their civilization, and with the hope— as the biblical prophet Joel had prayed—that Almighty God might "restore to [them] the years that the locust hath eaten."

Chapter 26

Descent into Hell: World War II and Its Holocausts

In August 1914 many Europeans cheered the outbreak of war, confident that their soldiers would march to victory and possibly be home by Christmas. In September 1939 there were no cheers or parades. This time, Europeans reacted to war like their medieval ancestors reacted to a famine or plague. A stoic silence fell over Paris, London, even Berlin (a fact that enraged Adolf Hitler). This time, Europeans expected a long, bloody, and inglorious war.

World War II would prove to be even more destructive than the Great War. But not in the same ways, for the German General Staff had spent twenty years studying the lessons of 1914–18 and had devised means to avoid the stalemate of trench warfare. The Germans combined the infiltration tactics pioneered by the storm troopers of the First World War with two, now mature, technologies: the tracked and armored vehicle known as the tank (*panzer* in German) and the airplane. Together, those machines restored mobility and surprise to the battlefield. The result was *Blitzkrieg* (lightning war), the twentieth-century equivalent of Napoleonic warfare, in that it combined mass, firepower, and especially battlefield maneuverability. German soldiers led by columns of tanks swept across boundaries, pierced defenses, and cut off the enemy's lines of retreat. The armored divisions, in turn, were supported from above by both the *Luftwaffe*'s shrieking Stuka dive bombers and large Junker bombers, which could obliterate enemy supply bases, not to mention frontline soldiers. *Blitzkrieg* tactics enabled the Wehrmacht to overrun whole countries in a matter of weeks, whereupon the German occupiers could mobilize captive nations' labor and materiel to support their next offensive.

The first victims were the Poles, whose soldiers fought bravely but were no match for their high-tech adversary. Of course, the Poles were also stabbed in the back by Hitler's new Soviet friends. Having quickly overrun all of Poland, the Germans and Soviets partitioned nearly all eastern Europe, with the USSR annexing Latvia, Lithuania, and Estonia, portions of Poland and Romania, and a sliver of Finland. The remaining countries, including Hungary and Yugoslavia, aligned with Germany to avoid being invaded themselves. Thus did the so-called successor states, born with high hopes at the 1919 Paris Peace Conference, disappear into the maws of the reborn dominions of Germany and Russia.

Over the winter of 1939–40 the western front remained eerily still. The French army hunkered down in the concrete fortresses of its Maginot Line, while the British buttoned up their air and sea defenses and began to raise an army for battle on the continent. This Phony War or *Sitzkrieg* ended abruptly in May 1940, when the Germans launched *Blitzkrieg* campaigns against Denmark and Norway, then took the Netherlands and Belgium, and finally raced through Luxembourg's rugged Ardennes forest into northern France. The *panzer* divisions thus outflanked the Maginot Line and rumbled toward the English Channel.

So swift was the enemy's advance that the British Expeditionary Force was obliged to make a heroic, if humiliating, evacuation by sea from the port of Dunkirk, leaving all its equipment behind. Within weeks the city of Paris fell to the invaders. The bulk of the French army, uselessly guarding its nation's eastward border, lost the will to resist. Mussolini then gratuitously declared war on France and Britain in the hope of seizing some spoils of victory for Italy. In June 1940, after just six weeks of serious combat, the government of the Third Republic surrendered. At Hitler's vengeful insistence, the French commanders were forced to sign an armistice in the same railroad car at Compiègne where the Germans had swallowed the armistice of November 1918. The Wehrmacht proceeded to occupy most of the country, while Hitler left southern France and France's African colonies to be governed by a fascist puppet regime based in the city of Vichy. That created the kind of anomalous situation in places such as Morocco that was depicted in the film *Casablanca*.

Britain now stood alone, with no hope of dislodging the Germans from their continental conquests. Members of the British cabinet seriously considered concluding a truce with Nazi Germany, but they were dissuaded by the defiant rhetoric of their "bulldog," Winston Churchill. Following Prime Minister Neville Chamberlain's resignation in June 1940, King George VI had asked Churchill to take command of the war effort. Churchill called those perilous weeks following the fall of France Britain's "darkest hour," yet he took to the radio waves to urge the king's subjects to fight on, promising them nothing but "Blood, Sweat, Toil, and Tears."

With the continent subdued, Hitler now planned a cross-channel invasion of Britain. But he rightly considered that move extremely risky unless and until Germany gained air and naval superiority over the English Channel. So he ordered the *Kriegsmarine* (German navy) to wage all-out submarine warfare against British shipping, and he instructed *Luftwaffe* commander Hermann Göring to launch bombing raids against England's cities. Week after week Londoners huddled in subway shelters as their houses, shops, factories, and churches exploded and burned in the streets above. Fortunately for them, British pilots in their Hawker Hurricane and Spitfire aircraft shot down so many German bombers that they managed to defeat the aerial Blitz by the late autumn of 1940. That ended the Germans' hopes for an amphibious invasion of England.

By the end of 1940 the war had reached an impasse. Germany and the Soviet Union were masters of the continent, while insular Britain fought on alone. Events just six and eleven months later brought the impasse to an end. When the Axis powers launched sneak attacks on the Soviet Union and the United States, thus awakening two sleeping giants, the "last European war" became a truly global war.

Why did the British refuse to make peace, wondered Hitler? It must be that they hoped to get help sooner or later from Soviet Russia. What was my principal war aim defined in *Mein Kampf*, asked Hitler? Conquest of *Lebensraum*—living space—in the East. Therefore, just like Napoléon in 1812, Hitler made the reckless decision to invade Russia. A successful *Blitzkrieg* in the

Soviet Union would result in Germany's control of the Ukraine breadbasket and the Caucasus oil fields. It would also give Hitler the opportunity to use millions of Slavic *Untermenschen* (subhumans) as slave labor. Finally, victory in the east would extinguish communism and wrench all hope of victory from the British.

Accordingly, on June 22, 1941, Operation Barbarossa commenced: the largest, cruelest military campaign in history. Over three million German soldiers, plus the armies of Romania and Finland (later augmented by Italian and Hungarian units), drove eastward along a continuous front more than two thousand miles long. During the campaign's initial months the Red Army retreated in disarray. Given that Stalin had purged his army's top officer corps, that was hardly surprising. But hundreds of thousands of Soviet soldiers also surrendered in the hope that the Germans had come as liberators rather than conquerors. They were sadly mistaken.

By December 1941 the German army had reached the outskirts of Leningrad (formerly Petrograd) and Moscow. Just then the Red Army began to be reinforced by hundreds of thousands of troops shipped from East Asia along the Trans-Siberian Railway. The Soviets launched counterattacks that stopped the German advance in its tracks as the dreaded Russian winter descended. For the first time, the *Blitzkrieg* had failed in its objective. The Nazi regime and German army were trapped once again in a gargantuan war of attrition.

Meanwhile, in 1940 the Japanese, who had been fighting a cruel war of aggression against China since 1937, joined with Germany and Italy in an alliance called the Tripartite Pact. The British and American governments wanted no part of this Asian war, but they did impose economic sanctions on Japan that culminated in a cutoff of precious oil desperately needed for the Japanese war effort. Rather than withdraw its armies from the Chinese front, the militant leaders in Tokyo decided to seize the rich raw materials of British Burma, French Indochina, the Dutch East Indies, and the American Philippine Islands. Since the United States' Pacific Fleet was the only military force able to frustrate their southeast Asian ambitions, the Japanese militarists decided to destroy the American ships lying at anchor in Hawaii's Pearl Harbor. On December 7, 1941, just as the Germans were being stopped outside of Moscow, dive bombers from Japanese aircraft carriers launched a sneak attack on Pearl Harbor. The US Congress declared war on Japan the next day. Three days later, Hitler honored his alliance with Japan by instructing the rubber-stamp Reichstag to declare war on the United States.

Descent into Hell

The two sleeping giants were thereby forced into an alliance that had no basis other than the common opposition of the United States and Soviet Union to Axis aggression. The alliance had an immediate effect. With the immense resources of Russia and America now fully engaged in the Allied war effort, the tides of battle turned quickly in all the major theaters. First, in June 1942 the US Navy sank four Japanese aircraft carriers at the Battle of Midway Island northwest of the Hawaiian chain. That battle broke the back of Japan's naval air power and soon enabled the US Navy, Marine Corps, and eventually Army to make island-hopping advances across the Pacific Ocean. Second, in autumn 1942 the British Eighth Army commanded by Field Marshal Bernard Montgomery defeated General Erwin Rommel's *Afrika Korps* at El Alamein, Egypt, and chased the Germans and Italians all the way back to Tunisia, where they were trapped by an Anglo-American-Canadian army advancing eastward from Morocco. In 1943, the Allies invaded Sicily and then Italy, where Mussolini's regime promptly collapsed. Third, the Germans' 1942 offensive in Russia ran out of steam around the city of Stalingrad (formerly Volgograd), where Soviet counterattacks encircled the entire German Sixth Army and killed or captured six hundred thousand soldiers. The strategic initiative thus passed to the Allied side in three major theaters of war. Churchill famously said at the time that this was not the end, nor even the beginning of the end, but rather the end of the beginning in the Allies' struggle for victory.

The beginning of the end really was D-Day—June 6, 1944—when American General Dwight D. Eisenhower ordered the commencement of the largest, riskiest amphibious assault in history. American, British, Canadian, and later some Free French divisions under General Charles de Gaulle invaded the beaches of Normandy in northern France. When German counterattacks failed to destroy the Allied beachhead, General George Patton's Third American Army led a breakout from Normandy that liberated Paris and swept all the way to the German frontier. During those same months the Red Army launched its most massive offensive to date, Operation Bagration, which drove the Germans out of Russian territory and carried Soviet soldiers to the outskirts of Warsaw. Those simultaneous campaigns doomed Nazi Germany to defeat.

Hitler refused to accept that reality. In December 1944 he hurled his last reserves against the western Allies. For several weeks his *panzer* divisions and mechanized infantry made alarming progress. But Eisenhower, Patton, and

Montgomery rushed in reinforcements to stem the tide until the wintry skies cleared. That allowed the Anglo-American air forces to assault German units from above, bringing their side another victory in what was known as the Battle of the Bulge. The following month Churchill, Roosevelt, and Stalin rendezvoused at Yalta, a resort town on Russia's Crimean peninsula, to negotiate plans for the peace soon to come. Three months after that the Red Army brought the storm of war to the German capital of Berlin. Hitler committed suicide in his bunker on April 30, 1945. Germany surrendered on May 8.

With that event European history, strictly speaking, came to an end. The wars of the twentieth century had bled and exhausted Europe's great nations into impotence. Germany was twice denied victory only because enormous extra-European resources from the United States and British Empire were thrown into the balance. Yet the outcomes of the world wars were curiously different. In the first war France held out in the west, Russia collapsed in the east, Europe's colonial peoples remained docile, and the Americans went home when it was over. In the second war France collapsed in the west, Russia held out in the east, the European colonies agitated for independence, and the Americans remained deployed. Those facts explain why in the years following 1945 Europeans were reduced to dependency on one or the other global superpower, while southern Asia, the Middle East, and (by 1960) most of Africa became independent. Europe's imperial order was crumbling. Europe's balance of power had already been destroyed.

There is a second sense in which World War II was the end of European history, using the word "end" to mean not its chronological culmination but its logical conclusion. That is a chilling claim, but one that cannot be denied. For the time had now come to jettison those pleasant Enlightenment myths to the effect that human nature is benign, people are rational, and history is a story of progress. The medieval era was for centuries supposed to have been the era when Europeans were cruel, violent, poor, ignorant, and superstitious. But compare that era now, with eyes wide open, to the conditions that prevailed in the postwar era.

During the decades following the outbreak of war in 1914, total war and totalitarian politics reached genocidal crescendos. As Churchill said, "War used to be cruel and glorious. Now it is cruel and squalid. 'Tis all the fault of democracy and science." Three developments made twentieth-century war especially horrific. The first was mass industrial society, mass military conscription, and mass mobilization of entire societies. The second was the application of advanced science and technology to weapons design. The third was the power of ideology and coercion, in democracies as well as dictatorships, to compel nations to commit wholesale slaughter and destruction. In sum, war became "progressively" more deadly through the spread of the ideologies born of the French Revolution and the techniques born of the Industrial Revolution. In the days of kings and mercenary soldiers, clear distinctions usually existed between civil and military, between combatant and noncombatant, between war and peace. Those distinctions began to break down during the French Revolution, which proclaimed military service to be the sacred duty of all male citizens, and they were further eroded during World War I, which reduced soldiers to mere cannon fodder, cogs in the machine, and also turned men, women, and children on the home front into targets of economic blockades designed to starve them into surrender.

World War II went further, utterly destroying any remaining distinctions between combatants and noncombatants and between war and peace. In the totalitarian regimes one might say that a perennial state of war existed. Those regimes were based on continuous struggle against national, racial, or class enemies. Hitler and Stalin butchered their enemies inside their own countries even before foreign wars began. Their government apparatus oversaw war economies, propaganda campaigns, and persecutions even before foreign wars began. Enemies came to be defined as whole categories of people (Jews, Slavs, capitalists, *kulaks*) even before foreign wars began.

Moreover, the "progressive" advance of technology made war against whole populations possible as never before. In 1937 Nazi and fascist mercenaries serving in the Spanish Civil War introduced the bombing of civilian targets, as depicted in Pablo Picasso's chilling canvas *Guernica*. In 1937, the Japanese carpet-bombed Shanghai and other cities, and their soldiers slaughtered one hundred thousand Chinese civilians in the Rape of Nanking. Once the war became global, the breakdown of distinctions between civilian and combatant became universal. Hitler attempted to break English morale by burning down London and Coventry. In Russia, Nazi SS brigades called *Einsatzgruppen* terrorized civilians and shot Jews on sight. Ethnic groups all over eastern Europe were encouraged by the Nazis or Soviets to commit local genocides against their ethnic rivals. Yugoslavia was one such arena of violence during the 1940s, as it would be again in the 1990s, with Serbs, Bosnians, Croats, and Kosovars butchering one another. Of course, Stalin needed no instruction in the use of such methods. In 1940 his NKVD shot twelve thousand Polish officers in the Katyn Forest Massacre to prevent them from leading a resistance movement against Soviet rule.

The democracies did not wage wars against their own people (although Britain's wartime exports of grain from its Bengal province in India caused the death by famine of between two and three million people). But all the Allied military and civil authorities were quick to carry the indiscriminate bombing of enemy civilians to its logical conclusion. The Royal Air Force under Sir Arthur Harris, and the US Army Air Force under General Curtis Le May, carpet-bombed dozens of cities. Armadas of B-17 Flying Fortresses and B-25 Billy Mitchell heavy bombers over Hamburg and Dresden, and armadas of B-29 Superfortresses over Tokyo and Yokohama, dropped so much napalm and high explosive warheads on enemy cities that the attacks kindled firestorms that sucked in oxygen like a hurricane and fanned hellish conflagrations. In Dresden some twenty-five thousand civilians were incinerated, and in Tokyo some ninety thousand.

Hence the atomic bomb that the American B-29 *Enola Gay* dropped on Hiroshima on August 6, 1945, was not some horrific aberration, but rather the logical conclusion of a total war in which governments turned terrorist on a gigantic scale, employing the latest technologies of destruction without regard for Europe's premodern principles of just-war theory and proportionality of force.

Last but by no means least in this chamber of horrors was the Nazi regime's war against the Jews. The premeditation and absence of any military justification made this the most infamous holocaust of them all.

As late as 1914 Germany had been one of the happiest locales for European Jewry in terms of security, toleration, assimilation, and opportunity. Russia, by contrast, was a veritable prison, in which Jews suffered severe restrictions and occasional violence. The depth of French anti-Semitism had been revealed in the Dreyfus Affair, the false accusation (and ultimately conviction) of a Jewish army officer on charges of espionage in a trial that dragged on from 1894 to 1906. In pre-1914 Vienna, anti-Semitic parties gained prominence. During that era a migration of *Ashkenazim*—European Jews—had occurred, with Germany and the United States being the chief destinations. That was also the era when Theodor Herzl promoted the modern Zionist movement, encouraging European Jews to emigrate to the Holy Land.

During the Great War British Foreign Secretary Arthur Lord Balfour pledged his government's support for a Jewish homeland in the region of Palestine (so named by the ancient Roman Empire). Indeed, Palestine became a British League of Nations mandate in 1920. But most European Jews in the years between the two wars did not emigrate, either because they did not want to leave their homes and jobs or because they were hindered by poverty, British travel restrictions, or Arab resistance. As a result, some eight million Jews remained in central and eastern Europe when the virulently anti-Semitic Hitler came to power in 1933. Roughly a quarter of them, mostly those residing in Germany and Austria, got out in time, having witnessed firsthand what Nazism was about. Nearly all the six million Jews who did not escape were captured in countries overrun by the German army during the war.

Hitler himself had warned in January 1939: "If international finance Jewry inside and outside of Europe succeed in plunging nations into another world war, the consequence will not be the Bolshevization of the earth and thereby the victory of the Jews, but rather annihilation of the Jewish race in Europe."

Just when the decision was made to exterminate Jews is still a matter of keen debate. Some historians argue it was a consequence of Hitler's belief that Germany seemed on the verge of winning the war. Others suggest that Hitler realized Germany was *not* on the verge of winning the war, given that the *Blitzkrieg* was failing. That meant the millions of Jews in eastern Europe formed a potential fifth column that must be disposed of. Still another theory holds that the German army's failure at Moscow, combined with America's entry into the conflict, caused Hitler to suspect the war might eventually be lost, so he had better speed up his personal war against the Jews. What is known for certain is that mass killing of Jews began with the invasion of the USSR and that the SS General Reinhard Heydrich was appointed Commissioner for the Preparation of a Final Solution to the Jewish Problem in January 1942.

At that time only one hundred and thirty thousand Jews remained in Germany. But nearly a million lived in western Europe and more than five million in eastern Europe. Their final destinations were already in place, for the Nazis had copied the Soviet system of concentration camps. In ghettos throughout Europe the SS and Gestapo arrested Jews and transported them to death camps whose names became infamous: Dachau, Belsen, Treblinka, Belzec, plus a camp in Poland especially designed for the Final Solution: Auschwitz. Here is the testimony of an SS officer at the postwar Nuremberg War Crimes Tribunal.

> I have been associated with the administration of concentration camps since 1934. On May 1, 1940, I was appointed to Auschwitz and commanded the camp until December 1943, during which time I estimate at least two and a half million victims were exterminated there by gassing and burning and at least another half million succumbed to starvation or disease. Deaths represent about 70 or 80 percent of the persons sent to Auschwitz, the remainder being selected for slave labor. . . . The final solution referred to the complete extermination of all Jews in Europe. I was ordered to establish extermination facilities in June 1941. So I visited Treblinka to find out how they carried out exterminations. The Commandant told me he had liquidated eighty thousand in the course of six months, principally Jews from the Warsaw ghetto. He used monoxide gas and I did not think his methods were very efficient. So when I set up Auschwitz I used Cyclon B, a crystallized acid dropped into the death chamber through a small opening. It took from three to fifteen minutes to kill the people, depending on climate conditions. We knew when they were dead because the screaming stopped. . . . We were required to carry out these exterminations in secrecy, but the foul stench from the burning of bodies permeated the area and all of the people in the surrounding communities knew what was going on at Auschwitz.

In all, about six million Jews were murdered by the Nazi authorities in the name of a regime in control of a nation whose culture had inspired such humanitarians as the poets Goethe and Schiller, such enlightened philosophers as Leibniz and Kant, and such sublime musicians as Beethoven and Brahms. Alas, the Germany of 1942 was no longer Beethoven's nation. It had become the nation of Nietzsche, where God is dead and everything is permitted. Thus did Nobel laureate Elie Wiesel, an Auschwitz survivor, record in his 1960 memoir *Night*:

Descent into Hell

German soldiers round up Jews in the Warsaw ghetto, 1943.

One day when we came back from work we saw three gallows rearing up in the assembly place. Roll call. SS all around us with machine guns trained. Three victims, in chains, and one of them the boy I called the little servant, the sad-eyed angel. The Commandant read the death sentence. All eyes were on the child, who was lividly pale, almost calm, biting his lip. The three victims mounted together on to the chairs of the gallows. Some one behind me hissed, "Where is God? Where is He?" And I heard a voice within me answer, "Here He is, hanging on this gallows."

It is hard to comprehend such horror. One is compelled to ask, How could such sadism happen? Did the German people know? Were the Allied leaders informed, and if so, why didn't they do something? Could such horrors happen again? Were Nazi extermination camps a "natural denouement" of European history, or were they an unnatural perversion of values that otherwise made Europe a great civilization? Such questions hang like ghosts in the air.

Some products of the Second World War were surely natural expressions of Western values, for they were astounding achievements born of modern science and technology. Indeed, the military impact of research and development had become so clearly decisive that the belligerent governments mobilized their national brain power as well as their national muscle power. The British set up a secret committee for military applications of science under Sir Henry Tizard, rector of Imperial College, London, and Oxford Professor F. A. Lindemann. In the United States Vannevar Bush, president of the Massachusetts Institute of Technology, headed the Office of Scientific Research and Development. The Nazi and Soviet regimes, of course, had pursued extensive military research and development programs even in peacetime. Churchill called it the Wizard War, a duel to invent new weapons and counterweapons and to crack the enemy's secret codes. The Wizard War was complex, ingenious, and nerve-wracking. Indeed, the round-the-clock stress broke the physical or mental health of a number of scientists. But a quick summary of its impact might focus on four "war babies"—that is, the inventions that illustrated the power of what might be called the fourth wave of industrial revolution, a wave that would define the entire postwar era.

The first war baby was radar, invented by a British team led by Sir David Watson-Watt. His scientists calculated that remote detection of airplanes and ships might be achieved by bouncing high-frequency radio waves off their metallic shells and measuring the time it took for the waves to return to their point of origin. The Battle of Britain might not have been won without the advance warning of incoming German bombers provided by the array of crude radar stations the government installed. Under the impress of war, both sides quickly developed additional technologies, such as underwater sonar, as their engineers learned to exploit an ever-wider range of frequencies on the electromagnetic spectrum. The new military science called electronic countermeasures hastened the postwar development of a host of civilian inventions ranging from television to lasers to microwave ovens.

A second technological war baby was the automatic calculating machine, or computer. It initially served two purposes and came in two types. A team of British mathematical geniuses was given the task of breaking the supposedly indecipherable code of the Germans' Enigma machine. They did it by inventing a mechanical computer that could process millions of bits of data and reveal internal patterns until human ingenuity cracked the code. Their machine was called ULTRA. Its decrypts of German military transmissions would prove invaluable to Allied intelligence. American scientists invented a similar machine called MAGIC, which cracked the Japanese diplomatic and naval codes.

In similar fashion, scientists at the University of Pennsylvania were put to work by the War Department on the problem of gunnery. The holy grail of artillerymen is first-round accuracy: how to calculate the azimuth and elevation needed to strike a distant target without a forward observer risking his life to adjust a battery's firing data via radio. The variables are immensely complex, since artillerymen must take into account the size of their weapons' explosive charge, the muzzle velocity of their shells, the range and direction of their targets, and the direction and strength of the winds at various atmospheric levels. The calculations of naval gunners are even more complex, because the pitch and roll of the waves and the speed and bearing of the target ships must also be accounted for. Scientists solved those problems by building the Eniac and Univac electronic computers, which were able to perform millions of calculations at the speed of light and provide data for the compilation of gunnery tables.

These first computers were enormous. Each circuit required its own vacuum tube. Younger generations doubtless do not know what vacuum tubes even looked like, because in the late 1940s two American inventors came up with the gadgets that eventually replaced them. They were called transistors, and they seemed miraculous at the time. By the late 1960s transistors were replaced by integrated circuits, and circuits were replaced during the 1980s by microchips. They are what make it possible to condense computing power that once required machines as large as a room onto a palm-sized mobile phone.

The third and fourth war babies shaped the postwar world in ways just as exciting, but they were also terribly threatening, as may be readily guessed. One was a German breakthrough that Wernher von Braun's design team code-named the A-4 and that Hitler called the V-2, or Vengeance Weapon Number Two. That sleek, silvery, forty-six-feet-tall rocket was the world's first medium-range ballistic missile. Rocketry had been invented in the thirteenth century by Chinese who used it mostly for fireworks. Modern rocketry research began in the 1890s, when a Russian mathematician named Konstantin Tsiolkovsky realized that rockets were the only practical way to accelerate a body to the speed required for earth orbit, about eighteen thousand miles per hour. Rockets do not need the atmosphere to burn fuel, since they carry their own oxidizers. Nor do rockets need air to provide aerodynamic lift. That is why rockets are the only known means of propulsion through outer space. By the 1920s spaceflight enthusiasts in Russia, Germany, and the United States had begun to experiment with rockets. In the 1930s the totalitarian regimes drafted their rocketeers into state service and put them to work on weapons. Thus did von Braun, who would later design the Saturn-5 rocket for the Apollo moon program, begin his career designing V-2 rockets for Nazi Germany. During the last year of the war, hundreds of V-2s were manufactured and launched against Antwerp and London. Ballistic missiles could not be decisive if all they could deliver was the same explosive payloads as airplanes. During the Cold War to come, however, Soviet and American engineers would compete to build intercontinental ballistic missiles that would threaten the whole human race with suicidal destruction.

Suicidal indeed, because of the fourth war baby: the nuclear warhead. In 1939 Albert Einstein wrote perhaps the most important letter of the twentieth century to President Roosevelt. "It may become possible," wrote Einstein, "to set up a nuclear chain reaction in a large mass of uranium by which vast amounts of power and large quantities of new radium-like elements would be generated. Now it appears almost certain that this could be achieved in the immediate future. This phenomenon would also lead to the construction of bombs, and it is conceivable—though much less certain—that extremely powerful bombs of a new type may thus be constructed." Roosevelt wrote three words on the letter and handed it to a military aide: "This requires action!" Fortunately, German scientists took some false steps in their own atomic program, perhaps because the Nazis had driven into exile brilliant Jewish physicists such as Einstein and Edward Teller.

At first no one knew how to build an atomic bomb, which is why the US Army put scientists to work in what was then the most expensive R&D program in history, the Manhattan Project, which included laboratories and test sites all over the country. On July 16, 1945, two months after the German surrender, the first atomic test occurred at Alamogordo, New Mexico. The warhead's mushroom cloud rose forty-one thousand feet, the shock wave broke windows over a hundred miles away, and the estimated yield was twenty thousand tons of TNT. Physicist Robert Oppenheimer, watching from a concrete bunker, recalled a verse from the Hindu Bhagavad-Gita: "I am become Death, the Destroyer of Worlds."

As it happened, the Alamogordo test occurred during the Potsdam Conference, where President Harry S Truman and Josef Stalin were conferring about the Allied occupation of Germany and other liberated countries. They reached no agreements whatsoever, and in the wake of the conference Stalin made clear his intentions to impose pro-Soviet governments on all countries liberated by the Red Army, while Truman made clear his intentions not to share America's atomic secrets with other countries or invite the Soviets to participate in the occupation of Japan following its imminent surrender. Stalin promptly ordered his own physicists to redouble their efforts to build a Soviet atomic bomb, which (thanks to his Communist espionage networks) they were able to do as early as 1949.

Thus, even before the political and ideological Cold War had begun, a technological race for doomsday weapons was underway within a post-European civilization divided into two hostile camps. Europeans had endured two world wars only to become trapped in a Cold War between superpowers, each possessing the capacity to destroy civilization. Could humanity survive such a predicament? That was the question haunting postwar peoples—not least Europeans, who had witnessed their own global hegemony self-destruct in the space of a single generation.

Chapter 27

Echternach Dance: The Cold War and the Revival of Europe

President Harry Truman was a combat veteran of the First World War. He had vivid memories of the muddy, shell-pocked moonscapes of the western front. Yet upon witnessing the wreckage in Berlin, he gasped: "I have never imagined such desolation." Berlin had been flattened by aerial bombing and house-to-house fighting. It was not alone. Nearly every city in central and eastern Europe had been leveled, beautiful cities with exquisite cathedrals, palaces, and museums that once displayed a thousand years of artistic treasures. All told, more than seventeen hundred European cities lay in ruins, plus seventy thousand rural villages. Such was the indiscriminate destruction of total war.

Most cruelly, people were destroyed: some twenty million Russians, five million Germans, three and a half million Poles, nearly a million French and a million British. Over twenty-five million refugees—what the armies of occupation called displaced persons—wandered homeless, many of them fleeing westward to escape the dreaded Soviet army or simply in search of food, shelter, or lost relatives. The continent they roamed was a nightmare of fallen power lines, shell-mangled roads, torn-up railways, blown-up bridges, and bombed-out buildings. The very survival of millions of these displaced persons depended on the charity of the American and British occupying armies. The Soviets, for their part, showed little mercy. With the tacit permission of their officers, Red Army soldiers wreaked vengeance on Germans, murdering, raping, and pillaging, while Communist officials arrested or shot everyone suspected of having collaborated with the Nazis. Soviet authorities stripped their eastern German occupation zone of natural resources, machinery, and crops in the name of reparations. By contrast, the Anglo-American authorities shipped food, fuel, and medical supplies to their zones of occupation, and they helped people in the war-torn regions of western Europe begin to clear the rubble and restore public utilities.

Yet how could anything like normal life be restored so long as Europeans were tormented by their memories of loss, their pain, or their agonizing guilt? If the First World War had bred disillusionment, the second bred horror. Exposure to Nazi extermination camps forced ordinary Germans to confront the evils their regime had committed and which they had supported, tolerated, or ignored. Millions of Romanian, Hungarian, Slovak, Italian, Scandinavian, Dutch, Belgian, and French men and women were forced to confront their own nation's collaboration with the enemy.

Europeans' psychological reactions varied enormously. One reaction was penitence and a return to religious faith. Many Catholics, Lutherans, and Anglicans judged that totalitarianism and the Second World War had been punishments for their continent's rejection of faith in, and obedience to, the author of the Ten Commandments. The late 1940s and 1950s were years when the writings of Catholic professor J. R. R. Tolkien, Anglican professor C. S. Lewis, Lutheran pastor Reinhold Niebuhr, Catholic philosopher Jacques Maritain, and others inspired a revival of traditional Christian theology. For a few years church memberships rose. But at least as many Europeans lurched in the other direction, judging that the world wars, the Holocaust, and the advent of atomic weapons rendered history, faith, even life itself, meaningless.

Existentialism emerged as a fashionable philosophy. Writers such as Jean-Paul Sartre claimed that the only thing human beings could be certain of was their own existence. It was as if Sartre had restated René Descartes's famous first principle—"I think, therefore I am"—only to stop there and to declare that everything other than the self was an illusion. Sartre famously wrote in his play *Huis Clos* (No exit): "L'enfer c'est les autres" (Hell is other people). The postwar "theater of the absurd" conveyed a similar message. Samuel Beckett's drama *Waiting for Godot* consisted entirely of two simpletons on an empty set engaging in incoherent conversation and periodically reminding each other what they were doing. They are waiting for Godot—God—who never shows up.

The films of the immediate postwar years likewise expressed the dark mood of a continent traumatized by radical evil. French and Italian directors pioneered the genre called *films noirs* (black films), whose scripts described lost, desperate people struggling to survive in a demimonde of crime, mystery, and betrayal. *Films noirs* were always shot in black and white on shadowy sets and featured antiheroes rather than heroes.

The Holocaust was an especially searing memory for Jews. They asked how the Lord could have permitted a catastrophe of biblical proportions. Whether or not Europe's Jewish survivors had been observant, most now concluded that Theodor Herzl had been right. Jews must establish their own nation-state, if only to serve as a refuge. Thus was the nation of Israel born—or rather, reborn—in 1948, when the United Nations General Assembly proposed a partition of the League of Nations' British mandate of Palestine into Jewish and Arab territories.

One nation that emerged from the war unscathed, confident, wealthy, and unprecedentedly powerful was, of course, the United States. Americans took for granted the fact that they were history's good guys, as opposed to the defeated fascists and victorious Soviets now oppressing eastern Europe. Europeans, helplessly trapped in the middle of the Cold War and reciprocal nuclear terror, resisted such black-and-white judgments. By the 1960s the younger generation in Europe was tempted to express resentment and suspicion of America as well as the Soviet Union, not only because those powers held Europe's fate in their hands but because they appeared to be so strikingly *similar*.

Consider the two countries whose armies bumped into each other, amid the wreckage of Nazi Germany, on April 25, 1945, near a town called Torgau on the River Elbe. Both the United States and the Soviet Union were creatures of European civilization, yet both were extra-European, continental. They were not merely great powers, but something new under the sun: superpowers. Both were multiethnic empires founded by pioneers who had struck out across vast frontiers until they reached the Pacific Ocean. Both were governed by regimes conceived in revolutions that abolished monarchies and forged a new sort of patriotism based not on ethnicity, holy soil, dynastic tradition, or folk memories but on ideologies expressing their faith in progress. Both the United States and the Soviet Union burst on the world scene in the year 1917 with their leaders' respective visions of a new world order. Both tried to isolate themselves from the conflicts of the 1930s and 1940s, only to be forced into World War II by sneak attacks in 1941. Both emerged from that war with power to impose their systems on Europeans.

Of course, the United States and the Soviet Union were profoundly different as well. American ideology, born of Enlightenment principles and British traditions, stressed limited government and capitalism. Soviet ideology, born of Marxist principles and Russian traditions, stressed total government and communism. But believers in both nations insisted their ideologies were universally valid and thus mutually exclusive. Given their reciprocal suspicions, fears, and military threats, it is hard to imagine how Truman's United States and Stalin's USSR could not become rivals in what came to be known as the Cold War. Recall that the only glue holding the Grand Alliance together had been the threat posed by Hitler's Germany. When that threat disappeared, the giants quickly parted ways. America's war aims, as expressed in the Atlantic Charter, carried echoes of Wilsonianism. The governments of the United States and the United Kingdom claimed to be fighting for human rights, national self-determination, economic opportunity for all, and a United Nations to keep peace in the future. At the Yalta Conference of January 1945, Churchill, Roosevelt, and Stalin issued the Declaration on Liberated Europe, which promised free elections to all the nations liberated by Allied armed forces. In the summer of 1945 an international convention in San Francisco approved the final draft of the United Nations Charter.

That Stalin's war aims sharply diverged from such liberal internationalist principles became painfully obvious during the war's latter stages. He was the dictator of a multiethnic empire. Hence, he dared not allow democratic or nationalist ideas to prevail in the territories under his sway. Stalin intended to seize as much land as possible, impose puppet regimes on his neighbors, and thereby secure the Soviet Union while expanding the reach of Marxism-Leninism. By 1948, when the Communist Party of Czechoslovakia seized power in a coup d'état, all the eastern European states had been subverted. In central and eastern Asia, too, Stalin hoped to recover the spheres of influence tsarist Russia had enjoyed before 1914.

The Grand Alliance of World War II began to unravel as early as that 1945 Potsdam Conference, when Stalin showed no inclination to cooperate over the occupation of Germany, or in the summoning of a peace conference, or in the establishment of real democracy in the countries of eastern Europe. In January 1946 Stalin launched his postwar Five Year Plan with a speech warning that the world was now divided into a peace-loving socialist camp led by the Soviet Union and a warmongering imperialist camp led by the United States. In February 1946 US Ambassador George F. Kennan sent the State Department his famous Long Telegram from Moscow, in which he explained the paranoid sources of Soviet conduct. The following month Winston Churchill declared in his Iron Curtain speech that Europe had become divided into two hostile blocs. Nevertheless, the Truman administration refrained from hostile acts in the hope that the Soviets might at least cooperate on a United Nations plan for international control of atomic energy. The American plan called on all nations to surrender their supplies of uranium and open their nuclear laboratories to United Nations inspectors, after which the United States would destroy its atomic bombs and reveal its nuclear secrets. But the Soviets insisted the Americans disarm first and refused to permit inspectors into their secretive empire. So arms control failed, and when the Soviets successfully tested their own atomic warhead in 1949, a nuclear arms race became inevitable.

Meanwhile, the British, left nearly bankrupt by another world war, began their painful retreat from the wide world. In March 1947 the Labour government of Prime Minister Clement Atlee (Churchill's Tories having been defeated in the 1945 elections) informed the White House that the United Kingdom could no longer assist Greece and Turkey against Communist pressures. The American government responded with unusual vigor. The president's Truman Doctrine pledged that US support would be forthcoming not only for Greece and Turkey but for any nation anywhere threatened by Communist subversion or assault. The Truman administration then persuaded Congress to pass an omnibus defense bill that created the US Air Force, a unified Defense Department, and a Central Intelligence Agency (CIA) to counter Soviet espionage and subversion.

Stalin countered in 1948 by ordering the Red Army to seal off the jointly occupied capital city of Berlin from western access, forcing the Americans and British to supply the now-isolated city through the gigantic Berlin Airlift. The Soviet use of military coercion frightened western European governments into forging a defensive alliance they begged the United States and Canada to join. They did. In 1949 the North Atlantic Treaty Organization (NATO) was founded during a trans-Atlantic conference in Washington, DC. That same year the three powers whose armies had occupied Germany's western zones—the United States, Britain, and France—gave the west German people a green light to establish their own federal republic under a constitution that safeguarded democracy. That was also the same year in which the US Congress approved a $13.6 billion aid package named for Secretary of State George C. Marshall. The idea was to give European governments outright grants they could invest in the economic recovery of their war-ravaged countries. The only condition the Americans attached to the Marshall Plan grants was that recipients cooperate with each other rather than compete. The Soviets, not surprisingly, forbade their eastern European satellite regimes from participating. The Marshall Plan therefore both hardened the division of Europe and triggered the beginning of western European economic integration.

Economic recovery had become politically urgent during the late 1940s because desperate citizens of Italy, France, and the west German zones showed signs of being tempted by communism. The Marshall Plan, plus some timely CIA subsidies to moderate parties in Rome and Paris, overcame that danger. By 1950 most west European countries had established stable democracies led either by center-right Christian Democrat parties or center-left Social Democrat parties. All the political parties now rejected the nationalism, let alone the fascism, that had prevailed during the 1930s and 1940s, and all pursued domestic policies that fostered regulated market economies and welfare states. In short, Europe's democratic nations now took it for granted that their future relied on cooperative international institutions.

Chief among those institutions was one that prior to the Second World War had been a mere aspiration: the ideal of European integration, perhaps even a United States of Europe, in which former enemies might work together for peace and prosperity. The prophets of a unified Europe included France's Foreign Minister Robert Schuman, Belgian Prime Minister Paul-Henri Spaak, Italian Prime Minister Alcide di Gasperi, and the first chancellor of the Federal Republic of Germany, Konrad Adenauer. Thanks to their leadership, "the original six," comprising the governments of France, Italy, West Germany, Belgium, Netherlands, and Luxembourg, formed the European Coal and Steel Community in 1949. It proved to be so successful that prophets of further integration, such as French economist Jean Monnet, inspired the six governments to conclude the

Treaty of Rome in 1957, which created the European Economic Community, or Common Market.

The momentum propelling European integration flagged for a season due to events in France, where the Fourth Republic, established after the end of the war, collapsed in 1958. To avert the very real threat of civil unrest, the national assembly called on General Charles de Gaulle to become president of a Fifth Republic devoted to the restoration of France's independence and grandeur. De Gaulle proceeded to do so with a vengeance. When the British government sought to join the Common Market in 1963, de Gaulle vetoed the application. When the Americans sought to impose their own strategic doctrines on their NATO allies, de Gaulle pulled French armed forces from under NATO command. When the United States and Great Britain (which had developed its own atomic weapons in 1952) refused to share their nuclear secrets with France, de Gaulle launched a crash program to develop a French nuclear arsenal.

In fact, the process of European integration inspired this chapter's title. The residents of the quaint town of Echternach in the Grand Duchy of Luxembourg had an old tradition. They would gather once a year in the town square, form a human chain, and then march around the perimeter of the square taking two steps forward followed by one step backward. The Echternach Dance is thus an apt metaphor for western Europeans' herky-jerky progress toward broader and deeper unity. Gaullist France's proud nationalism froze the Common Market's membership and prevented it from expanding its regulatory powers. But de Gaulle retired from office in the wake of riots and strikes that paralyzed Paris (and most other capital cities in western Europe) during the radical year of 1968. Under his successors, beginning with President Georges Pompidou, France reemerged as the principal champion of European integration. The European Economic Community (EEC) grew broader and deeper in 1973 when its members welcomed the British, Irish, and Danes into their club.

Momentum toward integration flagged again during the economic crises of the 1970s. But it revived following the deaths of the aged authoritarian rulers of Spain and Portugal, Francisco Franco and Antonio Salazar. After the Iberians succeeded in forming democratic governments, they too were admitted to the EEC in 1980. Just as important as geographic expansion was the institutional expansion inspired by an energetic EEC president named Jacques Delors. He argued that Europe must forge a genuine union with common social policies, common foreign and defense policies, and above all a single currency. The grand culmination arrived in 1993, when the Treaty of Maastricht transformed the European Community into the dynamic and far more assertive European Union, whereupon most member states traded in their historic francs, marks, and lire in favor of a new common currency called the euro.

What occurred in Europe after World War II was historically unprecedented. To say that western Europeans during the last half of the twentieth century enjoyed peace, security, and material prosperity would be a wild understatement. During the so-called Economic Miracle of the 1950s and 1960s Europeans not only recovered from the war but achieved phenomenal rates of economic growth. The United States government deserved much of the credit, given its Cold War defense of western Europe, the Marshall Plan, and its free-trade policies. But credit the Europeans themselves, who boldly reimagined their part of the continent as a transnational community freed from interstate rivalries and divisive ideologies. By the end of the Cold War in 1989, western Europeans had become so prosperous that even factory workers could afford expensive automobiles, color television sets, and four weeks of paid vacation per year. The only thing postwar Europeans lacked was a higher purpose beyond conspicuous consumption, something to give meaning and a humane calling to their collective lives, something derived from the nearly forgotten realm of *themis*.

Prior to 1914, Europeans wanted to believe that their meaning and humane calling was a *mission civilisatrice*, or civilizing mission in the colonial world. But the world wars had discredited imperialism and spawned independence movements throughout eastern, southern, and southwestern Asia. The British promised independence to the Indian subcontinent during World War II and granted it in 1947. Sadly, hundreds of thousands of Hindus and Muslims died in the violence accompanying the division of India and Pakistan. In 1948 the Arab kingdoms and the Israelis won independence, only to fall into a cycle of violence that persists to this day. The Dutch recognized the independence of gigantic Indonesia in 1949, but only after four bloody years of war. The French Fourth Republic tried to retain its overseas empire through a fiction they called *La Plus Grande France* (greater France) or *La France d'Outre-Mer* (overseas France), with the tragic result that the French military got dragged into lengthy, bitter, and ultimately futile conflicts in Vietnam and Algeria. In sum, the process of

European decolonization, far from being a civilizing mission, turned out to be far more cruel than the original process of colonization.

The first great turning point in decolonization—and the most symbolic, since it happened in the same country where the scramble for colonies began in 1882—was the Suez Crisis of 1956. After the war, the British had bestowed a nominal independence on Egypt under the dissolute King Farouk. But a colonel in the Egyptian army named Gamal Abdul Nasser led a revolt that overthrew the monarchy in 1952. Nasser was a pan-Arab nationalist determined to seize control of the Suez Canal and drive the Israelis into the sea. At length, the British, French, and Israeli governments formed a secret alliance to thwart Nasser. In October 1956 they launched preemptive strikes on the canal and the Sinai Peninsula. World opinion was shocked. The Soviets and Americans even joined forces at the United Nations to condemn the invasion and oblige the Europeans to withdraw. In the wake of that humiliation, the British government gave up on empire. Prime Minister Harold Macmillan, professing to feel the "winds of change" sweeping across Africa, promised rapid decolonization.

In 1957 Ghana emerged as the first sub-Saharan African republic. By 1966 all the British colonies, except the apartheid regimes in southern Africa, had gained independence. Under President de Gaulle, the Fifth Republic abandoned the war in Algeria and granted independence to France's African colonies in 1960. That same year the Belgian government abruptly pulled out of its gigantic empire in the Congo, whereupon that impoverished, divided, but mineral-rich expanse of jungles and savannahs collapsed into civil war.

Europeans nevertheless still felt a paternalistic responsibility for their former colonies. The preamble to their 1957 Treaty of Rome even made reference to their nations' historic mission of assisting Africans' economic and social development. But despite the foreign aid and technical assistance they provided to emerging African nations, Europeans did not succeed much more than the clumsy Americans or Russians in their efforts to help the new countries that a French sociologist dubbed *Le Tiers Monde* (the Third World). More often than not, the corruption of African leaders and their penchant for socialist policies, or else Africa's ubiquitous tribal conflicts, misuse of foreign capital, and dependence on fickle commodities markets, stymied the continent's efforts to achieve economic growth. The former European colonies in Africa and Asia also became pawns in the Cold War rivalries of the Soviet Union, United States, and, increasingly, the People's Republic of China, which emerged as a third force in world politics following the 1949 victory of Mao Zedong's Communist movement in the Chinese civil war.

A second mission pursued by various west European states was to serve as mediators between the two Cold War blocs. The first chance to do so arose in 1952, when Joseph Stalin died and a wave of de-Stalinization swept over eastern European capitals. Stalin's successor, Nikita Khrushchev, stunned the world with a speech to the 1956 Communist Party Congress in which he denounced Stalin as a criminal who had betrayed the Soviet Union and the Communist Party. But European hopes for a thaw in the Cold War were dashed that same year when the feisty Hungarians rose up against their own satellite government. By chance the revolt coincided with the Suez Crisis, which had temporarily thrown NATO into disarray. That emboldened Khrushchev to order the Red Army to reimpose Communist rule in Budapest by main force. Twelve years later Khrushchev's successor, Leonid Brezhnev, would do likewise in order to crush a liberalizing movement in Czechoslovakia known as the Prague Spring.

Meanwhile, western Europeans had grown restive and resentful of their dependence on the US nuclear umbrella, especially after October 4, 1957. On that historic day a team of Soviet scientists and engineers led by the brilliant Sergei Korolev shocked the world by launching into orbit Sputnik 1, the first artificial earth satellite. That event not only opened the Space Age; it also proved that the Soviets had developed an intercontinental ballistic missile able to deliver nuclear warheads to the United States. The consequences were enormous. Europeans began to ask whether Americans would really expose New York or Chicago to a nuclear war in response to some crisis threatening Paris or London. The British reaction to Sputnik was to halt their own missile program and lean on their so-called special relationship with the Americans. De Gaulle took the opposite tack. He developed French missile and space programs while simultaneously trying to mediate between Moscow and Washington. Meanwhile, the leaders of the West German republic, who had given up hope for national reunification when Khrushchev erected the Berlin Wall in 1961, extended olive branches to the Communist bloc. Beginning in 1969 the first Social Democratic chancellor of the Federal Republic, Willy Brandt, pursued an *Ostpolitik* (eastern policy) that led to bilateral treaties with the German Democratic Republic (East Germany), Poland, and the Soviet Union.

None of those initiatives brought the Cold War to an end. Nor did the American policy of *détente* (easing of tensions) pursued by Presidents Richard Nixon and Gerald Ford during the 1970s. Indeed, the events of that decade seemed disastrous for the western alliance. In 1973, just as Nixon was extricating American armed forces from their own calamitous Vietnam War, a domestic scandal called by the shorthand term Watergate ruined his presidency. Nixon would resign the office in August 1974. Meanwhile, Congress passed laws prohibiting any more military support for the South Vietnamese government (which would succumb to a massive invasion by the army of Communist North Vietnam in 1975).

The Middle East was another region where serial crises caused anxiety among NATO members. When the Yom Kippur War erupted between Egypt and Israel in 1973, the Arab-dominated Organization of Petroleum Exporting Countries (OPEC) punished the Western countries for their support of Israel. OPEC embargoed oil exports, and when they resumed sales the following year, the price of crude petroleum had quintupled. That threw the world economy into both a deep recession and rampant inflation—a phenomenon economists had once thought impossible—while it gave the Soviet Union, itself a large-scale exporter of oil, windfall profits.

Throughout the 1960s and early 1970s Brezhnev's Soviet regime had been quietly building its nuclear arsenal and strategic rocket force until it had achieved equality to that of the United States. The Soviets also supported left-wing insurgencies and the formation of client states abroad, such that ten Third World countries newly aligned with the Communist bloc between 1974 and 1979. Later, when Mikhail Gorbachev came to power in 1985, the world would learn that Brezhnev's Soviet Union had been a Potemkin Village of national proportions. The top-down command economy, bereft as it was of a profit motive or indeed private property, provided no incentives for managers and technicians to strive for innovation, while its sclerotic bureaucracy hindered productivity through its inefficiency, corruption, and favoritism. The Communist Party of the Soviet Union simply ran out of ideas—or else its members were too frightened to voice them. By the late 1970s the Communist regime was losing legitimacy, especially among the non-Russian nationalities of the Soviet bloc. Yet at the time it appeared as if the NATO powers were the ones losing the Cold War.

Then, over the years 1978 to 1982, a host of new factors combined to undermine Soviet power and confidence and to propel the Cold War toward its end game. First, a cohort of strong Conservative leaders emerged simultaneously within NATO's member states, including British Prime Minister Margaret Thatcher, American President Ronald Reagan, French President François Mitterand, and West German Chancellor Helmut Kohl. They had their differences regarding domestic policy, but all were determined to match the Soviets' military buildup and to assist anticommunist movements in the Third World. Second, inside the Soviet bloc courageous protest movements sprang up under leaders like the Polish dockworker Lech Wałesa and Czech intellectual Václav Havel. They boldly defied their police states and demanded they respect the human rights of their citizens. When instead their regimes cracked down on dissent, world attention focused on Soviet abuses more than at any time since the death of Stalin.

Third, the Roman Catholic College of Cardinals elected a new pope in the person of Karol Wojtyła, a Pole who became the first non-Italian pontiff since the year 1523. Wojtyła, who took the papal name of John Paul II, had grown up under both Nazi occupation and Communist rule, and he inspired his countrymen and eastern Europeans generally when he preached this simple message of faith: "Be not afraid." Fourth, President Nixon's policy of détente paid an enormous dividend when his diplomatic outreach to Chinese Chairman Mao Zedong and Premier Zhou Enlai flipped the People's Republic of China into a strategic partner of the United States, thus completing the encirclement of the Soviet Union. Fifth, the Soviets themselves made an unforced error when Brezhnev ordered the Red Army into Afghanistan in 1979. Islamic jihadis took to the hills to wage a fierce guerrilla war against the Soviet occupiers in what turned into a long war of attrition. Sixth, the Soviet economy lost its principal life-support system when OPEC cracked up in 1981 and the price of oil fell to less than $20 a barrel. The suddenly cash-strapped Soviet economy fell farther and farther behind, especially in the fields of cybernetics, which were just then taking off in the capitalist world.

Seventh and finally, Moscow finally got young, reform-minded leadership in 1985 in the person of Mikhail Gorbachev. His "new thinking" included détente

Berliners celebrate the fall of the Berlin Wall at the Brandenburg Gate in 1989.

and arms-control treaties with NATO plus *perestroika* (restructuring) of the economy and *glasnost* (openness) to encourage free speech. Gorbachev hoped to revitalize the communist system, but the effect of his reforms was to destroy it. Russians, cautiously at first, then more boldly, began to denounce the Communist Party's monopoly of power, while subject nationalities inside the Soviet bloc began to agitate for independence. Gorbachev's moment of truth arrived, with startling suddenness, in 1989, when human rights movements in Poland, Hungary, Czechoslovakia, and East Germany paralyzed the governments of those satellite states through massive demonstrations in which ordinary people cried out for free speech, free travel, and free elections. Would Gorbachev send in the Red Army as his predecessors had done? To his lasting credit Gorbachev said, "Nyet." He would not send in the tanks but instead would allow each nation to choose its own path toward socialism.

That was the signal for hundreds of thousands of people in Berlin to tear down the Berlin Wall, which had served as a symbol of Germany's—and all Europe's—east-west divide since 1961. Huge crowds also turned out in Warsaw,

Prague, and Budapest, eventually toppling their regimes in favor of democratic provisional governments. In 1991 the tidal wave reached the Soviet Union when the Baltic republics, the Ukrainians, and even the Russians themselves declared independence. Hardliners in the Politburo launched a belated coup, hoping to oust Gorbachev and reassert control. But the citizens of Moscow, now led by interim President Boris Yeltsin, defied the soldiers sent to arrest him until the demoralized soldiers disobeyed orders and deserted. The coup collapsed. The Soviet Union soon ceased to exist.

Thus did totalitarianism of the communist sort follow totalitarianism of the fascist sort into the dustbin of history, which meant the only ideology left standing was pluralistic democracy. Or so it seemed in the 1990s, when an American intellectual named Francis Fukuyama wrote of "the end of history." Fukuyama meant that all the ideologies born of the French Revolution had been tried, taken to extremes, and defeated: all except democracy. Moreover, he and other pundits, such as *New York Times* columnist Thomas Friedman, confidently predicted that computers, the Internet, and economic globalization were making it imperative for all countries to embrace liberal democracy and capitalist transparency if they wished to compete in the new world order.

During those optimistic years the European and Atlantic projects raced toward completion. Germany reunified, and the European Union and NATO expanded eastward to the very borders of Russia. Every post–World War II reverie seemed to come true, including Franklin Roosevelt's dream of a "One World" economy, Charles de Gaulle's dream of a single Europe from the Atlantic Ocean to the Ural Mountains, Konrad Adenauer's dream of a reunified Germany, Willy Brandt's dream of Europe as a peaceful bridge between superpowers, and President George H. W. Bush's dream of a "Europe Whole and Free."

Yet, ironically, victory in the Cold War did not strengthen the partnership between Europe and the United States. Rather, Europeans' resentment against what was now the "sole superpower," and what they described as Americans' arrogance, militarism, unilateralism, and insensitivity toward global issues, soon sharpened the tensions between them and Americans, despite or because of the repeated attacks on their common civilization by Islamic *jihadism* (terrorist movements or holy war).

Now that peace had broken out and the European Union had grown broader and deeper, its member states showed little interest in maintaining adequate defense budgets, and for that reason they remained dependent on the United States. Nor did Europeans make much progress toward their long-standing goal of a common foreign and defense policy. Nor did Europeans grow much richer, because their mature economies displayed sluggish growth and their governments increased their indebtedness, even as European firms were outcompeted in their own markets by manufactures from China and the "tiger economies" of Asian countries like South Korea, Taiwan, Vietnam, and Singapore. Moreover, European society was besieged by an influx of legal and illegal immigrants as well as refugees from the many wars scourging the Middle East.

Perhaps the most poignant evidence of a malaise at the end of history is that Europeans have stopped reproducing. Birth rates all over the continent have fallen far below 2.1 babies per woman, the benchmark for zero population growth. Demography, always and everywhere, is destiny. If the nations that dominated the world just a century ago have grown too demoralized, self-absorbed, or hedonistic even to have children, what future can their formerly dynamic civilization possibly have?

Think back on the long centuries this book has surveyed. Throughout modern history Europeans dreamed of the sort of peace and prosperity nearly all their progeny enjoy today. They wanted to believe in progress even though the religious wars of the Reformation, the wars of the French revolutionary and Napoleonic era, the world wars of the twentieth century, and finally the Cold War gave them manifold reasons to doubt that progress was real. When the Berlin Wall came tumbling down like the biblical walls of Jericho, it seemed that Europeans, like the children of Israel, were finally entering their promised land. Just three decades later, it is already apparent that Europeans could not stand their success and that they now face an identity crisis focused, above all, on two haunting questions: What is the purpose of cultural freedom? And what is the cause of civilizational decay?

The final chapter of this book will suggest some plausible answers.

Chapter 28

Be Not Proud, Be Not Ashamed: In Defense of the West

This book has surveyed the centuries during which the civilization founded in Europe, the one conventionally called Western, spread its technology, institutions, and values around the world—indeed beyond the world, if one includes the thousands of satellites and space probes launched since 1957. Europeans have exercised an enormous influence on world history through their geographical discoveries, commerce, colonization, wars, and cultural creations (what the political scientist Joseph Nye called "soft power").

When the Cold War ended, many journalists, scholars, and politicians believed that the culmination of globalization must inevitably create the first universal civilization. During those heady years of the 1990s they asserted that all peoples now had no choice except to embrace the supposedly universal values of democracy, human rights, transparent free markets, and the rule of law. The days of stubborn holdouts, such as the authoritarian governments of Iraq, Iran, China, Russia, and North Korea, appeared to be numbered, while Muslim *jihadis* (holy warriors) must soon become as extinct as those bomb-throwing nineteenth-century anarchists. The world had arrived at "the end of history." Yet from the perspective of the 2020s, it appears that "Western civilization," however defined, has become decadent, and is perhaps even dying.

Today, scholars and political activists harp constantly on the importance of understanding and respecting other civilizations and cultures, a contention that is surely undeniable. But if Europeans and their overseas progeny fail to understand and respect the identity and history of their own civilization and culture, they will have no frame of reference from which to observe other civilizations and cultures. Nor will they be able to grasp how similar to or distinct from their own those civilizations and cultures are. To hearken back to the ancient Greeks and Hebrews with whom this book began, we ought to recall Socrates's adage that to know thyself is the beginning of wisdom, and we should remember the Bible's adage that to fear God is the beginning of wisdom. Those are really two sides of the same coin, for in order to know ourselves we must look in the mirror, honestly confess our flaws and mortality, and become humble before whatever is holy and immortal.

Having said that, we encounter a paradox the moment we begin to study the so-called Western world, because, in the current age of globalization, nothing distinctly Western seems to exist anymore. For two decades Philadelphia's Foreign Policy Research Institute sponsored a seminar called the Center for the Study of America and the West. It hosted many erudite scholars who addressed aspects of the Western identity, but the Center's participants never arrived at answers to the question of how to define Western civilization. They could not even decide which peoples belong to it. A strictly ethnic definition might confine the West to countries in which Europeans and their descendants predominate, including most of the Americas, Australia, New Zealand, and much of South Africa. But if current demographic trends continue for another generation or two, whites will be in the minority even in much of Europe and North America. Indeed, birthrates for white women are so low that if DNA is the measurement used, one must admit that the West is shrinking. The demographic decline of "white people" in the decades since the end of the postwar baby boom has been nothing short of precipitous.

What if we discard an ethnic definition of Western civilization and substitute one based on values and institutions? If, in fact, the whole world is fast conforming to political and economic systems invented in Europe and its colonial offshoots, then any country that now embraces those systems may be considered part of the club. But that definition is problematic because a values-and-institutions model would imply that large portions of Europe itself—such as fascist Italy, Nazi Germany, and Soviet Russia—somehow dropped out of the West during the twentieth century when they abandoned representative government, human rights, and free markets, even though their totalitarian ideologies were themselves products of European history. What is more, a values-and-institutions definition would oblige us to recognize that the Western center of gravity has been migrating eastward. The world's largest democracies, such as India and Indonesia, and the most dynamic techno-capitalist economies, such as that of the People's Republic of China, are located in Asia.

The late Samuel Huntington, an acclaimed political scientist at Harvard University, suggested a third definition in his book *The Clash of Civilizations*, which predicted that the post–Cold War world would be defined by conflicts along cultural and religious divides. He noted that the Shinto Japanese, Buddhist and Taoist Chinese, Hindus of southern Asia, Arabs and others in the Islamic Crescent, and Eastern Orthodox Christians such as the Russians crafted indelible cultures very different from those informed by Catholic and Protestant Christians in Europe. Hence, those peoples can never really be "Western," even if they embrace democratic capitalism. Huntington's clash-of-civilizations prediction, however, clashes with those religious trends that reveal that Christian observance has been flagging in Europe, the United States, and the British dominions, whereas the most vibrant Christian churches today are flourishing in regions of Africa and Asia. Hence, if religion is one's yardstick, then one might conclude that in the twenty-first century the more Christian a nation is the less likely it is to be Western.

Surely an ironclad definition of the West would stress the material fruits of the scientific and industrial revolutions that arose in Europe and were exported abroad. Except that would mean that one must include most eastern and southern Asian countries—such as Singapore, whose late president Lee Kuan Yew loudly proclaimed the superiority of Asian values over Western values. It would also mean that one could exclude the more primitive regions of Latin America, despite those countries' Iberian and Catholic heritage. Moreover, to make science and technology the principal measures of Western civilization is to imply that *techne* is all that matters and that the things of *themis* are irrelevant.

What about a strategic, geopolitical definition that simply defines the West as the members of the North Atlantic Treaty Organization plus ancillary allies such as Japan, South Korea, and Israel? But that "us" vs. "them" definition ignores every feature other than foreign policy, not to mention history itself. For instance, thirty-five years ago Poland belonged to the Soviet bloc, and forty-five years ago the Iranian regime was a pro-American ally. Today, Muslim Turkey remains in the NATO alliance despite qualifications so dubious that the European Union refuses to consider its application for membership.

The only definition that makes sense is one based not on the characteristics of countries or peoples today, but on their historic roots. Thus did a textbook titled *Western Civilization* by authors Carlton J. H. Hayes, Marshall Baldwin, and Charles Cole describe the roots of its subject in these words:

> This European Civilization consists, first, in the fusing of ancient peoples of the Eastern Mediterranean into a conscious community of settled life, commerce, expansion, and artistic achievement. Second, in the Greco-Roman traditions of language, philosophy, art, law, and political concepts of monarchy, aristocracy, democracy, and dictatorship. Third, in the Judeo-Christian tradition, with its fruitful spirituality and ethical norms for personal and social behavior, and the distinctions it drew between the individual and society, liberty and authority, mercy and justice, and what is Caesar's and what is God's. Fourth, in traditions both of individualism and social responsibility, hence repeated revolt and revolution. Finally, it includes an expansionist tradition born of a missionary zeal, whether religious or political, ever pushing outward, first to Europe's frontiers, then across the Atlantic, and at last around the whole world.

In sum, the modern West is whatever sprouted from those ancient roots and bore fruit, whether sweet or bitter. Now, note that these authors wrote exclusively about traditions. Civilizations are defined by traditions, simply because people do not reinvent the structures of everyday life every morning at eight o'clock. Civilizations mean predictability of behavior, which is to say that most of the time most of the people behave and believe according to certain traditions, even if they are no more conscious of it than they are of breathing. Traditions cling like layers of skin. Of course, to study Europe is to notice that antitraditionalism is itself a powerful tradition. No wonder Europe's history has been not only creative and restless but destructive and self-critical.

Some seventy years ago professors teaching courses in modern European history invariably presented the continent's epic saga as a triumphant progression, at least by contrast to the histories of other civilizations. Moreover, most teachers and textbooks contrasted the relative dynamism of northern European Protestant peoples with the relative torpor of southern Catholic peoples. They also took for granted the superiority of the liberal regimes of western Europe over the authoritarian regimes that prevailed in eastern Europe. Indeed, the first "Western Civ" courses, such as the famous one developed at Columbia University, were invented during World War I as vehicles to indoctrinate students about what it was the Allied and Associated Powers were fighting for and what the Central Powers led by Germany were fighting against.

Such courses exhorted students to savor history as a progressive march, beginning with Athens, Jerusalem, and the glory that was Rome. They would then skip ahead to the fifteenth century Renaissance and the Age of Discovery, when Europeans really hit their stride. The Protestant Reformation was another great leap forward because it cast off the dead weight of church authority and bade Europeans think for themselves. The Scientific Revolution opened the cosmos to inquisitive Europeans and gave them the keys with which to unlock the secrets of the heavens and the earth. The Enlightenment extended such questing reason to social institutions, inspiring doctrines of natural rights and free markets. To be sure, the hot-blooded French made some faux pas on the road to liberty, the Germans frequently got it wrong, and the Russians never did get the message. But freedom in thought, politics, and economics triumphed—especially in the Anglophone world—until all men and eventually women achieved equality in the eyes of the law. Likewise, industrialization marched forward, with the most liberal countries in the vanguard, and catapulted Europeans and their progeny abroad to global hegemony.

What were Europeans to do with their power, wealth, and freedom? Why, spread their civilization abroad while sharing wealth and freedom more equitably at home. By the dawn of the twentieth century few Europeans doubted that the rise of the West was providential, or else the natural outcome of historical evolution, or else both. Christians, secular liberals, and Marxists all took for granted the superiority of European civilization.

Then came the Great War, a bloody civil war within Europe, followed by ideological schisms, the Great Depression, dystopian totalitarian regimes, another world war that spawned more holocausts, and finally a lengthy Cold

War marked by a nuclear balance of terror. Those serial catastrophes were more than enough to cause anyone to doubt the reality of progress. The West's material progress had delivered into the hands of a flawed human race the power to blow up the world. But in the fullness of time a new episode dawned. The Soviets' "evil empire" simply went poof like Sauron at the climax of Tolkien's *Lord of the Rings*. That was what inspired Fukuyama to extol the ideological victory of democratic capitalism over its dialectical rivals.

Yet by the time Fukuyama put down his pen the story of the Western march of progress was already being challenged in Europe and North America by new generations of postmodern intellectuals. They hotly denounced traditional Western values and institutions in the name of multiculturalism, deconstructionism, feminism, and environmentalism. The West is the best, they asked rhetorically? Nonsense, the West is the worst! What had Euro-American civilization ever given the world besides imperialism, war, racism, patriarchy, and oppression? When Europeans arrived in America, Asia, or Africa they came as conquerors greedy for gold and slaves, spreading terror and disease while their missionaries tore up indigenous cultures as if they were pulling weeds. Not content with plundering other countries, Western nations tormented themselves with incessant wars.

How could Western societies possibly expiate such a burden of guilt, asked the postmodern accusers? First, by ceasing to teach the history of Europe and America as a triumphal march—or indeed ceasing to teach history at all, as when students at Stanford University in 1987 chanted: "Hey hey, ho ho, Western Civ has got to go!" Second, by depicting other civilizations in a positive light and damning the crimes committed against them by Westerners. Third, by shutting down the economy of mass consumption that progressives believed was the principal cause of pollution, resource depletion, and global warning. Fourth, by paying trillions of dollars in reparations to the victims of Western oppression at home and abroad.

One can well imagine why many Chinese remain angry about the "century of humiliation" their great country suffered at the hands of Western (and Japanese) imperialists, or why many Muslims are angry about European imperialism in the Middle East, or why Latin Americans are angry about Yankee hegemony in their hemisphere. But why are postmodern intellectuals—most of whom are comfortable, well-educated Europeans and Americans—angry about the civilization their own ancestors built? Why do they condemn institutions and values that still attract millions of immigrants from other parts of the world? What progressive, postmodern critics ignore is the fact that the very values they invoke in order to condemn Western civilization—such as freedom, equality, social justice, toleration, human rights, feminism, and environmentalism—were themselves inventions of Western societies. They are involved not only in a logical contradiction, but also in some sort of self-loathing death wish.

Jacques Ellul was a twentieth-century French philosopher concerned with the cultural impact of technology. He was no blind apologist for European civilization. Yet Ellul warned against this postmodern suicidal syndrome. He granted that Europeans had been imperialistic. But he pointed out that every civilization has pursued conquest and empire when it had got the upper hand over others. What was distinctive about Europeans was their invention of *anti*-imperialism. He granted that whites had enslaved people of color. But he pointed out that all civilizations have known some form of slavery at some point in their histories. What was distinctive about Europeans was their invention of abolitionism. He granted that Westerners had a long tradition of patriarchy. But he pointed out that every civilization has been patriarchal. What was distinctive about Europeans was their invention of women's liberation. He granted that Western militaries had killed millions of innocent people in their myriad wars. But he pointed out that every civilization from Attila the Hun to Genghis Khan has killed innocent people indiscriminately. What was distinctive about Europeans was their invention of international law, self-determination, and human rights.

The myth that Western civilization has been uniquely evil may be traced in part to Jean-Jacques Rousseau's eighteenth-century concept of the noble savage. That allegedly enlightened philosophe postulated that human beings in the primitive state of nature had been morally pristine and happy and that it was society that corrupted human nature. If one accepts Rousseau's premise, then it follows that the more advanced a society becomes, the more corrupt it becomes. But if instead one postulates the biblical principle that human nature is fundamentally flawed (in Hebrew the word for sin simply means "missing the mark," like an archer who can never manage to hit the bull's-eye), then it follows that

Europeans are not more corrupt than people in other civilizations. Over time, they simply became more technically powerful. Hence the saying: "He who has no power has no power to do evil."

If Western peoples are no worse, man for man, woman for woman, than other peoples, have they not at least been self-righteous in their claim to be superior—for instance, by claiming to possess the one true religion or universally valid secular ideas? Once again, if one studies other civilizations, one finds that they, too, have been self-righteous and intolerant at various times. The Chinese used to believe (perhaps many still do) that theirs was the Middle Kingdom, a celestial realm whose emperors enjoyed a mandate of heaven, and that all other peoples were simply barbaric. The Japanese used to believe that they were literally descended from gods. Peoples in other Asian, Middle Eastern, and Latin American countries have at times been imperious, self-righteous, and indeed murderous.

What historians today need to do is to shift the arguments in the public square from the question of why there is evil and suffering in the world to the question of why there has sometimes been love, beauty, truth, peace, justice, and mercy. Selfish and predatory behavior needs no explanation—and that should go without saying whether one believes in biblical theology, Darwinian evolution, or both. So why is it that human beings sometimes practice charity? What was it about some people in the Western world that caused them to proclaim liberty, equality, and fraternity, if only as ideals to be pursued? What caused some people in the Western world to abolish slavery, work to improve labor conditions, fund social security programs, fight pollution, and resist tyranny—all the while seeking irenic methods to resolve conflicts? If Europe has been as wicked as its critics insist, how do they explain why there has been much good in its history? Those trickier questions compel the historian to revisit the Renaissance and ask what has become of *techne* and *themis* over the five centuries since.

But first it is necessary to ask why most people assume that their readers and listeners share their views about good and evil, as the previous paragraph just did. The reason is that nearly all people living in countries born of European traditions share the notions of morality contained in Jewish scripture, Greek philosophy, Roman law, medieval theology, and Enlightenment reason. Of course, other civilizations have remarkably similar notions of right and wrong. The Golden Rule, or something like it, is an expression of natural law akin to what we call conscience. For instance, we may all agree that murder, theft, and perjury are wrong. But why? Just because there are civil laws against them? Of course not; we can name all sorts of civil laws throughout history that were manifestly unjust. Rather, to call those sins wrong is a self-evident tradition as old as the Ten Commandments. But if an individual or entire culture turns—or is wrenched away—from its cultural roots out of falsehood or ignorance, then laws and morals begin to appear to be mere human constructions imposed by parents, teachers, priests, the police, and the hegemonic race, class, and gender of a given era. And if that is all they appear to be, why not rebel against them in the manner of Nietzsche's superman who is "beyond good and evil"?

Let us put the matter another way. Do you think it is wrong to kill whales? Why? Japan and Norway still allow whaling for economic gain. The Inuit people of Siberia and Alaska even endow pelagic hunting with sacred significance. What makes our notion of right and wrong more valid than theirs? Back in the 1970s an ironic message on a popular bumper sticker in San Francisco read "nuke the gay whales." Why not?

The answers to such questions clearly reside in the realm of *themis*. Science, technology, and majority vote cannot answer them to everyone's satisfaction or indeed anyone's satisfaction. Yet how often do people make snap moral judgments without reflecting on those judgments' basis? How often, when obliged to think about justice and mercy, do people sidestep the embarrassing precepts of *themis* and embrace utilitarian metrics drawn from *techne*? Why, for example, do many Americans choose to believe that theirs is an "exceptional" nation? Is it because the United States has the highest per-capita income, the mightiest military, the most advanced medical care? Or is it because of the ideals expressed in the Declaration of Independence? Now ask yourself how much of their liberty most Americans would speedily relinquish if the alternative was to have their standard of living cut in half?

Over the course of modern history Western societies have become so accustomed to measuring value on the basis of quantity that their citizens have become consumption machines. A revealing example of that was the gold-plated plaque that the National Aeronautics and Space Administration designed for the *Voyager 1* spacecraft in 1977. The plaque included some vital statistics about the race that launched the interstellar spacecraft—in the event that aliens might retrieve it in some distant future. It described the carbon-based DNA of which human beings are composed, depicted the two biological sexes, and revealed the astronomical location of planet Earth. A few selections of music were included, but no poetry, no art, indeed nothing to suggest why earthlings wanted to explore the cosmos in the first place.

The modern obsession with quantifiable things has hypnotized the West—and later the Rest—into believing that *techne* means progress and that progress is good. Never mind the fact that technologies such as cell phones and the Internet have become the most pervasive and addictive *drugs* ever invented. If you sometimes feel needs, desires, and longings for something less tangible but more genuine than mere things, that is your humanity gasping for air. What is it you long for in your heart of hearts? What makes you cry?

Think back to the Renaissance, when humanist scholars recovered much ancient art and philosophy and began to sow doubt among Europeans. Those doubts were not only about the authority of the Catholic Church—that had already been compromised—but about orthodox doctrines concerning the nature of God, the nature of man, and the relationship between the two. Was humanism an attack on the realm of *themis*? Not at all, because humanists focused intently on questions like how to live a good life and how to address timeless issues such as love, beauty, peace, justice, tragedy, and death. One product of humanism was the Protestant Reformation, which was driven by *techne* in the form of the printing press, but otherwise inspired Europeans to be all the more focused on questions of truth and meaning. Perversely, however, the religious divisions it caused within Christendom resulted in the subordination of national churches to political rulers, which surely marked a thematic retreat. The state-building monarchs cared more about the Machiavellian competition for power than about questions of truth and meaning.

The Scientific Revolution was another astounding achievement made by curious, rational Europeans who were in love with creation and wanted to discern the mind of God. But the scientific method put so much power into the hands of Europeans that they forgot the warnings of Sir Francis Bacon. They were tempted to fall into idolatries such as worshiping science itself or (worse yet) worshiping themselves for being clever enough to acquire such power. Through applied science, Europeans began to play God.

Enlightenment philosophes revealed both the potential for humane reforms and the potential for inhumane damage inherent in the application of amoral reason to social institutions. The hyperrational notions of the French Enlightenment tempted the revolutionaries after 1789 to imagine they possessed the power to redesign human laws, customs, and institutions from scratch without any reference to history, religion, and culture. The revolutionaries unpacked their triptych and turned its components into rigid ideologies such that the implications of liberty, equality, and fraternity haunted the continent for two hundred years. Occasionally, adherents of those ideologies made tactical alliances with the adherents of another ideology, but mostly the movements for radical liberty, radical equality, and radical nationalism engaged in wars of all against all in which the revolutionaries' ideals, though sublime in the abstract, became demonic in reality.

By the dawn of the twentieth century, Europe and its overseas transplants were becoming what Britain's Catholic philosopher G. K. Chesterton called a cut-flower culture. For a season that culture blossomed like roses in a vase, but it was certain to wilt over the long run. Its blossoms were evident during the nineteenth century, when liberal government, the rule of law, free markets, prosperity, education, and religious toleration spread far and wide. During that century slavery was ended, reforms were embraced, and science and industry burgeoned. But in the long run, it became evident that such advances alone could not satisfy thematic needs. The perverse response of modern Europeans was to deny the existence of those needs which could not be met by science and industry. Thus did Karl Marx claim to discover that dialectical materialism was the driving force behind history, that culture was mere superstructure invented by the ruling class of the day, and that religions were just the fables of mankind's childhood. Thus did Charles Darwin claim to debunk the notion that human beings were made in the image of God or indeed created at all. To quote Ellul again, following those great discontinuities "all that remained was the drab and insipid unfolding of implications." Gustave Le Bon, Georges Sorel, Sigmund Freud, and Friedrich Nietzsche regarded such expressions of *themis* as art and religion as mere psychological wish-fulfillment. Sociologist Max Weber wrote of the *Entzauberung* (disenchantment) of a bureaucratic industrial society in which human beings were turned into machines.

From the outside, Europe never seemed so mighty as in 1914. On the inside it was cracking up. The only way to restore the health of its civilization would have been to reconnect power with nurturing values, so that power would not become an end in itself. Instead, Europeans tried to expunge their increasingly lonely, meaningless, material existence by gorging on more power, more science, more technology, more hatred, more fear, more military mobilization until they blundered into a war so lethal and demoralizing that in its wake many people succumbed to ideologies of negation. The toxic products of that demoralized era included communism and fascism, which made bloodthirsty idols of materialism, racism, revolution, and war.

Recall how Elie Wiesel asked at Auschwitz what had become of God.

Ellul wrote an indirect answer to that question. "God's silence means only that man got what he wanted. . . . The West is dying because it told God to get lost, and He granted the wish." Ellul was a Catholic, but Protestants, Jews, and agnostics could reach similar conclusions so long as they believed in natural law.

In a thrilling book called *Zen and the Art of Motorcycle Maintenance* an American professor named Robert Pirsig wrote that a civilization in which people worship quantity over quality has already lost its soul. If, in fact, contemporary civilization is a cut-flower culture severed from its historical roots, there is no point in asking who or what constitutes Western civilization—because it no longer exists. One suspects that its mortal illness had already begun around the time of the First World War, when universities began to teach courses designed around the concept. Perhaps people sensed—if only subconsciously—the imminent *Decline of the West*, to cite the despairing title of Oswald Spengler's 1919 bestseller.

So that's how it ends, wrote the English journalist Malcolm Muggeridge: not with a bang or a whimper, but a death wish. American poet Robert Frost asked whether civilization will die by fire or ice. Nuclear fears notwithstanding, he said civilization would probably die by ice. Powerful indications of that prophecy include the following facts. Europeans (and most Americans) no longer reproduce themselves. Few people today read Greek and Latin classics, even in translation. Few people today listen to the music of giants like Bach, Mozart, Beethoven, and Brahms. Few people today meditate on the Bible or ponder the moral depths of authors like Dante and Dostoyevsky. Even highly educated people waste hours each day staring at computer screens, playing video games, and scanning social media. The printed book is going extinct.

The Russian novelist Aleksandr Solzhenitsyn, depicted here in 1974, had the moral wisdom to know that the line between good and evil ran not between nations, but through every human heart.

Artificial intelligence is making quantum leaps forward every year. Perhaps our future will indeed belong to the robots, in which case *techne* may prosper, but *themis* will die and never be resurrected.

Muggeridge, who was a wry wit as well as a cutting critic, said that he felt a certain kinship with gargoyles, those weird, grinning imps jutting from the walls of medieval cathedrals. Why, he wondered, had stonemasons carved such repugnant demons on their otherwise exquisite buildings? Most people assumed they were superstitious attempts to scare off real demons, but Muggeridge thought otherwise. He suspected that artists in the medieval era—their minds firmly fixed on heavenly things—placed gargoyles on the exterior walls to remind the busy people doing their deals in the markets below of their vanity and mortality. Muggeridge likened himself to a gargoyle, observing that in real life the only people who ever get to tell the truth are prophets and clowns.

As of this writing one may conclude that the civilization born in Europe had cause to claim universality because it bequeathed to posterity three precious gifts. The first gift was science and the technology derived from it, which are universally valid because no rational person can deny the scientific method. But science and technology simply represent power, and in the absence of ethical checks to constrain the exercise of power, science and technology may become what C. S. Lewis called "that hideous strength," an enabler of evil.

The second gift was the rule of law, which is the political equivalent of science. Law orders societies and makes people civil. But the rule of law cannot guide human beings on the use of their liberties any more than science and technology can. As the Nobel Prize-winning minstrel Bob Dylan put it in a ballad called "Jokerman": "Freedom, just around the corner for you. But with truth so far off, what good will it do?"

The third gift bequeathed by Western civilization was (and is) the Judeo-Christian religion, which instructs human beings on how to use their power and liberty. Two quotations from the Bible will suffice: "You shall love the LORD your God with all your heart and with all your soul and with all your mind and with all your strength. . . . You shall love your neighbor as yourself." "What does the LORD require of you but to do justice, and to love kindness, and to walk humbly with your God?"

In 1978 the novelist Aleksandr Solzhenitsyn, who survived years in the Soviet *gulag* before being exiled from the Soviet Union, was invited to deliver the commencement address at Harvard University (whose motto is *Veritas*—Truth). The title he chose—"A World Split Apart"—led the audience to assume that he would deliver a homily on the Cold War. Solzhenitsyn surprised them by denouncing capitalism and communism alike as materialist idolatries. In *The Gulag Archipelago*, his famous novel about life in a concentration camp, Solzhenitsyn pronounced the epitaph for civilization itself: "The line between good and evil passes not between countries, nor between classes, nor between political parties, but straight through the middle of each human heart. . . . No one on earth today has any way left to go, except upward."

Index

Aachen. *See* Aix-le-Chapelle
Abraham, 16–17
absolutism, 259
Abyssinia. *See* Ethiopia
Académie Française, 117
Academy of Sciences (France), 152
Academy of Sciences (Russia), 167
Act of Settlement, 136
Act of Supremacy (England), 75
Act of Union (1707), 136
Action Française, 367
Acts of the Apostles, 27
Adam and Eve, 20
Adenauer, Konrad, 398, 406
Aegean Sea, 8
Afghanistan, 404
Africa, 34, 37, 91, 104, 108, 178, 190, 192, 279, 282, 285, 287–89, 324, 382, 401
Africa and the Victorians (Gallagher and Robinson), 284
Age of the Democratic Revolution, The (Palmer), 202
Agricola. *See* Bauer, Georg
agriculture, 1, 6, 40, 104, 117, 188, 263, 286, 305, 334, 344, 353; advent of crop rotation, 41; climate and, 178; collectivization of, 369–70; development of the plow, 40; science and, 186, 235
aircraft, 353, 369, 377, 379, 384, 388
Aix-la-Chapelle (Germany), 34
Almagest (Ptolemy), 141, 143
Alamogordo (NM), 390
Alaska, 417
Alba Madonna, The (Raphael), *51*
Albania, 310
Alcibiades, 8
Alexander (the Great), 13, 22
Alexander I (Russian tsar), 215, 218, 221, 329
Alexander II (Russian tsar), 256, 273, 311, 334
Alexandra (Russian tsarina), 339
Alexandria, 13, 27
Algeria, 280, 400–401
Alhambra Decree, 79
Alighieri, Dante. *See* Dante
Allgemeine Elektrizitäts Gesellschaft, 267, 307–8
Alps, 322, 353
Alsace-Lorraine, 310, 324, 330

American Revolution, 103, 199
Amherst College, 3
Amsterdam, 95
anarchism, 273, 336
Anatomy Lesson of Dr. Nicolaes Tulp (Rembrandt), *146*
Andes Mountains, 98, 295
Angell, Norman, 308
Angles, 124
Anglicanism, 116, 125–26, 128–29, 132–33, 135–36, 231, 295, 394
Anglo-French Company, 279
Anschluss, 374
anti-Semitism, 299, 384–85
Antwerp (Belgium), 95, 187, 390
Apaches, 100
Aphrodite, 9
Apollo, 9, 10
Arabs, 49, 93–95, 143, 147, 211, 279, 324, 395, 401, 411
Aragon (region in Spain), 34, 42, 70, 79
Archangel (Russia), 339
Architect's Dream The (Cole), *4*
Ardennes forest, 378
Arendt, Hannah, 349
Argentina, 103, 365
Aristarchus of Samos, 12, 141
Aristotle, 8, 12, 42, 45–46, 50, 138, 141–42, 144, 150
Arizona, 100
Arkwright, Richard, 237
Armada (Spanish), 85, 127
Arouet, François-Marie. *See* Voltaire
Around the World in Eighty Days (Verne), 288
Artemis, 10
Arthur (English king), 37
artificial intelligence, 4
asceticism, 30
Asia, 6, 13, 23, 26, 32, 37, 43–44, 178, 279, 285, 288–89, 311

Assyria, 21
astronomy, 12
atheism, 342
Athena, 9, 10
Athens, 3, 7, 8, 9, 10, 27, 413
Atlantic Charter, 396
Atlantic Ocean, 80, 110, 191, 198, 221, 308, 406
Atlantis, 6
Atlee, Clement, 397
atomic energy, 390, 391, 394, 397
Attila the Hun, 415
Aufklärung (Enlightenment), 172, 178
Augustine of Canterbury, St., 74
Augustine of Hippo, St., 6, 30, 109
Augustinians, 63
Aurora (warship), 338
Auschwitz (concentration camp), 386, 420
Australia, 268, 279, 285, 367, 410
Austria, 63, 86, 120, 159, 172, 197, 211, 230, 249, 258, 267, 273, 300, 326, 328, 331, 351, 352, 385; Catholicism and, 88, 259; Habsburg era, 70, 83, 117, 161, 181, 194, 207–8, 226, 247, 249–50, 255–57, 260, 273, 309, 311–14; Hitler and, 354–55, 360, 374; loss of territories, 312; military alliances of, 196; Napoleon and, 214–15, 218–22; War of Succession and, 195; World War I and, 315–17, 322
authoritarianism, 169, 399, 409
Avars, 32
Azores, 94, 190
Aztecs, 80, 96, 98

Babylonia, 21, 22, 292
Bacchus. *See* Dionysus
Bach, Johann Sebastian, 89, 173, 420
Bacon, Francis, 138–39, 143–46, 148, 173, 175
Baden (German state), 258, 260

Index

Balbo, Italo, 353
Balboa, Vasco de, 96
Baldwin, Marshall, 412
Balfour, Arthur, 385
Balkans, 310, 315–16, 322
Baltic Sea, 87, 149, 158, 167, 330, 341, 406
Bank of England, 103, 198–99, 265, 365
Barbados, 190
barbarians, 31, 35–36
Barebone, Praise-God, 133
Barebones (movement), 133
Barmby, John Goodwyn, 271
Baroque (era and style), 88–89, 173
Bastille, 205
Battle of Blenheim, 121
Battle of Britain, 388
Battle of Königgrätz, 260
Battle of Lepanto, 84
Battle of Marathon, 9
Battle of Midway Island, 381
Battle of Mohacs, 70
Battle of Omdurman, 287
Battle of Passchendaele, 323
Battle of Poltava, 167
Battle of Pondicherry, 197
Battle of Salamis, 9
Battle of Temesvár, 255
Battle of the Bulge, 382
Battle of the Pyramids, 211
Battle of the Somme, 323
Battle of the White Mountain, 87
Battle of Thermopylae, 9
Battle of Tours, 34
Bauer, Georg, 147
Bavaria (German state), 258, 260, 354–55, 358
Bay of Biscay (France), 110
Bayer (firm), 307
Beagle, H.M.S. (ship), 295
Bebel, Auguste, 273, 309
Becker, Carl, 123, 183, 202

Beckett, Samuel, 394
Beer Hall Putsch, 355
Beethoven, Ludwig van, 173, 214, 231, 303, 337, 386, 420
Behaim, Martin, 95
Belgium, 120, 186, 198, 220, 239, 241, 269, 280, 317, 321, 324, 328–30, 378, 394, 398, 401
Belgrade (Serbia), 316
Bell, Daniel, 2, 292
Belsen (concentration camp), 386
Belzec (concentration camp), 386
Benedict of Nursia, St., 30
Benedictines, 81
Benin, 191
Bentham, Jeremy, 243
Beria, Lavrentiy, 371
Berlin (Germany), 158–59, 161, 167, 172, 249, 253, 281, 332, 377, 393, 397
Berlin Wall, 402, 405, *405*, 407
Bernini, Gian Lorenzo, 51, *80*, 81
Bernstein, Eduard, 274
Bessemer (firm), 307
Béthune, Maximilien de, duc de Sully, 111–13
Beyond Good and Evil (Nietzsche), 302
Bhagavad-Gita, 390
Bible, 3, 11, 15, 18, 20, 26, 62, 66, 73, 83, 140, 142, 145, 171, 177, 179, 183, 294, 296, 299, 410, 420, 422
Bill of Rights (England), 136
Billington, James, 163
Birmingham (UK), 373
Birth of Venus (Botticelli), 54
Bismarck, Otto von, 258–61, 273–74, 281, 286–87, 309–13, 375
Black Death. *See* bubonic plague
Black Hand Society, 315
Black Irish, 85
Blackshirts. *See* Fascio di Combattimento
Blake, William, *176*, 230

Blanc, Louis, 250
Blanqui, Louis-Auguste, 250
Blitzkreig, 376–80, 385
Blücher, Leberecht von, 221
Blum, Leon, 367
Boer War, 289
Bohemia, 35, 63, 70, 86–87, 254
Boleyn, Anne, 75
Bolivia, 100
Bolsheviks, 275–76, 327–28, 335, 337–40, 342, 349, 351, 355, 360, 371
Bonaparte, Louis Napoléon, 251–52, 260–61
Bonaparte, Napoléon, 133–34, 210–15, 217–21, 224, 228, 230, 240, 332, 356, 371, 377, 379, 407
Boniface VIII, Pope, 43
Book of Common Prayer, 75, 126
Bordeaux (France), 191
Borgias (family), 55
Borodino (Russia), 218
Bosnia-Herzegovina, 315, 384
Bossuet, Jacques-Bénigne, 110, 119, 180
Botticelli, Alessandro, 54
Boulton and Watt (locomotives), 239
Bourbon, House of, 109–10, 112, 121, 125, 127, 136, 157, 160, 194, 196, 198, 203, 215, 220–21, 226
Bourbon, Henri de, 74
Boxer Rebellion, 289
Boyle, Robert, 152
Brahe, Tycho, 149, 151, 177
Brahms, Johannes, 386, 420
Brandenberger, Jacques, 306
Brandenburg (German state), 86, 158–59, 167–68, 373
Brandenburg Gate, *405*
Brandt, Willy, 402, 406
Braudel, Fernand, 185
Braun, Wernher von, 389
Braunau-am-Inn (Austria), 354

Brave New World (Huxley), 349
Brazil, 83, 103–4, 190
Bremen (Germany), 158
Brezhnev, Leonid, 402–3
Briand, Aristide, 332
Bristol (UK), *240*
British Broadcasting Corporation (BBC), 263
British East India Company, 102–3, 117, 189, 195, 197, 279
British Expeditionary Force, 378
British Museum, 246
British North America Act, 257
British Parliament. *See* Parliament
British Petroleum, 267
Brittany (French region), 101
Bronstein, Lev. *See* Trotsky, Leon
Brownshirts. *See Schutzstaffel*
Brunelleschi, Filippo, 51
Brussels, 221
bubonic plague, 43, 49
Budapest, 248–49, 254, 402, 406
Buddha, 23
Buddhism, 178, 411
Bukharin, Nikolai, 371
Bulgaria, 310, 322
Bulgars, 36
Burgundy (French region), 70
Burke, Edmund, 202, 229–30
Burkhardt, Jacob, 45, 50
Burma, 380
Bush, George H. W., 406
Bush, Vannevar, 388
Butterfield, Herbert, 137, 138
Byelorussia, 340
Byron, George Gordon, 230
Byzantine Empire, 30, 32–34, 36, 49, 137, 143, 163–64

Cabot, John, 101
Cabot, Sebastian, 101

Index

Cabral, Pedro, 98
Caesar, Julius, 24, 29, 140, 211, 214, 303
Calcutta, 189, 197
Calvin, John, 71–73, 78, 81, 130, 133, 143
Calvinism, 72–73, 84, 86, 88, 110, 125–27, 133, 135, 159, 177, 181
Cambodia, 280
Cambridge University, 143
Cameroon, 281
Camino de Santiago de Compostela, 81
Canaanites, 18
Canada, 101, 257, 264, 268, 323, 365, 367, 381, 397
Canary Islands, 190
Candide (Voltaire), 174
Canterbury (UK), 75
Cape of Good Hope, 94–95
Cape of Storms. *See* Cape of Good Hope
capitalism, 192, 242, 266, 270, 272, 286, 302, 318, 334, 344–45, 349, 354, 383, 422
Caribbean (region), 98, 103, 104, 117, 190
Carlsbad Decrees, 225
Carmelites, 81
Carnot, Lazare, 209, 213
Carnot, Marie-François, 273
Caroline Islands, 281
Cartier, Jacques, 101
cartography, 96
Caspian Sea, 165
Castel Gandolfo, 139
Castile (region in Spain), 34, 70, 79
Castle Church, 66
Castlereagh, Robert Stuart, Viscount of, 220–22, 329
Cathedral of St. Sophia, 32
Catherine I (Russian empress), 334
Catherine II (Catherine the Great, Russian empress), 181, 197
Catherine of Aragon (British queen), 75
Catholic Center Party (Germany), 273

Catholic Reformation, 77–89, 99, 137, 300; art during, 80; monastic life and, 81
Catholicism, 15, 32-33, 50, 56, 61, 70, 73, 84, 87–88, 98, 112, 116–17, 121, 125–27, 129, 133, 139, 159, 166, 174, 178, 181, 203, 230, 231, 244, 259–60, 268, 273, 297, 299, 351, 358, 394, 404, 411, 413, 418–20; doctrine of, 63, 68, 71, 299, 394; Galileo and, 139, 149; Henry VIII and, 74–75, 125; James II and, 135; John Calvin and, 71–72; Martin Luther and, 68; monastic orders and, 38–39, 68, 125, 297; nobility and, 71, 87, 111, 115, 168; Reformation of, 77–89; taxation and, 43; universities and, 39, 82; wealth of church and, 35, 42–43, 75, 207. *See also* papacy
Caucasus (Eurasian region), 345, 380
Cauvin, Jean. *See* Calvin, John
Cavaliers, 130–31
Cavendish, Henry, 151
Cavour, Camillo di, 256
Celts, 124
Centennial Exhibition (1876), 294
Central Intelligence Agency, 397–98
Cervantes, Miguel de, 78
Chadwick, Owen, 43
Chamberlain, Joseph, 283, 299
Chamberlain, Neville, 373–76, *375*, 379
Champaigne, Philippe de, *113*, 114
Champlain, Samuel de, 101
Charlemagne, 34, 109, 215, 323
Charles I (British king), 109, 127–33
Charles II (British king), 134–35, 152
Charles the Great. *See* Charlemagne
Charles V (Spanish king), 70–71, 75, 83–84, 97, 100
Charles VI (Habsburg emperor), 194
Charles XII (Swedish king), 167
Charles Martel (Frankish king), 34
Chartism, 227, 244, 269

Chateaubriand, François de, 230
Chauvin, Nicolas, 212
Cheka. *See* KGB
Chernyshevsky, Nikolai, 275
Chesterton, G. K., 419
Chiaroscuro, 52, 55
Chicago, 402
Childers, Thomas, 358
Chile, 295
China, 83, 92, 104, 108, 163, 173–74, 179, 188–89, 192, 265, 277, 281, 287–89, 314, 348, 365, 368, 380, 383, 402, 407, 409, 411, 414, 416
Ch'ing Empire, 334
Christian Democrats (party), 398
Christianity, 15–16, 23–24, 40, 47, 50, 53, 57, 61, 81–82, 93, 105, 108, 126, 137–38, 141, 145, 151, 176, 181, 190, 192, 209, 221, 230, 298–99, 302, 342, 394, 411; Judaism and, 25, 372; justification by faith and, 65; medieval, 38; missionaries of, 26, 82, 163; Nietzsche and, 303; pacifism and, 29; politics and, 359; Roman Empire and, 28–29; separation from state, 29; virtues and, 55; Voltaire and, 178
Church of England, 75
Church of Scotland, 128
Churchill, John (Duke of Marlborough), 121
Churchill, Winston, 287, 368, 374, 379, 381–82, 388, 396–97
Cicero, 46, 50
Cincinnatus, 55
City of God, The (Augustine), 30
Civil Constitution of the Clergy, 207
Civil War (US), 210, 213, 256, 260, 265
Clash of Civilizations, The (Huntington), 411
Clemenceau, Georges, 329–30, 339
Cleves (Rhineland fief), 159

Clive, Robert, 197
Cluny, 39, 43, 139
coal, 186, 234–35, 237–38, 241, 264, 305–6, 331–32, 345, 369, 398
Colbert, Jean Baptiste, 119, 152
Cold War, 277, 288, 319, 390–91, 395, 400–4, 406–7, 409, 411, 413–14, 422
Cole, Charles, 412
Cole, Thomas, *4*
Coleridge, Samuel, 230
collectivism, 371
College of Cardinals, 39, 43, 83, 404
Cologne (Germany), 86
Colombia, 281
colonialism, 120, 229, 278–80, 282, 285–88, 299, 314, 331, 367, 382, 400, 402, 410
Columbia University, 413
Columbian exchange, 187
Columbus, Christopher, 55, 79–80, 92, 95–96, 98, 105
Comanches, 100
Comintern. *See* Communist International
Committee of Public Safety, 208–10
commodities, 117
Common Market. *See* European Union
Communards, 272, 273
communism, 246, 270, 274, 276, 332–33, 335, 337, 353–55, 367–68, 370, 375–76, 402–5, 420; coining of term, 271; fascism and, 348–351, 361; in Russia, 275, 327, 341–42, 369; Nietzsche and, 303; private property and, 245, 272; Solzhenitsyn and, 422; stages of history and, 271; World War I and, 319, 339; World War II and, 380, 396–98
Communist International, 343
Communist Manifesto, The (Marx and Engels), 246, 253, 271
Communist Party, 338–39, 341, 343–45,

356–57, 360, 367, 370–71, 391, 394, 396, 402–3, 405
Compagnie de Nouvelle-France,103, 117
Compiègne (France), 378
computers, 388, 389
Concert of Europe, 222
Concini, Concino, 113
Condition of the Working Classes in England, The (Engels), 246
Confederacy (US), 213
Confucianism, 285
Congo River, 280
Congress (US), 281, 326–27, 366, 380, 397–98, 403
Congress of Vienna, 221–23, 247, 329
Conquistadors, 80
Conservatism, 222, 229–31, 244, 249–50, 258, 260, 269, 350
Conservative Party (UK), 373–74, 404
Constant, Benjamin, 224, 293
Constantine, Donation of, 63
Constantine, 29, 32
Constantinople, 32–33, 40, 44, 49–50, 163, 310, 324
Copernicus, Nicolaus, 138–39, 148, 151
Corinth (Greece), 3, 6, 7, 10
Corn Laws, 226
Cornwall (British region), 101
Corporis humani fabrica, de (Vesalius),147
Corsica, 211
Cortés, Hernán, 96–98
Cossacks, 166, 219, 340
Council of Constance, 63
Council of Trent, 83
Counter-Reformation. *See* Catholic Reformation
Coventry (UK), 383
Cranach (the Elder), Lucas, 68
Cranmer, Thomas, 75, 238
Crete, 6, 80, 190
Crimea, 382

Crimean War, 256, 311, 334
Critique of Pure Reason, The (Kant),182
Croatia, 33, 254–55, 384
Cromwell, Oliver, 56, 123, 130–35, 208
Crusades, 39, 40, 42–43, 49, 79, 83, 137
Crystal Palace, 294
Cuba, 190, 194, 348
cubism, 304
Cyprus, 190
Cyril, St., 163
Cyrus (Persian emperor), 22
Czechoslovakia, 374–75, 396, 402, 404–5
Czechs, 220, 229, 254, 328, 374–75

da Gama, Vasco, 91–92, 94–95, 103
da Vinci, Leonardo, 48, 51–54, 146
Dachau (concentration camp), 386
Daedalus (myth of), 10
Dahlberg-Acton, John, Lord, 302
Dahomey, 191
Daladier, Édouard, 374
Damascus, 26
Danilevsky, Nikolai, 299
Dante, 42, 45, 420
Darius (Persian emperor), 8
Dark Night of the Soul, The (John of the Cross), 81
Darkness at Noon (Koestler), 371
Darwin, Charles, 175, 295–96, 298, 321, 419
Darwinism, 283–84, 287, 289, 300–301, 303, 309, 313, 354
Das Kapital (Marx), 246
David (Hebrew king), 19–20, 22–23, 37
Day of Dupes, 116
de Gaulle, Charles, 381, 399, 402, 406
De re Metallica (Agricola), 147
De Revolutionibus Orbium Coelestium (Copernicus), 148
Dead Sea Scrolls, 23
Declaration of Independence, 417

Declaration of the Rights of Man and Citizen, 214, 217
Declaration on Liberated Europe, 396
Decline and Fall of the Roman Empire, The (Gibbon), 172
Decline of the West (Spengler), 420
Defenestration of Prague, 86
deism, 183, 209
Delors, Jacques, 399
Demeter (Greek goddess), 9
Democracy in America (Tocqueville), 227
Democratic Party (US), 265, 331
demographics, 187, 263, 407
Denmark, 87, 159, 166, 253, 259, 330, 378, 394, 399
des Pres, Joaquin, 52
Descartes, René, 152, 394
Descent of Man, The (Darwin), 296
Descent of the Dove, The (Williams), 29
Deuteronomy, 16, 18
Deutscher Bund, 221
Dickens, Charles, 238, 268
Diderot, Denis, 184
Diesel, Rudolf, 306
Diet of Worms, 66
Dieu et Liberté (journal), 244
Diggers (socialist party), 131
Dionysius (god), 10
Discourse on Method (Descartes), 152
displaced persons. *See* refugees
Disraeli, Benjamin, 242, 310
Disrobing of Christ, The (El Greco), 80
Dnepr River, 163
Doctor Faustus (Marlowe), 143
Dolomites, 322
Dominic of Guzman, 39
Dominicans, 39, 58, 63, 99
Don River, 163
Don Quixote (Cervantes), 78
Doric (Greek culture group), 6
Dorn, Walter, 175

Dostoyevsky, Fyodor, 304, 420
Douhet, Giulio, 353, 368
Drake, Francis, 85, 101
Dreadnought, H.M.S., 306, 307
Dresden (Germany), 384
Dreyfus Affair, 384
duc de Gaston (third son of Henri IV), 115-16
duc de Montmorency (Mathieu Jean Felicité de Montmorency), 116
duc de Rohan (Henri II de Rohan), 115
dueling, 115
Dugommier, Jacques, 212
Duke of Alba, 84
Duke of Albuquerque, 95
Duke of Milan, 59
Duke of Wellington (Arthur Wellesley, First Duke of Wellington), 221
Duma, 336
Dunkirk (France), 378
Dürer, Albrecht, 54
Dutch East India Company, 102, 117, 189, 279
Dutch Sisters and Brothers of the Common Life, 63
Dutch West India Company, 103
Dylan, Bob, 422
Dzerzhinsky, Feliks, 340-41

Earl of Manchester, 130
East Anglia, 130
East Germany, 403, 405
East India Company, 190
East Indies, 80, 83, 85, 96
Eastern Orthodoxy, 163, 411
Eastern Question, 312
Eban, Abba, 25
Echternach, 399
Eck, Johannes von, 66
Éclaircissement. *See* Enlightenment
Economic Miracle, 400

Index

Economics and Empire (Fieldhouse), 285
Economist (magazine), 91, 94
Ecstasy of St. Teresa (Bernini), *80*, 81
Edict of Nantes, 74, 110, 112, 114–15, 120, 161
Edinburgh, 172
Edward VI (British king), 75
Egypt, 2, 7, 13, 17–18, 23, 25, 34, 178, 211, 245, 256, 279–81, 284, 310, 381, 401
Einstein, Albert, 175, 373, 390
Eisenhower, Dwight D., 381
Ekaterinburg (prison camp), *339*
El Greco, 54, 80
Elba (Italy), 220, 221
Elbe River, 158, 395
Elisabeth (Austrian empress), 273
Elizabeth (Russian tsarina), 196
Elizabeth I (British queen), 84, 85, 101, 125–27, 143
Ellul, Jacques, 415, 420
Emerson, Ralph Waldo, 231
Engels, Friedrich, 227, 245–46, 271–72, 275, 342
England, 34, 36–37, 42, 48, 58, 62, 111, 120, 123–24, 130–31, 143, 155, 158, 166, 172, 174, 179, 186, 190–92, 202, 228, 249, 271, 295, 306–7, 379; agriculture in, 187; Catholics in, 82, 84, 126, 129, 136; civil war, 129, 132–33 (*see also* English Civil War); colonies of, 101, 103; constitutional monarchy of, 123, 125, 168; exploration and, 101; industrialization of, 234–39; invasions and attempted invasions and, 128, 135, 215; labor in, 227, 244, 269, 335; Protestantism and 69, 71, 73, 75, 85; slavery and, 104. *See also* Great Britain, United Kingdom
English Channel, 85, 110, 124, 220, 251, 308, 322, 378–79
English Civil War, 128–31, 150, 160, 201

English Reformation, 74
Enlightenment, 31, 95, 171–75, 177, 179, 182–84, 192, 202, 230, 234, 236, 298, 350, 382, 396, 413, 416, 418
Enola Gay, 384
Entente Cordiale, 314
environmentalism, 415
Epicureanism, 8, 27
epistemology, 143, 149
Epistle to the Romans, 65
Erasmus, 60, 63, 82
Erfurt Program of 1891, 274
Escorial (palace), 84
Essay on Human Understanding, An (Locke), 176
Essenes, 23
Essex (British region), 130
Estates General, 37, 111–14, 116, 118, 120–21, 125, 127, 168, 198, 203, 205
Estonia, 341, 378
Ethiopia, 353, 368
Eucharist, 38, 68
Euclid, 12
Euphrates River, 1, 6
European Coal and Steel Community, 398
European Economic Community (EEC). *See* European Union
European Union, 155, 399–400, 406
evolution, 297
Execution of Charles I of England, The, 132
existentialism, 394
Expositions Universelles, 294
Ezra, 22

Fabri, Friedrich, 299
Factory Act (1833), 244
fairy tales, 231
Farben, I. G., 307
Farouk (Egyptian king), 401
Fascio di Combattimento, 352
fascism, 319, 348–54, 360–61, 398, 420

Fashoda Affair, 289
Fay, Sidney B., 308
Federal Reserve Bank, 365
feminism, 415
Ferdinand (Spanish king), 70, 79, 96, 133, 249, 254
Ferdinand II (Habsburg emperor), 86, 87, 88
Ferdinand III (Habsburg emperor), 88
Ferry, Jules, 287
feudalism, 34, 35–37, 125, 246, 272
Fieldhouse, David K., 285, 287
Fifth Monarchy Men, 131
film noir, 395
Finland, 327, 338, 341, 380
Fitch, Robert Elliot, 293
Five Year Plan (Soviet), 345, 359, 369, 371, 397
Florence (Italy), 48, 54, 57, 96, 112, 146
Foch, Ferdinand, 330
Ford, Gerald, 403
Foreign Policy Research Institute, 410
Fort Duquesne, 196
Four Year Plan (Nazi), 359
Fourth Republic, 399–400
France, 34, 37, 42, 70–71, 73, 82, 88, 124–27, 143, 150–51, 155, 157, 160, 169, 172, 174, 180–81, 185–86, 190–91, 194–97, 208–13, 219–21, 223–24, 226, 228–30, 236, 239, 241, 256–57, 260, 264, 266–67, 280–81, 283, 287–88, 307, 310–11, 315, 329, 331, 343, 350–52, 355, 359, 368, 375–76, 381, 393–95, 398–99, 401–2, 413; 1848 revolution, 227, 248, 250, 254; Catholicism and, 87–88, 135, 168, 203; colonialism and imperialism, 101–2, 159, 198, 282, 284–86, 289, 314, 366, 400–401; communism in, 367; EEC and, 399; Islam and, 34; John Calvin and, 71–73; labor in, 269, 274; militarism of, 156; monarchy of, 34, 48, 58–59, 73, 109–12, 115–21, 162, 205; Soviet Union and, 344; taxation in, 204, 282; textiles in, 189; World War I and, 317, 321, 324–26, 330–31; World War II and, 360, 367, 374, 378–79, 382
Francis II (Habsburg emperor), 219, 221
Francis of Assisi, St., 39
Francis Xavier, St., 83, 95
Franciscans, 38, 63
Franco, Francisco, 348, 351, 368, 399
Franco-Prussian War, 272, 309, 320
Franco-Russian Alliance, 313–14, 317
Frankenstein (Shelley), 303
Frankfurt Assembly, 252, 253, 258
Frankfurt-am-Main (Germany), 253
Franklin, Benjamin, 172
Franz Ferdinand, Archduke, 316
Franz Josef (Habsburg emperor), 254, 255, 260, 315, 326
free markets, 226, 241, 253, 265–66, 279, 350, 400
free will, 20, 57, 72
French and Indian War, 196–97
French East India Company, 103, 117, 189, 195, 197
French Revolution, 175, 194, 199, 201ff, 217–18, 223, 225–32, 234–35, 239, 244, 247, 250, 285, 320, 333–34, 338, 341, 358, 383, 406
Freud, Sigmund, 175, 181–82, 300–303, 309, 321, 419
Freudianism, 181
Friedman, Thomas, 406
Friedrich (crown prince of Germany), 312
Friedrich I (Prussian king), 161
Friedrich II (Prussian king), 162, 181, 195–97, 212, 364
Friedrich III (Frederick the Wise, Elector of Saxony), 66–67

Index

Friedrich V (Bohemian king), 86–87
Friedrich Wilhelm (Elector of Brandenburg), 159–61, 373
Friedrich Wilhelm I (Prussian king), 194–95, 228
Friedrich Wilhelm II (Prussian king), 228
Friedrich Wilhelm IV (Prussian king), 249
Fronde (French rebellion), 118
Frost, Robert, 420
Fukuyama, Francis, 406, 414

Galapagos Islands, 295
Galen (Greek physician), 12, 52, 142, 146, 147
Galilei, Galileo, 138–39, 145, 149–51, 177, 296
Gallagher, John, 284–85, 287
Gallicanism, 116
Garibaldi, Giuseppe, 256
Gascoyne-Cecil, Robert. *See* Salisbury, Lord
Gasperi, Alcide di, 398
Gatling gun, 287
Genealogy of Morals, The (Nietzsche), 302
Genesis, 16, 140, 295, 299
genetics, 297
Geneva (Switzerland), 72, 130, 133, 265
Genghis Khan, 415
Genie de Christianisme, Le (Chateaubriand), 230
Genoa (Italy), 55, 79, 86, 95, 187
George II (British king), 196
George III (British king), 199
George VI (British king), 379
Georgia (country), 345
Georgia (US state), 103
German Labor Front, 359
German Workers Party, 355
Germany, 34, 37, 41, 48, 52, 59–60, 62–63, 87, 108, 117, 121, 124, 131, 133, 148, 151, 155, 158–61, 166, 169, 172, 178, 186, 191–92, 198, 202, 213, 220–21, 223, 225, 228, 230, 236, 258, 260, 264–66, 272, 282–83, 287, 289, 302–3, 309–17, 322–24, 335, 343–44, 355, 359–60, 365–66, 368, 372, 374–76, 396–98, 405–6, 411, 413; 1848 revolution, 250–53, 254, 257; arts in, 54, 156; Catholicism and, 88; colonialism, 281, 284, 286; communism in, 271, 339, 343, 357; fascism in, 348, 350–51; Great Depression and, 363, 365–66; industrialization of, 239, 241, 258, 274, 307; Judaism and, 384–86, 372–73; labor in, 273–74; liberalism in, 224; nobility of, 72, 75, 83; printing press and, 67; Protestantism and, 64, 66, 68–69, 71; state-building and, 258; World War I and, 326–32, 337, 354, 367; World War II and, 378–82, 390–91. *See also* Holy Roman Empire, Prussia
Gestapo, 358, 372, 386
Ghana, 191, 401
Ghibellines, 59
Gibbon, Edward, 172
Gin Lane (Hogarth), *188*
Girondins, 207–8
Gladstone, William, 267, 280, 296, 310
Glasnost, 405
globalism, 406
Glorious Revolution, 136, 157, 160, 180, 235
Gobineau, Arthur de, 299
Goebbels, Joseph, 358, 372–73
Goethe, Johann Wolfgang von, 231, 386
gold, 70, 80, 85, 96, 105, 107, 120, 147, 188, 190, 256, 265, 267, 283, 328, 331, 335, 365
Gold Rush, 256
Golden Bull, 158
Golden Horde, 164

Google, xii, 52
Gorbachev, Mikhail, 403–5
Göring, Hermann, 359, 379
Gospel of John, 27, 65
Gosplan (State Economic Planning Commission), 342–44, 369
Granada, 79
Grand Alliance, 396
Great Britain, 124, 126, 136, 157, 184, 198, 208, 215, 218, 220, 236, 248, 256, 267, 270, 277, 285, 296, 315, 322, 325–27, 329, 331–32, 343, 351–52, 366, 375–76, 379, 381–82, 388, 393, 396–99, 401, 411, 413, 419–20; Christianity in, 178; colonialism, 85, 120, 194, 196–97, 199, 211, 235, 278–81, 283–84, 287, 289, 311, 384; concessions to Nazi Party, 360, 374; economy of, 204, 265, 286, 324, 359; industrialization of, 239–42; influence of Scottish Enlightenment on, 184; influence on United States, 136; liberalism in, 169, 223, 226, 228, 257; monarchy of, 127, 168; navy of, 214, 310, 313–14; Soviet Union and, 344; suffrage in, 257; textiles and, 237; tribes of, 124; unions and, 274; working class in, 238, 244. *See also* England, United Kingdom
Great Depression, 332, 349–50, 353, 355, 363–66, 413
Great Elector, 167–68
Great Instauration, 145
Great Northern War, 167
Great Wall of China, 105
Greece, 2, 4, 7, 15–16, 22–23, 26, 32, 40, 44, 49, 53–54, 62, 84, 95, 108, 137, 139, 147, 167, 192, 211, 218, 292, 397, 410; influence in Middle East, 13; mythology of, 9, 10; philosophy and, 10
Greek Orthodox Church, 33, 40, 163
Greenland, 40

Gregorian calendar, 140
Gregorian chant, 52
Gregory XIII, Pope, 140
Grimm brothers, 231
Guadeloupe, 117, 190
Guam, 281
Guelphs (family), 59
Guernica (Picasso), 383
Gulag Archipelago, The (Solzhenitsyn), 422
Gustavus Adolphus (Swedish king), 87, 130
Gutenberg, Johannes, 67

Habsburg, House of, 64, 70, 73, 83, 86, 88, 108, 117, 124, 162, 181, 194, 207, 219, 228–29, 253–54, 256, 259, 284, 297, 309, 316, 328, 354; start of Austria-Hungary and, 311
Habsburg, Maximilian von, 70
Hague, The, 309
Haig, Douglas, 323
Hamburg (Germany), 158, 384
Hamlet (Shakespeare), 183
Han dynasty, 265
Handel, George Frideric, 22, 89
Hanoi (Vietnam), 280
Hanover (German province), 196
Hanseatic League, 158
Hardenberg, Friedrich von, 221
Hardie, Keir, 274
Harding, Warren G., 332
Harris, Arthur, 384
Harvard University, 99, 235, 300, 411, 422
Harvey, William, 147
Havel, Václav, 404
Hawaii, 281, 381
Hawthorne, Nathaniel, 233
Haydn, Franz Josef, 173
Hayes, Carlton J. H., 412
Headrick, Daniel, 287, 288
Heathrow Airport, 375

Index

Heavenly City of the Eighteenth-Century Philosophers, The (Becker), 183
Hebrews. *See* Jews
Hegel, G. W. F., 214, 271, 295
Heilbron, John, 149
Helena, St., 221
Hellespont, 8
Hemholtz, Hermann von, 294
Hemingway, Ernest, 328
Henri II (French king), 73
Henri IV (French king), 74, 84, 110–12, 116, 159
Henry the Navigator (Portuguese king), 94
Henry VII (British king), 101
Henry VIII (British king), 74, 78, 116, 125
Hephaestus (god), 3
Hera (god), 10
Herf, Geoffrey, 359
Herodians, 23, 24
Herodotus, 9
Herzen, Alexander, 275
Herzl, Theodor, 385, 395
Heydrich, Reinhard, 385
Hindenburg, Paul von, *356*, 356
Hinduism, 173, 197, 359, 400
Hippocrates, 142
Hiroshima (Japan), 384
Hispaniola, 190
historical consciousness, 16
Hitler Youth, 359
Hitler, Adolf, 56, 192, 332, 346, 351, 354, *356*, 359–60, 367–68, 372–73, 375–83, 385, 389, 396
Hobbes, Thomas, 110, 179–80, 295
Hobsbawm, Eric, 236
Hobson, John, 282, 286
Hogarth, William, 188
Hohenzollern, House of, 159–61, 253, 260, 328
Holbein, Hans, 54
Holodomor, 369

Hollweg, Theobald von Bethmann, 317
Hollywood (CA), 100
Holocaust, 385–87, 394–95
Holstein, 253, 259
Holy Alliance, 221–22
Holy Roman Empire, 34, 37–38, 43, 48, 58–59, 63, 66, 68, 70, 73, 86–87, 124, 149, 158, 161–62, 165, 172, 186, 214, 220, 311
Holy Trinity, The (El Greco), 80
Homer, 6
Hooge Mogende, De, 108
Hoover, Herbert, 340, 366
Hoplites, 7
House of Commons, 125, 129
House of Lords, 125, 133
House of Orange, 86
Hudson River, 103, 134
Hudson River School, 231
Hudson, Henry, 101
Hughes, Charles Evans, 332
Hugo, Victor, 252
Huguenots, 73–74, 84, 104, 110, 114–15, 120, 161, 168. *See also* Calvinism
humanism, 47–48, 50, 54, 60, 62–63, 137, 173, 418
humanitarianism, 284
Hume, David, 172, 184
Hundred Years' War, 42, 111
Hungary, 35, 70, 220, 229, 254–55, 312, 351, 380, 394, 402, 405
Huns, 32
Huntington, Samuel, 411
Hus, Jan, 63
Huxley, Aldous, 349, 370
Huxley, T. H., 296
Huygens, Christiaan, 151
Hyatt, John, 306
hypnotism, 301

Iberian peninsula, 34, 42, 70, 96, 189, 411

Icarus (myth of), 10, 47
Iceland, 40
Icon and the Axe, The (Billington), 163
Idées Napoléoniennes, Les (Bonaparte), 251
Ignatius of Loyola, St., 81–83, 143
Iliad (Homer), 6
Imperial College, 388
imperialism, 188, 275, 277–78, 281, 283–84, 286, 288, 313, 318, 327, 345, 348, 397, 414–15; Greek, 8; technology and, 287
Imperialism, The Highest Stage of Capitalism (Lenin), 282
Incas, 80, 98
India, 85, 94, 103, 174, 188–89, 192, 197, 211, 237, 279, 284, 400, 411
Indian Ocean, 91–92, 94, 101
Indochina. *See* Vietnam
Indonesia, 279, 400, 411
indoor plumbing, 238
Indus River, 13
Industrial Revolution, 5, 223, 228, 234–36, 241, 244–45, 264, 268, 285, 305, 383, 388
industrialism, 235, 306, 314, 331, 345
industrialization, 238, 240, 242–43, 248, 258, 269–70, 275, 282, 419
Influence of Sea Power on History, The (Mahan), 313
Innsbruck (Austria), 254
Inquiry into the Nature and Causes of the Wealth of Nations, An (Smith), 184
Institutes of the Christian Religion, The (Calvin), 71–72
International Monetary Fund, 279
internationalism, 329
internet, 67
Ionic (Greek culture group), 6
Iran, 277, 281, 409, 412
Iraq, 409
Ireland, 103, 124–26, 129, 133, 136, 202, 248, 326, 399
Irish Republican Army, 326
Irish Sea, 127
Iron Age, 7
Iron Guard, 348
Iroquois, 83, 101
Isaac, 16, 17
Isabella (Spanish queen), 70, 79, 96
Isaiah, 21
Isaiah's Lips Anointed with Fire (West), *21*
Islam, 33–34, 40, 79, 93, 98, 117, 173, 178, 279, 342, 400, 404, 406, 409, 412, 414
isolationism, 367
Israel, 13, 14, 22, 109, 348, 395, 401, 403, 411
Isthmus of Suez, 245
Italian Fascist Party, 347
Italian-Turkish War, 289
Italy, 30, 34, 48–49, 52, 57, 66, 88, 112, 118, 149, 155–56, 186, 198, 202, 210–11, 214, 220, 223–24, 228, 269, 273, 283, 309, 312, 315, 321, 323, 329, 332, 343, 348, 350–52, 354, 366–67, 374, 380–81, 394–95, 398, 411; city states of, 107–8
Ivan II (Russian tsar), 167
Ivan III (Russian tsar), 163, 164, *165*
Ivan IV (Russian tsar), 164
Ivan the Terrible (Russian tsar), 109
Ivory Coast, 191

Jacob, 17
Jacobins, 207–9, 227, 341, 358
Jamaica, 190
James I (British king), 126–27
James II (British king), 109, 135
James VI of Scotland (king). *See* James I
James, William, 300–301
Jamestown, 103
Japan, 83, 95, 108, 156, 192, 236, 257, 279, 281, 284, 311, 314–16, 322, 328,

Index

331, 339, 348, 351, 366–68, 374, 380–81, 391, 411, 414, 416–17
Jefferson, Thomas, 225
Jelačić, Josip, 255
Jenkins, Robert, 194
Jerusalem, 413
Jesuits, 81–82, 84, 135, 272; adaptation of to different cultures, 83
Jesus, 13, 16, 22, 24–25, 29, 56, 62–63, 140
Jews, 3, 11, 13, 15–16, 21, 26–27, 95, 109, 135, 137, 192, 292, 331, 354, 372–73, 383, 385–86, 395, 410; diaspora of, 23
Joan of Arc, St., 42
Joel, 376
John (Gospel of). *See* Gospel of John
John (British king), 109, 125
John of the Cross, St., 81
John Paul II, Pope, 404
John the Baptist, 23
"Jokerman" (song), 422
Jordan River, 23
Josef II (Habsburg emperor), 181
Joseph, 17
Joshua, 19, 23
Judah, 21
Judaism, 16, 28, 40, 57, 79, 98, 177, 271, 300, 302, 342, 360, 420
Judea, 4, 13, 24, 299
Julian calendar, 140
Jülich (Rhineland fief), 159
July Monarchy, 250
Jupiter, 149
Justinian I (Byzantine emperor), 32, 33
Justitia (titaness), 3

Kadet Party, 335
Kaiser Wilhelm's Land, 281
Kalahari Desert, 286
Kamenev, Lev, 371
Kant, Immanuel, 172, 175, 179, 182, 386

Kapital, Das (Marx and Engels), 271, 336
Karl (Habsburg emperor), 326
Karl der Grosse. *See* Charlemagne
Katyn Forest Massacre, 384
Kaunitz, Wenzel, 196
Keats, John, 230
Kennan, George F., 397
kenosis, 81
Kenya, 280
Kepler, Johannes, 149, 151, 177
Kerensky, Alexander, 326–27, 336, 338
Keynes, John Maynard, 367
KGB, 341, 345, 371, 384
Khrushchev, Nikita, 372, 402
King of Prussia (PA), 195
Kingdom of the Two Sicilies, 70
Kipling, Rudyard, 284
Kissinger, Henry, 218
knights, 35–37, 39–40, 43, 70, 87, 164, 193; Teutonic, 158
Knox, John, 126
Koestler, Arthur, 371
Kohl, Helmut, 404
Königsberg, 175
Kopernik, Nikolaj. *See* Copernicus
Korea, 281, 314, 407, 411
Korolev, Sergei, 402
Kossuth, Louis, 254
Kotkin, Stephen, 346
Kristallnacht, 373
Kropotkin, Peter, 273
Krupp (firm), 267, 305, 307
Kuhn, Thomas, 149

"La Marseillaise," 208, 251
La Rochelle, 115
Labour Party, 269, 270, 274, 366, 374, 397
Lacombe, Georges, 291, 292, 304
Lamartine, Alphonse de, 251
Lammenais, Félicité de, 230, 244
Landes, David, 236

437

Landtag, 37, 259, 261
Langer, William L., 249
Laos, 280
L'Art de Jetter les Bombes, 152
Las Casas, Bartolomé de, 99
Laski, Harold, 370
Latvia, 341, 378
Laud, William, 127-28, 131
L'Avenir (journal), 244
Lavoisier, Antoine, 175, 294
Lawrence, Thomas, *219*
Le Bon, Gustave, 300, 321, 419
Le May, Curtis, 384
League of German Farmers, 359
League of German Women, 359
League of Nations, 327, 329, 331-32, 349, 360, 368, 373, 385, 395
League of Struggle for the Emancipation of the Working Class, 336
Leaning Tower of Pisa, 150
Leibniz, Gottfried, 151, 172, 174, 386
Lemaître, Frédéric, 250, 251
Lenin, Vladimir, 56, 192, 209, 276, 282, 286, 326-28, 335-39, 341-44, *344*, 369, 371, 396
Lent, 39
Leo X, Pope, 65-66
Leopold I (king), 280, 287
Leroy-Beaulieu, Paul, 298
Les Misérables (Hugo), 250
Levelers (socialist party), 131
Leviathan (Hobbes), 179
Levites, 20
Lewis, C. S., 394, 422
L'extinction du pauperisme (Bonaparte), 252
liberal arts, 42
Liberal Party (Britain), 224
liberalism, 222, 224-26, 228, 244, 250, 260, 267, 269, 282, 293, 302, 327, 349
libertarianism, 177

Library of Congress, 163
Libya, 289
Liebknecht, Wilhelm, 273
Life of Jesus, The (Strauss), 299
Lima (Peru), 99
Lincoln, Abraham, 256
Lindemann, F. A., 388
Lisbon, 95, 187
literacy, 41
Lithuania, 341, 378
Little Ice Age, 186-87
Liverpool, 191
Livingstone, David, 280
Livy, 46
Lloyd George, David, 329-30, 374
Lloyds of London, 192
Locarno Accords, 332
Locke, John, 136, 172, 176-77, 180
"Locksley Hall" (Tennyson poem), 293
logic, 11
logos, 12-13, 27
Lombardy, 254, 312
London, 95, 132, 136, 143, 172, 187, 237, 245, 294, 314, 323, 328, 370, 373, 375, 377, 383, 388, 390, 402; fire in, 135
London Conference (1924), 332
Long Parliament, 130
Lord of the Rings, The (Tolkien), 9, 414
Louis III (French king), 118
Louis Napoléon Bonaparte. *See* Bonaparte, Louis Napoléon
Louis Philippe (French king), 226, 249-51
Louis the Pious, 34
Louis XI (French king), 59
Louis XIII (French king), 113-17, 119, 124, 127, 167-68, 198, 203
Louis XIV (French king), 118-20, 124, 133, 135, 152, 161-62, 180, 189, 193-94, 198, 203, 261, 265
Louis XV (French king), 196, 198, 203-4
Louis XVI (French king), 199, 203-8, 211,

Index

228, 251
Louis XVIII (French king), 220–21
Louvre, 115, 207
Lübeck (Germany), 158
Lucretius, 46
Luddites, 242
Luftwaffe, 376–77
Lusitania, H.M.S., 326
Luther, Martin, 60–63, 65, 67, *68*, 69, 78, 81–83, 88, 92, 143; as composer, 68; persecution of religious life and, 68
Lutheranism, 63, 67–69, 86, 131, 159–60, 179, 231, 358, 394
Luxembourg, 378, 398–99

Macao, 103
Macbeth (Shakespeare), 55, 77–78
Maccabees, 23
MacDonald, Ramsay, 366
Machiavelli, Niccolò, 55, 59, 73, 109, 114, 256, 418
Machine in the Garden, The (Marx), 233
Macmillan, Harold, 401
Madeira Islands, 94
Madrid, 100, 224
Magellan, Ferdinand, 97–98
Maginot Line, 367, 378
Magna Carta, 37, 109, 125
Magnetogorsk (Russia), 369
Magyars, 36
Mahan, Alfred Thayer, 313
Mainz (Germany), 67, 86
Making of the English Working Class, The (Thompson), 243
malaria, 288
Malaysia, 280
Malthus, Thomas, 243
Mamelukes, 211
Man for All Seasons, A (film), 75
Manchester (UK), 237
Manchester School, 242–43, 271

Manchu Empire, 281
Manchuria, 281, 314, 368
Manhattan Project, 390
Manuel Fortunado (Portuguese king), 95
Mao Zedong, 402, 404
Maoris, 279
Marco Polo, 83, 95
Marcus Aurelius, 50
Maria Theresa (Habsburg empress), 181, 195–96
Marie Antoinette, 207–8
Marie Louise (Habsburg princess), 219
Maritain, Jacques, 394
Mark (Rhineland fief), 159
Marlowe, Christopher, 143
Mars, 149
Marseilles (France), 208
Marshall Islands, 281
Marshall, George C., 398, 400
Martinique, 117, 190
martyrdom, 23, 28, 30
Marx, Jenny von Westphalen, 271
Marx, Karl, 181–82, 227, 245–46, 253, 266–67, 271–73, 275, 293, 302, 342, 349–50, 419
Marx, Leo, 233
Marxism, 181, 188, 202, 205, 218, 236, 249, 269, 272–76, 282, 302, 335, 337, 341–43, 345, 353, 372–73, 396, 413
Marxist Social Democrats, 335–36, 338
Mary (mother of Jesus), 63, 157, 168
Mary (Princess of Orange, British queen), 135–36
Mary, Queen of Scots, 84–85
mass marketing, 266, 282
Massachusetts, 72
Massachusetts Bay, 103, 127
Massachusetts Institute of Technology, 388
materialism, 28, 57, 271, 300, 303, 353, 419
mathematics, 12, 40, 52, 141, 166

Matthew (evangelist), 29
Maxim gun, 287
Mayflower, 144
Mazarin, Jules, 118
McKinley, William, 273, 281
McNeill, William H., 2, 291
Medici, House of, 55, 58, 65
Medici, Catherine de, 73–74, 110, 112
Medici, Francesco de, 112
Medici, Marie de, 112–16
medievalism, 171
Mediterranean Sea, 3, 84, 110, 142, 198, 311
Meiji (Japanese emperor), 257
Meiji Restoration, 257, 281
Mein Kampf (Hitler), 355, 360, 373, 379
Mekong River, 280
Mendel, Gregor, 297
Mendeleev, Dmitri, 294
Mendelssohn, Felix, 231
Mensheviks, 335–36
mercantilism, 101–2, 116, 158, 174, 234, 266
Merriman, John, 46, 50
Mesmer, Pierre, 301
Mesoamerican tribes, 96, 99
Mesopotamia, 6, 7, 178
Messenes, 7
Messiah (Handel), 22
Metternich, Klemens von, 214, *219*, 220–21, 225, 230, 247, 254, 258, 329
Mexico, 80, 98–100, 190, 345, 365
Mexico City, 96, 99
Micah, 20
Michelangelo (Michelangelo di Lodovico Buonarroti Simoni), 48, 51–52, 303
Middle Ages, 34, 39, 42, 45–46, 110, 137, 160
Middle Passage, 191
Mighty Continent, The (BBC series), 263
"Mighty Fortress Is Our God, A" (Luther), 68
Milan, 48, 249
Miletus, 11–12
militarism, 212, 257, 275, 283, 327, 351, 406
Mill, John Stuart, 227, 244, 293
Milton, John, 132, 134
Ming Dynasty, 105
Ming Voyages, 92
mining, 104, 147, 186, 369
Minoans, 6
minstrelsy, 52
Mission, The (film), 100
Mississippi River, 195, 197
Mitchell, Billy, 384
Mitterand, François, 404
Modern History (Becker), 124
Molotov, Vyacheslav, 376
Moltke, Helmuth von, 259, 261
Mona Lisa (da Vinci), 53
monarchism, 48, 58, 108, 249, 340; in medieval era, 109; military and, 111; taxation and, 111
monasticism, 30, 37, 81, 139; in England, 74; inventions and discoveries and, 39, 297
Mongols, 105, 164
Monnet, Jean, 398
Montaigne, Michel de, 56, 143
Montcalm, Louis, 197
Montchrestien, Antoine de, 116
Monte Cassino, 30
Montesquieu (Charles Louis de Secondat, baron de La Brède et de Montesquieu), 156, 172, 178, 206
Monteverdi, Claudio, 52
Montezuma, 96
Montgolfier brothers, 217
Montgomery, Bernard, 381–82
Montreal, 197
Moors, 34, 42, 79

Moravia, 297
More, Thomas, 75
Morocco, 289, 381
Moscow, 163–64, 218–19, 315, 335–36, 338–39, 341, 343, 376, 380, 385, 397, 402, 404, 406
Moses, 17–19, 21, 24, 63, 140; law of, 20, 23
Mount Olympus, 10
Mozart, Wolfgang Amadeus, 420
Muggeridge, Malcolm, 370, 420, 421
Muhammad, 23, 33
Müller, Adam, 230
Munch, Edvard, 304
Munich, 355, 374, 376
Munich Agreement (1938), 375
Murmansk, 339
Mussolini, Benito, 348, 351–53, 355, 357, 368, 373, 375, 378, 381
My People: The Story of the Jews (Eban), 25
Mycenea, 6, 10
mysticism, 23, 80–81, 149, 173, 178, 245
mythology, 3, 10–11, 14, 47, 53

Nafis, Ibn, al-, 147
Namibia, 281
Nantes (France), 191
Naples, 353
Napoléon I. *See* Bonaparte, Napoléon
Napoléon III, 256, 260–61, 272, 310
Napoleonic Code, 156, 212
Napoleonic Wars, 228, 234–35, 239, 247, 319
Narkomindel (People's Commissariat of Foreign Affairs), 343
Nasser, Gamal Abdul, 401
National Aeronautics and Space Administration (NASA), 417
National Assembly (France), 205–7
National Book Award, 291
National Socialist German Workers' Party.
See Nazi Party
nationalism, 220, 222, 228, 283, 311, 325, 350, 354, 358, 360, 398, 419
Native Americans, 279
natural selection, 297
naturalism, 52, 295
Navigation Act (1651), 133–34
Nazi Party, 158, 348, 351, 355–58, 372, 374, 380–81, 386, 390, 394, 404
Nazism, 303, 332, 348, 358–60, 366, 373, 375, 379, 384–85, 388, 395, 411
Nazi-Soviet Non-Aggression Pact, 376
Nehemiah, 22
Nelson, Horatio, 211, 215
Neolithic Age, 9
Netherlands, 48, 60, 62, 70, 83–84, 86–87, 102–3, 108, 116, 120, 133–34, 143, 149, 158, 166, 177, 186, 190–91, 198, 210, 214, 220, 269; agriculture in, 187; art in, 52; Calvinism in, 71, 73; Catholicism in, 82; Charlemagne and, 34; colonialism and, 101, 279; England and, 135; exploration and, 101; navy of, 85; Protestantism in, 69; World War II and, 378, 394, 398
Nevada, 233
New Atlantis, The (Bacon), 145
New Deal, 366
New Economic Policy (USSR), 342, 344
New Guinea, 281
New Mexico, 100, 390
New Model Army, 130
New Testament, 16, 23–24, 69, 82
New York, 280, 328, 402
New York Times, 406
New York World, 308
New Zealand, 279, 367, 410
Newcomen, Thomas, 237, 239
Newfoundland, 101
Newport (RI), 191
Newton, Isaac, 11, 138, 145, 150–52, 173,

176–77, 294–96, 298
Nicholas I (Russian tsar), 249, 255
Nicholas II (Russian tsar), 315–17, 326, 336–39
Nicolson, Harold, 330, 332
Niebuhr, Reinhold, 394
Nietzsche, Friedrich, 302–4, 309, 316, 318, 346, 386, 417, 419
Niger River, 280
Nigeria, 280
Night (Wiesel), 386
Night of the Long Knives, 372
nihilism, 293, 350
Nile River, 1, 6, 280, 285, 289, 314
Nineteen Eighty-Four (Orwell), 349
Ninety-Five Theses, 66, 69
Ninth Symphony (Beethoven), 231
Nixon, Richard, 403–4
NKVD. *See* KGB
No Exit (Sartre), 394
Noah, 17
Nobel Prize, 386, 422
Nobel, Alfred, 306
nobility, 203, 218
noblesse d'épée, 36
Normandy, 381
Normans, 36, 124
Norsemen, 35, 124
North America, 40, 103–4, 136, 191, 197, 278
North Atlantic Treaty Organization (NATO), 277, 397, 399, 402–6, 411–12
North Korea, 348, 409
Northwest Passage, 101
Norway, 378, 394, 417
Novgorod (Russia), 164
Novum Organum (Bacon), 144
nuclear energy, 395, 397, 402, 414, 420
numeracy, 41
Nuremberg Laws, 372
Nuremberg War Crimes Tribunal, 386

Nye, Joseph, 409

Ockham, William of, 42, 63, 148
"Ode to a Nightingale" (Keats), 230–31
"Ode to Joy" (Schiller), 231
Oder River, 158
Odessa (Ukraine), 315
Odyssey (Homer), 6
Odyssey of the Self-Centered Self, The (Fitch), 293
Office for the Propagation of the Faith, 82
Ohio River, 196
oil, 19, 265, 267, 281, 324, 380, 403–4
Old Testament, 109, 295
Olympic games, 11
On Anatomical Procedure (Galen), 142
On the Origin of the Species (Darwin), 295
Operation Bagration, 381
Operation Barbarossa, 380
opium, 189
Opium War, 288
Oppenheimer, Robert, 390
Oration on the Dignity of Man (Pico della Mirandola), 56
Organization of the Petroleum Exporting Countries (OPEC), 403–4
Organum (Aristotle), 144
original sin, 20, 177
Orlando, Vittorio, 329, 352
Orleans (France), 226
Orthodoxy, 33, 40, 311, 338, 411
Orwell, George, 277, 349, 361
Osman (Turkish emperor), 44
Ottawa, 365
Otto, Nikolaus, 306
Ottoman Empire, 44, 49, 84, 93, 163, 190, 229, 256, 279, 310–12, 316, 324, 328–29, 334
Ovid, 46
Owen, Robert, 227, 245
Oxford, University of, 388

Index

Pacific Ocean, 96-98, 101, 104, 145, 281, 288, 311, 322, 335, 381, 395
Pact of Steel, 360
Padua (Italy), 48
paganism, 10, 16, 20, 30, 57, 98, 140, 142
Pakistan, 285, 400
Palestine, 385, 395
Palmer, R. R., 165, 202
Palmieri, Matteo, 51
Panama, 281
Pandora's Box, 10
pantheism, 177
papacy, 39, 43, 57, 62-63, 67, 93, 116, 140, 149; Babylonian captivity of, 16, 21-22, 43
Papen, Franz von, 356
Paris, 147, 172, 187, 202, 207, 217, 249, 251, 253, 261, 271-72, 294, 310, 314, 322, 328-29, 377, 398-99, 402
Paris Commune, 273-74
Paris Convention, 265
Paris Peace Conference, 349, 351-52, 354, 366
Parkes, Alexander, 306
Parlement de Paris, 118
Parliament (British), 37, 123, 125-29, 134-36, 150, 168, 180, 194, 199, 201, 204, 226, 244, 257, 269, 274, 374, 376
Parliamentary Recess (1653), 160
Parthenon, 13
Pascal, Blaise, 139
Passover, 18, 24
Patagonia, 97, 295
Patton, George, 381
Paul (apostle), 13, 26-27, 65
Paul III, Pope, 83
Paulskirche (Church of St. Paul), 253
Pavlov, Ivan, 301, 303
Pax Romana, 14
Peace of Augsburg, 71, 83, 86
Peace of Utrecht, 194
Peace of Westphalia, 88, 193
Pearl Harbor, 380
peasantry, 35-38, 41, 64, 69, 109, 159-60, 163-64, 166, 180, 186-87, 191, 203-4, 206-8, 218, 227, 230, 251, 275, 311, 326-27, 334-35, 337-38, 340-42, 344-45, 369-70
Peasants' War, 69, 131
Péguy, Charles, 78
Peloponnesia, 6
Peloponnesian War, 9
Pennsylvania, 196
Pensées (Pascal), 139
Pentateuch. *See* Torah
perestroika, 405
Persia, 7-9, 22; *see also* Iraq
Persian Gulf, 95, 281, 284
Peru, 80, 98-99, 101, 190
Peter (apostle), 26
Peter I (Russian tsar), 166-68, 256, 334
Peter III (Russian tsar), 196
Peterloo (UK), 226
Petrarch, 329
Petrograd. *See* St. Petersburg
petroleum; *see* oil
Pharisees, 13, 23, 26
pharmaceuticals, 288
Pharoah, 17
Philadelphia, 294, 410
Philip II (Spanish king), 80, 83-85, 100, 133
Philip III (Spanish king), 86
Philip IV (Spanish king), 86
Philip of Macedonia, 13
Philip the Fair (French king), 43
Philippines, 98, 103-4, 281, 314, 380
Philosophical Radicals, 244
philosophy, 10-14, 16, 23, 42, 56, 109, 138-39, 141, 143, 152, 171-72, 192, 224, 244, 271, 419

Philosophy of Christ, The (Erasmus), 60
Picasso, Pablo, 304, 383
Pico della Mirandola, Giovanni, 56–58
Piedmont-Savoy, 255–56
pilgrims (English), 103, 144
Pima Indians, 100
piracy, 101, 105, 194
Pirsig, Robert, 420
Pitt, William, 197
Pius IX, Pope, 300
Pius XI, Pope, 358
Pizarro, Francisco, 98
Plato, 8, 13, 27, 50, 59, 109, 141
Platonists, 17
Plessis, Armand Jean du. *See* Richelieu
Plutarch, 55–56, 58, 182
Plutarch's Lives, 55
Plymouth Rock, 103
Po River, 256
poetry, 230
Poincaré, Raymond, 316, 320
Poland, 35, 48, 148, 158, 191, 196, 219–21, 229, 254, 324, 328, 330, 340, 360, 375–76, 378, 384, 386, 393, 403–5, 412
Polányi, Karl, 267
Politburo, 341, 406
"Politics and the English Language" (Orwell), 277
Pompidou, Georges, 399
Pondicherry (India), 197
Pontius Pilate, 24, 56
Poor Laws, 134, 245
Pope, Alexander, 151
populism, 275
Portrait of Prince Metternich (Lawrence), *219*
Portugal, 34, 49, 83, 85, 91, 101–2, 143, 181, 189–90, 348, 399; exploration and, 94, 96, 100
Poseidon, 10

postmodernism, 181, 414–15
Potosí (Bolivia), 100, 104
Potsdam Conference, 390, 396
Prague, 248, 375, 406
Prague Spring, 402
predestination, 72
Presbyterianism, 72, 86, 123, 126, 128–29
Pride, Thomas, 131
Prince, The (Machiavelli), 59, 109
Princip, Gavrilo, 316
Principia Mathematica (Newton), 151–52, 295
progressivism, 222, 308, 415
Prometheus, 10
propaganda, 324, 340, 342, 348, 358, 372
Propaganda Society, 271
Protagoras, 8, 18
Protestant Reformation, 15, 20, 58–60, 77, 92, 131, 137, 146, 160, 173, 178, 201, 236, 257, 407, 413, 418; capitalism's emergence and, 78; causes of, 62–63; clergy and, 69; consubstantiation and, 68; England and, 74; peasantry and, 69; representational government and, 78; *sola scriptura* and, 63; view of Catholic sacraments and, 68
Protestantism, 77, 86, 98, 115, 117, 166, 178, 190, 257, 259, 268, 299, 413
Proudhon, Pierre-Joseph, 245, 271, 273
Prussia, 157–59, 161–62, 167, 169, 172, 175, 181, 191, 194–97, 212, 214, 218–21, 226, 228, 241, 249, 253, 257–58, 260–61, 269, 312, 320, 358–59, 364, 373
Psalm 137, 21
Ptolemy, 138–39, 141–42, 148, 150
Public Health Act (1870), 274
Pueblo Indians, 100
Puerto Rico, 281
Pufendorf, Samuel, 179
Puritanism, 72, 99, 126–30

Putin, Vladimir, 277
Pyrenees, 34, 88
Pythagoras, 11, 50, 149
Pythagoreanism, 8

quadrivium, 42
Quadruple Alliance, 220, 222
Quattrocento, 44, 48, 51, 55–57; *see also* Renaissance
Québec, 101, 103–4, 117, 120, 196
Québec City, 197
Quetzalcoatl, 97
quinine, 288
Qumran (Palestine), 23

radar, 388
Radetzky, Josef, 255
Ragpicker, The (play), 250, 253
railroads, 238, 248, 256, 258, 260, 264, 266, 288, 305–6, 311–12, 320, 326, 328, 337–38, 340, 345, 353, 369, 378, 380
Ranke, Leopold von, 156–57
Rape of Nanking, 383
Raphael, *51*
Rasputin, 337–38
Ravenna (Italy), 32
Reagan, Ronald, 404
realism, 222
Reconquista, 42, 79, 96
Red Army, 339–41, 371, 376, 380–82, 391, 394, 397, 402, 405
Red Cross, 340
Red River, 280
Red Sea, 95
Red Terror, 338, 341
Reflections on the Revolution in France (Burke), 229
Reflections on Violence (Sorel), 300
Reform Bill (1832), 226
refugees, 44, 49, 103, 393, 407

Reichstag, 37, 66, 261, 274, 317, 325–26, 331, 355–56, 380
Reign of Terror, 209–10, 227, 338
Reinsurance Treaty, 313
relativism, 300
Renaissance, 31, 42, 44, 62, 92, 109, 125, 137–38, 144, 146, 148, 167, 173, 182, 236, 292, 302, 413, 418; advances in technology during, 49; architecture in, 53; art in, 53; beginnings of statecraft and, 58; development of music during, 52; invention of Middle Ages and, 31; inventions of, 52; mathematics and, 52; papacy during, 57
Renan, Ernst, 299
Republic (Plato), 59
Republican Party (US), 332
Restoration Era (England), 134, 247
Rhine River, 86, 260, 306, 322, 374
Rhineland, 86, 88, 210, 214, 241, 253, 259, 271, 324, 330–32, 360, 373
Rhode Island, 191
Rhodes, Cecil, 283
Rhodesia, 280
Ribbentrop, Joachim von, 359, 376
Ricardo, David, 243
Richelieu, Cardinal (Armand Jean du Plessis), 113–16, 120, 124, 127, 129, 150, 167, 198, 206, 259; axioms of, 117–18; conquest/colonization and, 117; military and, 116–17;
Rijn, Rembrandt van, 89, *146*
Rio Grande, 100
Riot Acts, 226
Rise of the West, The (McNeill), 291
Robespierre, Maximilian, 56, 206, 209–10
Robinson, Ronald, 284–85, 287
Rocca, Enrico, 353
rocketry, 389–90
Roman Empire, 3, 4, 14–15, 23–24, 26, 28, 32, 34, 36, 53–55, 62, 81, 107–9, 121,

124, 137, 141, 190, 192, 350, 352–53, 385; engineering of, 31; fall of, 31
Romania, 229, 310, 322, 328, 348, 378, 380, 394
Romanov, Michael, 165
Romanov, House of, 165, 328, 339
romanticism, 222, 230–31, 244, 250–51, 255, 298, 350
Rome, 33, 249, 328, 398, 413
Rommel, Erwin, 381
Roosevelt, Franklin D., 363, 366, 382, 390, 396, 406
Roosevelt, Theodore, 281, 299
Rosetta Stone, 211
Rostow, Walt Whitman, 235–36
Roundheads, 130
Rousseau, Jean-Jacques, 172, 181–84, 202, 206, 415
Royal Dutch Shell (company), 267
Royal Navy (British), 197, 215
Royal Observatory (British), 152
Royal Society (British), 152
Ruge, Arnold, 271
Ruhr Valley, 305, 331, 350, 355
rule of law, 422
Rump Parliament, 131, 133
Rurik (Varangian chieftain), 163
Russia, 109, 133, 155–56, 158, 162, 172, 181, 196–97, 209, 225, 229, 236, 248–49, 255, 264, 273, 277, 281–82, 284, 301, 309–11, 313–16, 323–24, 331, 360, 378, 393, 396, 401, 406; agriculture in, 344; authoritarianism in, 409; Christianity in, 163; communism and, 333–34, 336–37, 340, 343; economy of, 191, 286, 344; France and, 214–215, 217–21; Germany and, 379, 381–83; Judaism and, 384; Lenin and, 326–27, 338, 342–43; rocketry and, 389–90; tsarist rule in, 165–68; working class in, 269, 275–76, 335; World War I and, 317, 321, 328, 339
Russian Orthodox Church, 163–64, 167
Russo-Japanese War, 314–15, 321
Russo-Turkish War, 289

Sahara Desert, 280, 287
Saigon, 280
Saint-Simon, Henri de, 227, 245, 252, 270–71
Saladin (Kurdish sultan), 40
Salazar, Antonio, 348, 399
Salisbury, Lord (Robert Arthur Talbot Gascoyne-Cecil, 3rd Marquess of Salisbury), 287, 310
Samuel, 19
San Francisco, 396, 417
San Francisco Bay, 101
Sancho Panza (character), 78
Sanskrit, 83
Santa Fe (NM), 103
Sarajevo (Bosnia-Herzegovina), 316
Sartre, Jean-Paul, 394
Savonarola, Girolamo, 58
Saxons, 124
Saxony, 35, 66, 86, 196, 221, 358
Say, Jean-Baptiste, 242
Sazonov, Sergei, 316–17
Scandinavia, 35, 37, 68–69, 163, 191; *see also* Denmark, Norway, Sweden
Schiller, Friedrich, 231
Schiller, Max, 386
Schleswig (Germany), 253
Schleswig-Holstein (German province), 259
Schlieffen Plan, 321–22
Schlieffen, Alfred von, 317
Schmalkaldic League, 71
Schneider-Creusot (firm), 267
Schönbrunn Palace, 254
Schubert, Franz, 231
Schuman, Robert, 398

Index

Schumpeter, Joseph, 282–83
Schutzstaffel, 358, 372, 383, 385–87
Scientific Revolution, 137, 145, 151–52, 167, 173, 236, 413
Scotland, 55, 73, 103, 124–25, 131, 136, 172, 184, 227, 237, 239, 280
Scott, Walter, 230
Scream, The (Munch), 304
Second Civil War, 131
Second Law of Motion (Newton), 11
Second Reform Bill (1867), 269
Second Socialist International, 274, 308, 325
Second Treatise on Government (Locke), 136
Secondat, Charles-Louis de. *See* Montesquieu
secularism, 11, 272–73, 302, 342, 413
Sedan (France), 261
Senate (US), 331, 366
Senegal, 280
Sepoy Mutiny, 279
September Massacres, 208
Serbia, 33, 229, 310, 312, 315–17, 322, 331, 384
serfs, 37, 191, 215, 218, 311, 334; *see also* peasantry
Seven Years' War, 196–98
Seville, 42, 83, 95
Seymour, Jane, 75
Shakespeare, William, 50, 55, 77, 183
Shanghai, 383
Shaw, George Bernard, 370
Shelley, Mary, 303
Shelley, Percy, 230
Shintoism, 411
Siberia, 163, 165, 275, 336, 339, 345, 369, 417
Sicily, 353, 381
Siemens (firm), 306–7
Sieyés, Emmanuel, Abbe, 205, 211, 356

Sigismund, Johann, 159
Silesia, 195–97, 241
silver, 104–5, 107, 188
Sinai Peninsula, 18, 401
Singapore, 189, 407, 411
Sino-Japanese War, 289
Skoda Works (firm), 267
slavery, 17, 104, 190–93, 246, 256, 272, 348, 351, 369, 415–16, 419
Slavs, 167, 192, 254, 311–12, 328, 360, 380, 383
Slovakia, 394
Smith, Adam, 172, 184, 234, 238, 241–43, 258, 278, 364
Smolensk (Russia), 218
Social Democratic Party (Germany), 269, 273–74, 325, 335, 357, 398, 402
Social Democrats (Russia), 275–76
Social Gospel, 284, 287
social media, 4, 420
Social Revolutionaries, 335, 338
Social Revolutionary Party (Russia), 275
social welfare, 274
socialism, 222, 227, 243, 245, 249, 269–70, 274, 308, 318, 336, 342–43, 349–50, 354, 358, 360, 367, 397, 405
Socialist International, 273
Society of Jesus. *See* Jesuits
sociology, 302, 401, 410
Socrates, 12–13, 145, 410
sola scriptura, 63, 71, 82
Solemn Covenant, 128
Solingen (Germany), 241
Solomon, 19, 20
Solon, 8
Solzhenitsyn, Aleksandr, *421*, 422
Sophists, 12, 17, 23, 141, 145
Sorbonne (France), 117
Sorel, George, 300, 304, 321, 351–52, 419
Sorrows of Young Werther, The (Goethe), 231

South Africa, 103, 283, 285, 289, 367, 401, 410
South America, 37, 97–98, 100, 103, 108, 178, 191, 295, 365
South China Sea, 314
Southeast Asia, 280
Southern Cross, 148
Soviet Union, 277, 333, 341, 343–45, 350, 360, 368–73, 376, 378–81, 383–85, 388, 393, 395–98, 402–6, 411–12, 414, 422
Spaak, Paul-Henri, 398
space exploration, 390, 402, 417
Spain, 35, 39, 58, 70, 73, 78, 86, 88, 102, 108, 112, 118, 120–21, 126–27, 133, 135, 143, 181, 190, 194, 198, 202, 220, 260, 269, 351; art in, 52, 54; authoritarianism and, 399; Catholicism and, 79–80; civil war in, 368, 383; colonialism of, 70, 85, 96, 99–100, 103–4, 121, 278; conquest of Incans, 98; Crusades and, 83; economy of, 79; exploration and, 49, 55, 94, 96, 98, 100; fascism and, 348; France and, 224; Ignatius of Loyola and, 81–82; introduction of wheel to Native Americans and, 97; Islam and, 34, 42; Judaism and, 79; liberalism in, 224, 257; mercantilism of, 101; United States and, 281
Spanish Civil War, 368, 383
Spanish Inquisition, 79, 372
Spanish-American War, 289
Sparta, 3, 7, 9–10
Spencer, Herbert, 298, 300
Spengler, Oswald, 420
Spice Islands, 97
spice trade, 49, 80, 95–97, 102, 188–89, 279
Spinoza, Baruch, 177
Spirit of the Laws, The (Montesquieu), 178
Spiritual Exercises (Ignatius of Loyola), 82

Spree River, 158
Sputnik, 402
Squadristi. *See* Fascio di Combattimento
St. Bartholomew's Day Massacre, 74
St. James (cathedral), 81
St. Lawrence River, 101, 197
St. Peter's Basilica, 65
St. Petersburg (Russia), 166–67, 172, 315–17, 326, 336, 338–39, 380
St. Petersburg Technological Institute, 335
Stalin, Josef, 333, 341, 344, 345–46, 357, 359–60, 369–72, 375–76, 380, 382–83, 390–91, 396–97, 402
Stalin: Paradoxes of Power (Kotkin), 346
Stalingrad. *See* Volgograd
Stanford University, 414
Stanley, Henry, 280
Star Chamber, 125
Star Wars, 9
state-building, 58, 157, 160, 162, 166, 168, 186, 259, 361
steamships, 288
steel, 239, 264, 286, 305, 307, 313, 323, 345, 353, 365, 369, 398
Steffens, Lincoln, 370
Stephenson, George, 238
Stoicism, 8, 27
Stolypin, Peter, 334
Strabo (geographer), 12
Strait of Malacca, 92, 95, 101
Strasser, Otto, 357
Strauss, David, 299
Stresemann, Gustav, 332
Stuart, House of, 123, 125–26, 135, 157, 168, 201
submarines, 326, 330, 379
Sudan, 280, 285, 287
Sudetenland, 374, 375
Suez Canal, 256, 279, 288, 311, 401–2
suffrage, 208, 226–27, 251, 260–61
sugar, 102–5, 117, 188, 190–91, 195

Index

suramin, 288
Sussex, 130
Sweden, 87, 102, 156, 159, 167, 181, 394
Switzerland, 68–72, 108, 155, 181, 210, 214, 220, 322, 327, 336–37
Syllabus of Errors, 300
syndicalism, 269, 273–74, 351–52
Syria, 23, 34

Tacitus, 46
Taiwan, 281, 407
Tallyrand, Charles Maurice de, 221
Tanzania, 281
Taoism, 178, 411
tariffs, 116, 119, 160, 226, 257, 282, 364, 365
Tatars, 164
taxation, 111, 116, 119, 160, 202, 235, 364
Taylor, A. J. P., 257
techne, 3, 5, 14, 30, 39, 42, 47, 88, 93, 152, 163, 241, 292, 346, 361, 411, 416–18, 421
technology, 2–3, 236, 239, 264, 287–89, 306, 383, 421–22; civilization and, 9; invention of printing press, 67; relationships and, 5
telegraph, 288, 326, 338
Telemann, Georg, 89
television, 263
Teller, Edward, 390
Ten Commandments, 18, 394, 417
Tennis Court Oath, 205
Tennyson, Alfred, 293, 298
Tenochtitlán, 96, 97
Teresa de Ávila, St., 81
Tetzel, Johann, 66
Teutonic Cross, 158
Texas, 100
textiles, 189, 237, 241, 245
Thatcher, Margaret, 404
Thebes, 7

themis, 3, 5, 14, 30, 39, 42, 47, 88, 152, 163, 241, 292, 346, 361, 400, 411, 416–18, 421
Theodora (Byzantine empress), 33
Theodosius (Roman emperor), 29
theology, 5, 13, 15, 24, 82
Theory of Moral Sentiments, The (Smith), 184
Theotokópoulos, Domenikos. *See* El Greco
Thermidorian Reaction, 210
Third French Republic, 274, 367
Third Socialist International. *See* Communist International
Thirty Years' War, 86–88, 117, 124, 133, 150, 158–60, 162, 193
Thirty-Nine Articles of Religion, 126
Thomas Aquinas, St., 42, 45, 140, 171
Thompson, E. P., 243
Thoreau, Henry David, 231
Thucydides, 9
Thus Spake Zarathustra (Nietzsche), 302
Tierra del Fuego, 97
Tigris River, 1, 6
Timbuktu, 280
Time of Troubles, 165
Tintoretto, 52
Titanic, 307, 309, 318, 326
Titian (Tiziano Vecellio), 52
Tizard, Henry, 388
tobacco, 102, 104–5, 117, 119, 188, 190–91, 195, 268
Tobago, 190
Tocqueville, Alexis de, 227
Togo, 281
Tokyo, 368, 380, 384
Toleration Act (1689), 136
Tolkien, J. R. R., 349, 394, 414
Tools of Empire, The (Headrick), 287
Torah, 16, 17
Torgau (Germany), 395
Tory Party, 368, 374

totalitarianism, 346, 364, 383, 406, 413
Tower of London, 129
Toynbee, Arnold, 1, 10
trans-Indian Railway, 288
Transcontinental Railroad (US), 288
Trans-Siberian Railway, 311, 314, 335, 380
transubstantiation, doctrine of, 68
Treaty of Brest-Litovsk, 327, 339
Treaty of Chaumont, 220
Treaty of Locarno, 359–60, 373
Treaty of Maastricht, 400
Treaty of Paris, 199
Treaty of Rome, 399, 401
Treaty of Utrecht, 121
Treaty of Versailles, 330–32, 351, 355, 359–60, 367, 373–74
Treblinka (concentration camp), 386
Trier (archbishopric), 86
Trinidad, 190
Tripartite Pact, 380
Triple Alliance, 309, 312, 314–15
Triple Portrait of Cardinal Richelieu (de Champaigne), *113*
trivium, 42
Trojan War, 6
Trotsky, Leon, 338–41, 343, 345, 369
Troy (ancient city), 6
Truce of God, 39
Truman, Harry S, 390–91, 393, 396–97
Tsiolkovsky, Konstantin, 389
Tudor, House of, 126
Tukhachevsky, Mikhail, 371
Turkey, 8, 32, 44, 49, 70, 84, 93–95, 117, 190, 256, 322, 328, 397, 412
Turkish Straits, 310
Turner, Frederick Jackson, 157
Twain, Mark, 199
Twenty-third Psalm, 19
Two Treatises of Government (Locke), 176

Uganda, 280

Ukraine, 163, 167, 340, 344–45, 369, 380, 406
Ulyanov, Vladimir. *See* Lenin, Vladimir
Umberto (Italian king), 273
unions, 269, *270*, 273–74, 335–36, 342, 399
United Kingdom, 240, 323, 365, 395–96; *see also* England, Great Britain
United Nations, 397, 401
United States, 25, 47–48, 85, 96, 103, 172, 184, 189, 194, 223, 229, 234, 241, 265, 268, 273, 277, 307, 313, 339–40, 348, 355, 382, 388–89, 398, 401, 404, 406–7, 410, 414, 420; Christianity and, 411; civil war in, 255–56; colonialism and, 279, 314; communism in, 343; economy of, 236, 286, 324, 400, 417; Great Depression and, 363, 365–66; immigration to, 264; independence of, 204, 278; isolationism of, 366; Judaism and, 385; League of Nations and, 331; nuclear energy and, 399, 402–3; rocketry and, 390; Soviet Union and, 344, 395–97; war with Spain, 281; World War I and, 326–27; World War II and, 379–81
United States Constitution, 210
Universal History (Voltaire), 178
Universal Postal Union, 265
University of Bologna, 41
University of California, 149
University of Cambridge, 41
University of Chicago, 2
University of Erfurt, 63
University of Glasgow, 239
University of Heidelberg, 41
University of Krakow, 41
University of Oxford, 41, 63
University of Padua, 147
University of Paris, 41, 71
University of Pennsylvania, 184, 389

Index

University of Prague, 41
University of Salamanca, 41
Ural Mountains, 165, 406
Urban II, Pope, 39
urbanization, 188
Ussher, John, 295
USSR. *See* Soviet Union
utilitarianism, 293
utopians, 270

Valois, 73, 110
Vandals, 32
Varangians, 163
Varennes (France), 207
Vatican Council I, 300
Venetia (Italian province), 254
Venice, 54, 84, 94–95, 107, 187, 249
Vera Cruz (Mexico), 96
Verdun (France), 34, 323
Vermeer, Johannes, 89
Verne, Jules, 288
Verona (Italy), 48
Versailles, 115, 119, 261, 272
Vesalius. *See* Wesel, Andreas van
Vespucci, Amerigo, 96
Vichy (France), 379
Vickers (firm), 267
Victor Emmanuel (Italian king), 256
Victor Emmanuel III (Italian king), 352
Victoria (British queen), 249
Victorianism, 267, 268, 294, 302
Vienna, 63, 71, 172, 195, 218, 221–22, 248–49, 254, 315, 317, 354, 384
Vietnam, 280, 285, 380, 400, 407
Vietnam War, 403
Vikings, 35–36, 40, 124
Vinland, 40
Virgil, 45
Virginia, 196
Virginia Company, 103
Visigoths, 32

Vistula River, 158
Vivaldi, Antonio, 89
Vladivostok (Russia), 335, 339
Volga River, 163, 164, 336
Volgograd (Russia), 381
Voltaire, 162, 172, 174, 178, 180, 183
Vormärz, 247
Voyager I (spacecraft), 417

Waiting for Godot (Beckett), 395–96
Waldseemüller, Martin, 96
Wales, 103, 124, 234, 239, 245
Wałesa, Lech, 404
Wall Street, 285
Wallenstein, Albrecht von, 87–88, 130, 133
war bonds, 324
War of Austrian Succession, 195
War of Jenkins' Ear, 194
War of the First Coalition, 208–9
War of the Spanish Succession, 121
Warsaw, 381, 386, 387, 405
Washington, DC, 398, 402
Washington, George, 196
Watergate, 403
Waterloo (Belgium), 221
Watson-Watt, David, 388
Watt, James, 234, 239
Wealth of Nations, The (Smith), 234, 241, 278
Weber, Max, 152–53, 302–3, 320, 419
Wehler, Hans-Ulrich, 283
Wehrmacht, 373–76, 378
Weimar Republic, 331, 355, 357, 360
Wells, H. G., 309
Wentworth, Thomas (earl of Stafford), 127–29, 131
Wesel, Andreas van, 146–47
Weser River, 158
Wessex (British region), 130
West Germany, 398
West Indies, 120, 188, 190

West, Benjamin, *21*
Western Civilization (Hayes, Baldwin, Cole), 412
Whigs, 135–36, 229
White House, 326, 363, 397
Wiesel, Elie, 386, 420
Wikipedia, 4
Wilhelm I (Prussian king), 258, 261, 273, 309, 312
Wilhelm II (Prussian king), 274, 312–15, 324, 328, 375
William of Orange (British king), 85, 135–36, 157, 168
William the Conqueror, 124
Williams, Charles, 29
Wilson, Woodrow, 326–27, 329–32, 339, 352, 366, 396; Fourteen Points of, 327–28, 330
Winding Passage, The (Bell), 2
Windischgrätz, Alfred von, 255
Windthorst, Ludwig, 273
Winter Palace, 338
Witte, Sergei, 311, 313, 335
Wittenberg, 65, 70
Wizard War, 388
Wojtyła, Karol. *See* John Paul II, Pope
Wolfe, Thomas, 197
Wordsworth, William, 217, 220, 232
World Bank, 279
"World Split Apart, A" (Solzhenitsyn), 422
World War I, 282–83, 289, 308, 318–21, 323–24, 326–28, 339, 348–52, 354, 364, 366–67, 374, 376–78, 383, 393–94, 413, 420
World War II, 277, 319, 367, 377, 382–83, 387, 393–94, 396, 398, 400, 406
Württemberg, 258, 260
Wycliffe, John, 63–64

Xerxes, 8–9

Yalta Conference, 382, 396
Yeltsin, Boris, 406
Yew, Lee Kuan, 411
Yokohama (Japan), 384
Yom Kippur War, 403
Yorkshire (British region), 130
YouTube, 263
Yugoslavia, 384

Zen and the Art of Motorcycle Maintenance (Pirsig), 420
Zeno, 11
zeppelins, 323
Zeus, 3, 10
Zheng He, 92
Zhou Enlai, 404
Zinoviev, Grigory, 371
Zionism, 385
Zola, Emile, 268
Zollverein, 226, 258–59
Zulus, 279
Zweig, Stefan, 308
Zwingli, Huldrych, 68–69

www.ingramcontent.com/pod-product-compliance
Lightning Source LLC
Chambersburg PA
CBHW030249010526
44107CB00031B/1370/J